# HISTORY
# OF A VOYAGE TO
## THE LAND OF BRAZIL

# LATIN AMERICA LITERATURE AND CULTURE

General Editor
Roberto González Echevarría
Bass Professor of Hispanic and Comparative Literature
Yale University

1. Manuel Bandeira, *This Earth, That Sky,* trans. Candace Slater

2. Nicolás Guillén, *The Daily Daily,* trans. Vera M. Kurzinski

3. Gwen Kirkpatrick, *The Dissonant Legacy of* Modernismo: *Lugones, Herrera y Reissig, and the Voices of Modern Spanish American Poetry*

4. Pablo Neruda, *Selected Odes of Pablo Neruda,* trans. Margaret Sayers Peden

5. Rosamel del Valle, *Eva the Fugitive,* trans. Anna Balakian

6. Jean de Léry, *History of a Voyage to the Land of Brazil, otherwise called America,* trans. Janet Whatley

7. Pablo Neruda, *Canto General,* trans. Jack Schmitt

8. Doris Sommer, *Foundational Fictions: The National Romances of Latin America*

9. Margarita Zamora, *Reading Columbus*

10. Alvar Núñez Cabeza de Vaca, *Castaways in a Strange Land: The Narrative of Alvar Núñez Cabeza de Vaca,* edited by Enrique Pupo-Walker, trans. Frances M. López-Morillas

11. Vicky Unruh, *Latin American Vanguards: The Art of Contentious Encounters*

JEAN DE LÉRY

# HISTORY
# OF A VOYAGE TO
# THE LAND OF BRAZIL,
## OTHERWISE CALLED
## AMERICA

Containing the Navigation and the Remarkable
Things Seen on the Sea by the Author; the Behav-
ior of Villegagnon in That Country; the Customs
and Strange Ways of Life of the American Sav-
ages; Together with the Description of Various
Animals, Trees, Plants, and Other
Singular Things Completely
Unknown over Here

translation and introduction by
## JANET WHATLEY

UNIVERSITY OF CALIFORNIA PRESS
Berkeley   Los Angeles   London

The publisher gratefully acknowledges the support of Joan Palevsky in the publication of this book.

University of California Press
Berkeley and Los Angeles, California

University of California Press, Ltd.
London, England

First Paperback Printing 1992

Library of Congress Cataloging-in-Publication Data
Léry, Jean de, 1534–1611.
    [Histoire d'un voyage fait en la terre du Brésil. English]
    History of a voyage to the land of Brazil, otherwise called
America / Jean de Léry : translated by Janet Whatley.
    p.  cm.—(Latin American literature and culture; 6)
    Translation of: Histoire d'un voyage fait en la terre du Brésil.
    "Containing the navigation and the remarkable things seen on the
sea by the author: the behavior of Villegagnon in that country: the
customs and strange ways of life of the American savages: together
with the description of various animals, trees, plants, and other
singular things completely unknown over here."
    Includes bibliographical references (p.
    ISBN 0-520-08274-5 (alk. paper)
    1. Brazil—Description and travel—To 1900.  2. Rio de Janeiro
(Brazil)—Description.  3. Indians of South America—Brazil—Social
life and customs.  4. Tupinamba Indians—Social life and customs.
5. Natural history—Brazil.  6. Villegagnon, Nicolas Durand de,
1510–1571?  7. Léry, Jean de, 1534–1611—Journeys—Brazil.
I. Title.
F2511.L655 1990
918.104'3—dc20                                    90-33487
                                                                                CIP

Printed in the United States of America

08   07   06   05
12   11   10   9   8   7   6

The paper used in this publication meets the minimum requirements of
ANSI/NISO Z39.48-1992 (R 1997) (*Permanence of Paper*). ∞

For my mother
ELINOR CHAPPLE SALTUS

# CONTENTS

## CHAPTER IV
Of the Equator, or Equinoctial Line: Together with the Tempests, the Fickleness of Winds, the Pestilent Rains, the Heat, the Thirst, and Other Inconveniences That We Endured in That Region

## CHAPTER V
Of the Sighting and First View That We Had Both of West India or the Land of Brazil and of the Savages That Inhabit It Together with Everything That Happened to Us on the Sea up to the Tropic of Capricorn

## CHAPTER VI
Of Our Landing at Fort Coligny in the Land of Brazil. Of the Reception That Villegagnon Gave Us, and of His Behavior, Regarding Both Religion and Other Aspects of His Government in That Country

## CHAPTER VII
A Description of the Bay of Guanabara Otherwise Called *Janeiro* in America; of the Island and Fort of Coligny, Which Was Built on It; Together with the Other Islands in the Region

## CHAPTER VIII
Of the Natural Qualities, Strength, Stature, Nudity, Disposition and Ornamentation of the Body of the Brazilian Savages, Both Men and Women, Who Live in America, and Whom I Frequented for about a Year

## CHAPTER IX
Of the Big Roots and the Millet of Which the Savages Make Flour That They Eat Instead of Bread; and of Their Drink, Which They Call *Caouin*

# CHAPTER X

Of the Animals, Kinds of Venison, Big Lizards, Snakes, and Other Monstrous Beasts of America

# CHAPTER XI

Of the Variety of Birds of America, All Different from Ours; Together with the Big Bats, Bees, Flies, Gnats and Other Strange Vermin of That Land

# CHAPTER XII

Of Some Fish That Are Common among the Savages of America, and of Their Manner of Fishing

# CHAPTER XIII

Of the Trees, Herbs, Roots, and Exquisite Fruits Produced by the Land of Brazil

# CHAPTER XIV

Of the War, Combats, Boldness, and Arms of the Savages of America

# CHAPTER XV

How the Americans Treat Their Prisoners of War and the Ceremonies They Observe Both in Killing and in Eating Them

# CHAPTER XVI

What One Might Call Religion among the Savage Americans: Of the Errors in Which Certain Charlatans Called *Caraïbes* Hold Them in Thrall; and of the Great Ignorance of God in Which They Are Plunged

CONTENTS

## CHAPTER XVII

Of Marriage, Polygamy, and Degrees of Consanguinity Observed by the Savages; and of the Treatment of Their Little Children

*152*

## CHAPTER XVIII

What One May Call Laws and Civil Order among the Savages: How Humanely They Treat and Receive Friends Who Visit Them; and of the Tears and Joyous Speeches That the Women Make to Welcome Them

*158*

## CHAPTER XIX

How the Savages Treat Each Other in Their Illnesses Together with Their Burials and Funeral Ceremonies and the Great Lamentations They Make over Their Dead

*172*

## CHAPTER XX

Colloquy upon Entry or Arrival in the Land of Brazil among the People of the Country Called Tupinamba and Tupinenquin: in the Savage Language and in French

*178*

## CHAPTER XXI

Of Our Departure from the Land of Brazil, Called America; Together with the Shipwrecks and Other Perils That We Escaped on the Sea during Our Return

*196*

## CHAPTER XXII

Of the Extreme Famine, Tempests, and Other Dangers from Which God Delivered Us as We Were Returning to France

*208*

# CONTENTS

# ACKNOWLEDGMENTS

Over the years of working on Jean de Léry, I have had a lot of help from a number of people, whom I now want to thank. I first learned of Léry in 1980, during a sabbatical leave provided by the University of Vermont. I spent that leave as a visitor in the Department of French Studies of Brown University, where Laura Durand and Henry Majewski offered me a scholarly home, warm hospitality, and encouragement in my initial research.

In 1987 the National Endowment for the Humanities (NEH) gave me a generous grant that helped subsidize a year-long sabbatical to work on this translation. Sharen Cohen and Martha Chomiak of the NEH staff made all the communications and transactions pleasant and straightforward, as did Lisa Ringey, of University of Vermont's Office of Sponsored Programs.

The staff of the Bailey-Howe Library at the University of Vermont have been responsive beyond any scholar's dreams. I want to thank particularly Nancy Crane and Bonnie Ryan of the Reference Department, John Buechler and Connell Gallagher of Special Collections, and William Dunlop of the Acquisitions Department. The John Carter Brown Library has been a prime resource; I owe particular thanks to Norman Fiering, Daniel Slive, Richard Hurley, and Patricia Arney for help with reproducing the illustrations. Kenneth Cain of the Newberry Library has helped me track down sources for the plates with the aid of Olive Dickason, who has given of her own valuable research time.

William Matheson of Washington University, who nurtures so many people's work with so much generosity, read the whole manuscript early on and brought to bear on it his craft of poet and translator. (He is not, however, responsible for the translations of the doggerel verse.) William Mitchell of the University of Vermont has offered me his ethnographer's insights on Léry's experience and his reading of the whole manuscript with an anthropologist's eye. Joseph Schall, of the Zoology Department of the University of Vermont, has helped me sort out the serpents and iguanas. I am greatly indebted to Lynn Bohs Sperry, a specialist in South American plant life (now at the University of Utah), who has made me a gift of her expertise; she has spent many hours checking, researching, and amplifying the notes on Brazilian flora.

I am deeply grateful to other friends and colleagues who have read and responded to this work in its various stages, and who have put up with my holdings-forth on Léry over the years: the list (which is not exhaustive) includes Philippe Carrard, Grant Crichfield, James Holstun, Philip Kennicott, Timothy Murad, Veronica Richel, Thomas Simone, Gretchen Van Slyke, and Susan Whitebook. Their friendship and their desire to see this book come forth have sustained me.

Stephen Greenblatt's delight in the work of Jean de Léry, his enthusiastic support of this project, and his efforts to have this translation see the light of day have been of great importance to me.

At the University of California Press, Scott Mahler has sponsored this project and has been unfailingly constructive and encouraging. My thanks to him, to Cathy Hertz for her careful and intelligent copy-editing of the manuscript, and to Shirley Warren, the Managing Editor.

My husband, Malcolm Whatley, has worked closely with me on all the details of this translation and on its documentation. His editorial skill and his concern that I preserve the integrity of Léry's thought, style, and grip on the world, inform every aspect of this book.

The illustrations have been made available through the courtesy of the John Carter Brown Library, at Brown University. These plates are reproductions of those that appeared in the 1580 edition, except for three: the Tupinamba family portrayed in Chapter VIII; the dancing figures in Chapter XVI; and the weeping greeting shown in Chapter XVIII. Those plates are taken from the 1600 edition. They are identical to those of 1580, but yielded better photographic reproduction.

# INTRODUCTION

*Once ashore, I ambled along the Avenida Rio Branco, where once the Tupinamba villages stood; in my pocket was that breviary of the anthropologist, Jean de Léry. He had arrived in Rio three hundred and seventy-eight years previously, almost to the day.*

—Claude Lévi-Strauss, in *Tristes Tropiques*,[1] recounting his arrival in Rio de Janeiro in 1934.

Jean de Léry's *History of a Voyage to the Land of Brazil* has not been made widely known in the English-speaking world, but those who turn their attention to French literature of New World exploration in the sixteenth century encounter it almost at once, with surprise and gratitude. For his vivid and subtle ethnography of the Tupinamba Indians and his minute description of the marvelous abundance of their natural setting provide one of the most detailed and engaging of the reports we have of how the New World looked while it was indeed still new; and it is rendered by a generous-minded, acutely observant man with a storyteller's gift.

The early chapters of the book are an account of an outbound sixteenth-century Atlantic crossing: the marvels and the terrors of riding over the "abyss of water that is the Western Sea." The encounters with the whales, porpoises, flying fish are recounted not only with wonder and delight but also with a zoological precision that gives a foretaste of the richness of the ethnography to follow. The tale is interwoven with scenes and examples of men employing the expanding expertise that was making the whole experience possible—the evolving instruments, the developing knowledge of winds and stars, of currents and tides. The final two chapters are a hair-raising account of the return voyage: the ship—a leaky, rotting hulk—blundered off course and soon exhausted its provisions. The voyagers were reduced to eating whatever on board could provide "juice and moisture," right down to the horn lanterns; Léry and his shipmates faced the imminent breakdown of all the inhibitions of civility as they cast the starved dead bodies into the sea.

But the book's heart is the long middle section: a portrait of a New World people just before it was engulfed by European colonization. Although Léry has often been cited as an early contributor to the myth of the "noble savage," his work is far too rich to be characterized by so simple an expression: his is a complex portrait of a people. They are human beings who command his admiration and respect on some points, elicit his ridicule or disapproval on others; people who delight him and who appall him; whom he envies for their life in this world while he fears for their souls in the next. He looks at them and their culture with the eyes of a Calvinist, a humanist, a craftsman, and of a guest among them in their villages.

The *Histoire d'un Voyage* is placed at the intersection of two great axes of early modern European experience: the Protestant Reformation and the discovery of America. At almost the last moment when such a collaboration was possible, a consortium that included both Catholics and Huguenots undertook to establish a colony and mission in the New World. Among fourteen representatives sent from Calvin's church in Geneva was the twenty-two-year-old Jean de Léry.

Léry was born in Burgundy in 1534. Almost nothing is known of his earliest years, and historians disagree as to whether he was an artisan or a member of the minor nobility.[2] Léry's life was shaped by the Wars of Religion (1562–1598), which were preceded by a long period of tension and persecution of the Huguenots. In the very year of Léry's birth, events took place that marked a sharp turning point for the Reformation in France: the "Affair of the Placards," in which Protestants denounced the Roman Mass as idolatry.[3] From then on, the French monarchy would fluctuate in attitude between the merest tolerance and active hostility. Léry was a child when in 1536 Calvin published his *Institutes of the Christian Religion,* and in 1541 established his theocracy in Geneva. By the time Léry was grown, the Genevan church was training native Frenchmen to return to France as missionaries of the Reformed Gospel, and he joined this missionary group. In 1556 he and his fellows were called on to go not to France but to Brazil, where they formed the first Protestant mission to the New World.[4]

Léry's account of that voyage was not merely a log of day-to-day notes. By the time he wrote the version to be published, he had experienced twenty more years, which included some of the most hideous in

French history. The St. Bartholomew's Day Massacre had flooded across the land in waves of such violence that Frenchmen were to be seen roasting and eating other Frenchmen's hearts. Léry himself had lived through the siege and famine of Sancerre. That period gave occasion for a focused meditation on the differences and similarities between the ways of Europeans and the ways of "savages," and indeed for the growth of a nostalgia for the Brazilian forests and for his Tupi friends.

Those years began for Léry in 1558, when he returned to France and from there went back to Geneva to resume his studies for the ministry.[5] Soon after his return he was married. (It is not known whether there were any children.) At this time Léry wrote an account of the deaths of three of his Huguenot companions at the hands of the colony's leader: *La Persécution des fidèles en terre d'Amérique* appeared in a Protestant martyrology, *l'Histoire des Martyrs*, edited by Jean Crespin.

Léry began his ministry in 1562 near Lyon. The violence that marked the beginning of the Religious Wars was particularly extreme in that region, where the Huguenots were meeting with reprisals for destroying the images in the Catholic churches. Léry opposed physical iconoclasm, for, like Calvin's, his war against graven images was on a different level. There are records of his trying, without success, to protect the churches against this kind of vandalism even as he was trying to establish the Reformed Religion.[6] In both his life and his writing, he was a man who preferred to build bridges rather than burn them, and who, in a time of fanaticism, could both give spirit to the resistance of his side and temper the violence around him.

In 1563 Léry returned to Geneva, where he wrote the first draft of his *Histoire d'un Voyage*. (The draft was lost, rewritten, lost again, and found later in its original version.) In 1564 he was serving the church of Nevers, and by 1569, he was at La Charité-sur-Loire. It was there, in August 1572, that the St. Bartholomew's Day Massacre caught up with him. Twenty-two Huguenots were slaughtered, but Léry managed to escape to Sancerre.

From January to August of 1573, Sancerre was besieged by royal Catholic forces and reduced to starvation. Léry's *Histoire mémorable de la ville de Sancerre* was published in 1574, four years before the publication of *Histoire d'un Voyage*.[7] The same ethnographic wholeness that distinguishes the later book is seen in the earlier. He observes and records how a community copes under such enormous pressure, and what characterizes the point of moral crisis, but he is also interested in practical human ingenuity: how does one manage to eat, when all ordinary foodstuffs have been consumed? How does one work one's way down, from dogs and cats to mice and rats, to shoe leather and parchment? Léry's experience, both on shipboard and in the Brazilian villages, helped his fellow Sancerrois survive, in ways ranging from the small but real comfort of the Tupi hammock, to the confidence that boiled leather really can sustain life.

Here, as in the Brazil book, Léry explores the outermost limits of permissibility: in such extremity, does eating the flesh of your dead neighbor fall within them? Léry's "No!" was not merely conventional: those limits had been candidly and concretely surveyed and reestablished in the New World and on the voyage back. In Sancerre, he saw them violated: the remains of a dead child, her flesh half-eaten, was the evidence that destroyed her desperate, demoralized family.

Léry was not only the recording spectator of Sancerre. As pastor, he bore responsibility for the moral health and courage of the community, and he was a chief negotiator with the royal representatives—who noted with a grudging admiration that Léry's recipes for fricasseed rats had allowed Sancerre to be obstinate for much longer than was convenient. After the siege, Léry took refuge in Berne, where he was received by the children of the Huguenot leader Admiral Gaspard de Coligny. It was there that he had the leisure and security to write down the Sancerre experience. In 1576, he was back in France, this time in his native Burgundy. It was at this point that he found in Lyon his original manuscript of the *Histoire d'un Voyage,* and the work appeared in its first edition in 1578.

Léry spent the last years of his ministry in the Vaud region of Switzerland. One of the last documents of his life records a baptism that he performed in 1613, the same year in which he died of the plague. He was seventy-nine.

Brazil had been claimed by Portugal in 1500, when it was discovered—by accident—by the Portuguese expedition of Pedro Alvarez Cabral.[8] The Treaty of Tordesillas (1494) had divided the New World between Spanish and Portuguese zones of influence, and this new discovery, falling on the Portuguese side of the line, was a windfall. By 1556, the Portuguese had established captaincies along the Brazilian coast and were exploiting its economic possibilities. Chief among these was the tree known as "brazilwood," which eventually gave its name to the country. Brazilwood was the source of a highly valued red dye, and it was not only the Portuguese who traded in it: since the early sixteenth century, French sailors and traders had been up and down the coast of Brazil. Great fortunes were built on shipments of the dyewood sent back to France—especially to Normandy.

Both the French and the Portuguese were continually dealing with the various tribes of the Tupinamba Indians of the coast. The Portuguese were largely bent on subduing the Indians and putting them to work in sugarcane factories. The French, on the other hand, had more informal and friendly relations with them, moving in and out of their villages as guests and traders, dealing on a basis of mutual benefit. Some Frenchmen—known in the French accounts as the "truchements de Normandie" or "Norman interpreters"—went even further: they moved into the villages, learned the language, cohabited with the women, had children by them, and (it was said) adopted all their practices—even cannibalism. While these "truchements" were a scandal to the French missionaries, they were undoubtedly immensely valuable to them as liaison agents.

For the first half-century after the discovery of Brazil, the French who were there had no official status, even with the French government. This was not on account of respect for the Treaty of Tordesillas—which the French by no means regarded as incontestable. Rather, the French monarchy was preoccupied with other matters. The expedition of 1555 was an attempt to change that state of affairs, and to get a foothold in Brazil.

Léry's motive for publishing his *Histoire* precisely when he did is stated in his Preface. That Preface, however, with its long tirades, is uncharacteristic of the book as a whole, and can be more a stumbling-block than a threshold to the work without some explanation of the origins of the enterprise, the controversy that had developed in France around rival accounts of it, and of its principal players: Nicolas Durand de Villegagnon, Admiral Gaspard de Coligny, and André Thevet.

Villegagnon, the leader of the expedition, had a long-established reputation as a valiant soldier and as a passionate and difficult man. He belonged to the Order of the Knights of Malta, and he frequently manifested the purity and intransigence that the chivalric orders intended to develop. In his distinguished military career, he had combatted the traditional foes of Christian Europe: the Moors in Algiers, the Turks in Hungary. He had played a role in the life of Mary Queen of Scots, commanding the ship that carried her off from Scotland to marry the future Francis II of France. He became Vice-Admiral of Brittany, but quarreled with the governor of the city of Brest, and found that the king sided against him. It may have been disgruntlement that set him to thinking of America, and sent him to ask Admiral Coligny for help in financing a colonial venture in Brazil. Hedging all his bets, however, he also acquired the support of the Cardinal de Lorraine, the leader of the Catholic clergy in France and a member of the uncompromisingly anti-Huguenot Guise family.

Gaspard de Coligny, Admiral of France, was a Huguenot sympathizer, and was to become one of the foremost leaders of the Protestant movement in France—and on St. Bartholomew's Day, one of its martyrs. Even before the religious wars erupted into their full virulence, he was interested in securing a refuge for the Huguenots. He was able to interest Henry II in the venture by presenting the prospects for profitable trade in brazilwood and other commodities from the New World, and for challenging Spanish and Portuguese hegemony.

Villegagnon had been acquainted with Calvin when they were both students in Paris. In the first chapter of the *Histoire*, Léry's claims—and the evidence is fairly strong—that Villegagnon wrote to Calvin from the colony and requested that the Reformed Church of Geneva send him some "ministers of the Word of God, along with other personages well instructed in the Christian religion." Later, Villegagnon denied sending any such letter, which in any case was no longer extant. Regardless of whether the letter was sent, the Calvinists who came did believe that they were summoned jointly by Admiral Coligny and Villegagnon to join the colony in Brazil, and to establish there a Reformed refuge and mission. The disintegration of the relations between Villegagnon and the Calvinists, recounted in Léry's Chapter VI, is perceived by him as a succession of betrayals on Villegagnon's part; most historians have come to think it was a misunderstanding.[9] In any case, Villegagnon eventually had three of Léry's party killed, and he plotted the deaths of the rest.

André Thevet was a Franciscan friar (or Cordelier) and a notable traveler, and was closely allied to the Catholic figures of authority: he was the chaplain of Catherine de Medici and Royal Cosmographer for Charles IX. Villegagnon took him on as chaplain at the beginning of the Brazil expedition. Thevet was in Brazil for only ten weeks or so, and had left before Léry and the Calvinist group arrived. His *Singularités de la France antarctique*, published shortly after his return in 1556, enjoyed a considerable vogue and did much to popularize the figure of the Brazilian Indian, and he himself was extravagantly praised by the major poets of his time as a new Jason or Ulysses. In 1575 he published his *Cosmographie universelle*, which included much of the *Singularités* material, with some important additions: it included a passage in which Thevet

*It claims it's the missionary's fault the village was destroyed*

accused the Calvinist ministers of cupidity and sedition, and blamed them for the wreck of the Villegagnon colony.

Léry's long, impassioned, and sometimes difficult Preface is his attempt to set the record straight. But it becomes clear over the ensuing decades that more is at issue than clearing the record on that one ten-month encounter. With successive editions of the *Voyage,* together with works of other writers, we see the Protestants staking out their ground of moral and intellectual influence over how the experience of discovery and expansion in the New World would be assimilated by Europe.[10]

Thevet was known to be careless and credulous, and Léry, with his meticulous habits of memory, verification, and logic, demolished Thevet's garbled accusations.[11] Nevertheless, a caveat is in order. There are certain areas where Thevet, a less selective collector of oddments, has given us valuable information that Léry either disregards or disparages. In the reportage of the two men there is more overlap than Léry would like to admit, even in anecdote and wording. It is likely that both authors supplemented their direct experience (of which Léry's was certainly the greater) with information from sources that they both used—the much-scorned Norman interpreters, for example. Indeed, it is almost certain that Léry was even to some extent indebted directly to Thevet.[12]

Villegagnon may not have been the turncoat that Léry claims, but he does seem to have been a violent and unstable man. It became clear at a certain point that his island compound was no safe place for Léry and his friends, and the task for them was now to escape with their lives. Since the next boat to Europe would be loading brazilwood for another two months, they established themselves at a tiny trading post—a few shacks—on the mainland, and for those two months depended for their survival on the good will of the Tupinamba. The experience of that period, together with those of previous extensive excursions while they were still with Villegagnon's colony, provided the material for Léry's ethnography.

The mission had failed; the colony was a fiasco, and by 1560, would fall to the Portuguese. The most lasting results of the venture were to be in the writing about it. While the duty of preaching the Gospel to all mankind was much on the minds of Léry and his friends, and they made a few modest attempts, their situation clearly precluded their making any lasting impact, and the quality of this "anthropologist's breviary" owes much to those circumstances. The reflectiveness and intimacy of this account may be due in part to a kind of detachment concomitant with the status of the refugee; knowing that he could not stay in Brazil long enough to have any permanent influence, Léry also knew that he had a unique chance to take in the sights, sounds, and smells of this New World that he would probably never see again.

What would Léry's contemporaries expect to find in a book about Brazil? What habits of imagining, categorizing, or judging would influence how they would assimilate and shape what they were to hear? Through what prisms would they refract the dazzling flood of images from the New World; on what patterns of likeness and difference would they project them?[13]

The New World discoveries did not immediately transform all European habits of mind; for a long time, Europeans would try to think of America in the ways already familiar—including ways of thinking about strange peoples that dated back to the ethnographies of Herodotus.[14]

The great transmitter of these ethnographies was Pliny the Elder (A.D. 23–79), whose *Natural History* was immensely important in the Middle Ages and the Renaissance for its lore on arts and industry and on flora and fauna, as well on as human populations. But what was incidental to Herodotus's descriptions became the hallmark of Pliny's work, and part of his legacy to the Middle Ages: a fascination with the monstrous and the fabulous at the expense of systematic inquiry into the normal functioning of ordinary, if foreign, societies.

All through the sixteenth century, one finds in travel books a semantic attraction between the term "America" and the terms "monster" and "marvel." The immensely popular voyage writing of Sir John Mandeville peopled the European imagination with headless men wearing their eyes in their shoulders, or with ears hanging down to their knees; and with human devourers of human flesh. Pierre d'Ailly's *Imago mundi,* which preserved the lists of monstrous populations from Pliny into the late medieval times, was read and annotated by Columbus himself, who kept seeking after one-eyed or dog-headed races of men.[15] According to medieval legend, in the forests of Europe itself could be found "wild men," degenerated from fully human status: hairy, solitary, deprived of language; often brutal, but sometimes gentle and strangely courteous.[16] These notions of half-human creatures whetted the European appetite for tales from the New World, for glimpses of such giants and Amazons as André Thevet provided. (Léry, aware of his readers' expectations about monsters and marvels, takes pains to establish himself as a credible witness rather than a fable-monger.)[17]

But something more than a mere fascination with the marvelous and monstrous would be needed if Europe was to assimilate the enormous new fact of America: this entirely new "other," neither Turk nor Jew, African nor Asian. And indeed, even as the news from America was arriving, the humanist enterprise was expanding the dialogue with ancient Greece and Rome beyond such fascinations to include a serious consideration of cultures that were not Christian, but yet could be regarded as admirable for their rationality and civility. Plutarch provided examples of stoic virtue; through the figures of Diogenes the Cynic, or the barbarous Germans of Tacitus, the classical world had reflected upon and criticized its own high civilization; through Ovid's *Metamorphoses,* an old form of "soft" primitivism pervaded the Renaissance: the Golden Age, when an innocent human race lived on acorns and honey, trees bore fruit all year around, the earth bore no scar of the plow and the sea no wake of ships, and no one distinguished between "mine" and "thine."[18]

The first popularizer of Columbus's voyages, Peter Martyr (Pietro Martire d'Anghiera), was an Italian humanist at the court of Ferdinand and Isabella. Through his *Decades de Orbo Novo* the earliest accounts of the New World were suffused with humanist idealization. While this undoubtedly encouraged receptivity and friendliness, it had some distinct disadvantages. Humanism could also represent New World peoples as preformed and familiar abstractions, and could thus obscure the specificity of their real cultures. Their very bodies were often portrayed in the forms and poses of the gods of classical antiquity (one sees this in the illustrations in Léry's *Histoire*).[19]

Sixteenth-century humanism was largely subordinate to Christianity. And for Christian Europe, the discovery of America quickened a whole series of latent questions. If the Bible was supposed to have accounted for all the progenitors in human creation, then where did these new-found peoples fit in? Where did they come from? Were they descended from Adam? After the Flood, which of the three sons of Noah was their ancestor? Is the Indian, like the African, a descendant of Ham, and condemned to be "a servant of servants unto his brethren"? And how could it be that the Indians knew nothing of one of the signal consequences of original sin, namely, that after the fall Adam covered himself from shame?

Were the Indians human beings at all? The answer came from Pope Paul III: in 1537 the Bull *Sublimus Deus* declared them to be "true men" and not to be treated as "dumb brutes created for our service." Thus the

Pope guaranteed the validity of New World evangelizing: only "true men" were candidates for salvation.[20]

But was it possible that they had already been evangelized; that they had received the Revelation and let it slip away? For there were legends that the Apostle Thomas had preached the Gospel in India, and even after the distinction between America and the East Indies had been clearly established, the belief persisted that St. Thomas had evangelized the New World.

America as fact and image, voyage account or speculation, reached Europe through a vast network of texts quickly translated into all the major European languages and disseminated by a burgeoning printing industry that was coeval with the discoveries.[21] For his general knowledge of the New World, Léry relied mainly on the *General History of the West Indies* by the Spanish historian Francisco López de Gómara, whose detailed account of the Conquest, while it judges Indians severely, casts a sardonic eye on the methods of the conquistadors.

Of all the New World peoples encountered by Europeans in the sixteenth century, the Tupinamba entered the most freely into the European imagination. They were to be given memorable literary form by Montaigne: they are the "Cannibals" of his famous essay (for which Léry was probably an important source). In fact, they were the all-purpose allegorical figure of "America" for the sixteenth and seventeenth centuries. The figure found in innumerable paintings, frescos, and friezes, with plumed skirt and headdress, carrying a wooden sword with a disk-shaped head: that figure is a stylized Tupinamba Indian.

Popularized by Vespucci and Thevet (and by countless sailors' and merchants' reports), the Tupi were irresistible. They were known to live in a lush tropical setting of brilliantly colored flora and fauna; their natural appearance accorded with European standards of beauty; and they were usually naked. The splendor of their feathered costumes rivaled the caparisoned horsemen of Agincourt; with their weapons they outdid the English bowmen. As European chivalry was on the wane, a nostalgia may have attached to the Tupinamba, who seemed like knights without horses, clad not in shining armor but in gleaming feathers. They were impelled to greater lengths for honor and vengeance than were even the feudal nobles, for in sinister and fascinating rites, they ate their enemies.

When Henry II paid a state visit to Rouen in 1550, there was a sort of Brazilian exotic package, ready to present to him as a spectacle: on an island in the Seine was set up a mock Brazilian village, where fifty real Tupinamba Indians, joined by two hundred fifty sailors in savage guise (naked and painted black and red) hunted, cut brazilwood, fought, and danced among trees swarming with monkeys and parrots. Brazil was already a consumer item.[22]

From the very beginning of the ethnographic section of the *Histoire*, we can watch Léry threading his way among these preconceptions, rejecting some and endorsing others, making distinctions and noting discrepancies between what he had heard and what he now saw. The question of the marvelous and the monstrous had first to be dealt with. The bodies of the Tupi are manifestly normal: "neither monstrous nor prodigious with respect to ours"—so much for Mandevillian expectations. In fact, even more "normal" than ours: stronger, more robust, freer of deformities.

Léry's Calvinism makes him proof against any simple Arcadian expectations, but his description nevertheless contains formulaic expressions of the Ovidian Golden Age: "woods, plants and fields always verdant"; they all drink at the Fountain of Youth, living to the age of one hundred twenty because of the "small care that they have of the things of this world"—whereas we Europeans drink of the corrosive waters of mistrust and avarice.

Léry re-creates the amazement (surely no longer fresh, even in his time) in the fact "no less strange than difficult to believe" that they go about "as naked as they came out of their mother's womb," in defiance of the shame that is natural to fallen man. Not only are they not hairy (like the Wild Man of European myths); they make their nakedness still more naked by plucking out all body and facial hair. This utterly exposed surface is then re-covered by layers of inscriptions and various kinds of ritual mutilations, and decorative or deforming stone inserts for their faces. Indeed, if they are given clothes, they simply miss the point: a shift, for instance, is worn pulled up above the navel, or wrapped around the head. In lieu of garments, they wear body paint; on certain occasions they cover themselves with a gum to which they attach the down of birds— and thus the hairy Wild Man is reconstituted, explained by Léry not as a prodigy of nature but as a product of culture.

In a rather troubling passage (one that compels us to take measure of the assumptions that separate us from Léry), he speaks of the women slaves at Fort Coligny: in spite of whippings, "It has never been in our power to make them wear clothes. . . . Secretly stripping off their shirts and other rags, they would not be content unless before going to bed they could promenade naked all around our island." The image of the naked, incorrigible *femme sauvage* (Vespucci had popularized a particularly lurid version) is inevitably the focus for erotic attraction and fear in many of these narratives. Léry, however, seeks to defuse the image of the New World woman as an incitement to lust. "This crude nakedness," he says, "is much less attractive than one might think." It is, he says, the rouge, the ruff, the wig, the farthingale, the "robes upon robes" that drive men wild, rather than "the ordinary nakedness of savage women, who, however, for natural beauty, are in no way inferior to ours." Léry accords the Brazilian woman an intrinsic beauty on which man can look without sin. Desire, suggests Léry, has little to do with the accessibility of the naked body and much more to do with the inexhaustible play of the imagination, the never-ending manipulation of cultural signs.

The section on natural history (Chaps. IX–XIII) is a veritable encyclopedia of flora and fauna, rendered with such precision that modern botanists and zoologists have been able to identify almost every item he mentions: from the palms and hardwoods to the glorious panoply of birds, from the manatee to the sloth; by Léry's description, the ethologist can readily recognize the threat display of the iguana. For his classification, Léry uses an informal hybrid of various systems.[23] He follows the general outline of Pliny's *Natural History,* beginning with man as the sovereign creature; but unlike Pliny, he puts, for instance, insects and bats with birds, "things that fly." A touch of popularized Aristotelianism appears in his mention of plants as things with "vegetative soul." His approach is an improvisational and empirical one, allowing expression of astonishment at the splendor of the parrots' plumage, of ecstasy at the smell and taste of pineapple.

The taxonomy of the natural world here (as in most botanical and zoological works of the time) is defined mainly by the use human beings can make of it: what is good to eat, what can be used for ornamentation or shelter. You can learn the different preparations for the poisonous and nonpoisonous forms of manioc (cassava); given the materials, you could make the brew *caouin* yourself from Léry's instructions; or build the *boucan* for grilling meat (human or other); or assemble an intricate, finely fitted arrow.

He continually interweaves ethnographic detail and anecdote with natural history to show the interpenetration of the animal and the human realms. There are odd glimpses of personal exchange, or recognition on the part of the wild things. The *sagouin* is so proud and touchy that if you hurt its feelings it will "let itself die of chagrin." A terrifying "monstrous lizard" encountered in the forest transfixes them with his gaze, and in retrospect, seemed to have "taken as much pleasure in looking at us as we had felt fear in gazing upon it."

The relationship of the Tupi to their abundant and generous world is a revelation to the Old World visitor. They move about the Brazilian forest and seashore as sovereigns. They cavort in the water like dolphins, and hoot with laughter at the Europeans who officiously come to rescue them in their boats.

The marvels of America, the *difference* that Léry never fails to proclaim, are to him a fresh revelation of what God can do. In the words of another Calvinist, Urbain Chauveton, America is the providential gift of a "tableau tout neuf"—a wholly new picture—to reanimate our jaded sense of wonder and revivify our adoration of God.[24] But Léry will say repeatedly that the great error of the Tupi is that in their own praise of the abundance in which they live, they attribute to nature what should be attributed to the Creator of nature. Just "how far they are removed from such knowledge" is exemplified in the subjects of Chapters XIV, XV, and XVI: on war; on cannibalism; on religion.

Léry's description of Tupi wars reveals an ambivalence. They do not fight for lands, or spoils, or ransoms; they fight for vengeance. And in the code of European chivalry, vengeance is the price exacted by honor. But for Léry, these inveterate, unremitting hatreds bear too much resemblance to the viciously retaliatory relations between Catholics and Protestants at the very time of his writing. He knows that the *point d'honneur* is deadly, in Brazil or in France.

And yet, he admires. The councils of war are exemplary in their order and eloquence, and can be assimilated to the discourse of Renaissance magnanimity, the ideal of *générosité,* or large-hearted uncircumspect valor. And as for the magnificence of the Tupi warrior in his full regalia, Léry gives way to sheer delight in the "marvel" of the "great featherings of red, blue, green, scarlet" sparkling in the light.

The sequel of these splendid combats was the ritual slaughter and eating of captured enemies, and in European culture this is said to be the most forbidden of all acts, the insurmountable barrier to sympathy or understanding. But in fact, there was a rich and elaborate European discourse of cannibalism, in which the travelers' New World reports were only one strand among many.[25]

In the first place, the anthropophagic metaphor had moved to the center of Protestant polemic in the harrowing controversies over the Eucharist and transubstantiation (as when Léry compares the savage tribe of Ouetaca with Villegagnon, who "wanted to eat the flesh of Jesus Christ raw").

Furthermore, Léry's readers knew firsthand about real, literal cannibalism. There were the sieges, like that of Sancerre, which on occasion produced the cannibalism of desperation. And there were the riots and lynchings of the St. Bartholomew's Day Massacre, in which mobs or individuals, in paroxysms of hatred, threw themselves on the bodies of slain Huguenots and tore into them to devour their hearts or livers. Even when the specific act of cannibalism was not involved, mutilation and dismemberment of the corpses were everyday events during the Wars of Religion. The body of Admiral Coligny himself, the most revered and beloved of French Protestant political leaders and the prime target of the Massacre, was castrated and strung up on display.

Thus, when Léry discusses the horror of Tupi cannibalism, it is not a horror that disqualifies the Tupi as members of the human species. Their cannibalism is first and foremost ritual—a socially interpretable act—and it is that aspect that makes it, if not redeemable, at least tolerable to contemplate. Léry could see in it an order and a containment that was reassuring and even, one senses, aesthetically compelling—a "tragedy," as he calls it.[26]

The victim was an established enemy. According to different phases of the ritual, he was at certain moments incorporated into the community, at others rejected from it; but he had his own moment, his own song of defiance, when he was allowed to assert his own dignity and valor. The killing took place without torture, by a single great blow to the head. The cannibal feast was a social event: the distribution of the cooked flesh among neighboring groups was a gesture of solidarity and also of shared responsibility, implicitly entailing allegiance. (As a Frenchman, Léry belongs to an allied group, and he narrowly avoids offending his Tupi hosts by refusing to partake.)

What does it all mean? All the chroniclers asked this question; the explicit answer is not the only one that the ethnographer is looking for, but it is a starting point. "Vengeance" was the most frequent reply, and in fact the various warring tribes among the Tupi seemed to have been locked into systems of automatic retaliations; the victim could always say, "In eating my flesh you are eating the flesh of your own kinsmen, which I have devoured." One group affirms its own integrity and strength by demoralizing the other, "pursuing the dead and gnawing them right down to the bone."

A wife is granted to the prisoner while he is awaiting execution, which may be months or even years away; that wife will then, on the appointed day, eat her erstwhile husband and the children she has had by him—enough, as Léry says, to make your hair stand on end. But if you "consider what goes on every day over here, among us"—and here Léry matches intensity for intensity, detail for detail: the human fat sold to the highest bidder, the human heart roasted over coals, on the familiar streets of towns such as Lyon and Auxerre. These orgies of hatred unleashed by the St. Bartholomew's Day Massacre may have had their own laws and rituals that emerge under the analysis of the anthropologist and historian; but as Léry saw them, they were utterly horrible because they signaled the utter breakdown of European order—a convulsion, a formless, aberrant manifestation of savagery in which neighbor devours neighbor.[27] Tupi cannibalism, with its containment, keeps categories of friend and enemy stable; it makes possible large, well-defined areas of trust that will, as we shall see, be the basis of his relationship with them.

Léry speaks of the books that will bear "witness for posterity." The Wars of Religion have been for the French the ultimate bad news concerning what civilized human beings are capable of doing to each other. For Léry and many other Protestants, it was urgent that the hideous facts not be forgotten or swept under the carpet. The histories and martyrologies of Théodore de Bèze and Jean Crespin kept alive both these memories and the French Protestant identity, even if the cause did not prevail.[28]

Yet, for all that he gives examples of European conduct that are worse even than Tupi cannibalism, he would not obscure the central fact of what he regards as their fallen state: the ignorance of their Creator which has allowed them to stray into such dreadful practices.

From Léry's Chapter XVI one learns less about Tupi religion than about how Léry, as a devout sixteenth-century European Protestant, reconciles his faith, his doctrines, and his experience of these people. What he does present of Tupi religious practice is as ammunition assembled in his two-front war with Roman Catholicism and with a nascent movement of free-thinking, and the reader is given a review of the repertoire of Protestant polemical devices.

Chapter XVI is permeated, both textually and ideologically, with Calvin's *Institutes of the Christian Religion,* and in fact Léry's opening words, "There is no people, however barbarous and savage, that lacks the feeling that there is a divinity," are taken from it almost verbatim, by way of a quotation from Cicero.[29] Léry begins his chapter by amassing evidence that would seem to make the Tupinamba an exception: they are "ignorant of the sole and true God"; "they neither confess nor worship any gods"; "they do not pray by any religious form to anything whatsoever"; they are at the zero degree of religious awareness. Or so they are presented at the beginning of the chapter; but we will see the polemic and the rhetorical effects for which Léry is laying the groundwork.

"Can it be that, like brute beasts, these Americans live without any religion at all? Indeed they do, or with almost none." With that "almost," Léry begins to qualify his absolute negation. In fact, they do possess the merest glimmer of religious awareness, for they do believe in the immortality of souls and in an afterlife: those who are good dance eternally with their ancestors in beautiful gardens behind the mountains, while the worthless are "incessantly tormented" by Aygnan, who is the figure in Tupi lore that Léry identifies with Satan. Even if they define the virtuous life as one of killing and eating many enemies, they at least make the distinction.

And particularly, they suffer the torments of the devil even in this life. From the description of the Tupi in their natural setting, they might seem to be happy pagans, too content to feel any need for redemption. The point of entry for the Christian message is their pain: their fear of Aygnan, which makes them sweat with anguish—and which makes them infinitely more salvageable than the European atheist. Like the vast majority of his contemporaries, Léry fully believes in devils, and will not tolerate any metaphorizing or psychologizing about them. And now we can see the rhetorical strategy underlying the hyperbolically negative description of Tupi religious sense. *Even these savages,* the most benighted imaginable, could serve as theologians to the European atheist. Through their belief in the immortality of the soul and the reality of the devil, they have more access to the divine than the European free-thinker who has rejected the Christian revelation.

As Léry builds up the dossier on the Tupi religious sense, he counts as evidence even their submission to those "impostors," those "charlatans," the *caraïbes,* or Tupi shamans, who appear every few years to engage them in certain mysterious ceremonies. Like most missionaries, Catholics or Protestant, Léry regards these shamans as competitors for the souls of the Indians; and like other Huguenot writers, he sees their "idolatrous" practices as analogous to the Roman Catholic cult of saints and relics (the *caraïbes* dance in and out of villages like "popish indulgence-bearers").[30] But Léry is capable of a candid admiration and even a delight in what he does not rationally approve of. As a clandestine witness of a religious ceremony, he is enraptured with the "marvelous harmony" of the chanting voices; two decades later he can say "It seems to me that I still have their voices in my ears."

When Léry asks the meaning of those chants, the interpreter provides a schematic and fragmentary answer: laments for ancestors, anticipation of the afterlife, the story of a deluge. That last item commands Léry's attention, which is chiefly available for whatever can be reconciled with Scripture. Their deluge story must be a degraded, eroded version of Noah's flood. But that degradation does not really surprise him, because "being deprived of writing, it is hard for them to retain things in their purity." Their variants of the story occur because it is spoken: it is *fable*, therefore distorted every time it is transmitted—unlike Scripture, the fixative for truth.

"They know nothing of writing, either sacred or secular," neither *Ecriture* nor *écriture*, Scripture nor script. For early Protestantism the written word had a central importance: script makes possible Scripture, the pure source of religious truth fixed in permanent form, unadulterated by the accretions and distortions of Roman Catholicism. The passages in this chapter concerning the written word are charged with Léry's awareness of its implications as a medium for retention, for reinforcing the slippery aural memory; for communication independent of presence; and even for domination.[31]

Like most missionaries of the time, Léry was too preoccupied with finding the resemblance between Tupi religion and Scripture to perceive the shape of their cosmogony, their own sacred history. In the notes to Chapter XVI there is an outline of that cosmogony, as anthropologists have been able to reconstruct it from the sixteenth-century European chroniclers—particularly André Thevet—and from native informants of groups descended from the Tupi. While Thevet is no model of reliability, his account of Tupi myth in his *Cosmographie universelle*, swarming with heroes and demigods performing or undergoing metamorphoses, has too many points in common with other early sources and with modern ethnography to be dismissed. Thevet's penchant for collecting, and the absence in him of the Protestants' violent antipathy to "idolatry" and "superstition," has resulted in a fuller record of Tupi religious beliefs than the one Léry has left us.

Léry's report is a mere suggestion of a mythology whose richness he did not explore, and of which he may have been unaware. He refers briefly to the deluge, but not to the great culture heroes, who gave the earth its shape through ordeals of fire and water, and who taught humanity the cultivation of manioc. He knows the term *Mair* for "Frenchman" or "stranger," but does not mention that it is also the name of one of those early culture heroes. He understood something of the prestige of the *caraïbes* as shamans, but he did not seem aware that they had also an important messianic function.[32]

No entity in Tupi religion seems to have been actually worshiped: neither the culture heroes, nor the *caraïbes,* nor Toupan, the spirit of thunder. Could not that vacuum be filled by a belief in the Christian God? Is there, for Léry, any basis for hope of their conversion? He does not find it in their ceremonies, however enthralling, nor in their myths; for the Reformed missionary, gesture and fable—which Catholic missionaries tended to turn to their own purposes—are associated chiefly with error and superstition. Léry's religion is tending toward the abstract and contemplative praise of the Creator and His works.

As for the association that other chroniclers make between the Indians and the malediction of Ham, the only taint that Léry can be sure of is the one that they share with all humanity in a fraternal bond: they are "issued from the corrupt race of Adam." But are they convertible? The question remains, I think, unresolved for him, as indeed, Calvinist thought resists pronouncing on another's salvation or damnation.[33] Of the anecdotes Léry relates, one tells of failure, the other—their response to the celebration of the Creation in Psalm 104—suggests the possibility of eventual success. And however problematic such success might be in the mind of the modern reader, in the mind of Léry the Tupi's becoming Christians of the "pure Gospel" would have been the realization and the crowning of their humanity.

The final chapters of the ethnography in which Léry turns to ordinary human dealings in this earthly life—marriage and childbirth, civil order and hospitality, healing and funeral rites—offer an implicit answer to a question underlying all the early speculation about the New World: is it possible for a people living outside the Christian dispensation to live a morally coherent life?

The account that Léry gives is of an ordered polygamy resembling the patriarchal society of Biblical times. Léry sees and praises Tupi society as one—for all that its people go naked—in which there is no sexual tension, no imaginative elaboration of the erotic, no "romance." Tupi women are offered as admirable examples for European women: hardworking in the growing and preparing of food, courageous and resilient in childbirth, unsparing of their bodies in nourishing their children. While there are other sides to Léry's representation of women—the naked nocturnal wanderers, the demon-possessed celebrants at the religious rites, the devourers of human flesh—in their families they are domestic and maternal beings, producers of the Tupi babies whom they raise with much humane good sense.

Probably no part of the whole book is more important than Chapter XVIII, on civil order and hospitality. It is the obverse of the one on cannibalism: it treats of the trust within the tribe, and the laws of hospitality that apply to any stranger who is recognized as an ally.

This is also the chapter that comes the closest to the heart of any ethnographer's experience. The rules of ethnographic fieldwork require that one immerse oneself in an alien culture, retain the bare minimum of comforts and associations from home, and submit to a profound disorientation. You are reduced for a time to a level of infantile dependence and incomprehension of what is going on around you. Everyone, down to the little children, is smarter than you are. You are never in on the joke.

Léry gives us stories of himself in exactly such states. In this chapter, there are episodes full of false alarms, of unnecessary panics, of complete loss of dignity and composure. He is "surrounded by savages," divested of hat, sword, belt, and tunic; he is made to spend a night trying to sleep through a cannibal feast; he is offered a roasted foot while he contemplates his future as the *plat du jour*. The eventual clarifications take place amid great hoots of Tupi laughter. The future defender of the Calvinist faith at one point surrenders his baptismal name of Jean (impossible to pronounce or remember) and renames himself "*Léry-oussou*," or "Big Oyster."

These scenes are also the obverse of Léry's experience with Villegagnon, who seemed to offer welcome and refuge, and who proved to be a mortal enemy. Here, in scene after scene, the Tupi seem threatening, and in fact enfold him in a benevolent embrace—albeit one that is, at times, overwhelming (rather like the affectionate gaze of the enormous lizard).

In all the early New World literature, the theme of hospitality was one of the most compelling and the most charged with hope or regret: the first encounter of mutual amazement between naked inhabitants in their setting of flowers and feathers, and the bearded Europeans encased in metal and bearing swords. The early texts record those initial welcomes, the free offering of food and shelter, and the gradual souring of relations as the Europeans reveal their greed and violence, and as the Indian cultures are themselves degraded. But for Léry, Indian hospitality is still intact; the most memorable descriptions are of encounters not on a beach with European ships in the background, but deep within the Tupi setting, in the heart of the forest villages. The description of the "weeping greeting" or the "welcome of tears" shows Léry's ethnography at its best: the meaning of advance or retreat, of touching or refraining from touching, of expansiveness or reserve, of the inversion of codes in the expression of joy. The illustration that accompanies the account epitomizes the entire book: the welcomed guest sitting in the hammock is a European, in doublet and hose, also shedding tears and fully performing his part in the ceremony.[34]

Léry's description of Tupi life begins with the beautiful natural body and follows it, as he says, "all the way to the grave." The weeping women mourn their dead husbands and kinsmen: "he who was so valiant and who gave us so many prisoners to eat"; "he avenged us well." Léry perceives an equivalence between their laments and those of the women of Béarn and Gascony celebrating the vitality of their beloved and unregenerate men; he points to the particular codes of expression that in each culture will celebrate its own values and guarantee its own continuity.

The Tupi-French colloquy that ends the ethnographic section (Chapter XX) may or may not be of Léry's composition. (Thevet claimed not.)[35] Certainly Léry put his mark on it, because the French interlocutor identifies himself early on as "Big Oyster" (Léry-oussou). As in the best modern foreign language textbooks, so in Léry's colloquy we find the chief characteristics of the language and a basic vocabulary displayed in typical situations that foreigners find themselves in. It displays the nuances of etiquette, the forms of indirection and reserve that modulate all transactions; it shows the rules of barter, the strategies on both sides for making one's own desire for an object seem less than it is, or for making the rarity of an object seem greater than it is. One sees also a particular moment in New World–Old World technological exchange, which is well under way but has not yet submerged the indigenous cultures. The Tupi already know who is the best European maker of pruning hooks; the steel knife has replaced the sharpened stone. We see a European trying to explain European power structure, the monarchical system, the cities of stone houses.

The author of this dialogue had made an effort that already suggests an attentive respect for the alien language—a respect not to be taken for granted in sixteenth-century Europe, but absolutely necessary for sailors, traders, or missionaries; and particularly for a refugee from an abortive colony stranded beyond the furthest outpost.[36]

When Léry leaves the Tupi village for his return home, he leaves a place where the "savage" tells the truth in a strange language for a place where a countryman tells lies in a familiar language. Of Villegagnon's treachery, dissimulated by his apparently benevolent farewell, Léry learns, and tells his readers, only later on. But it is an element in a plot that would serve for Shakespeare or Boccaccio. For when Léry and his companions reach Europe—after a voyage that itself would strain credulity in a work of fiction—, it is revealed that Villegagnon had placed in the ship captain's hands a casket to be delivered to the authorities back home. The casket contained instructions to burn the returning Calvinists as heretics.

When the ship is only a few days out on the return voyage, five of his fellow Huguenots, judging the vessel unsafe, determined to take a dinghy from the ship and return to Fort Coligny. Léry himself is already in the boat when a friend persuades him to stay with the ship. Of the five who return, three will be put to death by Villegagnon. (It was of these that Léry gave an account in Crespin's *Histoire des Martyrs*.)

The return passage, in a leaky tub commanded by an incompetent captain, is another introduction to an exotic culture—the culture of famine. The ship does, in the end, bring most of its passengers home; but the specimens of New World fauna go into the pot. The gastronomically exotic was disorienting enough—from parrots and monkeys to tapir-skin shields and grilled rats' feet—but now the unthinkable is thought, and not in the "savages' " context of ritual and meaning, but out of degrading hunger: The captain begins his calculations as to the moment when one of them will provide meat for the others.

Léry, when he is writing this, partly looks back on the voyage as a rehearsal for his role at Sancerre. Not only his recipes for extraordinary comestibles, but his comprehension of what is involved in resorting to them are to be called on. There again, among his neighbors, the unthinkable will be thought—and this time enacted.

For Léry, the frustration of Villegagnon's deadly plot (the casket falls into Protestant hands), his surviving the desperate voyage, his friend's last-minute appeal as the dinghy was loading—all these pile meaning on Providential meaning. "Delivered . . . from so many abysses of death," he acknowledges a sense of election to record their martyrdom (which he carried out in his contribution to the Crespin martyrology) and to bear witness to the power of the Eternal.

That, at least, is the explicit sense in the work of an obligation peculiarly Léry's own. There are other and larger recognitions throughout the work of a kind of grace central to Renaissance literature of the pastoral mode. The plot of the *Histoire* invites a comparison with *The Tempest;* the exile from Europe voyages to the edge of the world; exiled even from Europe's colony of exiles, he flees into the very wilderness of a land already wild, there to encounter trustworthy forms of human goodness in its inhabitants. It is a rule of pastoral plots that you must stay in your place of exile only long enough for certain profound and beneficent transformations to take place; in this case, for Léry's bone-deep "experience" of America. You must then return—to Milan and resume your dukedom, or to Geneva to take up your ministry—arriving back in Europe wracked and exhausted by tempests that are withal blessed.

What lay ahead for Léry was the St. Bartholomew's Day Massacre. In the compacted violence of walled cities choked with hatred, the memory of the Brazilian forests and the Tupi people is still present: "I often regret that I am not among the savages." Not, it would seem, as a paralyzing regret, but as a sustaining memory, in the unacquisitive spirit of Léry's family motto: "Plus voir qu'avoir"—"More to see than to have."

The tonus, the vitality of this text is due largely to a tension in Léry between disapproval and delight. A small but significant marker: as a theologian Léry speaks with contempt of the "Rabélistes," yet Rabelais is omnipresent—sometimes by explicit reference, and sometimes just beneath the surface. At the end of Chapter XII, Léry enunciates the criteria for entry into the Tupi world in terms that are almost identical with those for admission to the Abbey of Thélèmes: "Just as they love those who are gay, joyful, and liberal, on the contrary they hate those who are taciturn, stingy and melancholy; and I can assure any who are sly, malicious, gloomy, niggardly, or who munch their bread alone in a corner, that they will never be welcome among our Tupinamba." This evocation of the elements of the festive and the chivalric: Is it to preserve them? To exorcise them? It may be that displaced onto America, they can have sanctuary and be loved in their "savage" guise even as they are being combatted at home by those very forces with which Léry is doctrinally allied.

As Léry describes them, the exotic New World cultures resemble the Old World in just those aspects that modernity—via the Reformation—would suppress in the name of a purer religion or a more efficient economic structure. The plumed display, the unmeasured consumption of feast days with their gigantic *cahouinages,* the young Tupi men dancing "like morris dancers" through the villages at night with their maracas, the splendid warriors, the widows' outpourings for the prowess of their dead husbands—all this speaks directly to European traditions of chivalry, to rituals that bear pre-Christian traces, to ancient codes of valor, to a festive tradition of unparsimonious expenditure.

Léry wrote not of a Golden Age, but of a real society with its own anxieties, its own internal tolls and compensations—some of them violent—and its own recognizable kind of coherence. For all that they are a people destitute of divine knowledge they are, at their worst, not worse than "some bearing the name of Christian"; at their best they are exemplary of what earthly human beings can be. Léry's word to characterize them is *rondeur;* it is glossed as "frankness," but it inescapably connotes integrity and wholeness—like that of the earth, newly perceived in its complete roundness.

Léry intended this work for the ordinary literate person, curious about other lands and peoples. His language is salty and vigorous, a storehouse of popular and proverbial expressions. Léry shared with other Reformation writers an aesthetic of a conscious and chosen simplicity; he explicitly eschews the "fine flowers of rhetoric."

Nevertheless, his thought does not reach us in a series of discrete statements, but rather through long parenthetical expressions, intensifying locutions, and concatenations such as "not only . . . but also." One can wait a long time for the main verb, which is often preceded by a number of clauses, themselves introduced by strings of absolute constructions. Occasionally Léry even loses himself in his own syntax and emerges from an elaborate sentence having neglected to provide the long-awaited verb at all. These labyrinthine sentences, however, do express the unifying quality of Léry's thought: he establishes priorities, makes concessions, and offers comparisons and caveats.

I have kept in mind both Léry's idiosyncrasy and the needs of the reader, and have tried to avoid making Léry's text too smooth and bland, or obliterating the complex relationships among the elements of his thought. But I would not want him to be less intelligible to the modern English reader than he was to the French reader of his time; therefore, I have sometimes divided a particularly tortuous sentence into two or three separate ones, transposed the order of clauses, and so forth.

One of the pleasures of the translator's task is finding, for instance, the appropriate term of abuse from a diction that may include "windbag," or "blockhead," but that will sound neither too quaintly archaic nor too jarringly modern. My constant companion has been Randle Cotgrave's *Dictionarie of the French and English Tongues,* a treasurehouse of language both colloquial and technical, which was published in

1611. I have sought words and expressions that have existed in English at least since the seventeenth century and that are familiar today: the pool of language common to Léry's time and to ours.

I have used both footnotes (in the text) and endnotes (gathered at the end of the text, in the "Notes" section). The unbracketed footnote material is from Léry's marginal notes. The bracketed material contains either my additions to Léry's notes, or the brief explanation of terms unfamiliar to many modern readers. The endnotes treat more problematic questions and refer to background material, historical and critical sources, and so on.

This translation is based on the second edition, that of 1580. Between the first (1578) and the second (1580) editions, Léry made a number of additions and corrections. The later editions (1585, 1600, 1611) bear a heavy load of polemic and of compiled allusions. While these are of great interest to the specialist, for the general reader they tend to obscure the clean line of narrative, ethnography, and commentary that characterize the 1580 edition. The availability of this edition through the facsimile published by Jean-Claude Morisot (Geneva: Droz, 1975) is yet another reason for choosing it: a reader with enough French to profit from consulting the original work to check details can easily consult both the original and the English versions.

The numerous references to *Viagem* indicate my use of the notes in the Brazilian Portuguese translation: *Viagem à Terra do Brasil* (São Paulo: Editora da universidade de São Paulo, 1980), translated by Sergio Milliet and with notes by Milliet and by the Tupi specialist Plinio Ayrosa.

# HISTORY
# OF A VOYAGE TO
## THE LAND OF BRAZIL

# DEDICATION

### ❧

# TO THE ILLUSTRIOUS
## AND POWERFUL LORD FRAN-
## COIS, COMTE DE COLIGNY, SEIGNEUR
## DE CHATILLON. GOVERNOR FOR THE
## KING IN THE CITY OF MONTPELLIER,
## ETC.[a]

Monsieur:

The blessed memory of him through whom God has shown me the things from which I have built the present history inspires me to show my gratitude; therefore it is not without cause that I now have the boldness to present it to you, his successor. It is my intention to perpetuate here the memory of a voyage to America undertaken for the express purpose of establishing the pure service of God, both among the French who had retreated there, and among the savages living in that land; therefore I have judged it my duty to make it known to posterity how greatly he who was the cause and the motive of it all is forever to be praised. Indeed, I dare affirm that in all past history there will not be found any French and Christian captain who has extended both the reign of Jesus Christ, King of Kings and Lord of Lords, and the boundaries of his sovereign prince, into so distant a land.

All this being duly considered, who can exalt highly enough such a holy and truly heroic enterprise? Some may say that given how short a time these things lasted, and that at present there is no more news of the true religion in that land than there is name of Frenchman living there, this enterprise merits little esteem. But in spite of such allegations, what I

---

[a][François de Coligny was the son of Gaspard de Coligny, Admiral of France. Admiral Coligny obtained the royal support for Villegagnon's Brazilian venture. He was to become a revered Protestant leader and martyr; he was killed in the St. Bartholomew's Day Massacre (1572), of which he was the chief target. For more details on Coligny, see Translator's Introduction and Léry's Chapter I.]

have said remains true: just as the Gospel of the Son of God has been declared in our own time in that fourth part of the world, called "America," it is also very certain that if the affair had been as well pursued as it had been auspiciously begun, the two reigns, spiritual and temporal, would have been so securely founded in our time that more than ten thousand persons of the French nation would be there now, as fully and surely in the possession of it for our king as the Spanish and Portuguese are, in fact, now established there in the name of theirs.

Therefore, unless one would wish to impute to the Apostles the destruction of the churches that they had first erected, and the ruin of the Roman Empire to the brave warriors who had adjoined to it so many fair provinces, similarly—since they are to be praised who first laid the foundations in America of the things I have mentioned—one must attribute the fault and the discontinuation both to Villegagnon and to those with him, who instead of advancing the work they had begun (as they had promised to do) abandoned both the fortress that we had built, and the country that had been named "Antarctic France," to the Portuguese: who found that it very well suited their needs. It will forever be known that the late Gaspard de Coligny of blessed memory, Admiral of France, your virtuous father, who carried out his enterprise through those whom he sent to America, besides making a part of that land subject to the French crown, also gave ample proof of his zeal to have the Gospel declared not only throughout this kingdom, but throughout the entire world.

Since I consider you, Monsieur, to represent the person of that excellent Lord, to whom the country will be perpetually indebted for so many generous acts, I have published this little labor of mine under your authority. Moreover, by this means it will be you to whom Thevet[a] will have to respond, not only in general, for condemning and slandering the cause for which we made this voyage to America, but also in particular, when he speaks of the Admiralty of France in his *Cosmography,* for daring to rail against the good name, revered by all people of good will, of him who was the cause.

Moreover, Monsieur, your constance and magnanimity in the defense of the Reformed Churches of this realm manifest each day how fitly you follow the footsteps of him who, having left you in his place to sustain that same cause, shed even his own blood for it: that, I say, was my second reason for addressing you, as well as to recognize in some way

---

[a][See Translator's Introduction.]

the good and gracious hospitality that you offered me in the city of Berne, where, after my deliverance from the siege and famine of Sancerre, I sought you out. By all these circumstances I have been led to address myself directly to you. I very well know, however, that although the subject of this history is such that if sometimes you desired to hear it read, there are things in which you could take some pleasure, nevertheless with respect to its language, which is crude and ill polished, it is not for the ears of a lord so well instructed from his earliest years in the cultivation of letters. But having assured myself that by your natural graciousness, receiving my good affection, you will be indulgent to this fault, I have no reluctance in offering and dedicating what I have been able to accomplish, both to the holy memory of the father and as token of the humble service that I desire to continue for the children.

Upon which, Monsieur, I shall pray the Eternal that together with my lords your brothers, and Madame de Teligny your sister (plants bearing fruits worthy of the trunk from which they spring), keeping you all in His holy protection, He may bless and make prosper ever more your virtuous and generous actions.

The twenty-sixth of December 1577.

> Your very humble and affectionate servant
> J. de Léry

# PREFACE

One might well be amazed that, having made the voyage to America eighteen years ago, I have waited so long to bring this history out: therefore it has seemed only proper that I explain what has impeded me. Early on, after I came back to France, I would show people my memoirs, most of them written with brazilwood ink,[1] and in America itself, containing the notable things that I observed during my voyage, and I would give spoken accounts to those who wanted to know yet more; but I had not intended to go any further with them than that. However, some of those with whom I often spoke maintained that, rather than let so many things worthy of memory remain buried, I should set them down in writing at more length, and in a more orderly fashion.

Upon their entreaties and solicitations, in the year 1563 I wrote a rather full report of them. As I was leaving the place where I had been living at that time,[2] I lent it to a reliable person; it so happened that, as the people to whom he had given it to return to me were passing through Lyon, it was taken from them at the city gate, and was so utterly lost that in spite of all my efforts, I could not recover it. Since I was distressed by the loss of this book, a while later, when I retrieved the rough draft that I had left with the person who had transcribed it for me, I managed to have another fair copy made (except for the colloquy of the savage language, which you will see in the twentieth chapter, and of which neither I nor anyone else had a copy). I finished it at a time when I was living in the town of La Charité-sur-Loire; violence was descending in France on those who were of the Religion, and I was constrained, in order to avoid that fury, to leave in haste all my books and papers and take refuge in Sancerre.

Immediately after my departure everything was ransacked, and this second American collection disappeared; so I was a second time deprived of the fruits of my labors. However, one day I was recounting to a notable Seigneur the first loss in Lyon, and mentioned to him the name of the person to whom, I had been told, my work had been given. He was so taken with this matter, and gave it so much attention that he finally recovered it, and last year (1576), as I was passing by his house, he returned it to me. So that is how it has come about that what I had written about America, which had kept slipping out of my hands, could not until now see the light of day.

But to tell the truth, there was another reason. I had felt that I did not have the necessary qualities to take pen in hand. The same year that I returned from that land, which was in 1558, I saw the book entitled *Of the Singularities of America*, which M. de la Porte, following the tales and memoirs of the friar André Thevet, had prepared for publication.[3] Although I was not unaware of what M. Fumée, in his preface to the *General History of the West Indies*[4] has justly remarked—that the *Singularities* are singularly stuffed with lies—, if the author had been content with that and had gone no further, I might still have suppressed the whole thing.

But in this present year 1577, reading Thevet's *Cosmography*,[a] I saw that he has not only revived and augmented his early errors, but what is more (perhaps supposing that we were all dead, or that if one of us were still alive he would not dare contradict him), with no other pretext than the desire to backbite and, with false, stinging, and abusive digressions, to slander the ministers and those—of whom I was one—who in 1556 accompanied them to go join Villegagnon in Brazil, he has imputed to us crimes. Therefore, in order to refute these falsehoods of Thevet, I have been compelled to set forth a complete report of our voyage. And before I go on, lest you think that I am complaining about this new "cosmographer" without just cause, I will record here the libels that he has put forth against us, contained in Volume II, Book 21, Chapter 2, page 908:

> Moreover [*says Thevet*] I had forgotten to tell you that shortly before, there had been some sedition among the French, brought about by the divisiveness and partiality of the four ministers of the new religion, whom Calvin had sent in order to plant his bloody Gospel. Chief among them was a seditious minister named Richier, who had been a Carmelite and a Doctor of Paris a few years before his voyage.[5] These gallant preachers, who were trying only to get rich and seize whatever they could, created secret leagues and factions, and wove plots which led to the death of some of our men.

---

[a][*La Cosmographie universelle* (Paris, 1575), hereafter abbreviated "*Cosmog. univ.*"]

*But some of these mutineers were caught and executed, and their carcasses went to feed the fishes: the others escaped, one of whom was the said Richier, who soon after went to be minister at La Rochelle, where I believe he still is. The savages, incensed by such a tragedy, nearly rushed upon us to put to death all who were left.*

Those are Thevet's very words, which I ask the reader to note well.[a] For since he never saw us in America, nor we him, and since even less was he (as he says) in danger for his life because of us, I want to show that he has been in this respect a bold-faced liar and a shameless calumniator. Therefore, to anticipate what he might want to say in order to save face— that his report does not refer to the time when he was in that country, but that he means to be recounting an act that took place since his return—I ask him in the first place whether this deliberate expression that he uses, "The savages, incensed by such a tragedy, nearly rushed upon us to put to death, etc.," can be meant otherwise than, by this "us," to include himself in this supposed danger. However, if he wanted to quibble further, and still deny that his intention was something other than to have it believed that he really saw, in America, the ministers that he speaks of, then let us listen to the language he uses in another passage:

*Moreover (says this Cordelier) if I had stayed longer in that land, I would have tried to win the lost souls of this poor people, rather than endeavoring to dig in the earth and seek the riches that nature has hidden there. But since I was not yet well versed in their language, and since the ministers that Calvin had sent there to plant his new Gospel were undertaking this charge and were envious of my resolution, I abandoned this enterprise of mine.*[b]

"Believe the bearer," goes the saying that mocks such paid liars.[6] Therefore, if this good Roman Catholic has given no other evidence of having abandoned the world (as required by the order of Saint Francis, to which he belongs) than by, as he says, "having scorned the riches hidden in the bowels of the earth in Brazil," nor performed any other miracle than the conversion of the American savages living there, "whose souls" he says "he had meant to to win, if the ministers hadn't prevented him"— when I have shown that such is not the case—he is in great danger of

---

[a][Léry's quotations from Thevet are in the main highly accurate.]

[b]Volume II, Book 21, Chapter 8 (p. 925). [The quotation is accurate except for Léry's substitution of "Evangile" (Gospel) for "Eglise" (Church).]

neither being put on the Pope's calendar to be canonized, nor being hailed after his death as Monsieur Saint Thevet.

So to prove that everything he says is so much nonsense: it is hardly likely that Thevet—who in his writings turns everything to his own purpose and "makes his arrows out of any wood," who picks up any bits and shards he can find to lengthen and color his tales—would have been silent in his *Singularities* on the subject of the ministers if he had seen them in that country, much less if they had committed what he accuses them of in his *Cosmography*, printed sixteen or seventeen years later. By his own testimony in the *Singularities,* he arrived at Cape Frio in 1555, the tenth of November, and arrived four days later at the Bay of Guanabara in America, which he left the last day of the following January to return to France;[a] we, however, as I will show in this history, did not arrive at the Fort of Coligny, situated on that same bay, until the beginning of March 1557. Since it is obvious that Thevet had left more than thirteen months earlier, how has he made so bold as to say and write that he saw us there?

The gulf of almost two thousand leagues of sea between him, who had long since returned to Paris, and us, who were under the tropic of Capricorn—is that not warrant against his seeing us? So it might be; but he had an itch to push on and to lie "cosmographically": that is to say, to the whole world. Since I have proved him false on this first point, whatever else he says deserves no answer. Nevertheless, to resolve all the replies he might make concerning the sedition that he presumes to mention, I say in the first place that no such sedition will be found to have existed at Fort Coligny while we were there; and even less was a single Frenchman killed there in our time. If Thevet claims nonetheless that there was a conspiracy of Villegagnon's people against him in that country, and wants to impute it to us, I ask nothing more than Villegagnon's own testimony to serve as our defense and to show that the conspiracy had taken place before we arrived. The letter that Villegagnon wrote in Latin to M. Jean Calvin, in response to the one that we brought to him from the latter, has already been translated and published elsewhere long since; even if someone doubts what I say, the original, written in brazilwood ink and still legible, bears witness to the facts. However, since it will do double service in this matter—both to refute Thevet, and to show what religion Villegagnon pretended to hold at that time—I have inserted it here word for word.[7]

---

[a] See Chapters 1, 24, 25, and 60 of the *Singularities.*

## The Content of the Letter that Villegagnon Sent
### from America to Calvin

*Words cannot express the joy that has come to me through your letters and by the brothers who brought them. They found me reduced to such a state that I had to fill the offices both of magistrate and of minister of the Church; which was a cause of great anguish to me, for the example of King Ozias[8] turned me from such a way of life. But I was compelled to do it, for fear that the workers whom I had hired and brought over here might, by frequenting the native people of this land, be besmirched with their vices, or, for lack of continuity in the practices of the Religion, fall into apostasy. This fear was allayed by the arrival of the brothers. There is also this advantage, that if henceforth I must engage in some enterprise and incur dangers, I will have no lack of persons to console me and help me with their counsel—an aid that had been taken from me by the fear of the dangers amongst which we live. For the brothers who had come over here from France with me, distressed by the difficulties of our affairs, had withdrawn into Egypt,[a] each offering some excuse. Those who had remained were poor, wretched folk, and mercenaries, such as I had been able to procure at the time. The disposition of the latter was such that it behooved me to fear them rather than to take any comfort from their presence.*

*Now the cause of this is that upon our arrival all sorts of vexations and difficulties arose, so that I did not know what counsel to heed or where to start. The country was all wilderness, and untilled; there were no houses, nor roofs, nor any use of wheat. On the contrary, there were wild and savage people, remote from all courtesy and humanity, utterly different from us in their way of doing things and in their upbringing: without religion, nor any knowledge of honesty or virtue, or of what is just or unjust; so that it seemed to me that we had fallen among beasts bearing a human countenance. We had to provision ourselves astutely and swiftly against all these difficulties, and take the necessary measures while the ships were preparing to go back, for fear that the native inhabitants, coveting the goods we had brought, might catch us off guard and put us to death. There was also the proximity of the Portuguese, who do not wish us well; having been unable to hold on to*

---

[a]["Egypt" is a Huguenot code-word for Papism. See text below.]

*the land that we now possess, they take it very ill that we have been well received here, and bear us a mortal hatred. So all these things were confronting us at the same time: that is, we had to choose a place to settle, clear it and level it, arm and provision it throughout, erect forts, build roofs and sheds to protect our gear, gather materials from all around and, for lack of beasts of burden, carry it on our shoulders to the top of a hill through thickets and dense woods. Furthermore, since the native inhabitants live from day to day, with no concern for ploughing the earth, there was no particular place where food supplies were stocked; we had to go gather them and seek them far and wide, so that our company, already small, of necessity dispersed and diminished.*

*Because of these difficulties, my friends who had followed me, considering our affairs to be in a desperate state (as I have already shown), went back the way they came; and for my part I too was sorely distressed. However, I reminded myself that I had assured my friends I was leaving France in order to deploy for the advancement of the reign of Jesus Christ the care and pains that I had formerly expended on the things of this world (the vanity of which endeavor I had recognized); I deemed it likely that I would give others reason to speak ill of me and to reproach me, and that I would harm my reputation if I let myself be turned away from this task through fear of toil or danger. Furthermore, since it was a question of Christ's business, I assured myself that He would assist me, and would bring everything to a good and happy outcome. Therefore I have taken courage, and have entirely applied my mind to accomplish the thing that I had undertaken with such ardent desire and to employ my life in it. And it has seemed to me that I could arrive at my ends by this means: if I bore witness to my intention and design by a good and steadfast life, and if I withdrew the troop of workers that I had brought with me from the company and acquaintance of the heathen. When I stopped to reflect on that, it seemed to me that it was not without the Providence of God that we are involved in these affairs, but rather that this has happened to keep us from being spoiled by too great idleness, and thus from giving free rein to our disorderly and fretful appetites. And afterward it occurred to me that there is nothing, however high and difficult, that cannot be overcome by striving. Therefore one must find one's hope and help in patience and firmness of spirit, and I must engage my family in continual labor; then the goodness of God will aid such a desire and undertaking.*

1

*Therefore we moved to an island about two leagues from the mainland, and there I chose our dwelling-place, so that having removed all means of escape, I might retain our troop in its duty; and since the native women would not come to us without their husbands, the occasion to sin in that respect was cut off.*

*Nonetheless it happened that twenty-six of our mercenaries, lured by their carnal appetites, conspired to put me to death.[9] But on the day set for the assassination, the plot was revealed to me by one of the accomplices, at the very instant that they were speeding toward me to strike me down. We avoided death by this means: I began to make straight for them, with five servants I had armed; the conspirators were gripped with such fear and astonishment that, without encountering any difficulty or resistance, we seized and imprisoned four of the principal instigators of the plot, who had been denounced to me. The rest of them, terrified, abandoned their arms and went into hiding. The next day we released one of them from his chains, so that he might plead his case in greater liberty; but breaking into a run, he threw himself into the sea, and drowned. When the others who remained were led forth in bonds to be interrogated, they confessed, of their own free will and without torture, to what we had already learned from him who had accused them.*

*One of them, whom I had punished a short while earlier for having dealings with a whore, showed somewhat more ill will. He said that the conspiracy had started with him, and that he had bribed the wench's father, so that the latter might rescue him from my power if I pressed him to abstain from the girl's company. That one was hanged for his misdeed; the two others we pardoned, but on condition that they plough the earth in chains. As for the rest, I chose not to inform myself further concerning their guilt, lest I leave unpunished a known and verified crime; or, if I wanted to do justice, and if it should turn out that the whole troop was guilty, there might not be any left to finish the work we had undertaken. Therefore concealing my displeasure, we pardoned them, and told them to be of good cheer; nonetheless we were not so sure of them that we did not seek and sound out, through his actions and behavior, what each of them had in his heart. And thus by not sparing them, but rather by making them work in my very presence, not only have we blocked the path to their evil designs, but also in a short time we have solidly armed and fortified our island all around.*

*However, insofar as I was able, I did not cease to admonish*

*them and turn them away from their vices, and instruct them in the
Christian religion, having for that purpose established public prayers
every day, morning and evening; and by means of such duty and
provision we spent the rest of the year in greater peace. Furthermore,
we were delivered from such cares by the arrival of our ships. For
there I found persons whom I not only had no need to fear, but whom
I could even trust with my life. With such help ready at hand, I chose
ten of the whole troop, to whom I handed over the power and
authority to command. Henceforth nothing might be done except by
the advice of council; so that if I were to order anything prejudicial to
someone's interests, it would be invalid and without effect, unless it
were authorized and ratified by the council. However, I reserved for
myself one right: if a sentence was pronounced, I would be permitted
to pardon the malefactor, so that I might be of benefit to everyone,
without harming anyone.*

*Those are the means by which I have purposed to maintain
and defend our state and dignity. May our Lord Jesus Christ defend
you and your companions from all evil, fortify you with his Spirit,
and grant you a long life for the work of his Church. I entreat you
to greet for me affectionately my very dear and faithful brothers,
Cephas and De la Flèche. From Coligny, in Antarctic France, the
last day of March 1557.*

*If you write to Madame Renée of France, our mistress, I beg
you to greet her humbly in my name.*[10]

At the end of this letter of Villegagnon there is a clause written in his
own hand; but since I will cite it against him in the sixth chapter of this
history, I have removed it from this place so as to avoid repetitions. Be
that as it may, it is evident from this narration of Villegagnon that Thevet
has committed a falsehood in his *Cosmography*, in noising it abroad and
babbling that we had been the instigators of a sedition at Fort Coligny,
seeing that we had not yet arrived there when it occurred. It is a marvel
how much this digression pleases him (he never gets enough of talking
about it), so that even when he treats of the loyalty of the Scots,[a] he works
that falsehood into his discourse, and has this to say about it:

*whose fidelity I have also come to know in the example of a certain
number of gentlemen and soldiers accompanying us on our ships to*

---

[a][These Scots were members of Villegagnon's personal guard.]

*these distant countries of Antarctic France, on the occasion of certain conspiracies against our company by Norman Frenchmen, who, because they understood the language of this savage and barbarous people (who are so brutish as to possess almost no reason), were plotting with two petty kings of the country, to whom they had promised the few goods that we possessed, to kill us all. But these Scots, being warned of this, revealed the plot to the Seigneur de Villegagnon and to me also. For which these impostors were well punished, as well as the ministers that Calvin had sent, who, having been included in the conspiracy, drank a little more than their fill.*[a]

Once again Thevet, piling one thing on another, entangling himself more and more, doesn't know what he means here: for he confounds three different episodes, one of which is false and invented by him (which I have already refuted), and two others that occurred at different times. He was among those whom Villegagnon reproached in his letter for returning into Egypt (that is, to the Papacy)—from which one can also gather that everyone, before leaving France, had promised Villegagnon to join the Reformed Religion, which he said that he wanted to establish in the place where he was going. It is, indeed, the case that the Scots had revealed the conspiracy that Thevet speaks of; however, Thevet was no more included in this second and real danger than in the first imaginary one, forged in his brain.

Concerning the statement about the third episode, that "some seditious companions of Richier were executed, and their carcasses went to feed the fishes": this is far from the truth, at least in the way that Thevet puts it. On the contrary—as will be seen as this story unfolds—although Villegagnon offered us very ill treatment after his revolt from the Religion, nonetheless, since he did not feel himself to be the strongest, he did not put any of our company to death before the departure of Richier and our guide Du Pont (with whom I made the return voyage); what is more, since he neither dared nor was able to hold us by force, we left that country with his permission—albeit a fraudulent permission, as I shall recount elsewhere. What is true, as you will see in due time, is that five men of our band, after our first near-shipwreck about eight days after our departure, returned in a boat to the land of the savages. He did, indeed, cruelly and inhumanely, have three of these five thrown into the sea; not, however, for any mutiny that they might have undertaken, but, as the

---

[a][*Cosmog. univ.,*] Volume II, Book 16, Chapter 8, p. 665.

report of it in the history of the martyrs of our time testifies,[a] on account of their confession of the Gospel, which Villegagnon had rejected.[11]

Furthermore, in saying—either mistakenly or maliciously—that they were ministers, and again in attributing to Calvin the sending of four of them into that land, Thevet commits another, and double, fault. For in the first place, the election and the calling of pastors in our Churches is done by the order which is established through the consistories of the local congregations, and through several persons chosen and authorized by all the people; therefore, there is no one among us who, like the Pope, has the absolute power to do such a thing.

Secondly, as to the number, it will not be found that more than two ministers, Richier and Chartier, were in America at that time (and I think that none have gone since). If on this last point, however, and on that of the vocation of those who were drowned, Thevet replies that, not being finicky, he calls all those who were in our company "ministers," I respond that, just as he knows that in the Roman Catholic Church not everyone is a Cordelier as he is, so too (without making comparisons), we who profess the Christian and Evangelical Religion, are not—as in his hodge-podge of terms—all "ministers."

And furthermore, because Thevet—who has as honorably called Richier "minister" as he has falsely called him "seditious" (granting, however, that Richier did, indeed, abandon his title as doctor of the Sorbonne)—might take it amiss that in reply I accord him here no other title than that of Cordelier, I am content to gratify him so far as to name him not only simply "cosmographer" but also, what is more, so general and universal a one, that—as if there were not enough remarkable things on this entire globe, nor in this world (of which, however, he writes both what is and what is not)—to fill out and augment his idle tales, he goes so far as to seek his nonsense in the realm of the moon. Nonetheless as the native Frenchman that I am, jealous of the honor of my prince, it angers me all the more that he of whom I speak, inflated with the title of Royal Cosmographer, draws from it money and wages that are so badly used; and, what is worse, that by this means these inanities, unworthy even of being put down in a mere letter, are protected and authorized by the royal name.

Furthermore, so that I shall have sounded all the strings that he has touched: It shows that he measures all others by the yardstick and rule of

---

[a][Jean Crespin, *Histoire des Martyrs*.]

St. Francis, whose Friars Minor,[a] like him, shove all they can into their sacks, that he has falsely put it forth that "the preachers" as he says "having arrived in America, trying only to get rich, seized whatever they could." This I deem unworthy of response. However, in saying such a thing—which is no truer than the fables of the *Cordeliers' Koran*[12]— Thevet is knowingly and willingly attacking those that he never saw in America and from whom he never received any grievance elsewhere. Therefore, since I am one of the defendants, I must, throwing back into his garden the stones he tried to hurl at us, uncover some of his other deceits.

So—to beat him still with his own cudgel—what will he reply to the fact that, having first said expressly in his *Singularities* that he "remained only three days at Cape Frio,"[b] he nevertheless then wrote in his *Cosmography* that he "stayed there several months"?[c] At least if he had said "a month," in the singular, and had then persuaded us that in that country the days last a little more than a week, then someone who wanted to believe him might have done so; but to extend the stay of three days to several months—unless I am mistaken, we have not yet learned that the days in the Torrid Zone and near the tropics, which are more equal in length than those in our climate, are, for all that, transformed into months.

Furthermore, he still thought to dazzle the eyes of those who read his works, and, to hear him hold forth far and wide, you would say that he has not only seen, heard, and observed in his own person all the customs and manners of that multitude of diverse savage peoples living in that fourth part of the world, but that he has also surveyed all the countries of the West Indies—for which, however, for many reasons, the lives of ten men would not suffice. Now I have shown by his own testimony that he remained only about ten weeks in America—that is, from the tenth of November 1555 until the last of the following January—during which time (as I have heard from those who have seen him over there), he was waiting for the return ships to be loaded, and hardly budged from the uninhabitable island where Villegagnon had his fort. Indeed, because of the wildness and the inaccessibility of those regions, and also for fear of the Margaia, who are sworn enemies of our nation, and whose land is not

---

[a][The order of the Friars Minor was founded by St. Francis of Assisi.]
[b]Chapter 24, p. 21.
[c]Book 21, Chapter 4, p. 913.

far from the place we were living, there is not one among the French interpreters—not even among those who had lived there nine or ten years—who would boast of having gone forty leagues into the interior (I am not speaking here of distant navigations along the shores). Nonetheless Thevet says he went "sixty leagues and more with the savages, traveling day and night in thick and dense woods, without finding any animal who tried to harm them."[a] Now *that* I believe—that he was not in danger from wild beasts—as firmly as I do that no thorns scratched his hands and face and no rocks bruised his feet on that journey.

But above all, who would not be amazed, when he says in one place, "that he was more certain of what he has written of the savages' way of life after he had learned to speak their language,"[b] and then nonetheless gives such poor proof of it that he translates *pa*,[13] which in the Brazilian language means "Yes," as "And you too"?[c] So considering (as I shall show elsewhere) what good and solid judgment Thevet has displayed when he wrote that before the discovery of fire in that land there was smoke to dry meat,[14] and taking what he says here as a sample of his competence in understanding the savages' language, I will let you judge whether, failing to understand even this one-syllable affirmative adverb, he may fairly boast of having learned it. The person[15] who reproaches him for chewing over what he learned of obscure and fearsome words after having frequented two or three peoples for a few months will have reason to laugh when he sees what I have said.

Without inquiring further, you see how far you can trust Thevet for the confused and disordered things that he will babble at you about the language of the Americans in the twenty-first book of his *Cosmography;* and you can be sure that when he gets to *Maïr momen* and *Maïr pochi* he will offer you the most grotesque and bawdy tales.[16]

And again what shall we say about the fact that, although in his *Cosmography* he vehemently attacks those who call this land of America West India, and claims that he wants it to keep its name of "Antarctic France" (which, he says, he was the first to give it, while elsewhere he says that the name was used by all the French who arrived in that country with Villegagnon), he has nonetheless himself in several places called it

---

[a]Book 21, Chapter 17, p. 951.

[b]Book 21, Chapter 7, p. 921.

[c]Book 21, Chapter 5, p. 916.

"American India"?[a] In short, although he contradicts himself, one would nonetheless say, considering the censures, corrections, and rebuttals that he makes of the works of others, that all of those authors had been raised in bottles, and that only Thevet has seen everything, peeping out from the hole of his Cordelier's hood.[17]

And I am sure that if, when he reads this history of mine, he sees some details of things that he had touched on in any way at all, then immediately, in his usual style and with his high opinion of himself, he will not fail to say, "Aha! You stole that from my writings." And indeed, if Belleforest, who is not only a cosmographer just like him, but who moreover had crowned his *Singularities* with a fine ode in his praise, has nevertheless been unable to escape being scorned by Thevet any number of times as "poor philosopher," "poor tragedian," "poor Comingeois"[18]—since he cannot bear that any person, even one who blasts the Huguenots as readily as he, be compared to him—what can *I* expect from him, who with my frail pen have dared to touch such a Colossus? Already I see him, like a Goliath, armed cap-a-pie, cursing me to his gods; when he sees that I have revealed some of his tricks, I have no doubt that he will gape wide to swallow me up, and employing the canons[b] of the Pope, will fulminate against me and my little work.

But even if, to combat me, he were, with the aid of his Saint Francis the Younger,[19] to resuscitate Quoniambegue[20] with his two pieces of artillery on his bare shoulders (as he has preposterously represented him in his *Cosmography*,[c] thinking that we could believe that this savage would fire them without fear of skinning himself, or of having his shoulders torn off by the recoil), nevertheless, in addition to the charges that I have already made to repel him, I intend hereafter not merely to attack him in passing, but, what is more, to assail him so vigorously that I will level and reduce to nothing this proud Ville-Henry, which he so fantastically built in the air for us in America.

But while I am closing in for the attack, and while he—since he is warned—is preparing either valiantly to sustain the assault or else to surrender, I entreat the readers (who will remember that, as I said, the impostures of Thevet against us have in part been the cause of my publish-

---

[a]*Singularities,* Chapter 1, p. 2, line 30, and elsewhere.
[b][In French, the words for "cannon" and "canon" are identical: *canon.*]
[c]Book 21, [Chapter 17,] p. 952.

ing this history of our voyage) to excuse me if I have taken rather long in this preface to refute him, convicting him by his own writings. I will insist no further on this point, although since the first printing of my work I have been warned that Thevet was looking for memoirs of the events to use against me in his writing; and that even some of those who say they are of our religion had offered him information—by which, if that is the case, they show their true zeal. For, as I have said elsewhere, never having seen Thevet, as far as I know, nor having received any offense from him in my own person, I have contradicted him in this history only to remove the blame that he had tried to put on the Gospel, and on those who were the first in our time to have proclaimed it in the land of Brazil.

This will serve also to respond to that apostate Mathieu de Launay,[21] who, the better to reveal his apostasy, has been impudent enough to write in his second book that, even when there was not a question of the Religion, the ministers would unceasingly snap at the most excellent personages of their time, among whom he places Thevet—who had himself however, in the passage which I have particularly refuted, attacked without any cause the Reformed religion and those who profess it. This shameless De Launay, who in that same passage called me a scoundrel (knowing me well, he says—which is an impudent lie, for I have never had any dealings with him, nor he with me, praise God), having himself abandoned Jesus Christ, the fountain of living waters, and returned to drink in the Pope's stinking cisterns and to beg in his kitchen,[a] takes it on himself to defend it, until he and his fellows—who, it will finally be said, have hardly given off an odor of faith—get themselves scalded there, after being used, wretched in the eyes of God and men.

So to conclude this discussion: let Thevet answer, if he wishes, whether what I have said against him is true or not, for *that* is the point; and let him not, in the style of bad lawyers, confound the issue by seeking to know who I am—although, by the grace of God, I go about with my head held high, as boldly as he might do, for all that he is a cosmographer; and I can assure him that if he puts forward anything other than the truth, I will confront him with arguments so firm, citing his own writings as evidence, that you will not have to go as far as America to judge their worth.

In the same vein, I trust that no one will be scandalized—as though I

---

[a]["Kitchen" was commonly used at the time in satirizing the politics of Roman Catholicism. It still means "dirty politics" in France.]

wanted to stir up quarrels concerning people now dead—that I have recounted in this history the conduct of Villegagnon in America while we were there: for beyond its relevance to the subject that I have chiefly proposed to treat (that is, to show for what purpose we made this voyage), I have not said nearly all that I might say if he were alive now.

Let me speak now of my own concerns, and first, of religion, since that is one of the principal issues that can and must be attended to among men. Even though later, throughout Chapter XVI, I will explain what the religion of the savage American Tupinamba is (as far as I have been able to understand it), still, seeing that I begin that discussion with a problem which I continually wonder at, and can by no means resolve as well as one might wish, I will now touch on it in passing.

Those who have spoken best, according to common feeling, have not only said but also recognized that being human and having the intuition of dependence on a greater Being than oneself, indeed, than any created thing, are so conjoined with each other that, however different may be the ways of serving God, there remains the fundamental fact that man must naturally have some religion, true or false. Nonetheless, having thus soberly judged of the matter, when it is a question of understanding what the nature of man most willingly submits to regarding religious duty, they have also admitted that we all recognize the truth of what the Latin poet[a] said:

> Man's own cupidity
> Is his chief deity.[22]

If we then apply these two testimonies to our American savages: in the first place, regardless of what is particular to them, one certainly cannot deny that as natural men they have that disposition and inclination common to all, which is to understand something greater than man, on which depends good and evil—or such at least as they imagine good and evil to be. And to that is related the honor they pay to those whom they call *caraïbes*, whom we will speak of later, who, they believe, bring them good or bad fortune at certain times.

But the goal that they hold as their happiness and sovereign point of honor is the pursuit and vengeance on their enemies (as I shall show later when I speak of their wars); deeming this so great a glory, both in this life and after (just as it was, in part, by the ancient Romans), they hold such

---

[a]"Sua cuique Deus fit dira Cupido." *Aeneid*, Book IX [v. 185].

vengeance and victory to be their chief good. In short, as will be seen in this history, with respect to what one calls religion among other peoples, it must be said frankly that these poor savages have none whatsoever, and that if there is a nation in the world that exists and lives without God, it is truly this one. However, on this point they are perhaps not utterly condemnable: in admitting and confessing somewhat their misfortune and blindness—although they do not understand it in such a way as to be troubled by it, nor to seek a remedy even when one is presented to them—they do not pretend to be other than what they are.

Concerning other matters, the summary headings of the chapters at the beginning of the book show clearly enough what they are; also, the first chapter explains our motives for making this voyage to America. As I promised in the first edition, we have added to the five original illustrations of savage men several more for the pleasure and satisfaction of the readers; if it had been up to me, there would have been more, but the printer was not willing this time to go to the expense that would have been necessary for their engraving.

Furthermore, since I am not unaware of what is commonly said—that since old people and travelers to distant lands cannot be contradicted, they give themselves license to lie—I will say a word about that. As much as I hate lying and liars, if there are some who are unwilling to give credence to a number of things (strange things, indeed) that are to be read in this history, let them be advised, whoever they may be, that I have no intention of taking them to see those places. I will not trouble myself over that any more than I do over hearing that people doubt what I have written and published about the siege and famine of Sancerre: which, however, as you will see, was assuredly not as severe (although much longer) than the famine we endured on the sea during the return voyage to France.[23] For if those of whom I speak will not believe what was done in the very middle of this kingdom of France, to the public knowledge of more than five hundred persons still living, how will they believe what can only be seen two thousand leagues from where they live: things never known (much less written about) by the Ancients; things so marvelous that experience itself can scarcely engrave them upon the understanding even of those who have in fact seen them?

I do not endorse the fabulous tales found in the books of certain people who, trusting to hearsay, have written things that are completely false; yet I am not ashamed to confess that since I have been in this land of America, where everything to be seen—the way of life of its inhabitants, the form of the animals, what the earth produces—is so unlike what we have in Europe, Asia, and Africa that it may very well be called a "New World" with respect to us, I have revised the opinion that I formerly had of Pliny and others when they describe foreign lands, because I have seen things as fantastic and prodigious as any of those—once thought incredible—that they mention.

As for style and language, beyond what I have already said—that I recognize my incapacity in that regard—still, I know very well that, because I will not have used phrases and terms precise enough to explain and represent the art of navigation and various other things that I mention, there will be some who will not be satisfied—in particular our Frenchmen, who have such delicate ears and are so enamored of fine flowers of rhetoric that they will not approve or receive any writing without new-fangled and high-flown words.[24] Even less will I please those who deem all books not only puerile, but also sterile, unless they are enriched with stories and examples taken from elsewhere: for although I could have put forth a great number of them concerning the matters that I treat of, nevertheless except for the historian of the West Indies,[25] whom I cite often because he has written several things about the Indians of Peru that are consistent with what I say about our American savages, I have only rarely used others.

And indeed, in my modest judgment, a history that is not bedecked with the plumes of others is rich enough when it is full of its own subject; furthermore, the readers, who then do not stray from the goal proposed by the author that they have in hand, understand all the better his intention. I ask those who read the books that are printed every day, about wars and other things, whether the multitude of quotations taken from elsewhere, even if adapted to the matters being treated, do not weary them.

However, one might well object that, having rebuked Thevet on that point, and now reproving others, I am myself committing the same faults. If someone finds it ill that hereafter, when I speak of savage customs, I often use this kind of expression—"I saw," "I found," this happened to me," and so on (as if I wanted to show myself off)—I reply that not only are these things within my own subject but also I am speaking out of my own knowledge, that is, from my own seeing and experience; indeed, I will speak of things that very likely no one before me has ever seen, much less written about.[26] I mean this, however, not about all of America in general, but only about the place where I lived for about a year: that is, under the tropic of Capricorn among the savages called the *Tupinamba*. Finally, I assure those who prefer the truth simply stated over the adorned and painted lie of fine language, that they will find the things put forth by me in this history not only true, but also, since they have been hidden to those who lived before our age, worthy of wonder. And I pray the Eternal Author and Preserver of this whole universe and of all the beautiful creatures contained therein, that this little work of mine may redound to the glory of His Holy Name. Amen.

# HISTORY
# OF A VOYAGE TO
# THE LAND OF BRAZIL,
## OTHERWISE CALLED
## AMERICA

———

Containing the Navigation and the Remarkable
Things Seen on the Sea by the Author; the Behav-
ior of Villegagnon in That Country; the Customs
and Strange Ways of Life of the American Sav-
ages; Together with the Description of Various
Animals, Trees, Plants, and Other
Singular Things Completely
Unknown over Here

# C H A P T E R   I

ॐ

# OF THE MOTIVE
## AND THE OCCASION THAT
### MADE US UNDERTAKE THIS DISTANT
### VOYAGE TO THE LAND OF BRAZIL

A number of cosmographers and other historians of our time have already written about the length, width, beauty, and fertility of that fourth part of the world called "America"—or the land of Brazil, together with the islands near it and the lands adjacent to it (lands completely unknown to the Ancients)—as well as of the various navigations in the eighty years since it was first discovered; therefore I will not pause to summarize those matters at length or in a general fashion. My intention and my subject in this history will be simply to declare what I have myself experienced, seen, heard and observed, both on the sea, coming and going, and among the American savages,[1] with whom I visited and lived for about a year. And, so that the whole enterprise may be better understood by everyone, beginning with the motives for our undertaking so arduous and distant a voyage, I will speak briefly of what occasioned it.

In the year 1555 a certain Villegagnon, Knight of Malta (that is, of the Order called "St. John of Jerusalem"), discontented in France and having had some unpleasant dealings in Brittany, where he was living at the time, let it be known to several distinguished personages of various ranks throughout the realm of France that he had long yearned to withdraw into some distant country, where he might freely and purely serve God according to the reformation of the Gospel, and, moreover, that he desired to prepare a place for all those who might wish to retire there to escape persecution: which, indeed, at that time was such that many persons, of both sexes and of all stations of life, in all parts of France, by edicts of the king and by decrees of the Parlement were being burned alive, their goods confiscated, on account of the Religion.

Villegagnon declared, moreover, both by word of mouth and by letter, that having heard so many good reports of the beauty and fertility

3

of the part of America called the "land of Brazil," he was ready to set forth in order to settle there and to put his plan into effect. And in fact, under this fine pretext, he won the hearts of some of the nobility who were of the Reformed Religion, who, with the same motives that he claimed to have, wished to find such a retreat. Among them was Gaspard de Coligny of blessed memory, Admiral of France,[2] who enjoyed the favor of King Henry II, the reigning monarch at that time. Admiral Coligny proposed to the king that if Villegagnon made this voyage he might discover great riches and other commodities for the profit of the realm; thereupon the king gave Villegagnon two fine ships fitted out and furnished with artillery, and ten thousand francs for the voyage.

Before leaving France, Villegagnon promised several honorable persons who accompanied him that he would establish the pure service of God in the place where he would reside. After providing himself with sailors and artisans to take with him, in May of 1555 he embarked on the sea, where he underwent many tempests and tribulations; but finally, in spite of all difficulties, he reached his destination the following November.

Upon his arrival, he disembarked, and at first considered settling on a rocky islet at the mouth of an arm of the sea and a saltwater bay called by the savages *Guanabara,* which (as I shall describe) is located twenty-three degrees beyond the Equator—that is, right under the tropic of Capricorn; however, the heavy seas drove him away. He advanced about a league toward land, and set himself up on a previously uninhabitable island. Once he had unloaded his artillery and his other gear, so as to enjoy greater security against both the savages and the Portuguese, who already have so many fortresses in that country, he began to build a fort.

Furthermore, still pretending to be burning with zeal to advance the reign of Jesus Christ, and attempting to persuade his people of the same, when his ships were loaded and ready to return to France, he wrote and sent a man to Geneva expressly to request that the Church and its ministers help him as much as possible in his holy enterprise. But above all, in order to pursue and speedily advance the work that he had undertaken, and which (he said) he desired to continue with all his strength, he urgently entreated them to send him not only ministers of the Word of God, but also to send a number of other persons well instructed in the Christian religion to accompany the ministers, the better to reform him and his people, and even to bring the savages to the knowledge of their salvation.[3]

When the Church of Geneva received his letters and heard his news, it first rendered thanks to God for the extension of the realm of Christ into so distant a country, even into so strange a land, and among a nation that was indeed completely ignorant of the true God.

The late Lord Admiral, to whom Villegagnon had written for the same reason, solicited by letter Philippe de Corguilleray, Sieur du Pont (who had retired near Geneva, and who had been his neighbor in France near Châtillon-sur-Loing) to undertake the voyage in order to lead those who wanted to join Villegagnon in that land of Brazil. The same request was made by the Church and the Ministers of Geneva, and although he was already old and feeble, the Sieur du Pont, out of the strong desire that he had to employ himself in so good a work, agreed to do what was asked of him, postponing all his other business, even leaving his children and his family to go so far away.

That being done, it was next a question of finding ministers of the Word of God. Du Pont and other friends of his spoke of this to a number of students of theology in Geneva, and several of them, including Pierre Richier (already more than fifty years old) and Guillaume Chartier, promised him that if they were recognized according to the ordinance of the Church to be fitted to that charge, they were ready to take it on. Thus after these two had been presented to the ministers of Geneva, who heard them expound on certain passages of the Holy Scripture, and exhorted them concerning the rest of their duty, they willingly accepted, with the leader Du Pont, to cross the sea to join Villegagnon, and undertake to spread the Gospel in America.

Now there still remained to be found some other persons instructed in the principal articles of the faith, and also, as Villegagnon had ordered, artisans expert in their craft. But so as not to deceive anybody, Du Pont told of the long and tedious path to be taken: that is to say, about a hundred and fifty leagues by land and more than two thousand leagues by sea.[a] He added that upon arrival in that land of America, one would have to be content to eat, instead of bread, a certain flour made from a root; and as for wine, not a trace, for no grapevines grow there. In short, just as in a New World (as Villegagnon intones in his letter) one would have to adopt ways of life and nourishment completely different from those of our Europe. Therefore anyone preferring theory to practice in these things, and unwilling to undergo a change of air, or to endure the waves of the sea and the heat of the Torrid Zone, or to see the Antarctic

---

[a][Comparing Léry's reports with known distances, we find his league to be about two and a half miles (see Cotgrave).]

Pole,[4] would by no means choose to accept such a challenge, or to enlist and embark on such a voyage.

Nevertheless, after several summonses and inquiries on all sides, the following men, more courageous, it would seem, than the others, presented themselves to accompany Du Pont, Richier, and Chartier: Pierre Bourdon, Matthieu Verneuil, Jean du Bordel, André La Fon, Nicolas Denis, Jean Gardien, Martin David, Nicolas Raviquet, Nicolas Carmeau, Jacques Rousseau, and I, Jean de Léry,[5] who, as much out of an earnest desire that God had given me to serve His glory, as out of curiosity to see this New World, was of the company. So we were fourteen in number who left the city of Geneva to make this voyage the tenth of September 1556.

We wended our way to Châtillon-sur-Loing, where we met with my Lord Admiral, who not only encouraged us to pursue our enterprise, but also, promising to help us in naval matters and offering much good advice, gave us hope that by God's grace we would see the fruits of our labors. From there we set forth for Paris, where during the month that we stayed there, several gentlemen and some others, who had heard why we were making this voyage, joined our company. From there we passed on to Rouen, and went to the seaport of Honfleur, which was our appointed place in Normandy; there we remained for about a month, making our preparations and waiting for our ships to be ready to set sail.

ใช

# OF OUR EMBARKATION
## AT THE PORT OF HONFLEUR
IN NORMANDY, TOGETHER WITH THE
TEMPESTS, ENCOUNTERS, SEIZURE
OF SHIPS, AND THE FIRST LANDS
AND ISLANDS THAT WE
DISCOVERED

The Sieur De Bois le Comte, a nephew of Villegagnon, had come to Honfleur before us and had had three fine ships fitted out for war at the king's expense; once they were fully equipped with supplies and necessities for the voyage, we boarded them on the nineteenth of November. The Sieur de Bois le Comte, with about eighty people—both soldiers and sailors—was in a ship called the *Petite Roberge;* he was elected our Vice-Admiral. I boarded another ship called the *Grande Roberge,* where there were about one hundred twenty of us in all; we had as captain the Sieur de Sainte Marie dit l'Espine, and as ship's master a certain Jean Humbert of Harfleur—a good pilot, and, as he was to demonstrate, very well experienced in the art of navigation. In the other ship, called *Rosée,* from the name of its captain, there were about ninety people. These included ten young boys, whom we took along to learn the language of the savages, and five young girls, with a woman to watch over them. (These were the first Frenchwomen taken to the land of Brazil; the savages of that country, as we shall see later, who had never seen any women clothed, were amazed upon their arrival.)

Thus that very day, around noon, we put our sails to the wind at the exit from the Honfleur harbor; there was no lack of cannonades, trumpets, drums, fifes, and other triumphal honors usually accorded to ships of war that set forth. First we went to anchor at the harbor of Caux, which is one league by sea beyond Le Havre de Grâce. There, according to the custom of sailors undertaking a voyage to distant countries, after the masters and captains had reviewed and made certain of the number of soldiers and sailors, they gave the command to weigh anchor, and we thought to put to sea that evening. However, the cable of the ship I was in broke, and the anchor could only be hauled with great difficulty; thus we were not ready until the following day.

So on the twentieth of November, leaving the land behind us, we sailed out onto that great and impetuous Ocean Sea. We could see in the distance the coast of England, and sailed alongside it, leaving it on our right. Then we were seized by a surge of the sea that continued for twelve days, during which—even aside from being very ill from the usual sea-sickness—there was not one of us who was not terrified at the ship's swaying. Those especially who had never smelled sea air, nor danced such a dance, and who saw the sea so high and roiled up, thought at each instant that the waves were about to take us to the bottom. It is an amazing thing to see a wooden vessel, however large and strong, resist the fury and force of that terrible element. For even though the ships are built of heavy wood tightly bound and pegged, and heavily tarred—indeed, the one I was in was probably about one hundred ten feet long and twenty-seven feet wide—, what is that compared with the width and depth of that gulf, that abyss of water that is the Western Sea? Without enlarging upon the subject, let me say at this point that it is impossible to overestimate both the excellence of the art of navigation in general, and in particular the invention of the mariner's compass with which it is practiced—the use of which dates back only about two hundred fifty years.

We were, then, tossed about, and we navigated with great difficulty until the thirteenth day after our embarkation, when God pacified the swell and storms of the sea.

The following Sunday we met two English merchant ships that were coming from Spain. When our sailors accosted them, and saw that there was much to be had aboard, they nearly pillaged them. And indeed, as I have said, our three vessels were well furnished with artillery and other munitions; our sailors therefore were overbearing and arrogant, and when weaker vessels found themselves at their mercy they were by no means safe.

I must say here, since it has come up in connection with this first encounter with a ship, that I have seen practiced on the sea what is also done most often on land: that is, he who has weapons in his fist, and who is the strongest, carries the day, and imposes the law on his companion. The way it goes is that these mariner gentlemen, striking sail, and meeting with the poor merchant ships, usually claim that they have been unable to approach any land or port because of tempests and calms, and that they are consequently short of supplies, for which they are willing to pay. But if, under this pretext, they can set foot on board their neighbors' ship, you need hardly ask whether, as an alternative to scuttling the vessel, they relieve it of whatever takes their fancy. And if one then protests (as in fact we always did) that no order has been given to pillage indiscriminately, friends as well as enemies, they give you the common cant of our land soldiers, who in such cases offer as sole reason that it's war and custom, and that you have to get used to it.

I will add this, by way of preface to some episodes that we will see further on: the Spaniards boast, and even more do the Portuguese, of having been the first to discover the land of Brazil and, indeed everything from the Straits of Magellan, fifty degrees on the side of the Antarctic Pole, to Peru, and on through to this side of the Equator; they consequently maintain that they are the lords of all those countries. They claim that the French who travel in those parts are usurpers, and if they find them on the sea and at their mercy, they wage such war on them that they have even flayed some of them alive, or put them to some other kind of cruel death. The French, who maintain the contrary—that they have their due share in these new-found countries—, not only refuse to be beaten by the Spaniards (and even less by the Portuguese) but defend themselves valiantly, and often render blow for blow to their enemies who (to speak of them dispassionately) would not dare to accost or attack them if they did not see themselves to be stronger and to outnumber them in vessels.

Now to return to our journey. The sea swelled again, and for six or seven days it was so rough that sometimes I saw the waves leap about the upper deck. Putting into practice what is said in Psalm 107, all of us, our senses reeling, staggered about like drunkards; the vessel was so shaken that no sailor, however skillful, could keep himself on his feet. And indeed, as it is said in the same Psalm, when in such turbulence one is suddenly lifted so high on these terrifying mountains of water that it seems one must rise to heaven, and just as abruptly one plummets so low that it seems one must penetrate to the hollows of the deepest gulfs and abysses—to dwell thus, I say, in the midst of a million sepulchres, is this not to behold the great wonders of the Eternal?[1] Assuredly, it is. In this tumult of the furious waves, danger comes nearer than the thickness of the planks that the ship is made of; and it occurs to me that the poet who said that those who go on the sea are only four fingers from death puts them at too great a distance from it.[2] To give a more pointed warning to sea-goers, I have not only translated but also amplified these verses in this fashion:

Though the sea by boisterous swells
Makes shudder him who on it dwells,
Yet in wood his faith vests man
Whose width five fingers—nay four will span
(The ship's thin strakes that him does bear),
Not seeing that he lives ever where
Death bides four fingers' width away.
So any man is mad we'll say
Who, faith not in God, sets out on the sea,
For none but God can life's savior be.[3]

After the tempest had ceased, He who renders the weather calm and tranquil when He pleases sent us a wind to our liking; we arrived in the Spanish Sea, and found ourselves on the fifth of December at the level of Cape St. Vincent. There we met a ship from Ireland, from which our seamen, under the pretext I have mentioned—that we were short of supplies—took six or seven kegs of Spanish wine, figs, oranges, and other goods with which it was laden.

Seven days later we approached three islands, named by Norman pilots *la Gracieuse, Lancelote,* and *Forte-Aventure,* which are the Fortunate Isles.[a] There are seven of them counted at present, I think, all inhabited by the Spanish. Now, although there are those who mark on their maps and teach in their books that these Fortunate Isles are located only eleven degrees this side of the Equator, and therefore would be in the Torrid Zone, I have seen their latitude taken with the astrolabe, and I can say with assurance that they are situated twenty-eight degrees toward the Arctic Pole.[b] So these authors, who are mistaken themselves and who mislead others as well, are putting these islands at a distance from us that is too great by seventeen degrees.

At this point we took the boats down from our ships, and twenty of our people, both soldiers and sailors, boarding them with small cannon, muskets, and other arms, thought to plunder those Fortunate Isles; but as they were about to land, the Spaniards, who had seen them coming,

---

[a][The Canary Islands. These are Graciosa, Lanzarote, and Fuerteventura; there are five others.]

[b][Léry is correct.]

drove them back with such force that instead of making a landing, they beat a hasty retreat. Nevertheless, they swerved and wheeled around until finally they encountered and seized a caravel belonging to some fishermen, who, seeing our men coming toward them, had made for the land and abandoned their vessel. Not only did our men take a great quantity of dried dog-fish, some mariner's compasses, and the rest of what was aboard, even down to the sails which they carried off but also—since they could do no worse to the Spanish, on whom they wanted to avenge themselves—with great ax-blows they sank a bark and a boat that were nearby.

During the three days that we remained near these Fortunate Isles, the sea was very calm; we took such a great quantity of fish with nets and hooks that after we had eaten our fill, having no fresh water at our disposal, and fearing that it might make us too thirsty, we were forced to throw more than half of it into the sea. The kinds of fish were dorado, dog-fish, and others whose names we didn't know. There were some that the mariners call *pilchard,* a kind of fish that has so little body that it seems that the head and tail (which is reasonably large) are joined together; its head is shaped like a crested helmet, and all in all it is rather strange in form.

Wednesday morning the sixteenth of December, the sea became turbulent again, and the waves so suddenly filled the boat, which had been tied to our ship since our return from the Fortunate Isles, that it was submerged and lost; the two sailors who had been guarding it were in such great danger that we just barely managed to save them by hastily throwing them ropes and pulling them into the ship. And here is a remarkable thing. During that storm, which lasted four days, our cook had put some bacon to soak in a great barrel, to remove the salt. There came a great swell of the sea, which in its impetuosity, leaping over the hatch, carried it more than a pike's length away from the ship; another wave suddenly came from the other side, and without turning the barrel over, threw it back with great force on the same hatch, with all its contents. Thus the sea returned our dinner to us, which, as you might say, had gone down the stream.

On Friday the eighteenth of December we discovered the great Canary Island, to which we drew near on the following Sunday. But because of the contrary wind, although we had planned to renew our supply of fresh water there, it was not possible to make a landfall. It is a beautiful island, inhabited at present by the Spaniards, rich in sugarcane and good wines; it is so high that you can see it from twenty-five or thirty

11

leagues. Some also call it the "Peak of Tenerife," and think that it is what the Ancients called "Mount Atlas," from which we get the word "Atlantic." However, others assert that the Great Canary and the Peak of Tenerife are two separate islands; I will defer to the facts, whatever they may be.[a]

That same Sunday we saw a Portuguese caravel; since it was downwind of us, those who were in it saw that they could neither resist nor flee, so they struck sail and came to yield themselves up to our Vice-Admiral. Our captains had decided long before to "equip themselves" (as we say today) with a ship of this kind, which they had always vowed to take from either the Spanish or from the Portuguese; the more surely to take possession of it, they immediately put some of our people in it. However, because of certain considerations regarding the master of this ship, they told him that if he could speedily find and seize another caravel nearby, they would give him back his own. For his part, he preferred to have the loss fall rather on his neighbor than on himself; so he was given, according to his request, one of our barks armed with muskets and filled with twenty of our soldiers and some of his men, and like the true pirate that I think he was, the better to play the part and not get caught, he sailed well out in front of our ships.

Then we sailed along the Barbary Coast, inhabited by Moors, at a distance of scarcely two leagues. As was carefully observed by several of us, it is a flatland—in fact, so low that as far as our view could extend, we could see no mountains or other objects; it seemed to us that since we were higher than that whole land, it should be immediately submerged, and that we and our ships should be able to pass over it. Although it seems this way to the eye on almost any seacoast, it is especially noticeable in that place. And indeed, when I looked on the one side at this big, flat country, which appeared to be a valley, and on the other side at the sea, which, although calm, seemed in comparison a great and dreadful mountain, I remembered the words of Scripture,[b] and contemplated this work of God with great admiration.[4]

To return to our sea-rovers, who, as I have said, had gone ahead of us in the bark. On the twenty-fifth of December, Christmas Day, they met a caravel of Spaniards and fired a few musket shots at them, seized them and brought them alongside our ships. And because it was not only a fine

---

[a][They are, in fact, two separate islands.]
[b]Job 38, 8–11; Psalm 104, 9.

ship, but also loaded with white salt, it greatly pleased our captains. Since, as I have said, they had decided long before to "equip themselves" with one of these, they took it with us to Villegagnon's settlement in Brazil. It is true that they kept their promise to the Portuguese, who had seized this ship, to return his caravel; but our seamen (cruel in this respect), who had put all the Spaniards, dispossessed of their goods, pell-mell in with the Portuguese, not only left no morsel of biscuit or of other supplies with these poor people, but what is worse, they tore their sails, and even took away their ship's boat, without which they could not approach land. I think that it would have been better to send them to the bottom than to leave them in such a state. And indeed, abandoned thus to the mercy of the water, if some ship did not come to their rescue, they must certainly have either drowned or died of hunger.

After this pretty piece of work, committed to the great regret of a number of us, we were pushed by a favorable wind south-southwest, and thrown forward onto the high sea. And lest I weary the reader by recounting in detail so many of our seizures of caravels on the voyage over, I will merely say that the next day and again on the twenty-ninth of December we took two others, which offered no resistance. As for the first, which was Portuguese, although our mariners and especially those who were in the Spanish caravel had a great desire to pillage it, and therefore fired a few cannon shots around it, nonetheless after our masters and captains had spoken to those who were in it, and received their respects, they let them go without taking anything from them. From the other, which belonged to a Spaniard, they took wine, biscuits, and other food. The Spaniard lamented above all the loss of a hen which was taken from him: for, as he said, whatever tempests raged, she never stopped laying, and every day furnished him a fresh egg in his ship.

The following Sunday, the watch in the maintop of our ship gave out the customary cry of "Sail! Sail!" and we sighted five caravels, or some other kind of large ships (for we couldn't clearly make them out). Our sailors—who may not be pleased at my recounting of their courtesies—had no question but "Where are they?" that is, so that they could maneuver to surround them. Singing *Te Deum* before the victory, they thought that the ships were as good as taken. But they were to windward of us (so the wind was against us) and they were cutting the water and fleeing as fast as they could. So in spite of the violence that our men did to our vessels out of greed for booty, arming them with all the sails at the risk of capsizing and sinking us, it was impossible for us to overtake them.

One might find it strange that, as we were thus venturing on the sea

13

to reach the land of Brazil, every ship would flee or strike sail before us. On this point I will say that although we had only three vessels (albeit armed with eighteen bronze pieces and more than thirty small cannon and iron muskets in my ship alone, not counting other munitions), nevertheless our captains, masters, soldiers, and mariners, for the most part Norman—a nation as hardy and belligerent at sea as any who sail on the ocean today—had not only resolved to attack and combat the naval army of the King of Portugal if we met with it but also sworn to carry the victory.

# CHAPTER III

## OF THE BONITOS, ALBACORE, GILT-FISH, PORPOISES, FLYING FISH, AND OTHERS OF VARIOUS KINDS THAT WE SAW AND TOOK IN THE TORRID ZONE

From that time on we had a frothy sea and so fair a wind that we were pushed to three or four degrees this side of the Equator. There we caught a great many porpoises, dorado, albacore, bonitos, and a large quantity of several other kinds of fish. I had always thought that the sailors who spoke of flying fish were telling us tall tales; however, experience showed me that they really did exist.

We began to see big schools of them jump out of the water and soar into the air (just as larks and starlings do on land), flying almost as high as a pike's length, and sometimes to a distance of more than a hundred paces. Since often it even happened that some would hit against the masts and fall into our ships, we could easily catch them in our hands. Now to describe this fish (and I have seen and held any number of them going and coming from Brazil): it is something like a herring in form, but a little longer and rounder, with little barbels under the throat, and wings like those of a bat, almost as long as the whole body; it is very flavorful and good to eat. Since I have not seen any of them this side of the tropic of Cancer, I am of the opinion (although I am not completely sure) that, liking a warm climate, they remain in the Torrid Zone, and do not venture out of it in the direction of either of the poles. There is still another thing that I have observed: these poor flying fish, whether they are in the water or in the air, are never at rest. For when they are in the sea, the albacore and other big fish, pursuing them to eat them, wage continual war; and if they try to escape by flight, there are certain sea-birds that seize and feed on them.

These sea-birds, which live as predators, are so tame that often, when they light on the coamings, rigging and spars of our ships, they let themselves be caught by hand. Since I have eaten some—and therefore seen both the inside and the outside—here is a description. They are of gray plumage, like sparrow-hawks; although they seem from the outside to be as big as crows, when they are plucked, you see that they have hardly more flesh than a sparrow, so it is a wonder that, being so small of body, they can still seize and eat fish bigger than they are. They have only one bowel, and their feet are flat like those of ducks.

To get back to the other fish that I have mentioned just now: the bonito, who is one of the best to eat that can be found, is very much like our common carp; however, it has no scales. I have seen a great many of them, for during the whole six weeks of our voyage they hardly left our ships, which they apparently followed because of the pitch and tar that the ships were rubbed with.

As for the albacore, they resemble the bonitos, but in size, there is no comparison between the two kinds, for I have seen and eaten my share of albacore that were almost five feet long and as big as a man's body. The albacore is not at all viscous; its flesh is as flaky as a trout's. With only one bone in its whole body and very little in the way of entrails, it must rank as one of the best seafish. Indeed, since we didn't have on hand everything necessary to prepare it well (nor do any passengers who make these long voyages), we did nothing but salt it and put big round slices of it on the coals, and we found it wonderfully good and flavorful even cooked in this fashion.

Those gentlemen who are so fond of delicacies, who refuse to venture onto the sea, and yet want fish to eat (as one says of cats who want the same without getting their feet wet)—if they could obtain this fish on land as easily as they do other seafood, and could have it prepared with a German sauce or in some other way, do you doubt that they would lick their fingers? I say expressly, if they could have it at their disposal on land: for as I have said of the flying fish, I don't think that these albacore, whose habitat is mainly in the deep ocean between the two tropics, come close enough to the shore for the fishermen to be able to get them home before they spoil. However, this holds only for us who live in this climate; as for the Africans to the east, and those of Peru and the regions on the west, it may well be that they have plenty.

The dorado—which I think bears that name because in the water it appears yellow, and shines like gold—has a shape something like that of a salmon; nonetheless, it is different in that it has a sort of hollow place in the back. But from having tasted it, I maintain that this fish is better than

16

all those I have just mentioned; neither in salt water nor in fresh water is there a more delicate one.

Concerning porpoises, there are two kinds. While some have a face almost as pointed as a goosebeak, in others it is so rounded and blunt that when they lift their nose out of the water it looks like a ball.[1] Because of the resemblance between these and hooded monks, when we were on the sea we called them "monks'-heads." I have seen some of both kinds that were five to six feet long, with a wide, forked tail; they all had an opening on the head, through which they not only took in wind and breathed, but also sometimes sprayed out water. But especially when the sea begins to stir itself up, these porpoises, appearing suddenly on the water in the midst of the waves and billows that toss them about, even at night turn the sea green, and indeed seem themselves to be all green. It is a great amusement to hear them blow and snort; you would think that they really were ordinary pigs, such as we have on land.[2] When the mariners see them swim about and bestir themselves in this way, they take it as a sure sign of an approaching storm, which I have often seen borne out. In moderate weather, when the sea was only frothy, we sometimes saw them in such great abundance that all around us, as far as our view could extend, it seemed that the sea was all porpoises; however, since they did not let themselves be caught as easily as did many other kinds of fish, we didn't have them as often as we wished.

Since we are on the subject, to better satisfy the reader, I want to describe the means I saw the sailors use to catch them. The one among them who is most expert and experienced in this kind of fishing lies in wait along the bowsprit, holding an iron harpoon hafted with a pole of the thickness and about half of the length of a pike, tied to four or five fathoms of line. When he sees a school of porpoises approach, he picks out one to aim for, and throws this weapon with such force that if it reaches its target it does not fail to pierce it. Once he has struck it, he lets out the rope, still firmly holding on to the end. The porpoise, in struggling, works the harpoon deeper into himself, and loses blood in the water. When he has lost a little strength, the other mariners, to help their companion, come with an iron hook called a "gaff" (also hafted with a long wooden pole), and by the strength of their arms they haul the porpoise into the ship. On the voyage over we caught about twenty-five of them in this fashion.

As for the insides of a porpoise: its four flippers are lifted off, just as you would remove the four hams from a pig; it is split, and the tripes (the backbone too if so desired) and the ribs are removed; open and hung in that fashion you would say that it is an ordinary pig—indeed, his liver has the same taste, although it is true that the fresh meat is too sweetish in smell and is not good. As for the lard, all those that I have seen had only an inch of it, and I think there are none that have more than two inches. Therefore no longer be duped when those merchants and fishwives, both in Paris and elsewhere, say that their Lenten bacon, which is four fingers thick, is porpoise: for it is certainly whale fat. There were little ones in the bellies of some that we caught (which we roasted like sucking pigs), and therefore, whatever others may have written to the contrary, I think that porpoises, like cows, carry their litters in their bellies instead of multiplying by eggs, as almost all the other fishes do. Even though I would not make any decision here, lest anyone would argue the point by citing to me those who have firsthand experience—rather than those who have only read books—, no one will meanwhile prevent my believing what I have seen.

We also caught many sharks; found in the sea even when it is calm and quiet, they seem all green. Some are more than four feet long, and proportionately thick. Still, since their flesh is not very good, the mariners don't eat it unless they are forced to it by lack of better fish. They have a skin almost as coarse and rough as a file, and a flat, wide head with the mouth as deeply cleft as that of a wolf or an English mastiff. These sharks, moreover, are not only monstrous in appearance but also, since they have very sharp and cutting teeth, are so dangerous that if they grab a man by the leg or some other part of the body, they either carry that member off, or drag him to the bottom. When the sailors, in time of calm, bathe in the sea, they are much afraid of them; when we fished for them (as we often did with fishhooks as thick as a finger) and got them on to the deck of the ship, we had to be as careful as you would have to be on land with ill-tempered and dangerous dogs. Not only are these sharks no good for eating, but whether they are caught or whether they are in the water, they do only harm. So, just as you do with dangerous beasts, after we had stabbed and tormented those that we could catch, as if they were mad dogs, either we beat them with great blows of iron clubs, or else, having first cut their flippers and tied a barrel ring to their tails, we threw them back into the sea. Since they floated and struggled a long time on the surface of the water before sinking, we had much good sport watching them.

Although the sea tortoises in this Torrid Zone are far from being so huge and monstrous that you could roof a whole house or make a navigable ship from a single shell (as Pliny claimed for the ones from the Indies and the islands of the Red Sea),[a] nevertheless, because you see some that are so long, wide, and thick as to be scarcely believable for those who haven't seen them, I will mention them here in passing. And without making a longer discourse on the subject, I will let the reader judge what they can be like by the following sample. One that was caught by the ship of our Vice-Admiral was so big that eighty people in the ship had a good meal off it (at least by the standards of shipboard life). The oval upper shell, which was given to our captain the Sieur de Sainte-Marie, was more than two and a half feet wide, and proportionately strong and thick. Moreover, the flesh is so much like veal that, especially when it is larded and roasted, it has almost the same taste.

This is how I saw them caught on the sea. During fair and calm weather (you rarely see them otherwise), when they come up out of the water, the sun warms their backs and their shells until they can no longer stand it, and to cool off they flip over and lie belly up. The mariners who see them in that state approach in their boat as quietly as they can; when they are near they hook them between two shells with the iron gaffs I have mentioned. Then it is as much as four or five men can do with the strength of their arms to haul them into the boat. This, in brief, is what I wanted to say about the tortoises and fish that we caught at that time; for I will speak later about dolphins, as well as whales and other sea monsters.

---

[a]Pliny, *Natural History*, Book 9, Chapter 10.

# C H A P T E R I V

## OF THE EQUATOR,
### OR EQUINOCTIAL LINE:
TOGETHER WITH THE TEMPESTS, THE
FICKLENESS OF WINDS, THE PESTI-
LENT RAINS, THE HEAT, THE THIRST,
AND OTHER INCONVENIENCES THAT
WE ENDURED IN THAT REGION

To return to our navigation. Our good wind ran out on us at three or four
degrees this side of the Equator; we then had very troublesome weather,
mixed with rain and calm. Navigation is difficult and indeed very dangerous near this equinoctial line; because of the fickleness of various winds,
all blowing at the same time, even though our three ships were quite near
each other, I saw each vessel being pushed by its particular wind, and
those who manned the tillers and the rudders were unable to prevent it:
so that they formed a triangle, one going to the east, another to the north,
and the other to the west. This didn't last long, for suddenly there came
up a kind of whirlwind that the mariners of Normandy call *grains,* which
sometimes would stop us short, and then the next minute would blow so
hard in the sails of our ships that it is a marvel that they didn't turn us top
down and keel up a hundred times over.

Furthermore, the rain that falls in the region of this line not only
stinks, but it is so pestilent that if it falls on the flesh, it raises pustules and
big blisters, and even stains and spoils garments.[1] Then, too, the sun is so
burning hot that in addition to the violent heat that we endured, we were
so sorely pressed by thirst—aside from two small meals a day, we had no
fresh water or other drink at our disposal—, that for my part my breath
failed me, and, as I know from having tried it, I lost the ability to speak
for more than an hour. And that is why in such extremity, during these
long voyages, the seamen regularly wish, for better luck, that the sea were
changed into fresh water. At this point someone might ask whether, so as

not to imitate Tantalus dying of thirst in the middle of the waters, it would not be possible in this extremity to drink, or at least to refresh the mouth, with sea water. I reply that whatever recipe one might cite to me, such as passing it through wax or distilling it some other way (and the swaying and tossing of ships at sea hardly lends itself to making ovens, or to keeping bottles from breaking), unless you want to vomit up your guts as soon as the sea water is in your body, there is no question of tasting it, much less swallowing it. Nevertheless when you see it in a glass, it looks as clear, pure, and clean as any fountain or spring water. And furthermore (something that has amazed me, and that I will let the philosophers dispute) if you use sea water for leaching bacon, herring, or other meat and fish, as salty as you please, they will be unsalted better and sooner than in fresh water.

To get back to what I was saying. When our afflictions under this burning zone were at their worst, we found that because of the heavy and continual rains that had penetrated the hold, our biscuit was spoiled and mouldy; each of us had but a very little, and not only did we have to eat it rotten, but also—for it was this or die of hunger, since we could afford to throw nothing away—we swallowed as many worms (of which it was half-composed) as we did crumbs. Furthermore, our fresh water was so polluted, and likewise so full of worms, that merely in drawing it from the containers where it is kept on board ship, even the least squeamish of us could not keep from spitting; but the worst was that when you drank, you had to hold the cup in one hand and stop up your nose with the other because of the stench.

What do you say to that, my finicky gentlemen, who, when you are a little oppressed by the heat, after changing your shirt, and having your hair freshly curled, enjoy resting in a fine cool room, seated in a chair, or on a bed of ease, and could not think of taking a meal unless the dishes are shining, the glasses polished, the napkins white as snow, the bread nicely cut, the meat, as delicate as you please, properly prepared and served, and the wine or other draught clear as emerald? Are you willing to board ship to live in such a fashion? For you, I don't advise it; and it will tempt you even less when you hear what happened on our return. Therefore, let me entreat you that, when people talk of the sea, and especially of such voyages, you who know nothing of it except through books (or what is worse, having only heard tell of it by those who never made the journey) do not insist on holding forth, and (as the saying goes) sell your cockleshells to pilgrims from Mont-Saint-Michel:[2] that is to say, I ask you to defer a little to those who have endured such torments, and

21

have experienced things, which, to tell the truth, cannot slip into the brain nor into the understanding of men unless (as the proverb says) they have been through hungry times.[3]

I would add to this something here that concerns as much my first remarks on the variety of winds, storms, foul rains, and heat, as the things that are generally seen on the sea, especially under the Equator. One of our pilots, called Jean de Meun, of Harfleur, although he didn't know A from B, had nevertheless by long experience with his maps, astrolabes, and Jacob's staff[a] become so expert in the art of navigation that often, and especially during storms, I would see him silence a learned personage (whom I shall not name) who in calm weather would pride himself on teaching the theory of it. Not, however, that I condemn or wish in any way to disparage the sciences that are acquired and learned in schools, and by the study of books; such is far from my intention. But I must ask that you not so settle on a mere opinion, whosesoever it may be, that you cite me reason against the experience of a thing. So I entreat the readers to bear with me if, remembering our mouldy bread and our stinking water, along with the other discomforts we endured, and comparing all that with the fine meals of these great critics, I have been a bit choleric in this digression. For to be sure, because of the difficulties that I have mentioned, and for reasons that I will discuss more fully elsewhere, many seamen, after having consumed all their provisions in these places—that is, under the Torrid Zone—could not pass beyond the equator and were forced to give up and to go back to where they had come from.

As for us, after we had veered and wheeled around in this wretched state for about five weeks in the region of that line, and had finally little by little drawn near to it, God, taking pity on us, sent us a wind out of the north-northeast, and the fourth day of February we were pushed right under it. Now it is called the "equinoctial line," not only because in all times and seasons the days and nights are of equal length there, but also because when the sun is straight overhead there, which happens twice a year on the eleventh of March and on the thirteenth of September,[4] the days and the nights are of equal length the world over: so that those who live under the Arctic and the Antarctic Poles, participate only those two days of the year in the day and the night; the very next day the one or the other (each in turn) loses the sun from sight for a half a year.

---

[a][An instrument used for taking the altitude of the sun.]

The fourth of February, then, when we passed the center, or rather the girdle of the world, the sailors performed their customary ceremonies in this troublesome and dangerous passage. So that those aboard who have never before passed under the Equator are sure to remember it, they are bound with ropes and plunged into the sea; or else their faces are blackened and besmeared with an old cloth rubbed on the bottom of the cauldron. One can, however, buy the sailors off and be exempted from all that, as I did, by paying for their wine.

Thus, without further delay, we cut the sea, running before a fair wind from the north-northeast, until we were four degrees beyond the equinoctial line. From there we began to see the Antarctic Pole, which the Norman mariners call the "Southern Star," around which, as I noticed then, there are certain stars arranged in a cross, which they call the "Southern Cross." Another author[a] has written that the first in our time to make this voyage reported that you can always see next to the Antarctic Pole, or due south, a little white cloud[b] and four stars in a cross, with three others that resemble our Ursa Major. Now we had already lost the Arctic Pole from view a long time before: and I will say here incidentally that (contrary to what some people think, and to what would seem possible, given the sphere) not only are you unable to see both poles when you are right under the Equator, you cannot see either one; you have to be about two degrees off the Equator, either north or south, to see the Arctic or the Antarctic Poles.

On the thirteenth of February the weather was fine and clear; after our pilots and ships' masters had taken the height with the astrolabe, they assured us that we had the sun right at the zenith, and so directly overhead that it could not be more precise. And in fact although to test it we planted daggers, knives, and awls on the upper deck, the sun's rays were so exactly perpendicular that on that day, especially at noon, we saw no shadow on our ship. When we were at twelve degrees, we had a storm that lasted three or four days. And after that (going to the other extreme) the sea was so tranquil and calm that during this time our ships stood fixed on the water, and if the wind had not risen to make us move on, we would never have budged from the spot.

Now during our whole voyage we had as yet seen no whales; but in

---

[a]Gómara, *Histoire générale des Indes [occidentales]*, Book 3, Chapter 98. [Léry used M. Fumée's translation from the Spanish.]

[b][The Magellanic Cloud, either of two irregular galaxies.]

that region, we saw some rather close at hand. There was one that rose up near our ship and gave me such a fright that until I saw it move, I thought it was a rock against which our ship was about to crash and be shattered. I observed that when it was about to dive, it raised its head above the sea and spewed more than two casks of water from its mouth into the air. Then, sounding, it made such a horrible roiling of the water that I was afraid that it would draw us in after it, and that we would be engulfed by it. And in truth, as it is said in the Psalm and in Job,[a] it is a fearsome thing to see these sea monsters frolic and play at their ease amidst these great waters.[5]

We also saw dolphins, which, followed by several kinds of fish, all disposed and arranged like a company of soldiers marching after their captain, appeared in the water to be of a reddish color; and there was one that swam around and around our boat six or seven times, as if to proffer endearments and caresses. In recompense, we tried everything we could think of to catch it, but again and again it nimbly beat its retreat, blowing its trumpet, and we could not do it.

---

[a]Psalms 104.26. Job 40.28 [in the French Protestant Bible; in the King James Version, Job 41.8].

# CHAPTER V

# OF THE SIGHTING AND
## FIRST VIEW THAT WE HAD
BOTH OF WEST INDIA OR THE LAND
OF BRAZIL AND OF THE SAVAGES
THAT INHABIT IT, TOGETHER WITH
EVERYTHING THAT HAPPENED TO US
ON THE SEA UP TO THE TROPIC OF
CAPRICORN

After that we had a favorable west wind, which lasted so long that on the twenty-sixth of February 1557 (as determined with the astrolabe and planisphere),[1] at about eight o'clock in the morning, we sighted West India, the land of Brazil, the fourth part of the world, unknown to the Ancients: otherwise called "America" (from the name of him who first discovered it in about 1497).[2] You can well imagine that when we saw we were so near the place that we had set out for, with some hope of soon putting foot to ground, we were filled with joy and gave whole-hearted thanks to God. Indeed, since we had been tossing and afloat on the sea almost four months without putting in to port, it had often occurred to us that we were in exile out there, and it seemed as though we would never escape it. After we had ascertained that what we had sighted was, indeed, dry land (for you can often be deceived on the sea by the clouds, which then vanish), having a fair wind and heading straight for the land, the same day (our Admiral having gone on ahead) we cast anchor a half a league from a mountainous place that the savages call *Huuassou*.

After we had taken the boat down out of the ship, and, according to the custom in that land when one arrives, had fired the cannon several times to warn the inhabitants, we suddenly saw a great number of savage men and women on the seashore. However (as some of our seamen who had been there before recognized), they were of the nation called

*Margaia*,[3] allies of the Portuguese, and therefore such enemies of the French that if they had had us at their mercy, we would have paid no other ransom except being slain and cut to pieces, and serving as a meal for them.

We also began to see for the first time, even in the month of February (just when over here, and in almost all of Europe, everything is closed up and hidden in the womb of the earth because of the cold and frost), the forests, woods, and plants of that country as green and flourishing as those of our France are in May and June. And it is that way all year long, and in all seasons in that land of Brazil.

Notwithstanding this enmity of our Margaia with respect to the French, which both they and we dissimulated as best we could, our master's mate, who could stammer out a few words in their language, got into the ship's boat with a few other sailors and went over to the shore, where the savages continued to assemble in big troops. However, since our people put no trust in them except for some express purpose, they stayed beyond an arrow's reach from land so as to avoid the danger of being seized and *boucané*—that is, roasted. From a distance, our sailors displayed for them knives, mirrors, combs, and other trifles, and called out to them asking for food supplies in exchange; some of the savages, who had drawn as near as they could, upon hearing this did not wait to be asked again, but hurried off to get food for them. So when he returned, our master's mate brought back flour made from a root (which the savages eat instead of bread), hams, and the meat of a certain kind of boar, with an abundance of other food and fruits that are found in that country. Not only that, but, to present themselves to us, and to bid us welcome, six men and one woman embarked straightaway to come see us on the ship. And because these were the first savages that I had seen up close, you can well imagine that I looked at them and studied them attentively. I will postpone describing them at length until a more appropriate place, but still even now I want to say something in passing.

First, both the men and the woman were as utterly naked as when they came out of their mother's womb; however, to bedeck themselves, they were painted and blackened over the entire body. The men had their heads shaved close in front, like a monk's tonsure, and wore their hair long in back; but, in the style of men's wigs over here, their locks were clipped around the neck. Furthermore, they all had the lower lip pierced, and each one wore in the hole a green stone, well polished, carefully placed, and mounted in the lip as in a setting; the stone was of about the size of a testoon,ᵃ and they would take it out and put it back whenever they pleased. They wear such things thinking to be the more handsomely adorned; but to tell the truth, when this stone is removed and this great split in the lower lip appears like a second mouth, they are greatly disfigured. As for the woman, besides not having a split lip, she wore her hair long like the women over here; her ears were so cruelly pierced that you could have put a finger through the holes; she wore great pendants of white bone in them, which swung almost to her shoulders. I will wait until later to refute the error of those who would have had us believe that the savages were covered with hair.

However, before these visitors left us, the men, and especially two or three elders who seemed to be the most important men in their parishes (as we say over here), claimed that their region grew the finest brazilwood that could be found in the whole country, and they promised to help us cut and carry it; furthermore, they would provide us with food—in short, they did everything they could to persuade us to load our ship right there. But because, as I have said, they were our enemies, all this was merely to lure us and trick us into coming ashore so that afterwards, having the advantage over us, they could cut us to pieces and eat us. So aside from the fact that we intended in any case to go elsewhere, we had no mind to stop there.

After our Margaia had taken a good look at our artillery and at whatever else they wanted to see in our ship, since we wanted neither to detain them nor to offend them (bearing in mind the consequences of our deeds for other Frenchmen who would come there unwarned in the future and who might suffer as a result of our acts) and since they were asking to return to their people who were waiting for them on the shore, it was a question of paying them what they wished for the food they had brought us. And because they have no use of currency, the payment we made them was in shirts, knives, fishhooks, mirrors, and other merchandise and small wares fit to peddle among this people. But here was the best of it. Upon their arrival these good people, all naked, had not been sparing in showing us everything they had; and now at their departure, not being in the habit of wearing undergarments or, indeed, any other kind of clothes, when they put on the shirts that we had given them and came to seat themselves in the ship's boat, they tucked them clear up to the navel so as not to spoil them, and, revealing what should be hidden,

---

ᵃ[A silver coin.]

insisted that we see their behinds and their buttocks as they took their farewell of us. Were these not courteous officers, and was this not a fine ambassadorial civility? For notwithstanding the proverb that is so common to us over here, that the flesh is nearer than the shirt,[4] they on the contrary, as if to show us that they were not of that mind, and perhaps as a display of their magnificent hospitality, favored their shirts over their skin by showing us their behinds.

After we had refreshed ourselves a little there (for although the food that they had brought us seemed strange, nonetheless out of necessity we ate heartily of it), the next day, a Sunday, we weighed anchor and set sail. Skirting the land, and working our way toward our destination, we had not sailed more than nine or ten leagues before we found ourselves at the place of a Portuguese fort, called by them *Espirito santo* (and by the savages *Moab*). Recognizing both our equipage and that of the caravel that we had in tow (which they judged correctly that we had taken from their countrymen), they fired three cannon shots at us, and we fired three or four at them in reply. But because we were too far for the reach of their shot, they did us no harm, and I think we did none to them, either.

Then going on our way, still skirting the land, we passed near a place called *Tapemiry,*[a] where at the entry to the land, and at the mouth of the sea, there are some little islands; I think that the savages who live there are friends and allies of the French.

A little farther on, at around twenty degrees, live other savages called *Paraïbes,* in whose land, I noticed as we passed, you can see little pointed mountains shaped like chimneys.

The first of March we were at the latitude of the Little Shallows, that is, an area of reefs and points of land mingled with small rocks that stick out into the sea, which mariners avoid as much as possible lest their ships hit against them.

At these shallows we had a clear sighting of a flatland that for about fifteen leagues of its length is possessed and inhabited by the Ouetaca,[5] savages so fierce and wild that, just as they cannot live in peace with each other, they wage open and continual war against all their neighbors as well as against strangers in general. They are so swift of foot and run so fast that not only do they evade all risk of death when they are pressed and pursued by their enemies (who have never been able to vanquish them or tame them), but also when they hunt they catch certain wild

---

[a][Today, the river and town of Itapemirim.]

animals—kinds of stags and does—by running them down. Although like other Brazilians they go entirely naked, nonetheless, contrary to the most ordinary custom of the men of that country (who, as I have already said and will later expand upon, shave the front of their head and clip their locks in back), these wear their hair long, hanging down to the buttocks. In short, since these devilish Ouetaca remain invincible in this little region, and furthermore, like dogs and wolves, eat flesh raw, and because even their language is not understood by their neighbors, they are considered to be among the most barbarous, cruel, and dreaded nations that can be found in all the West Indies and the land of Brazil. Furthermore, since they neither have nor wish to have any acquaintance or commerce with the French, Spanish, Portuguese, or with any from our side of the ocean, they know nothing about our merchandise.

However, according to what I have heard since then from a Norman interpreter, when their neighbors have goods that they want, this is their manner of bartering. The Margaia, Cara-ia, or Tupinamba (which are the names of the three neighboring nations), or one of the other savages of that country, without trusting or approaching the Ouetaca, shows him from afar what he has—a pruning-hook, a knife, a comb, a mirror, or some other kind of wares brought over for trade—and indicates by a sign if he wants to exchange it for something else. If the other agrees, he shows in turn a bit of featherwork, or some of the green stones that they set in their lips, or some other thing that they have in their region. Then they will agree on a place three or four hundred steps from there; the first, having carried the thing that he wants to exchange and set it on a stone or log, will then withdraw, either back or to one side. The Ouetaca then comes to take it and leaves the object he had displayed at the same spot; then he too will retreat and will allow the Margaia (or whoever it may be) to come and get it: so that up to that point they keep their promises to each other. But as soon as each one has returned with his object of exchange, and gone past the boundaries of the place where he had first come to present himself, the truce is broken, and it is then a question of which one can catch the other and take back from him what he was carrying away. You can well imagine that the Ouetaca, who can run like a greyhound, has the advantage, and presses hard on the heels of the one he is chasing. Therefore, unless the lame, gouty, or otherwise slow-footed folk from over here want to lose their merchandise, I do not recommend that they negotiate or barter with the Ouetaca.

Now it is similarly true of the Basques that they have an entirely separate language, and that, as everyone knows, being lively and nimble, they are held to be the best running footmen in the world;[6] since on these two points they could be compared with our Ouetaca, it seems that they might well be a match for them on the field. You could also rank with them certain men who live in a region of Florida, near the Palm River, who (as someone writes) are so strong and light of foot that they can overtake a stag, and run for a whole day without rest; then too, there are great giants on the river La Plata, which also (according to the same author) are so agile that merely by running and using their hands they can catch certain deer of the region.[a] But to these coursers I will let go the reins; to these two-footed hounds I will let slip the leash: let them run as swift as the wind though they fall thick as rain (tumbling onto their noses) in their three places in America (places nonetheless far from each other, for the regions of La Plata and of Florida are over fifteen hundred leagues apart) or their fourth place back in our Europe. These I will leave, to return to the thread of my story.

After we had sailed along the shore of the Ouetaca territory and left it behind us, we passed into the view of another neighboring country named *Macaé*, inhabited by other savages of which I will say nothing except that, for the reasons I have mentioned, you can guess that they do not have an easy time of it, and have no mind to be lulled to sleep next to such brusque and fidgety alarm-clocks as their neighbors are. On the shore of their land there can be seen a big rock shaped like a tower, which, when the sun strikes it, glistens and sparkles so brightly that some think it is a sort of emerald; indeed, the French and Portuguese who travel there call it the "Emerald of Macaé." They say, however, that the site cannot be approached with ships because of the innumerable rocky points just above the water which project about two leagues into the sea; they also maintain that it is inaccessible from the land.

There are also three little islands called the "Islands of Macaé,"[b] near which we cast anchor and slept for a night. The next day, setting sail, we thought that we could arrive at Cape Frio that same day. However, instead of advancing, we had such a contrary wind that we had to give up and turn back to where we had come from that morning, and stay there at anchor until Thursday evening; and as you will hear, we nearly stayed there for good. For Tuesday the second of March, the day called "Shrove-Tuesday," after our sailors had made merry according to their custom,[7] it

---

[a][Gómara,] *Histoire générale des Indes,* Book 2, Chapters 46 and 89.
[b][The Santa Ana and Papagayos Islands.]

happened that around eleven o'clock at night, just as we were about to retire, a storm came up so suddenly that the cable holding the anchor of our ship was unable to sustain the violence of the furious waves, and it suddenly snapped. Our vessel, tossed about by the billows and pushed toward the shore, came in to where we had only twelve feet of water (which was the least it could float in even when it was completely empty), and we very nearly ran aground. In fact, the master and the pilot, who were sounding the depth as the ship was drifting, instead of being more confident and giving courage to the others, when they saw that we had come to that point cried out two or three times, "We are lost! We are lost!" Our sailors, however, speedily cast another anchor, which thanks to God held firm, and we were prevented from being carried onto the rocks of these Islands of Macaé, which without a doubt would have entirely wrecked our ship, and—with the sea being as high as it was— would have left us with no hope of saving ourselves. This fright and shock lasted around three hours, during which time there was not much use in shouting, "Larboard! Starboard! Raise the helm! Luff! Haul the bow line! Let go the sheet!"—for all that kind of yelling goes on out on the high seas, where the seamen do not fear a storm as much as they do close to land, where we were at that time.

Since our drinking water was spoiled, when morning came and the storm had ceased, some of us went to get fresh water in these uninhabitable islands. We found the land covered with eggs and birds of various kinds, utterly different from our own; and because they were unaccustomed to seeing men, they were so tame that they let themselves be caught by hand, or killed by blows of a stick. We filled our bark with them, and brought back to the ship as many as we pleased. Although it was the day called "Ash Wednesday," nonetheless our sailors—even the most Roman Catholic among them—, who had a good appetite from their work of the night before, had no scruples about eating them. And, after all, since he who (contrary to the doctrine of the Gospel) has forbidden Christians to eat meat on certain days has not yet set foot in this land, where consequently no one has heard of observing the laws of such superstitious abstinence, it seems that the place gave them sufficient dispensation.[8]

The Thursday that we left these three islands, we had such a favorable wind that the next day, around four o'clock in the afternoon, we arrived at Cape Frio, the best-known port and harbor for French navigation in that country. There, after casting anchor and firing several cannon shots as a signal to the inhabitants, the captain and the ship's master, with some of us others, went ashore. First we found on the shore a great number of savages called *Tupinamba,* allies and confederates of our nation, who brought us, along with their courtesies and welcome, news of *Paycolas*[a] (for so they called Villegagnon), which made us very happy. In this same place we caught, both with a net and with hooks, a great quantity of several kinds of fish, all different from those over here; but among the others, there was one, perhaps the oddest, most deformed and most monstrous that one might ever see, and for that reason I wanted to describe it here.[b] It was almost as big as a yearling calf, and had a nose about five feet long, and a foot and a half wide, armed with teeth on each side, as sharp and cutting as a saw: so that when on the land we saw one of them suddenly move this great nose, we all were wary of it, lest we be marked by it, and cried out to each other, "Watch your legs!" Its flesh was so hard that, although we all had a good appetite, and we even boiled it more than twenty-four hours, still, we could never eat it.

It was there, too, that we first saw flocks of parrots flying high above, like pigeons and crows in France; they are always joined together as couples in the air, almost like our turtledoves.

Having thus arrived at twenty-five or thirty leagues from our destination, we desired nothing more than to get there as soon as possible, and for that reason we did not make as long a stay at Cape Frio as we might otherwise have done. So the evening of that same day, having made ready and set sail, we cut the water so swiftly that on Sunday the seventh of March 1557, leaving the high sea on the left (to the east), we entered the inlet of the sea, the saltwater estuary called *Guanabara* by the savages, and *Janeiro* by the Portuguese (who gave it that name because they discovered it on the first day of January). So, as I mentioned in the first chapter of this history, and as I will describe hereafter at more length, we found Villegagnon settled, as he had been since the preceding year, on a little island situated in this estuary. When we had saluted him with cannon fire from about a quarter of a league off, and he had answered us, we drew near the shore and cast anchor. So that, in sum, was our navigation, and what happened to us and what we saw on our way to the land of Brazil.

---

[a][*Paycolas* means Lord or Father Nicolas (*Paï* is a term of respect used for elders, chiefs, or shamans).]

[b][Probably a sawfish.]

❧

# OF OUR LANDING AT
FORT COLIGNY IN THE LAND
OF BRAZIL. OF THE RECEPTION THAT
VILLEGAGNON GAVE US, AND OF HIS
BEHAVIOR, REGARDING BOTH RELI-
GION AND OTHER ASPECTS OF HIS
GOVERNMENT IN THAT COUNTRY

When our ships were in harbor in the bay of Guanabara, near the main-land, each of us put his baggage in the boats, and we went ashore to the island and fort called *Coligny*. And seeing ourselves delivered from the perils and dangers by which we had so often been surrounded on the sea, and so fortunately guided to the desired port, the first thing that we did after putting foot to ground was to give thanks to God. That done, we went to find Villegagnon, who was waiting for us and whom we each greeted in turn; he, for his part, with an open countenance (or so it seemed), embracing us and clasping us around the neck, warmly welcomed us. After that, the Sieur du Pont—our guide, with Richier and Chartier, ministers of the Gospel—briefly explained to him our principal motive for this voyage, and for making the difficult crossing to join him: which was, in response to the letters that he had written to Geneva, to establish a Reformed Church according to the word of God in that country.[1] Here are the very words he used in his answer:

"As for me," he said, "I have long desired this, with all my heart, and I receive you very willingly under these conditions: because I want our Church to be renowned as the best reformed of all, from now on I intend that all vices be repressed, that sumptuousness of apparel be re-formed, and, in short, that everything that could prevent us from serving God be removed from our midst." Then, raising his eyes to heaven and clasping his hands, he said, "Lord God, I thank thee for having sent what I have so ardently prayed for." Then, addressing our company again,

"My children (for I wish to be your father), just as Jesus Christ when He was in this world did nothing for himself, but rather did everything for us, so too (in the hope that God will preserve my life until we are well established in this country and you are able to do without me), everything that I mean to do here is for you, and for all those who come here with the same purpose as yours. For I intend to make here a refuge for the poor faithful who are persecuted in France, in Spain, and elsewhere across the sea, so that, fearing neither king, nor emperor, nor any other potentates, they can serve God purely according to his will." Those are the first words that Villegagnon spoke to us upon our arrival, which was a Wednesday, the tenth of March 1557.

After that, Villegagnon having commanded that all his people promptly gather together with us in a little room in the middle of the island, the minister Richier pronounced an invocation to God, and the Fifth Psalm, "Give ear to my words, O Lord," was sung in the assembly; then Richier, taking as his text these verses of the twenty-seventh Psalm, "One thing have I desired of the Lord, that will I seek after; that I may dwell in the house of the Lord all the days of my life," preached the first sermon at Fort Coligny in America. But during that time, Villegagnon, who intended to expound that text, was incessantly clasping his hands, raising his eyes to the heavens, heaving great sighs, and assuming other such postures, to the point that we were all amazed. At the end, after the solemn prayers, which were performed on a day of the week ordained for the purpose according to the customary rules of the Reformed Churches in France, the company dispersed. However, we newcomers remained and dined that day in the same room, where our only food was flour made from roots, fish *boucané* (that is, roasted in the savage style), and other roots cooked in ashes (these foods and their properties I will treat elsewhere, rather than interrupt my story); for drink, since in this island there is neither fountain, well, nor river of fresh water, we had water from a cistern—or rather a gutter containing all the island's rainfall—, which was as green and filthy as an old frog-covered ditch. It is true, however, that compared with the foul and stinking water that we had drunk on the ship, we found it good.

Finally, as our last course, to refresh us from our sea-toil, they took us to haul stones and earth in this Fort of Coligny that they were continuing to build. Such was the fine treatment that Villegagnon offered us from the very day of our arrival.

Furthermore, in the evening, when it was a question of lodging, the Sieur du Pont and the two ministers were provided with a room of very indifferent comfort in the middle of the island. In order to accommodate the rest of us who were of the Religion, they gave us a little house on the seashore, which a savage slave of Villegagnon's was finishing, building it in the native fashion and covering it with grass; in the style of the Americans, we hung sheets and cotton beds there, so that we slept suspended in the air.

The next day and the following ones, Villegagnon took no notice of our being weakened by the sea passage, nor of the heat of the climate, nor of the little nourishment that we had, which was two cups of hard flour a day for each of us, made of the roots I have mentioned (we made gruel of some of it with the muddy cistern water, and ate the rest dry, as the natives do); even though he was not constrained by necessity, he made us haul earth and stones into his fort—indeed, at such a rate that, given our discomforts and infirmities, in compelling us to sustain that labor from daybreak until night, he seemed to be treating us a little more roughly than might be warranted by the duty of a good father toward his children (as he had said upon our arrival he wanted to be).

However, because of our great desire for the completion of the building and refuge that he said he wanted to make for the faithful in that land, and because Master Pierre Richier, our oldest minister, to encourage us further said that we had found in Villegagnon a second Saint Paul (and indeed, I have never heard a man speak better on religion and on Christian reformation than he did at that time), there was not one of us who did not joyfully employ his strength to the utmost in this task, even though we were unaccustomed to it. On this point I can say that Villegagnon has not been able to complain justly that he did not get out of us all the service that he wished as long as he professed the Gospel in that land.

Now to return to my main subject. The first week after we had arrived there, Villegagnon not only consented to but also himself established this order of services: that is, that aside from the public prayers, which were held every evening after the day's work, the ministers would preach for an hour on all working days and twice on Sundays. He also expressly declared that he intended the Sacraments to be administered according to the pure Word of God, without any human addition, and, moreover, that ecclesiastic discipline be practiced against those who faltered. Following that ecclesiastical policy, on Sunday the twenty-first of March, when the Last Supper of Our Lord Jesus Christ was celebrated for the first time in the Fort of Coligny in America, the ministers had prepared and catechised beforehand all those who were to take Communion.

Because they did not have a good opinion of a certain Jean Cointa (who asked to be called "Monsieur Hector"), a former doctor of the Sorbonne who had crossed the sea with us, he was requested by them, before presenting himself, to make a public confession of the faith—which he did, and at the same time, in front of everyone, abjured Papism.

Similarly, when the sermon was finished, Villegagnon, seemingly still full of zeal, rose and declared that the captain, ship's masters, sailors, and others, who were present but who had not yet professed the Reformed Religion, were not able to comprehend such a mystery; he made them leave, and would not permit them to see the bread and wine administered. He himself, both to dedicate his fort to God, and to profess his faith before the Church, kneeled on a square of velvet (which his page usually carried behind him) and pronounced aloud two prayers. Since I have a copy of them, and so that everyone can better understand how difficult it was to know the heart and inner conscience of that man, I have inserted them here, word for word, without changing a single letter.

> My God, open the eyes and the mouth of my understanding, dispose them to make unto Thee confession, prayers, and thanksgiving for the supreme benefits Thou hast granted us! Almighty God, living and immortal, Eternal Father of Thy Son Jesus Christ Our Lord, who by Thy Providence with Thy Son governest all things in heaven and on earth, as in Thine infinite goodness Thou hast made known to Thine elect since the creation of the world, and especially through Thy Son, whom Thou has sent to earth, and through whom Thou manifestest Thyself, having said aloud, "Hear Him";[a] and after His Ascension by Thy Holy Spirit descending on the Apostles: I acknowledge to Thy Holy Majesty from my heart, in the presence of Thy Church, planted by Thy grace in this land, that I have never found, through the trial and attempt of my own strength and prudence, that there comes from my own efforts anything but pure works of darkness, the wisdom of the flesh, polluted with the zeal of vanity, tending only to the aim and use of my body. Therefore I protest and frankly confess that without the light of Thy Holy Spirit I am fit only to sin: thus stripping myself of all glory, I desire it to be known of me that if there be a glimmer or spark of virtue in the work that Thou hast undertaken through me, I confess it to be due

---

[a][Luke 9.35: "And there came a voice out of the cloud, saying, This is my beloved Son: hear him.]"

*solely to Thee, source of all good. In this faith then, My God, I render unto Thee thanks with all my heart, that it hath pleased Thee to call me away from the affairs of this world, amidst which I lived by the appetite of ambition, and by the inspiration of Thy Holy Spirit to put me in a land where I can freely serve Thee with all my strength for the increase of Thy Holy Kingdom, and in so doing to prepare a place and a peaceful dwelling for those who are being forbidden to invoke Thy Name in public, where they can sanctify Thee and adore Thee in spirit and in truth, and recognize Thy Son our Saviour Jesus Christ as our only mediator, our way and our life, and the sole merit of our salvation.*

*Moreover, I thank Thee, O God of all goodness, that, having led me into this land among those ignorant of Thy Name and Thy greatness, but possessed by Satan as his inheritance, Thou hast preserved me from their malice, although I was destitute of human strength: Thou hast, rather, put them in terror of us, so that at the mere mention of us they tremble with fear, and Thou hast dispersed them so as to nourish us with their labors. And to restrain their brutal violence, Thou hast afflicted them with cruel maladies, preserving us from the same all the while; Thou hast removed from the earth those who were the most dangerous to us, and hast reduced the others to such weakness that they dare undertake nothing against us. By which means we have the leisure to take root in this place, and for the company that it has pleased Thee to bring here without hindrance, Thou hast established the rule of a Church to keep us in the unity and fear of Thy Holy Name, so as to lead us into eternal life.*

*O Lord, since it has pleased Thee to establish in us Thy Realm, I beseech Thee through Thy Son Jesus Christ, whom Thou hast given in sacrifice to confirm us in Thy love, to increase Thy mercies and our faith, sanctifying us and illuminating us by Thy Holy Spirit, and to dedicate us to Thy service, that all our endeavor may be for Thy glory: may it please Thee too, Our Lord and Father, to extend Thy benediction to this place Coligny, and to this land of Antarctic France, to be an impregnable retreat for those who in good faith and without hypocrisy seek refuge there, to dedicate themselves with us to the exaltation of Thy glory; and where we may, without disturbance from heretics, invoke Thee in truth. Grant also that Thy Gospel may reign in this place, fortifying Thy servants, lest*

37

*they stumble into the error of the Epicureans[2] and other apostates; may they rather be constant in persevering in the true adoration of Thy Divinity according to Thy Holy Word.*

*May it please Thee too, God of all goodness, to protect the King our sovereign according to the flesh, his wife, his descendants, and his council; Messire Gaspard de Coligny, his wife and his descendants, preserving them in the will to maintain and favor this Thy Church; and grant me, Thy humble bondsman, the prudence to guide me so that I may never stray from the straight and narrow path, and that I may resist all the hindrances that Satan might put in my way without Thine aid. May we recognize Thee perpetually as our merciful God, our just judge and the preserver of all things with Thy Son Jesus Christ, reigning with Thee and with Thy Holy Spirit, descended upon the Apostles. Create then in us an upright heart, mortify us to sin, regenerating in us the inner man to live for justice, subduing our flesh to make it fit for the actions of the soul inspired by Thee, that we may do Thy will on earth, as the angels do in heaven.*

*But lest a lack of the necessities cause us to stumble into sin through mistrust of Thy bounty, may it please Thee to provide for the needs of our life, and maintain us in health. And even as earthly meat by the heat of the stomach is converted into blood and nourishment for the body, grant so to nourish and sustain our souls with the flesh and blood of Thy Son, so that he may be formed in us, and we in Him; driving away all malice (food for Satan), and putting in its place charity and faith, so that we may be known by Thee as Thy children.*

*And when we have offended Thee, may it please thee, O Lord, in thy mercy, to wash our sins in the blood of Thy Son, having remembrance that we were conceived in iniquity, and that by the disobedience of Adam sin is naturally in us. Moreover, I know that our soul cannot fulfill the holy desire to obey Thee through the organ of the imperfect and rebellious body. May it please Thee then by the merit of Thy Son Jesus, not to impute to us our faults, but rather the sacrifice of His Death and Passion, that we have suffered with Him through faith, having been grafted onto Him by the receiving of His Body in the mystery of the Eucharist. Likewise grant us grace so that, by the example of Thy Son, who prayed for those who perse-*

*cuted Him, we pardon those who have offended us, and that instead of vengeance we procure their good as if they were our friends. And when we are importuned by the memory of the riches, splendors, pomps, and honors of this world, being on the contrary, downcast by poverty and by the weight of the Cross of Thy Son (to which may it please Thee to inure us so as to render us obedient, lest fattened by worldly felicity, we rebel against Thee), sustain us and soften the harshness of our afflictions, that they may not stifle the seed that Thou hast placed in our hearts. We pray Thee also, Heavenly Father, to guard us from Satan's undertakings, by which he seeks to lead us astray; preserve us from his ministers and from the furious savages, in the midst of whom it pleases Thee to keep and maintain us, and from the apostates from the Christian Religion scattered among them;[3] but may it please Thee to recall them to Thine obedience, that they may be converted, and that Thy Gospel be published through all the earth, and that Thy salvation be declared to all nations. Who livest and reignest with Thy Son and the Holy Spirit would without end. Amen.*

## Another Prayer to Our Lord Jesus Christ, Which Villegagnon Uttered Immediately After

*Jesus Christ Son of God, living, eternal, and consubstantial, His living image by which all things were made, Thou hast seen mankind condemned by the infallible judgment of God Thy Father through the transgression of Adam, who, to enjoy the life of the eternal kingdom, was made by God of earth unpolluted by male seed (from which he might draw the necessity of sin), endowed with all virtue, in freedom of will to preserve himself in his perfection; he, nonetheless, enticed by the sensuality of his flesh, solicited and aroused by the flaming darts of Satan, let himself be vanquished, on account of which he incurred the wrath of God, from which would have followed the infallible perdition of men, had it not been for Thee, Our Lord, who, moved by thine immense and inexpressible charity offered Thyself to God Thy Father, humbling Thyself in deigning to substitute Thyself for Adam, to endure all the waves of the indignation of God Thy Father, for our purification. And even as Adam had been made of uncorrupted earth, without male seed, Thou wast conceived by the Holy Spirit in a Virgin, to be made and formed in true flesh like that of Adam, and continually subjected to trials above those of all other human creatures, without sin: and finally, desiring to graft onto Thine own body that of Adam and all his posterity, nourishing their souls with Thy flesh and Thy blood, Thou hast been willing to suffer death, so that as a member of Thy Body they may be nourished in Thee, and that they may please God Thy Father, offering Thy death in payment for their offenses, as if it were their own body. And even as the sin of Adam was descended to his posterity, and through sin death, Thou hast willed and obtained from God Thy Father that Thy justice be ascribed to believers, who by their eating of Thy flesh and blood, Thou has made one with Thee and transformed into Thee, nourished by Thy flesh and substance, their true bread, to live eternally as children of justice and no longer as children of wrath. Since it has pleased Thee to do us so much good, and that being seated on the right hand of God Thy Father, Thou art there eternally ordained our intercessor and sovereign priest according to the order of Melchizedek,[4] have pity on us, preserve us, fortify and increase our faith, offer to God Thy Father the confession that I make with both heart and mouth, in the presence of Thy Church, sanctifying me by Thy Spirit, as Thou hast promised, saying, "I will not leave you orphans."[a] Advance Thy Church in this place, so that Thou mayest be worshiped here in all peace. Who livest and reignest with Him and the Holy Spirit forever, world without end. Amen.*

These two prayers finished, Villegagnon was the first to present himself to the Lord's Table, and received kneeling the bread and wine from the hand of the minister. However, in brief, just as an ancient writer has said—that is, that it is hard to feign virtue for long—it became evident that there was only ostentation in his deeds, and that although he and Cointa had publicly abjured papistry, they nevertheless had more desire to debate and contest than to learn and profit; thus they were not slow to stir up disputes concerning doctrine. But principally on the point of the Lord's Supper: for although they rejected the transubstantiation[5] of the Roman Church, as an opinion which they openly said was stupid and absurd, and although they did not approve of consubstantiation[6] either, still they were not content with what the ministers taught and proved by the Word of God, that the bread and wine were not really changed into the Body and Blood of the Lord, which also was not con-

---

[a][John 14.18: "I will not leave you comfortless."]

tained within them; rather that Jesus Christ is in heaven, whence, by virtue of his Holy Spirit, he communicates himself in spiritual nourishment to those who receive the signs in faith. Well, however that may be, said Villegagnon and Cointa, the words "This is my Body; this is my Blood" cannot be taken other than to mean that the Body and the Blood of Jesus Christ are contained therein. What then if you ask: "Then how did they mean it, since you said that they rejected the doctrines both of transubstantiation and of consubstantiation?" I have no notion of what they meant, and I firmly believe that they didn't, either; for when they were shown by other passages that these words and expressions are figures—that is, that Scripture is accustomed to calling the signs of the Sacraments by the names of the things signified—although they could not provide any proof to the contrary, nonetheless they remained obstinate; to the point that, without knowing how it might be done, nevertheless they wanted not only to eat the flesh of Jesus Christ grossly rather than spiritually, but what was worse, like the savages named *Ouetaca*, of whom I have already spoken, they wanted to chew and swallow it raw.[7]

However, Villegagnon, still putting on a fair countenance and protesting that he desired nothing more than to be rightly instructed, sent the minister Chartier back to France in one of the ships (which, after it was loaded with brazilwood and other merchandise of the country, left on the fourth of June for its return) so that on this dispute over the Lord's Supper he might bring back the opinions of our theologians, and especially that of Master Jean Calvin, to whose opinion Villegagnon said he was willing to submit everything.[8] And, indeed, I have often heard him repeat this remark: "Monsieur Calvin is one of the most learned personages who has lived since the Apostles: and I have not read any theologian who to my mind has better or more purely set forth and treated Holy Scripture than he has." Moreover, to show that he revered him, in the answer that he made to the letters that we brought him, he not only informed him at length about his state in general but also particularly (as I have said in the Preface, and which will be seen again at the end of the original of his letter dated the last day of March 1557, which is in safekeeping) he wrote in his own hand, with brazilwood ink, what follows:

> *I will take the counsel that you have given me in your letters, and endeavor with all my power not to stray from it in the least. For indeed, I am fully persuaded that there can be none holier, truer, or more entire. Therefore we have also had your letters read in the assembly of our council, and afterward registered, so that if we*

*should chance to wander from the straight and narrow path, we
may be recalled and corrected by the reading of them.*

A certain Nicolas Carmeau, who was the bearer of these letters, and
who left the first of April in the ship Rosée, said to me while taking leave
of us that Villegagnon had ordered him to say to Monsieur Calvin that he
beseeched him to believe that, in order to perpetuate the memory of his
counsel, he would have it engraved in bronze; Villegagnon had also
charged Carmeau to bring him from France a number of persons—men,
women, and children—promising that he would pay all the expenses that
~~those of the Religion would incur in going to join him.~~

Before continuing, I want not to omit the mention here of ten
savage boys, nine to ten years of age and younger, who had been captured
in war and sold as slaves to Villegagnon by savages who were friendly to
the French. Minister Richier had placed his hands on them at the end of a
sermon, and we had prayed God all together that He might do them the
grace to be the first fruits of this poor people, and to be drawn to the
knowledge of their salvation. They then embarked in the boats that left
on the fourth of June to return to France, where upon their arrival they
were presented to King Henry II, who was reigning then. The latter made
a gift of them to several great lords; among others, he gave one of them to
the late Monsieur de Passy, who had the boy baptized, and after my
return I recognized him there.

Furthermore, the third of April two young men, servants of Villegagnon, were joined in marriage at the sermon (in the style of the Reformed churches) to two of the young girls that we had brought into this
country from France. I mention this here, not only because these were the
first marriages made and solemnized in the Christian manner in the land
of America, but also because many of the savages who had come to see us
were more astonished at seeing women clothed (for they had never seen
such before) than they were amazed at the ecclesiastical ceremonies,
which, however, were also completely unknown to them. Likewise, the
seventeenth of May, Cointa married another young girl, who was related
to a certain La Roquette of Rouen who had crossed the sea at the same
time we had. Having died some time after our arrival, he had left this
kinswoman heir to the merchandise that he had carried over, which
consisted of a great quantity of knives, combs, mirrors, colored woolen
cloth, fishhooks, and other small wares fit for trade among the savages:
and that very well suited Cointa, who knew how to make use of everything. The two other girls (there were five in all) were also immediately

married to two Norman interpreters; so there were no more Christian women or girls left to marry.

So as not to omit what was praiseworthy in Villegagnon any more than what was reprehensible, I will add something here in passing. Certain Normans, having escaped from a shipwreck long before his arrival in that country, had remained among the savages, where, having no fear of God, they lived in wantonness with the women and girls (I have seen some who had children by them already four or five years old). Both to repress that behavior, and to prevent any men who lived on our island and in our fort from abusing them in that fashion, Villegagnon, by the advice of the council, forbade on pain of death that any man bearing the name of Christian live with the savages' women. It is true that the ordinance permitted that if some of these women were drawn and called to the knowledge of God, then after they had been baptized it would be permitted to marry them. But in spite of the remonstrances that we have made several times to this barbarous people, there was not one of them who would leave her old skin and confess Jesus Christ as her savior;[9] thus, in the whole time that I lived there, not a single Frenchman took one of them to wife. Nevertheless, as this law was doubly founded on the Word of God, it was so well obeyed that not one of Villegagnon's men transgressed it.

Moreover, whatever I have heard said of him since my return—that when he was in America he defiled himself with savage women—I will bear this witness for him, that he was in no way suspected of it in our time. What is more, he set such great store by the execution of his ordinance that, had it not been for the pressing request, made by some whom he loved most, on behalf of an interpreter who had gone to the mainland and had been convicted of fornication with a woman whom he had thus abused earlier on, instead of having him punished merely by being chained by the foot and put among the slaves, Villegagnon would have had him hanged. So according to what I have known of him, with regard both to himself and to others, he was to be praised on this point; and would to God that, for the advancement of the Church and for the fruit that many good people would receive from it now, he had conducted himself as well in all other respects.

But possessed as he was by a spirit of contradiction, he was unable to content himself with the simplicity that Holy Scripture shows true Christians should observe concerning the administration of the Sacraments. It happened that the day of the next Pentecost, when we were celebrating the Lord's Supper for the second time, he—directly contraven-

43

ing what he had said when he set up the order of the Church: that is, that he wanted all human inventions to be rejected—claimed that Saint Cyprian and Saint Clement had written that, in the celebration, water must be mixed with the wine. He not only obstinately insisted that this must be done but also affirmed and wanted it to be believed that the consecrated bread profited the body as much as the soul; furthermore, that it was necessary to mix salt and oil with the baptismal water; and that a minister could not marry a second time. This last he tried to justify by the words of Saint Paul to Timothy, "A bishop then must be blameless, the husband of one wife."[a] In short, he no longer wished to depend on any counsel other than his own; without basing what he was saying on the Word of God, he wanted to alter everything to suit his appetite.

But so that everyone may be warned just how invincible his arguments were: among several verses of the Scripture that he put forth, claiming them as proof of what he was saying, I will cite only one here. This is what I heard him say one day to one of his people: "Have you not read in the Gospel about the leper who said to Jesus Christ, 'Lord, if thou wilt, thou canst make me clean'? And immediately Jesus said to him, 'I will; be thou clean.' And immediately his leprosy was cleansed.[b] Thus," said this fine expositor, "when Jesus Christ said of the bread, 'This is my Body,' one must believe without any other interpretation, that his Body is contained in the bread; and let those Genevans prate as they will." Is that not a fine way to interpret one passage by another? It is certainly as much to the purpose as what was once claimed in a council, that since it is written "God created man in his own image," one must therefore have images.[10] Therefore you may judge by this swatch of the motley theology of Villegagnon, who has got himself so much talked about, whether (with his fine understanding of Scripture) he would be able—as he has boasted since his apostasy—equally to shut Calvin's own mouth, and to hold his own against anyone who would take his part.[11] I could add many other remarks as ridiculous as these, which I have heard him make concerning the Sacraments. But when he was back in France, Petrus Richelius portrayed him in all his colors, and others since then have dusted him off and curried him so well that it needs no redoing;[12] lest I weary my readers, I will say no more about it here.

At the same time Cointa, who also wanted to show off his learning,

[a]I Timothy 3. 2.

[b]Matthew 8.2–3.

began to give public lessons; but having begun the Gospel according to Saint John (the highest and most difficult matter known to theologians), he spoke about as much to the purpose as those who sing the Magnificat at matins;[a] and yet he was the only follower of Villegagnon to impugn the true doctrine of the Gospel. "How then of the Friar Cordelier André Thevet," someone will ask at this point, "who complains so in his *Cosmography* 'that the ministers that Calvin had sent to America, envious of his wealth, and encroaching on his charge, prevented him from winning the lost souls of the poor savage people?' (for these are his own words). Did he remain silent then? Did he bear more affection toward the barbarians than toward the defense of the Roman Church, of which he makes himself out to be such a pillar?" The answer to this falsehood of Thevet will be—just as I have said elsewhere—that he had already returned to France before we arrived in that country. So again I ask the readers to note here in passing, that I have not made, and will not make, any mention of him in connection with the disputes that Villegagnon and Cointa had with us at Fort Coligny in the land of Brazil; likewise, he never saw the ministers whom he speaks of, nor they him. Therefore, as I have proved in the Preface of this book, since this good Catholic Thevet was not there in our time, and had a gulf of two thousand leagues of sea between him and us to prevent the savages from rushing on him and putting him to death because of us (as he has falsely written that they were about to do)—rather than feed the world such nonsense, let him cite some other example of his zeal than this conversion of the savages that he would have accomplished if the ministers hadn't prevented him, for I say again that that is false.

Now to return to my account. Immediately after this Pentecostal Lord's Supper, Villegagnon declared openly that he had changed the opinion concerning Calvin that he had formerly claimed to have; and, without waiting for the answer that he had sent the minister Chartier to France to obtain, he said that Calvin was a wicked heretic who had strayed from the faith. From then on it was a hostile face that he turned to us; he said that he wanted the sermon to last no more than a half an hour, and from the end of May on, he attended it only rarely.

To conclude, the dissimulation of Villegagnon was so clearly revealed to us that, as the saying goes, we knew very well what stuff he was made of. If you ask what caused that revolt: some of our people main-

---

[a][An adage: The Magnificat is to be sung at vespers, not at matins.]

tained that the Cardinal de Lorraine[a] and others had written him from France through the master of a ship that came to Cape Frio (thirty leagues from our island), and in their letters had reproved him very harshly for leaving the Roman Catholic religion, so that Villegagnon suddenly changed his opinion out of fear. However, I have heard since my return that even before he left France, Villegagnon, the better to exploit the name and the authority of the late Admiral of Châtillon,[b] and also the more easily to take advantage of both the Church of Geneva in general and Calvin in particular (for, as we have seen in the beginning of this history, he had written to both parties, in order to have people go join him) had conspired with the Cardinal de Lorraine to feign the Religion. But whatever the case may be, I can assert that at the time of his revolt, he became so moody—as if his conscience had become a torturer—swearing every other minute by the body of Saint James (which was his habitual oath) that he would break the head, arms, and legs of the first one who irked him, that no one dared come into his presence.

While we are on the subject, I will recount the cruelty that I saw him exercise at the time on a Frenchman named La Roche, whom he held in chains. He made him lie flat on the ground, and he had him beaten on the belly by one of his sergeants with great blows of a cudgel, so hard that the breath was nearly gone from him. After the poor man was beaten black and blue on one side, this inhuman creature said, "By the body of Saint James, lecher, turn the other side." Although in his amazing pity he left this poor body stretched out, broken, and half dead, nonetheless the man could not leave off his regular work, which was that of carpenter. Likewise, some other Frenchmen whom he kept chained for the same offense as La Roche's—that is, they had conspired to throw him into the sea on account of his ill treatment of them before our arrival, for he had worked them harder than galley-slaves—some of them, carpenters by trade, abandoned him, preferring to go over to the mainland and join the savages (who treated them more humanely) than to stay any longer with him. Thirty or forty savage men and women of the Margaia, whom our allies the Tupinamba had taken in war and had sold to him as slaves, were treated still more cruelly. And in fact, I once saw him make one of them, named "Mingant," clasp his arms around a piece of artillery while hot

---

[a][A member of the powerful Guise family, Grand Inquisitor of France, and head of the most intransigently anti-Protestant Catholic faction.]

[b][Coligny.]

grease was poured onto his buttocks—and this for an offense that was hardly worth a reprimand; so these people often would say in their language: "If we had thought that Paycolas (for so they called Villegagnon) would treat us this way, we would have let ourselves be eaten by our enemies rather than come to him."

So there you have in passing some idea of his humanity, and I would be content to put an end to talking about him, if it were not for what I have mentioned above: that when we had first landed on his island, he said that he wanted the superfluity in dress to be reformed.

So I must tell of the good example and practice that he showed in that respect. He had a great quantity of silk and woolen cloth, which he preferred to let rot in his coffers than be used to clothe his people (some of whom nonetheless were almost naked). He also had camlet in all colors, and of this he had six garments made, so that he could have a different one for each day of the week: that is, the coat and the breeches always matched—red, yellow, tan, white, blue, and green. You may judge for yourselves just how fitting this was to his age and to his profession and rank. We could tell by the color of the outfit he had put on just what his mood would be that day; when we saw green and yellow, we would tell that there would be foul weather. And especially when he was splendidly decked out in one particular long robe of yellow camlet, banded with black velvet, the jokers among his people would say that he looked like a true buffoon. No doubt if those over here who portrayed him standing naked as a savage on the bottom of an overturned pot had known about the gorgeous robe, they would not have left him standing there adorned only with his cross and his flageolet around his neck.[13]

If someone now says that it is out of place for me to examine these things so closely (and, indeed, I confess that this last point especially was hardly worth putting down), I reply that, since Villegagnon has been such an Orlando Furioso[14] against those of the Reformed Religion, especially since his return to France: having, I say, turned his back on them in that fashion, it seems to me that he deserves to have everyone know how he has conducted himself in all of the religions he has followed. I will add that, for the reason I mentioned in the Preface, I am not saying nearly all that I know about it.

Finally, we had the Sieur du Pont inform him that since he had rejected the Gospel, we were in no way his subjects, and did not intend to be his servants any longer; even less were we willing to continue carrying earth and stones to his fort. Thereupon thinking to intimidate us, and even starve us if he could, he denied us the two cups of root flour that each of us was used to having every day. But far from being vexed by this, on the contrary, since in our trade with the savages (either they came to see us in the island in their little barks, or else we went to seek them out in their villages) we were getting more for a billhook or two or three knives than he would have given us in half a year, we were very pleased by such a refusal in that it released us entirely from subjection to him. If he had been the stronger, however, and if a number of his men and chief officers had not taken our part, then he would have made a very bad business for us—that is, he would have tried to subdue us by force.

In fact, he did test to see whether he could succeed in this. On one occasion Jean Gardien and I had gone over to the mainland, where we stayed that time about two weeks among the savages. He pretended to know nothing of our leave—which we had requested from M. Barré his lieutenant—and, claiming that we had violated his ordinance forbidding anyone to leave the island without permission, he had not only tried to have us arrested, but what was worse, he ordered that we both be chained by the foot, like his slaves. Our danger was all the greater in that the Sieur du Pont, our leader (who, as some said, was too submissive to him, considering his rank), instead of supporting us and opposing him, entreated us to endure this for a day or two, and assured us that when Villegagnon's anger subsided he would have us set free. But since we had not disobeyed the ordinance, and particularly since (as I have said) we had already announced to him that, because he had broken the promise he had made us to maintain the observance of the Evangelical Religion, we did not intend to take anything more from him—added to which, there was the example of so many others whom he kept chained, whom we saw so cruelly treated by him daily before our very eyes—we flatly declared that we would not endure it.

Hearing that response, and knowing that if he wanted to take this further, there were fifteen or sixteen of our company who were so well united and bound in friendship that to strike one was to strike us all, he realized that he could not take us by force, so he relented and conducted himself more civilly. Furthermore, as I mentioned just now, the leaders among his people were of our Religion, and consequently angry with him because of his revolt. If we had not feared the displeasure of the Admiral, who had sent him under the King's authority, and who did not yet know him as he had come to be (we had other hesitations as well), there were those who would have seized this occasion and gratified their desire to fall upon him and throw him into the sea, so that, as they said, his flesh and his big shoulders could go to feed the fish.[a] Most of them, however, found it more expedient that we behave courteously. Although we still held the sermon (which he dared not or could not prevent), nonetheless, to keep him from disturbing us and harassing us further when we celebrated the Lord's Supper, from then on we did it at night, when he was unaware of it.

After the last Lord's Supper that we had in that country, there remained only about a glassful of all the wine that we had brought from France, and since we had no way of replenishing our supply, the question arose among us whether, for lack of wine, we could celebrate Communion with other kinds of drink. Some, citing among other passages the one in which Christ at the Last Supper, after giving thanks, expressly said to his Apostles, "I shall drink no more of the fruit of the vine, etc.,"[b] were of the opinion that when wine was lacking, it would be better to abstain from the sign than to change it. Others said, on the contrary, that when Christ instituted the Lord's Supper, being in the land of Judaea, he had spoken of the ordinary drink of that region, and that if he had been in the land of the savages it is probable that he would have made mention not only of the drink that they use instead of wine, but also of the root flour that they eat instead of bread; they concluded that while they would not change the signs of the bread and the wine as long as they could be obtained, nonetheless if they were not to be had, there would be no obstacle to celebrating the Lord's Supper with the commonest things for human nourishment that took the place of bread and wine in the land where they were. But while the majority were of the latter opinion, since we had not yet come to that extremity, the matter remained undecided. The question, however, by no means engendered dissension among us; rather, by the grace of God, we remained always in such union and concord, that I could wish that all those who make profession of the Reformed Religion today were on such a friendly footing as we were then.

Now to finish what I had to say regarding Villegagnon. The proverb has it that he who would withdraw from someone seeks the occasion; thus, it happened at the end of October that he, detesting more and more both us and our doctrine, said that he was no longer willing to endure having us either in his fort or on his island, and commanded us to leave.

---

[a][Villegagnon was known for his physique, and especially his massive shoulders.]

[b]Matthew 26.28; Mark 14.25 ["until that day that I drink it new in the kingdom of God"].

The fact is that we had the means to drive him off ourselves if we had wanted to; but, beyond the reasons mentioned above, we were aware that it was widely known all over France and the other countries that we had gone over there to live according to the reformation of the Gospel; so, fearing to stain the latter, and wanting to leave him no occasion to complain of us, we preferred to obey Villegagnon. Therefore without contesting it further, we yielded the place to him.

Thus it is that after we had stayed about eight months on the Island and Fort of Coligny, which we had helped to build, we withdrew and went over to the mainland. There we remained two months, while we waited until a ship from Le Havre de Grâce, which had come there to be loaded with brazilwood (we had bargained with its master to take us back to France), was ready to leave. We set ourselves up on the seashore on the left side, at the entrance to the Bay of Guanabara, in the place that the French call "La Briqueterie," or the "Brickyard," which is only about half a league from the fort. From there we would come and go, visiting, eating, and drinking among the savages (who were, beyond comparison, more humane to us than he—I do him no injustice—who could not bear to have us with him); and they, for their part, often came to visit us, bringing us food and other things we needed.

Now having briefly summed up and described in this chapter the inconstancy and changeability that I have known in Villegagnon in the matter of religion, the treatment he offered us under that pretext, his disputes and the opportunity he seized to turn away from the Gospel, his habitual demeanor and discourse in that country, the inhumanity he showed his people, and the way he was splendidly arrayed, I shall reserve for my account of our return voyage both the leave he granted us and his treachery toward us upon our departure from the land of the savages. In order to treat other points, I will leave him for now, beating and tormenting his people in his fort, which, along with the estuary where it is situated, I shall describe next.

ぞ

# A DESCRIPTION OF
## THE BAY OF GUANABARA[1]
OTHERWISE CALLED *JANEIRO* IN
AMERICA; OF THE ISLAND AND FORT
OF COLIGNY, WHICH WAS BUILT ON
IT; TOGETHER WITH THE OTHER
ISLANDS IN THE REGION

This arm of the sea, or Bay of Guanabara, as it is called by the savages (the Portuguese call it *Janeiro*, because they discovered it the first of January), is situated at twenty-three degrees beyond the Equator, directly under the tropic of Capricorn. It has been one of the Brazilian seaports the most frequented by the French, and therefore it has seemed to me appropriate to describe it in some detail at this point. I will begin without lingering over what others have chosen to write about it, having myself lived in and sailed around this land for about a year. As you enter it and advance toward land, the bay is about twelve leagues long, and in some places seven or eight leagues wide; although the mountains that surround it on all sides are not as high as those that border that large and spacious body of fresh water, Lake Geneva, nevertheless with the mainland lying close by on all sides, Guanabara rather resembles it in its situation.

As you leave the open sea, you must sail alongside three small uninhabitable islands,[a] against which the ships, if they are not, indeed, well handled, will dash and be shattered; so the mouth is rather troublesome. After that, you must pass through a strait that is barely an eighth of a league wide, bounded on the left side as you enter by a mountain, or pyramidal rock; not only is this of an amazing and extraordinary height but also, seeing it from a distance, one would say that it is artificial. And

---

[a][Cotunduba, Pae, and Mae (Lussagnet 10, n. 2).]

indeed, because it is round, and like a big tower, we French hyperbolically named it "Butter Pot."[a] A little farther up into the bay there is a rather flat rock, perhaps one hundred or one hundred twenty paces around, which we called the "Ratcatcher",[b] on which Villegagnon thought to build a fortress, having off-loaded his equipment and artillery there upon his arrival; but the ebb and flow of the sea drove him away. A league beyond lies the island where we stayed, which, as I have already mentioned, was uninhabitable before Villegagnon arrived in that country. Moreover, since it is only about a half a league around, and six times as long as it is wide, surrounded by little rocks that just break the surface of the water and which keep the ships from coming closer than the reach of a cannon shot, it is a superb natural stronghold. And in fact, even with the little boats, we could only land there from the inland side, which is to say from the side opposite to an approach from the open sea; so that if it had been well guarded it would have been impossible to take it by force or in a surprise attack—as the Portuguese, by the fault of those whom we left there, have done since our return.[2]

There was a hill at each end of the island, and on each of them Villegagnon had built a little dwelling; on a rock fifty or sixty feet high, at the middle of the island, he had had his own house built. On either side of this rock, we had leveled some small areas on which to build the rooms where we assembled for the sermon and for dining, and some other buildings where all eighty of us, including Villegagnon's men, installed ourselves. But note that except for the house on the rock, where there is a little timbered structure, and for some bulwarks where the artillery was placed, and which are covered with some kind of masonry, all the other buildings are huts, which, since the savages were their architects, were built in the native style—that is, of wooden logs, and covered with grasses.

So there you have, in brief, the workmanship of the fort, which Villegagnon named "Coligny in Antarctic France," thinking he would please Messire Gaspard de Coligny, Admiral of France (without whose favor and assistance, as I said at the beginning, he would never have had the means to make the voyage, nor to build any fortress in the land of Brazil). But while he pretended to perpetuate the name of this excellent lord, whose memory will be forever honorable among all people of good

---

[a][Today, Sugar Loaf.]
[b][Today, Lage.]

will, I will let you judge how Villegagnon, besides rebelling against the Religion (contrary to his promise, which he had made before leaving France, to establish the pure service of God in that land) by abandoning the fortress to the Portuguese, gave them occasion to make trophies of the names both of Coligny and of Antarctic France, which had been placed there.

While I am on the subject, I will say that I never cease to be amazed that Thevet—similarly seeking to please Henry II, who was reigning then—in the year 1558, some two years after his return from America, had drawn on the left side of a map that he had made of the Bay of Guanabara and the Fort of Coligny, on the mainland, a city that he called "Ville-Henry." And what is more, even though he had had enough time since then to realize that it was pure nonsense, he nevertheless had it put yet again into his *Cosmography*.[3] For when we left this land of Brazil, which was more than eighteen months after Thevet, I maintain that there was no kind of building, much less a village or a city, in the place where he marked down this one, created out of his fantasy. And being uncertain himself as to what should come first in the name of this imaginary city, like those who argue over *bonnet rouge*, or *rouge bonnet*, he named it "Ville-Henry" on his first map, and "Henry-Ville" in the second, which makes one conjecture that all that he says about this is only his imaginings. So without fear of equivocation, the reader can choose as he pleases between these two names, and will find that it's all one thing—that is, nothing but counterfeit. I conclude, nonetheless, that Thevet not only made freer with the name of King Henry than Villegagnon did with that of Coligny, which he gave to his fort, but also, by repetition, profaned a second time the memory of his Prince.

So as to anticipate everything he might declare on the subject (and I flatly deny that the site he claims to be so is the one we call the Brickyard, where our workmen built several little houses), I admit that there is a mountain in that land, which the French, who settled there first, named "Mount Henry," in memory of their sovereign lord; just as also, in our time, we named another "Corguilleray," from the surname of Philippe de Corguilleray, Sieur du Pont, who had led us there. But if there is a difference between a mountain and a city, just as there is between a bell-tower and a cow, then it follows either that Thevet, marking this "Ville-Henry" or "Henry-Ville" on his maps, is seeing things, or else that he is deliberately trying to dupe us. So that nobody might think that I am speaking anything but the truth, I defer to those who have been on this voyage, and even to Villegagnon's own people—some of whom are still alive—as to whether there was a trace of a city where he has tried to situate this one, which I dismiss with the fictions of poets.[4]

Therefore, as I said in the Preface, since Thevet has, without any occasion, sought a scrimmage with me and my companions, if he finds this refutation of his works on America hard to stomach (seeing that, to defend myself against his calumnies, I have razed a city), let him be aware that these are not all the errors I have noticed: as I am witness, if he is not satisfied with the little that I touch upon in this history, I will show him them in detail. I am sorry nonetheless that I have again been compelled to digress in this way; but for the reasons I have mentioned—that is, to show the truth of what has happened—I will let the readers judge whether or not I am wrong.

So to pursue what remains to be described, both of our bay of Guanabara and of what is situated in it: four or five leagues farther into the bay from the fort, there is another island, beautiful and fertile, which is about six leagues around, and which we call the "Great Island."[a] And because there are several villages there inhabited by the savages called Tupinamba, who are allies of the French, we ordinarily went there in our boats to get flour and other necessities.

There are many other little uninhabited islets in this arm of the sea, where, among other things, good big oysters are to be found. The savages, diving off the seashore, bring back big stones, around which there are innumerable little oysters of another kind that they name leripés, which are so firmly attached—you would think they were glued—that they have to be torn off by main force. We often had big potfuls of these leripés boiled; in some of them, as we opened and ate them, we found little pearls.

Furthermore, the bay is filled with various kinds of fish: many good mullet, sharks, ray-fish, porpoises, and others, small or middling in size, some of which I will describe more fully in the chapter on fish.[b] But chiefly, I don't want to forget to mention here the horrible and frightful whales: when they displayed their great flippers out of the water while playing in that wide and deep bay, they often came so close to our island that we could shoot at them with our harquebuses and hit them. However, since their skin is so tough, and their fat so thick that I don't believe

---

[a][Today, Ilha do Governador.]
[b][Chapter XII.]

54

the ball could penetrate deep enough to injure them, they survived our attacks, and continued on their way.

While we were over there, ten or twelve leagues from our fort, in the direction of Cape Frio, there was a whale that drew too near the shore. Since the water wasn't deep enough for it to return to the open sea, it was washed up on the shore and there remained beached. However, no one dared approach it before it had died by itself. While it was struggling, it made the earth tremble all around; the noise and tumult could be heard more than two leagues along the shore. Although several of the savages, and some also of our men who dared approach it, carried away as much as they wanted of it, still there remained more than two-thirds of it, which was wasted and left sinking at the site. Even the fresh meat was not very good, and we used very little of what was brought to our island aside from some pieces of fat that we melted, to illuminate the night by the oil that came out of it; so we left it out in heaps exposed to the rain and the sun, and took no more account of it than if it were dung. The tongue, however, which was the best, was salted in barrels and sent to France to my Lord Admiral.

To conclude: as I have already mentioned, the mainland surrounds this arm of the sea on all sides; at the far and closed end of it there are two other fine freshwater rivers that enter it; I have sailed on these in ships' boats nearly twenty leagues into these lands, and have been in many villages among the savages who live in various parts.

There in brief you have what I have observed in this Bay of Janeiro or Guanabara: the loss of which, and of the fort that we had built there, I regret all the more in that if the whole area had been well guarded, as was possible, it would have been not only a fine refuge but also a great convenience for sailing in that region for all those of our French nation. Twenty-eight or thirty leagues beyond, in the direction of the river La Plata and the Strait of Magellan, there is another great arm of the sea called by the French the "Vases Bay,"[5] and it appears that when they are voyaging in those parts they use it for a harbor; they also put in at Cape Frio, where, as I said earlier, we first went ashore in the land of Brazil.

### ঽ

# OF THE NATURAL
## QUALITIES, STRENGTH,
### STATURE, NUDITY, DISPOSITION AND
### ORNAMENTATION OF THE BODY OF
### THE BRAZILIAN SAVAGES, BOTH MEN
### AND WOMEN, WHO LIVE IN AMERICA,
### AND WHOM I FREQUENTED FOR
### ABOUT A YEAR

Thus far I have recounted both what we saw on the sea on our way to the land of Brazil, and what took place on the Island and Fort of Coligny, where Villegagnon was staying while we were there; I have also described the bay called *Guanabara*. Since I have gone so far into these matters, before reembarking for France I also want to discuss what I have observed concerning the savages' way of life, as well as other singular things, unknown over here, that I have seen in their country.

In the first place then (so that I begin with the chief subject, and take things in order), the savages of America who live in Brazil, called the *Tupinamba*, whom I lived among and came to know for about a year, are not taller, fatter, or smaller in stature than we Europeans are; their bodies are neither monstrous nor prodigious with respect to ours. In fact, they are stronger, more robust and well filled-out, more nimble, less subject to disease; there are almost none among them who are lame, one-eyed, deformed, or disfigured.[1]

Furthermore, although some of them reach the age of a hundred or a hundred twenty years (for they know how to keep track of their ages and count them by moons), few of the elderly among them have white or gray hair. Now this clearly shows not only the benign air and temperature of their country (in which, as I have said elsewhere, there are no frosts or great cold, and the woods, plants, and fields are always greening), but also—for they all truly drink at the Fountain of Youth—the little care or worry that they have for the things of this world. And indeed, as I will later show in more detail, since they do not in any way drink of those murky, pestilential springs, from which flow so many streams of mistrust, avarice, litigation, and squabbles, of envy and ambition, which eat away our bones, suck out our marrow, waste our bodies, and consume our spirits—in short, poison us and kill us off before our due time—nothing of all that torments them, much less dominates or obsesses them.[2]

As for their natural color, considering the hot region where they live, they are not particularly dark, but merely of a tawny shade, like the Spanish or Provençals.

Now this next thing is no less strange than difficult to believe for those who have not seen it: the men, women, and children do not hide any parts of their bodies; what is more, without any sign of bashfulness or shame, they habitually live and go about their affairs as naked as they come out of their mother's womb. And yet, contrary to what some people think, and what others would have one believe, they are by no means covered with hair;[3] in fact, they are not by nature any hairier than we are over here in this country. Furthermore, as soon as the hair begins to grow on any part of the body, even the beard and eyelashes and eyebrows, it is plucked out, either with their fingernails, or, since the arrival of the Christians, with tweezers that the latter have given them—which makes their gaze seem wall-eyed, wandering, and wild. It has been written that the inhabitants of the island of Cumana in Peru do the same.[a] As for our Tupinamba, they make an exception only of the hair on the head, which on all the males, from their youth onward, is shaved very close from the forehead to the crown, like the tonsure of a monk; behind, in the style of our forefathers or of those who let their hair grow, they have it trimmed on the neck.

To leave nothing out (if that is possible), I will also add this. There are certain grasses in that land with leaves about two fingers wide, which grow slightly curved both around and lengthwise, something like the sheath that covers the ear of the grain that we call "Saracen wheat." I have seen old men (but not all of them, and none of the young men or children) take two leaves of these grasses and arrange them together and bind them with cotton thread around their virile member; sometimes they wrapped it with handkerchiefs and other small pieces of cloth that we

---

[a][Gómara,] *Histoire*, Book 2, Chapter 79.

gave them. It would seem, on the face of it, that there remains in them some spark of natural shame, if indeed they did this on account of modesty, but, although I have not made closer inquiry, I am still of the opinion that it is rather to hide some infirmity that their old age may cause in that member.[4]

To go on, they have the custom, which begins in the childhood of all the boys, of piercing the lower lip just above the chin; each of them usually wears in the hole a certain well-polished bone, as white as ivory, shaped like one of those little pegs that we play with over here, that we use as tops to spin on a table. The pointed end sticks out about an inch, or two fingers' width, and is held in place by a stop between the gums and the lip; they can remove it and put it back whenever they please. But they only wear this bodkin of white bone during their adolescence; when they are grown, and are called *conomi-ouassou* (that is, big or tall boy), they replace it by mounting in the lip-hole a green stone (a kind of false emerald), also held in place inside by a stop, which appears on the outside to be of the roundness and width of a testoon, with twice its thickness.[a] There are some who wear a stone as long and round as a finger (I brought one such stone back to France). Sometimes when these stones are removed, our Tupinamba amuse themselves by sticking their tongues through that slit in the lip, giving the impression to the onlooker that they have two mouths; I leave you to judge whether it is pleasant to see them do that, and whether that deforms them or not. What is more, I have seen men who, not content with merely wearing these green stones in their lips, also wore them in both cheeks, which they had likewise had pierced for the purpose.[5]

As for the nose: our midwives over here pull on the noses of newborn babies to make them longer and more handsome; however, our Americans, for whom the beauty of their children lies in their being pugnosed, have the noses of their children pushed in and crushed with the thumb as soon as they come out of their mothers' wombs (just as they do in France with spaniels and other puppies). Someone else has said that there is a certain part of Peru where the Indians have such outlandishly long noses that they set in them emeralds, turquoises, and other white and red stones with gold thread.[b]

Our Brazilians often paint their bodies in motley hues; but it is

---

[a] [In French, *teston;* in English, "testoon," a silver coin.]

[b] [Gómara,] *Histoire*, Book 4, Chapter 108.

especially their custom to blacken their thighs and legs so thoroughly with the juice of a certain fruit, which they call *genipap*,[a] that seeing them from a little distance, you would think they had donned the hose of a priest; and this black dye is so indelibly fixed on their skin that even if they go into the water, or wash as much as they please, they cannot remove it for ten or twelve days.

They also have crescent shaped pendants, more than half a foot long, made of very even-textured bone, white as alabaster, which they name *y-aci*, from their name for the moon; they wear them hung from the neck by a little cord made of cotton thread, swinging flat against the chest.

Similarly, they take innumerable little pieces of a seashell called *vignol*, and polish them for a long time on a piece of sandstone, until they are as thin, round, and smooth as a penny; these they pierce through the center and string onto cotton threads to make necklaces that they call *boüre*, which they like to wear twisted around their necks, as we do over here with gold chains. I think this is what some people call "porcelain shell";[b] we see many women over here wearing belts of it. When I arrived back in France, I had more than fifteen feet of it, as fine as you might ever see. The savages also make these *boüre* of a certain kind of black wood, which is very well suited to this since it is almost as heavy and shiny as jet.

Our Americans have a great many ordinary hens, which the Portuguese introduced among them and for which they have a use that I will now describe. They pluck the white ones, and after they have boiled the feathers and the down and dyed them red with brazilwood, they cut them up finer than mincemeat (with iron tools since they have acquired them—before that with sharpened stones). Having first rubbed themselves with a certain gum that they keep for this purpose, they cover themselves with these, so that they are feathered all over: their bodies, arms, and legs all bedecked; in this condition they seem to be all downy, like pigeons or other birds newly hatched. It is likely that some observers, who upon their arrival saw these people thus adorned, went back home without any further acquaintance with them, and proceeded to spread the rumor that the savages were covered with hair. But, as I have said above, they are not so in their natural state; that rumor has been based on ignorance and too easily accepted.

---

[a] *Genipa americana* L.

[b] [In modern usage, the cowrie.]

In the same vein, someone has written that the people of Cumana anoint themselves with a certain gum or sticky unguent, and then cover themselves with feathers of various colors; they are not unhandsome in such a costume.[a]

As for the head ornaments of our Tupinikin,[b,6] aside from the tonsure in the front and the hair hanging down in back, which I have mentioned, they bind and arrange wing feathers of rosy or red hues, or other colors, to make adornments for their foreheads somewhat resembling the real or false hair, called "rackets" or "batwings," with which the ladies and young girls of France and of other countries over here have been decorating their heads; you would say that they have acquired this invention from our savages, who call this device *yempenambi*.

They also have pendants in their ears, made from white bone, of almost the same kind as the bodkin that the young boys wear in their pierced lips. Furthermore, they have in their country a bird that they call *toucan,* which (as I will later describe more fully) has a plumage as black as a crow's, except for a patch under the neck, which is about four fingers' width long and three wide, all covered with fine little yellow feathers, edged with red on the bottom. They skin off these patches (which they also call *toucan,* from the name of the bird that bears them), of which they have a large supply; after these are dry, they attach them with a wax that they call *yra-yetic,* one on each side of the face in front of the ears. These yellow plaques, worn on their cheeks, seem like two ornaments of gilded copper on the ends of the bit of a horse's bridle.

If our Brazilians go off to war, or if—as I will recount elsewhere— they ceremonially kill a prisoner in order to eat him, they want to be more gallantly adorned and to look more bold and valiant, and so they put on robes, headdresses, bracelets, and other ornaments of green, red and blue feathers, and of other various true and natural colors of extreme beauty. When these feathers have been mixed and combined, and neatly bound to each other with very small pieces of cane and cotton thread (there is no featherworker in France who could handle them better, nor arrange them more skillfully), you would judge that the clothes made of them were of a deep-napped velvet. With the same workmanship they make the ornaments for their wooden swords and clubs, which, decorated and adorned

---

[a][Gómara,] *Histoire,* Book 2, Chapter 79.

[b][Léry means Tupinamba. See note 6.]

with these feathers so well suited and fashioned to this use, are a marvelous sight.

To finish off their outfitting: they procure from their neighbors great gray-hued ostrich feathers (which shows that there are some of these huge, heavy birds in certain parts of those lands, where, however, not to misrepresent anything, I myself have not seen any).[7] Binding all the quill ends together, with the other ends of the feathers spread out like a little tent, or like a rose, they make a great cluster of plumes that they call *araroye*. They tie this around their hips with a cotton string, the narrow part next to the flesh, and the spread-out feathers facing outward. When they are rigged out in this you would say (as it has no other purpose) that they were carrying a chicken-coop attached to their buttocks.

I will explain more fully in another place how the greatest warriors among them, in order to show their valor—especially to show how many enemies they have killed, and how many prisoners they have massacred to eat—make incisions in their breast, arms, and thighs; they then rub these slashes with a certain black powder, which makes the scars visible for life, as if they were wearing hose and doublets slit with great gashes in the Swiss fashion.

If it is a question of leaping, drinking and *caouinage*[8] (which is just about their daily occupation), to have—besides their voices and the chants that they customarily use in their dances—something more to arouse their spirits, they gather a certain rather firm-skinned fruit of the size and approximately the shape of a water-chestnut. When these are dried and the pits removed, they put little stones inside them and string several of them together, making leggings that, when tied on, make as much noise as snail shells—indeed, almost as much as the bells we have over here (which they greatly covet).

They have a kind of tree in that region, which bears a fruit as big as an ostrich-egg, and of the same shape.[a] The savages pierce it through the middle (as you see children in France pierce big walnuts to make rattles), then hollow it out and put little round stones into it, or else kernels of their coarse grain (of which I will speak later); they then pass a stick about a foot and a half long through it. In this way they make an instrument that they call a *maraca,* which rattles louder than a pig bladder full of peas, and which our Brazilians usually have in hand. When I discuss their religion, I will tell you the idea they have about this *maraca* and its

---

[a]The calabash tree, *Crescentia cuhete* L.

sound once they have adorned it with beautiful feathers and consecrated it to the use that we will see.

There you have their natural condition, and the accoutrements and ornaments with which our Tupinamba customarily outfit themselves in their country. Besides all that, since we had carried in our ships a great quantity of cloth in red, green, yellow, and other colors, we had coats and multicolored breeches made for them, which we exchanged for food supplies, monkeys, parrots, cotton, long peppers, and other things of their region with which our seamen usually load their ships. Now some, with nothing else on their bodies, would sometimes put on these wide, sailor-style trousers, while others, on the contrary, would leave aside the trousers and put on only the jackets, which came down just to their buttocks. After they had gawked at each other a while and paraded around in these outfits (which gave us our fill of laughing), they would take them off and leave them in their houses until the desire came to don them again; they also did this with the hats and shirts we gave them.

Now that I have fully treated what can be said concerning the exterior of the bodies of the American men and of the male children, if you would picture to yourself a savage according to this description, you may imagine in the first place a naked man, well formed and proportioned in his limbs, with all the hair on his body plucked out; his hair shaved in the fashion I have described; the lips and cheeks slit, with pointed bones or green stones set in them; his ears pierced, with pendants in the holes; his body painted; his thighs and legs blackened with the dye that they make from the *genipap* fruit that I mentioned; and with necklaces made up of innumerable little pieces of the big seashell that they call *vignol*. Thus you will see him as he usually is in his country, and, as far as his natural condition is concerned, such as you will see him portrayed in the following illustration, wearing only his crescent of polished bone on his breast, his stone in the hole in his lip, and, to show his general bearing, his unbent bow and his arrows in his hands. To fill out this plate, we have put near this Tupinamba one of his women, who, in their customary way, is holding her child in a cotton scarf, with the child holding on to her side with both legs. Next to the three is a cotton bed, made like a fishing net, hung in the air, which is how they sleep in their country. There is also the figure of the fruit that they call *ananas,*[a] which, as I shall describe hereafter, is one of the best produced in this land of Brazil.

---

[a][Pineapple.]

For the second contemplation of a savage, remove all the flourishes described above, and after rubbing him with a glutinous gum, cover his whole torso, arms, and legs with little feathers minced fine, like red-dyed down; when you have made him artificially hairy with this fuzzy down, you can imagine what a fine fellow he is.

In the third place, whether he remains in his natural color, or whether he is painted or covered with feathers, attire him again in his garments, headdresses and bracelets so laboriously wrought of these beautiful natural feathers of various colors that I have described to you; when he is thus outfitted, you might say that he is in his full Papal splendor.[9]

For the fourth description, leave him half-naked and half-dressed, in the way I have described him; give him the breeches and jackets of our colored cloth, with one of the sleeves green and the other yellow; you will judge that he no longer needs anything but a fool's bauble.

Finally, if you add to these the instrument called the *maraca* in his hand, the plumed harness that they call *araroye* on his hips, and his rattles made of fruits around his legs, you will then see him (as I will show him again later) equipped as he is when he dances, leaps, drinks, and capers about.

As for the rest of the devices that the savages use to bedeck and adorn their bodies, according to the description that I have just given: you would need several illustrations to represent them well, and even then you could not convey their appearance without adding painting, which would require a separate book. However, beyond what I have already said about them, when I come to speak of their wars and their arms, lacerating their bodies, and putting in their hands their wooden swords (or clubs), and their bows and arrows, I will portray them as more furious.

But for now let us leave a little to one side our Tupinamba in all their magnificence, frolicking and enjoying the good times that they know so well how to have, and see whether their wives and daughters, whom they call *quoniam* (and in some parts, since the arrival of the Portuguese, *Maria*) are better adorned and decked out.

First, besides what I said at the beginning of this chapter—that they ordinarily go naked as well as the men—they also share with them the practice of pulling out all body hair, as well as the eyelashes and eyebrows. They do not follow the men's custom regarding the hair of the head: for while the latter, as I have said above, shave their hair in front and clip it in the back, the women not only let it grow long, but also (like the women over here), comb and wash it very carefully; in fact, they tie it up sometimes with a red-dyed cotton string. However, they more often let it hang on their shoulders, and go about wearing it loose.

They differ also from the men in that they do not slit their lips or cheeks, and so they wear no stones in their faces. But as for their ears, they have them pierced in so extreme a fashion for wearing pendants that when they are removed, you could easily pass a finger through the holes; what is more, when they wear pendants made of that big scallop shell called *vignol,* which are white, round, and as long as a medium-sized tallow candle, their ears swing on their shoulders, even over their breasts; if you see them from a little distance, it looks like the ears of a bloodhound hanging down on each side.

As for their faces, this is how they paint them. A neighbor woman or companion, with a little brush in hand, begins a small circle right in the middle of the cheek of the one who is having her face painted; turning the brush all around to trace a scroll or the shape of a snail-shell, she will continue until she has adorned and bedizened the face with various hues of blue, yellow, and red; also (as some shameless women in France likewise do), where the eyelashes and eyebrows have been plucked, she will not neglect to apply a stroke of the brush.

Moreover, they make big bracelets, composed of several pieces of white bone, cut and notched like big fish-scales, which they know how so closely to match and so nicely to join—with wax and a kind of gum mixed together into a glue—that it could not be better done. When the work is finished, it is about a foot and a half long; it could be best compared to the cuff used in playing ball over here. Likewise, they wear the white necklaces (called *boüre* in their language) that I have described above, but they do not wear them hung around the neck, as you have heard that the men do; they simply twist them around their arms. That is why, for the same use, they find so pretty the little beads of glass that they call *mauroubi,* in yellow, blue, green, and other colors, strung like a rosary, which we brought over there in great number for barter. Indeed, whether we went into their villages or they came into our fort, they would offer us fruits or some other commodity from their country in exchange for them, and with their customary flattering speech, they would be after us incessantly, pestering us and saying "*Mair, deagatorem, amabé mauroubi*":[10] that is, "Frenchman, you are good; give me some of your bracelets of glass beads." They would do the same thing to get combs from us, which they call *guap* or *kuap,* mirrors, which they call *aroua,* and all the other goods and merchandise we had that they desired.

But among the things doubly strange and truly marvelous that I observed in these Brazilian women, there is this: although they do not paint their bodies, arms, thighs, and legs as often as the men do, and do not cover themselves with feathers or with anything else that grows in their land, still, although we tried several times to give them dresses and shifts (as I have said we did for the men, who sometimes put them on), it has never been in our power to make them wear clothes: to such a point were they resolved (and I think they have not changed their minds) not to allow anything at all on their bodies. As a pretext to exempt themselves from wearing clothes and to remain always naked, they would cite their custom, which is this: whenever they come upon springs and clear rivers, crouching on the edge or else getting in, they throw water on their heads with both hands, and wash themselves and plunge in with their whole bodies like ducks—on some days more than a dozen times; and they said that it was too much trouble to get undressed so often. Is that not a fine and pertinent excuse? But whatever it may be, you have to accept it, for to contest it further with them would be in vain, and you would gain nothing by it.

This creature delights so much in her nakedness that it was not only the Tupinamba women of the mainland, living in full liberty with their husbands, fathers, and kinsmen, who were so obstinate in refusing to dress themselves in any way at all; even our women prisoners of war, whom we had bought and whom we held as slaves to work in our fort— even they, although we forced clothing on them, would secretly strip off the shifts and other rags, as soon as night had fallen, and would not be content unless, before going to bed, they could promenade naked all around our island. In short, if it had been up to these poor wretches, and if they had not been compelled by great strokes of the whip to dress themselves, they would choose to bear the heat and burning of the sun, even the continual skinning of their arms and shoulders carrying earth and stones, rather than to endure having any clothes on.

And there you have a summary of the customary ornaments, rings, and jewelry of the American women and girls. So, without any other epilogue here, let the reader, by this narration, contemplate them as he will.

When I treat the marriage of the savages, I will recount how their children are equipped from birth. As for the children above the age of three or four years, I especially took great pleasure in watching the little boys, whom they call *conomi-miri;* plump and chubby (much more so than those over here), with their bodkins of white bone in their split lips, the hair shaved in their style, and sometimes with their bodies painted, they never failed to come dancing out in a troop to meet us when they saw us arrive in their villages. They would tag behind us and play up to us, repeating continually in their babble, "*Contoüassat, amabé pinda*": that is, "My friend and my ally, give me some fishhooks." If thereupon we yielded (which I have often done), and tossed ten or twelve of the smallest hooks into the sand and dust, they would rush to pick them up; it was great sport to see this swarm of naked little rascals stamping on the earth and scratching it like rabbits.

During that year or so when I lived in that country, I took such care in observing all of them, great and small, that even now it seems to me that I have them before my eyes, and I will forever have the idea and image of them in my mind. But their gestures and expressions are so completely different from ours, that it is difficult, I confess, to represent them well by writing or by pictures. To have the pleasure of it, then, you will have to go see and visit them in their own country. "Yes," you will say, "but the plank is very long." That is true, and so if you do not have a sure foot and a steady eye, and are afraid of stumbling, do not venture down that path.

We have yet to see more fully, as the matters that I treat present themselves, what their houses are like, and to see their household utensils, their ways of sleeping, and other ways of doing things.

Before closing this chapter, however, I must respond both to those who have written and to those who think that the frequenting of these naked savages, and especially of the women, arouses wanton desire and lust. Here, briefly, is what I have to say on this point. While there is ample cause to judge that, beyond the immodesty of it, seeing these women naked would serve as a predictable enticement to concupiscence; yet, to report what was commonly perceived at the time, this crude nakedness in such a woman is much less alluring than one might expect. And I maintain that the elaborate attire, paint, wigs, curled hair, great ruffs, farthingales, robes upon robes, and all the infinity of trifles with which the women and girls over here disguise themselves and of which they never have enough, are beyond comparison the cause of more ills than the ordinary nakedness of the savage women—whose natural beauty is by no means inferior to that of the others. If decorum allowed me to say more, I make bold to say that I could resolve all the objections to the contrary, and I would give reasons so evident that no one could deny them. Without going into it further, I defer concerning the little that I have said about this to those who have made the voyage to the land of Brazil, and who, like me, have seen both their women and ours.[11]

I do not mean, however, to contradict what the Holy Scripture says about Adam and Eve, who, after their sin, were ashamed when they recognized that they were naked, nor do I wish in any way that this nakedness be approved; indeed, I detest the heretics who have tried in the past to introduce it over here, against the law of nature (which on this particular point is by no means observed among our poor Americans).[12]

But what I have said about these savages is to show that, while we condemn them so austerely for going about shamelessly with their bodies entirely uncovered, we ourselves, in the sumptuous display, superfluity, and excess of our own costume, are hardly more laudable. And, to conclude this point, I would to God that each of us dressed modestly, and more for decency and necessity than for glory and worldliness.

# CHAPTER IX

🌿

# OF THE BIG ROOTS
## AND THE MILLET OF
## WHICH THE SAVAGES MAKE FLOUR
## THAT THEY EAT INSTEAD OF BREAD;
## AND OF THEIR DRINK, WHICH THEY
## CALL *CAOUIN*[1]

Since we have heard in the preceding chapter how our savages are out-
wardly adorned and equipped, to relate things in order it seems to me
appropriate to treat next their common and ordinary sources of food. In
the first place, one must note that although they do not have, and therefore do not sow or plant, wheat or vines in their country, nevertheless, as I
have seen and experienced, they dine and feast well without bread or
wine.

In their country our Americans have two kinds of root, which they
call *aypi* and *maniot*,[2] which in three or four months grow as big around
as a man's thigh, and about a foot and a half long. Once they have pulled
them up, the women—for the men don't concern themselves with this—
dry these roots over a fire on the *boucan* (which I shall describe later), or
else sometimes take them green, and grate them on a flat piece of wood in
which certain little pointed stones have been set, just as we grate cheese
and nutmeg; thus they reduce them to a flour as white as snow. This raw
flour, like the white juice that comes out of it (of which I shall speak in a
moment) has the fragrance of starch made of pure wheat soaked a long
time in water, when it is still fresh and liquid. After I came back over here,
whenever I happened to be in a place where starch was being made, the
scent of it made me remember the odor one usually picks up in the
savages' houses when they are making root flour.

To prepare it, the Brazilian women then take big earthen pots that
hold more than a bushel each, which they themselves make very skillfully
for this use, and put them on the fire, with a quantity of flour in them;

69

while it cooks, they stir it continually with split gourds, which they use as we use dishes. As it cooks this way the flour forms something like little hailstones, or apothecary's pills.[a]

Now they prepare this two different ways: some, which the savages call *ouy-entan,* is cooked hard, and this they take with them when they go to war, because it keeps better, and some, called *ouy-pou,* is less cooked and more tender, and it is so much better than the first that when you eat it fresh you would say that it is the center of a loaf of warm white bread.[3] For either method, as the flour is cooked, its taste changes and becomes more agreeable and delicate.

Although these flours taste good, and are nourishing and easy to digest, especially when they are fresh, nonetheless, as I discovered, they are by no means suitable for making bread. It is true that one can make with it a kind of dough, which, rising like that made of wheat flour with leavening, is as fine and white as if it were, indeed, wheat bread; but as it cooks, the crust and all the top dries out and burns, and when it comes to cutting or breaking the bread, you find that the inside is all dry and has turned back into flour. For that reason I think that he who first reported that the Indians who live at twenty-two or twenty-three degrees south of the Equator—who must be our Tupinamba—lived on bread made from wood shavings, had probably heard of the roots I am speaking of, but failing to observe what I have recounted, made a mistake.[b]

Both kinds of flour are good for making a porridge which the savages call *mingant.* This is especially good when they soak it in some fat broth, for then it becomes lumpy like rice, and has a very good flavor. But for all that, our Tupinamba—men, women, and children— are accustomed from their youth upward to eating it dry instead of bread, and are so adept in their style of eating it that when they take it with four fingers from their earthen pot or some other vessel, they can toss it from a considerable distance, and it lands so neatly in their mouths that they don't spill a bit of it. We Frenchmen, wanting to imitate them, tried to eat it that way; but not being adept at the method, instead of throwing it into our mouths, we spread it all over our cheeks and covered our entire faces with flour. So unless we wanted to be got up like clowns—especially those of us who wore beards—we were compelled to eat it with spoons.

---

[a]Léry is describing the process whereby tapioca is made.

[b][Gómara,] *Histoire,* Book 2, Chapter 92.

After these *aypi* and *maniot* roots are grated green, in the way I have described to you, the women will sometimes make big balls of the fresh, damp flour that comes from them; squeezing them and pressing them hard between their hands, they will extract from them a juice almost as white and clear as milk. This they catch in earthen plates and dishes and put it out to warm in the sun, which makes it clot and congeal like curds. When they want to eat it they pour it into other earthen pans, and in those they cook it over the fire as we do omelettes; it is very good prepared in that way.

The *aypi* root is good not only for its flour, but also when cooked whole on the ashes or in front of the fire; when it gets tender and splits and becomes floury, you can eat it like a chestnut roasted on hot coals, which is what it tastes like. However, it is not the same with the *maniot* root, for that is only good as a well-cooked flour, and it is poisonous if it is eaten any other way.

The plants or stems of both, which are only slightly different from each other in form, grow to the height of small juniper trees, and have leaves rather like the peony. But what is to be noticed and admired in these *aypi* and *maniot* roots of our land of Brazil is the way they multiply. The branches are almost as tender and easy to break as hemp; nevertheless, however many you can break and stick as deep as you can into the earth, then without any other cultivation, that many big roots you will have at the end of two or three months.

The women make holes in the earth with a pointed stick, and by this means also plant two kinds of coarse millet, red and black, which is popularly known in France as "Saracen wheat" (the savages call it *avati*). From this they also make a flour, which is cooked and eaten in the same way as that made from roots. And I think now (contrary to what I said in the first edition of this history, where I made a distinction between two things that, now that I have thought about it, I believe are the same) that this *avati* of our Americans is what the historian of the Indies calls *maize*, which he says also serves as wheat for the Indians of Peru. For here is the description he gives of it.

"The maize stalk," he says, "grows to the height of a man, and more; it is rather thick, and puts forth leaves like those of marsh reeds. The ear is like a wild pine cone; the grain is coarse, and is neither round nor square, nor as long as our grain. It ripens in three or four months, and in countries that are irrigated by streams, in a month and a half. For one seed it yields one, two, three, four, five hundred, and it has been found that some have multiplied to six hundred: which also shows the fertility of this land now owned by the Spaniards."ᵃ Another has written that in some places in East India the soil is so good that, by the report of those who have seen it, wheat, barley, and millet grow more then twenty feet high.ᵇ

And that is all I have seen of the customs concerning what is used for all kinds of breads in the country of the savages in the land of Brazil, called "America."

The Spanish and Portuguese, presently settled in several places of the West Indies, now have a great deal of wheat and wine that Brazil produces for them, so they have proved that it is not for lack of the right soil that the savages have none. We Frenchmen also brought wheat-seed and vine-stock on our voyage, and I have seen by experience that if the fields were ploughed and cultivated as they are over here, both would flourish. Indeed, the vine that we transplanted took very well, and put forth very fine stalk and leaves, clearly showing the bounty and fertility of the country. It is true that during the year that we were there the vine produced only small and sour grapes, which instead of ripening got hard and dry; but, as I have learned since from certain good wine growers, it is to be expected that new plants in their first and second years produce nothing but wild and sour grapes that are not of much use. I am of the opinion that if the Frenchmen and others who followed us and who are living now in that country continued to cultivate that vine, in the following years they must have had good, handsome grapes.

As for the wheat and rye that we sowed there, it was defective in this: although the plant came up well, and even came forth with the ear, nevertheless the seed did not form at all. But since the barley did form its seed and came to proper maturity, and even greatly multiplied, it is likely that this soil was too rich, and hastened so much the growth of the wheat and rye (which, as we see over here, want to remain longer in the earth than barley does before producing their fruits) that they grew high too soon and didn't have the time to flower and form their seeds. So whereas in our France to improve our fields and make them more fertile we fatten them with dung, I think that to make this new land yield more wheat and other such seed, when it is ploughed one should fatigue it and make it more lean for several years.

And certainly, since the country of our Tupinamba is capable of nourishing ten times more people than it has—I myself when I was there

---

ᵃ[Gómara,] *Histoire,* Book 5, Chapter 215.
ᵇChalcondyle, *De la guerre des Turcs,* Book 3, Chapter 14.

could boast of having at my disposal more than a thousand acres of land, better than any in all of Beauce—who can doubt that if the French had remained there (which they would have done, and there would now be more than ten thousand of them, if Villegagnon had not rebelled against the Reformed Religion) they would have drawn the same profit from it as the Portuguese, who have adapted themselves so well to that land? Let that be said in passing, to satisfy those who wonder whether wheat and vines, if sown, planted, and cultivated in the land of Brazil, could not come to fruition.

Now to resume my discussion. So as better to distinguish the matters that I have undertaken to treat, before I speak of the flesh, fish, fruits, and other foodstuffs utterly unlike those of our Europe with which our savages nourish themselves, I must speak of their drink, and the way it is made.

In the first place, it must be noted that just as their men have no hand in the making of the flour, but rather leave that whole task to their women (as you have already heard), they do likewise concerning their drink, and are even more scrupulous in their refusal to meddle in the making of it. These roots, *aypi* and *maniot,* serve as their chief nourishment, prepared in the way that I have just described; now here is how they handle them to make their customary drink.

After the women have cut up the roots as fine as we cut turnips for stewing, they let the pieces boil in water in great earthen vessels; when they see them getting tender and soft, they remove the pots from the fire and let them cool a little. When that is done, several of the women, crouched around these great vessels, take from them these little round pieces of softened root. First they chew them and twist them around in their mouths, without swallowing them; then they take the pieces in their hands, one after the other, and put them into other earthen vessels which are already on the fire, and in which they boil the pieces again.[4] They constantly stir this concoction with a stick until they see that it is done, and then, removing it from the fire a second time, without straining it, they pour it all into other bigger earthen jars, each having the capacity of about an eleven-gallon Burgundy wine-measure. After it has clarified and fermented, they cover the vessels and leave the beverage until people want to drink it, in the manner that I will shortly describe. To give you a better picture of all this, these last big vessels that I have just mentioned are made almost like the big earthen vats that I have seen used for laundry in some parts of the Bourbonnais and the Auvergne, except that they are narrower at the mouth and in the upper part.

Our American women likewise boil and then chew the coarse millet they call *avati,* and make a brew like that made from the roots I have mentioned. I repeat expressly that it is the women who perform this task: for although I have seen no distinction made between the young girls and the married women in this respect,[5] the men nevertheless hold the firm opinion that if they were to chew the roots or the millet to make this beverage, it would be no good. They even consider it as unseemly for their sex to deal with it as people over here find it strange (rightly, I think) to see those great clumsy peasant men of Bresse take the distaff to spin. The savages call this beverage *caouin.* It is cloudy and thick like wine lees, and has almost the taste of sour milk; they have it both red and white, just as we do our wine.

Since these roots and the coarse millet that I have spoken of grow in their country the year round, they make this beverage in all seasons, and sometimes in such quantity that I have seen more than thirty of these big vessels (which, as I have told you, hold more than fifty quarts each) set out in a row in the middle of their houses, where they remain covered until it is time to have a *caouin* celebration.

But before we get to that point, I beg permission to offer (without any implied approval of this vice) a prologue: Yield, you Germans, Flemings, Lansquenets, Swiss, and all you over here who profess to drink and carouse, for after you have heard how our Americans acquit themselves in this domain, you will confess that compared to them you know nothing about it, and you will have to abandon the field to them.[6]

When they set to it, and especially when they formally execute a prisoner of war to eat him in the ceremonies that we will see later, their custom (quite the contrary of ours concerning wine, which we like cool and clear) being to drink this *caouin* warm, the first thing that the women do is to make a little fire around the earthen vessels, where it will be heated lukewarm. That done, they begin by uncovering the first vessel at one end, and stir up the beverage; they dip it out with big gourd-halves, each holding about three pints. The men dance past the women, one after the other, and the women, serving as cupbearers, present to each man one of these big cupfuls—not forgetting to quaff it themselves; and neither one nor the other ever fails to toss it off in one gulp. But do you know how many times? Until the vessels—even if there were a hundred—are all empty, and there is not a single drop of *caouin* remaining. And in fact I have seen them go three days and three nights without ceasing to drink, and even after they were so sated and drunk that they could take no more—since to abandon the game would have been to be reputed womanish, and more than *schelm*ª among the Germans—, when they had vomited they went at it again, more valiantly than before.

Now what is still stranger and more remarkable among our Tupinamba is that, just as they eat nothing during their drinking bouts, so, too, when they eat they drink nothing during their meal; therefore when they saw us mingle the two, they found our custom very strange. If someone says at this point, "So they do as horses do?" the answer given by a joker in our company was that at least you don't have to bridle them or bring them to the river to drink, and there is no danger of their breaking their cruppers.

One must note, however, that while on the one hand they do not observe particular hours for dinner, supper, or light repasts, as we do over here, and do not hesitate if they are hungry to eat as readily at midnight as at noon, on the other hand, since they never eat when they are not hungry, you could say that they are as sober in their eating as they are excessive in their drinking. Some of them have the cleanly habit of washing their hands and their mouths before and after meals; however, I think they do this because otherwise their mouths would always be pasty from those root and millet flours, which, as I have said, they customarily use instead of bread. While they are eating they preserve a marvellous silence, so that if they have something to say, they save it until they have finished. When they heard us prating and chattering during our meals, as is the custom of Frenchmen, they made great fun of us.[7]

As long as this *caouinage* lasts, our American rakehells and carousers heat their brains hotter and hotter, singing, whistling, egging each other on, and exhorting each other to behave valiantly, and to take many prisoners when they go to war; lined up like cranes, they dance unceasingly, going back and forth through the house where they are assembled, until it is all over: that is, they never leave as long as they think there is anything left in the vessels. As proof of what I have said—that they are first and supreme in drunkenness—I believe there are some of them who on a single one of these occasions drink more than twenty pots each of *caouin*. Throughout all this they are covered with feathers, as I described them in the preceding chapter, and in this costume they kill and eat a prisoner of war; drunk as priests, they are enacting the Bacchanales of the ancient pagans, and it is a sight to see them roll their eyes. It does sometimes happen that neighbors with neighbors, seated in their cotton

---

ª[*Schelm* is German for "base."]

beds hung in the air, will drink in a more modest fashion; but their custom being such that all the men of a village, or several villages, usually assemble to drink (which they do not do for eating), these private drinking parties rarely take place.

Whether they drink a little or a lot, in addition to what I have said—that they never breed melancholy, but rather assemble every day to dance and make merry in their villages—the young marriageable men have this particular custom: each of them dons one of those feather clusters called *araroye* that are tied on the hips, sometimes with the *maraca* in hand, and those little dried fruits—the ones I mentioned, that rattle like snailshells—tied around their legs. They do almost nothing else every night but come and go in this get-up, leaping and dancing from house to house; seeing them and hearing them so often at this business, I was reminded of those over here whom we call "morris dancers," who, during the festivals of the patron saints of each parish, go about in fools' garb, scepter in hand and bells on their legs, dallying and dancing the morris in among the houses and town squares.

But it must be noted that in all savages' dances, whether they line up one after another, or (as I shall describe when I speak of their religion) arrange themselves in a circle, neither the women nor the girls ever join the men, and if they want to dance, they do it separately.

Before I finish this discussion of the drinking style of our Americans, and so that the readers may know that if the savages had as much wine as they please, they would gallantly continue to raise their cups, I will recount a tale both comic and tragic, told to me one day in his village by a *moussacat* (that is, a good father of a family who offers hospitality to people passing through the village).

"One day," he said, "we surprised a caravel of Peros" (that is, Portuguese, who, as I have mentioned elsewhere, are mortal and irreconcilable enemies of our Tupinamba). "After we had slain and eaten the men who were in it, as we were taking possession of their merchandise, we found some big wooden *caramemos* (that is what they call barrels and other vessels) full of drink. Setting them upright and staving in the tops, we tried tasting what was in them. However," said this savage elder, "I know not what kind of *caouin* they were filled with, and whether you have any such in your country; but I will tell you that after we had drunk our fill, we were so stunned and stupefied that for three days, it was not in our power to wake up." It seems likely that these were casks full of some good Spanish wines, of which the savages, without knowing it, had enjoyed a truly bacchanalian celebration; it is no wonder if, after such a blow on the head, they found themselves also, in their turn, suddenly helpless.

As for us, when we were first in that country, we thought that we could avoid the spitting that, as I have mentioned, the savage women use in the composition of their *caouin*. So we pounded *aypi* and *maniot* roots with millet, which we boiled together, thinking to prepare this beverage in a more seemly fashion. But to tell the truth, experience showed us that, made thus, it wasn't any good; so little by little, we accustomed ourselves to drinking the other as it was. We didn't usually resort to it, however, because we had all the sugarcane we could want. We would leave it to soak for several days in water that we had cooled a little, because of the warm climate; we drank the sugared water with great pleasure. Because of the temperature of that country, the beautiful, clear freshwater springs and rivers are so good (in fact, I will say, incomparably more healthful than those over here) that you can drink from them all you like, without suffering any ill effect; we usually drank the water pure, without adding anything to it. The savages call fresh water *uh-ete,* and salt water *uh-een.* They pronounce these words with the throat, as the Hebrews do with the letters that they call guttural (these were the most troublesome to pronounce of all the words in their language).

To conclude: I have no doubt that some of those who have heard what I have said concerning the chewing and twisting around of the roots and millet in the mouths of the savage women when they concoct their *caouin,* will have been nauseated, and will have spit. To allay this disgust, I entreat them to remember what we do when we make wine over here. Let them consider merely this: in the very places where the good wines grow, at the time of grape-harvest the wine-makers get into the tubs and vats, and with their bare feet and sometimes with their shoes, they tread the grapes; as I have seen, they crush them again the same way on the winepresses. Many things go on which are hardly more pleasing than this custom of chewing among the American women. If thereupon someone says, "Yes, but as it ferments in the vats the wine expells all that filth," I reply that our *caouin* is purged the same way, and that therefore on this point the one custom is as good as the other.

≈&

# OF THE ANIMALS,
## KINDS OF VENISON, BIG LIZ-
### ARDS, SNAKES, AND OTHER MON-
STROUS BEASTS OF AMERICA[1]

Concerning the four-footed animals, I will say first of all that in general and without exception there is not a single one in that land of Brazil in America that is in all respects exactly like any of ours; what is more, our Tupinamba rarely raise any domestic ones. So to describe the wild animals of their country—for which their generic name is *sóo*[2]—I will begin with those that are edible. The first and most common one, which has a reddish and rather long coat, they call *tapiroussou*.[a] It is of about the height, bulk, and shape of a cow; however, it has no horns, and has a shorter neck, longer and more pendant ears, thinner and more agile legs, and an unsplit hoof shaped like that of a donkey. In fact, you could say that it partakes of both, and is half cow and half donkey.[3] But it is entirely different from either, in its tail, which is very short (there are many animals in America that have almost none at all), and in its teeth, which are much more cutting and sharp; however, since it has no means of resistance other than flight, it is not at all dangerous. The savages kill it and various other animals with arrows, or else they catch it in traps and with other devices that they make quite skillfully.

This animal is immensely valued by them because of its skin; when they flay it, they cut all the hide off the back in a circle, and after it is dry they make disks from it as big as the bottom of a medium-sized barrel, which serve as shields against the arrows of their enemies when they go to war. Indeed this skin, dried and prepared, is so tough that there is, I think, no arrow, however forcefully shot, that could pierce it. I was bringing two of these shields back to France as curiosities; but during our return we were afflicted with famine on the sea, and after all our food supplies

---

[a][The tapir. The suffix *-oussou* or *-ouassou* means "big."]

had been used up, and the monkeys, parrots, and other animals that we were bringing back from that country had been used for nourishment, we finally had to eat our leather shields grilled over coals—in fact, as I shall recount at the right moment, we ate all the other leather and all the skins that we had in the ship.

The flesh of this *tapiroussou* has almost the same taste as beef; but as for the way of preparing and cooking it, our savages usually have it *boucané*. Now I have mentioned before and shall often need to repeat this term, *boucaner*, and since the occasion presents itself conveniently, to end the reader's suspense, let me explain this way of doing things.

Our Americans first stick four wooden forks deep into the earth, each fork as big as an arm, to form a square about three feet on a side, and about two and a half feet high; across these forks they place sticks at intervals of about an inch, or two fingers' width. In this manner they make a big wooden grill, which in their language they call *boucan*.[4] They have several of these planted in their houses. Those who have some meat put it on the grill in pieces, and with very dry wood, which doesn't give off much smoke, they make a slow little fire underneath; turning the meat over and over, twice every quarter-hour, they let it cook until it suits them. Since they don't salt their meat to make it keep, as we do over here, they have no other way of preserving it except to cook it; so if in one day they were to take thirty wild beasts, or other animals that we will describe in this chapter, to avoid having it stink they would immediately place the meat in pieces in the *boucan*. Turning it over and over again as I have described, they leave it there sometimes more than twenty-four hours, and until it is cooked all the way through to the bone, the middle as well as the outside. They do the same thing with fish; when they have a great quantity (especially of those that they call *piraparati,* which are a kind of mullet, of which I will speak again elsewhere), they thoroughly dry them and make flour of them. In short, these *boucans* serve them as salting tubs, drying-hooks, and cupboards. You could hardly enter their villages without seeing them not only furnished with venison or fish, but also most often (as we shall see later) you would find them covered with thighs, arms, legs, and other big pieces of human flesh from the prisoners of war whom they ordinarily kill and eat.

And there you have the *boucan* and *boucanerie,* that is, the rotisserie of our Americans. By the way (with all due respect to him who has written otherwise), they do not abstain from boiling their meat whenever that suits them.[5]

To pursue the description of their animals. The biggest that they have after the donkey-cow, of which I have just spoken, are certain kinds of deer that they call *seouassous*.[a] Besides being not nearly as big as ours, and having much smaller horns, they are also different in having a coat as long as that of the goats over here.

The boar of that country, which the savages call *taiassou*,[b] in its shape resembles those of our forests. Its body, head, ears, legs, and feet are also the same, as well as its teeth, which are long, hooked, pointed, and consequently very dangerous; however, it is much thinner and more scraggy, and has a horrible grunting cry. It also has another strange deformity: a natural opening on the back, like the one that the porpoise has on its head, through which it blows, breathes, and takes in air whenever it wants to. Lest you find that so strange, the author of the *General History of the Indies* says that there are also pigs in the country of Nicaragua, near the kingdom of New Spain, that have the navel on the backbone, which are surely of the same kind as those that I have just described.[c] The three animals just mentioned, the *tapiroussou,* the *seouassou,* and the *taiassou,* are the biggest in the land of Brazil.

Going on to other wild game of our Americans, there is a russet-colored beast that they call *agouti*,[d] about as big as a month-old pig, which has a cleft foot, a very short tail, and a muzzle and ears almost like those of a hare; it is very good to eat. There are others of two or three kinds, which they call *tapitis*,[e] all rather like our hares, and of about the same taste; but their coat is more reddish. In the woods they also catch certain rats, as big as squirrels, and with almost the same reddish coat, whose flesh is as delicate as that of rabbits.

*Pag,* or *pague*[f] (one can hardly distinguish which of the two they are uttering) is an animal about as big as a medium-sized pointer, with an irregular and badly shaped head. Its flesh tastes almost like veal; its skin is very beautiful, dappled with white, gray, and black, and if we had any like them over here, they would be highly valued as fur.

There is another in the form of a polecat, with a grayish coat, which

---

[a][The generic Tupi name for deer.]

[b][The peccary, of the genus *Tayassu*. The opening on the back is not an orifice for breathing, but a gland producing strong-smelling secretions.]

[c][Gómara, *Histoire*,] Book 5, Chapter 204.

[d][The modern English term is the same.]

[e][The tapiti (*Sylvilagus minensis*) is of the same genus as the cottontail rabbit.]

[f][The paca, or spotted cavy: a large rodent.]

the savages call *sarigoy*,[a] but it stinks so that they don't willingly eat of it. We skinned several of them, however, and when we realized that it is only the fat over the kidneys that gives off the foul odor, we removed it and went ahead and ate the meat, which in fact is tender and good.

As for the *tatou*[b] of the land of Brazil, this animal (like the hedgehogs over here) usually drags itself through the brush and cannot run as fast as some others; but to compensate, it is so well armed, and covered with scales so strong and hard that I think even a sword-blow would have no effect. When it is skinned, the scales move and can be handled with the skin, from which the savages make little containers that they call *caramemo;* you would say, seeing it folded, that it was an armored gauntlet. The flesh is white, and of rather good flavor. But as for its form, if the animal that Belon, in the third book of his *Observations*, calls the *tatou* of Brazil is indeed mounted as high on its four legs as he has shown it in a picture there, I have seen none of them in this country.[6]

Besides all these animals, which are the commonest ones for the sustenance of our Americans, they also eat crocodiles, which they call *jacaré*, and which are as thick as a man's thigh and correspondingly long. But they are so far from being dangerous that, on the contrary, I have seen the savages on several occasions carry them home alive, and their children would play around them without being hurt. I have heard the old men say, however, that as they travel through the country they are sometimes attacked, and have to defend themselves with their arrows against a kind of *jacaré*, huge and monstrous, which, when it has perceived them and picked up their scent from a distance, comes out from the reeds of the watery places where they have their dens.

While we are on the subject, aside from what Pliny and others tell of those of the Egyptian Nile,[7] the author of the *General History of the Indies* says that near the city of Panama, crocodiles have been killed that were more than one hundred feet long, which is almost incredible. I have noticed that the medium-sized ones that I have seen have a deep-cut mouth, long thighs, and a tail that is neither rounded nor pointed, but flat and thin at the end. I must confess that I have not carefully noted whether, as is commonly maintained, they can move their upper jaw.[c]

Our Americans also catch lizards, which they call *touous;* not green

---

[a][The opossum.]

[b][The armadillo.]

[c][The crocodile in fact cannot move its upper jaw.]

ones like ours, but gray and with a smooth skin, like our little lizards. They are four to five feet long, proportionately thick, and of a shape hideous to see; however, they ordinarily stay on the riverbanks and in marshy places, and are no more dangerous than the frogs that live there. I must add that when you have skinned, gutted, and cleaned them, and cooked them thoroughly (their flesh being as white, delicate, tender, and flavorful as the white meat of a capon), it is one of the best kinds of meat that I have eaten in America. It is true that at the beginning I was horrified at the notion, but after I had tasted it, as far as meat was concerned, I sang the praises of nothing but lizards.

Our Tupinamba also have certain big toads, which when they are *boucané* with the skin, tripe, and entrails, serve as food. Our physicians teach, and people back over here generally believe, that the flesh, blood, and whole body of the toad are deadly; however, from what I have said about those of Brazil, the reader can easily gather that either because of the temperature of the country, or perhaps for some other reason that I am unaware of, they are not vile, venomous or dangerous as ours are.[a]

They also eat snakes as big as your arm and about three feet long; and (as I said they do with crocodiles) I have seen the savages drag back some of them that are streaked with black and red, which they would throw alive in the middle of their houses among their wives and children, who instead of being afraid of them would grasp them with both hands. They prepare and cook these big terrestrial eels in sections; but from what I know of it, the meat has an insipid, sweetish taste.

It isn't that there are not other kinds of snakes: especially in the rivers one finds certain long, slender ones, as green as a beet, whose sting is extremely venomous; and in the story I am about to tell, you will hear that, besides these *touou* I just spoke of, there are other and larger lizards in the forest that are very dangerous.

One day two other Frenchmen and I were rash enough to set forth to visit the region without the savages whom we customarily had along as guides. Having lost our way in the woods, as we were going along a deep valley, we heard the sound of a beast making its way toward us. Thinking that it was some savage, we continued on our path without disquiet and thought no more about it. But suddenly on our right, and about thirty feet from us, we saw on a little rise a lizard much bigger

---

[a][Some toads of Brazil are poisonous and some are harmless; the same is true for various parts of their bodies.]

than a man's body, six or seven feet long, which seemed covered with whitish scales, as sharp and rough as oyster shells; with one of its front feet lifted, its head raised high and its eyes gleaming, it stopped short to look at us.[8] We had not a single harquebus or pistol among us, but only our swords, and, savage-fashion, each a bow and arrows in hand—weapons that could not serve us very well against such a furious and well-armed animal. Seeing him, and fearing that if we took flight he would outrun us and, having caught us, would swallow us up and devour us, we looked at each other stunned, and remained stock-still. This monstrous and terrible lizard opened its maw; because of the great heat (for the sun was shining and it was about noon), it was breathing so hard that we could easily hear it. After it had stared at us for about a quarter of an hour, it suddenly turned around; crashing through the leaves and branches where it passed—with a noise greater than that of a stag running through a forest—it fled back uphill. As for us, we had had such a scare that we had no desire to run after it; praising God for delivering us from this danger, we went on our way. It has occurred to me since, in accord with the opinion of those who say that the lizard takes delight in the human face, that this one had taken as much pleasure in looking at us as we had felt fear in gazing upon it.

There is also in that country a predatory beast that the savages call *jan-ou-are*,[a] which is almost as long-legged and light-footed as a greyhound. It has long hairs around the chin, and a beautiful spotted skin like that of a lynx, which in general it closely resembles. The savages have great fear of this beast, and not without cause; for since it lives off its prey, like the lion, if it catches them it does not fail to kill them and then to tear them to pieces and eat them. And for their part, too, being cruel and vindictive against anything that hurts them, when they can catch one in a trap (which they do often), they do their worst: they pierce and wound it with arrows, and make it linger in its misery for a long while in the pit where it has fallen, before they finish it off. So that you can better understand how this beast deals with them: one day when five or six other Frenchmen and I were passing by the big island, the savages warned us to look out for the *jan-ou-are*, which, that very week, had eaten three people in one of their villages.

To go on, there is a great abundance of those little black monkeys, which the savages call *cay*, in the land of Brazil; but since they are to be

---

[a][The jaguar. It holds an important place in Tupi myths and ceremonies.]

seen in fair numbers over here I won't give any further description of them. Nevertheless, I will mention this: being forest-dwellers, their natural inclination is to stay in the tops of certain trees which bear a fruit with pods almost like our big beans, from which they get nourishment. They often gather there in troops, especially in time of rain (as cats sometimes do on rooftops over here); it is quite a sport to hear them calling out and crashing around up in the trees.

This animal gives birth to only one infant at a time; the little one has the innate ability to embrace and cling to the neck of its mother or father as soon as it is out of the womb. If they are pursued by hunters, they can save it by leaping from branch to branch, carrying it. For that reason the savages cannot easily take either the young ones or the old ones: they have no other means of catching them but by knocking them out of the trees with arrows or other missiles. They fall to the ground stunned and sometimes wounded; after the savages have healed their wounds and tamed them a little in their houses, they barter them for various merchandise with the foreigners who are traveling over there. I say "tamed" advisedly: when these monkeys are first caught, they are so wild that they bite your fingers, even putting their teeth clear through the hands of those who are holding them; the pain is so great that one is compelled to stun them with blows to make them let go.

There is also in the land of Brazil a marmoset, which the savages call *sagouin,* no bigger than a squirrel and having the same kind of russet fur. It has the face, neck, front, and almost all the rest of the body like a lion, with the same proud bearing; he is the prettiest little animal that I have seen over there. And indeed, if he were as easy to take across the ocean as the monkey is, he would be much more valued.[a] But besides being so delicate that he cannot tolerate the tossing of the ship on the sea, he is so proud and touchy that for the slightest offense offered him, he lets himself die of chagrin. There are some to be seen over here, however, and I think that this is the animal Marot[9] is referring to when, writing of how his servant Fripelipes answered a certain Sagon who had accused him of something, he says:

> Combien que Sagon soit un mot
> Et le nom d'un petit marmot.
> [Although Sagon is a word
> And the name of a little marmoset.]

---

[a][The *sagouin,* or marmoset, is in fact a species of monkey.]

84

I must confess that, in spite of my curiosity, I have not observed all the animals of the land of America as well as I had wished. But to conclude, I want to describe two that are stranger and more curious in form than all the others.

The bigger of these, which the savages call *hay*,[a] is of the size of a big spaniel, with a face rather like a monkey's, approaching the human; it has a belly hanging down like that of a pregnant sow, a gray coat with a smoky-brown tinge like the wool of a black sheep, a very short tail, hairy legs like those of a bear, and very long claws. And although when he is in the woods he is very wild, once he is caught, he is not hard to tame. It is true, nevertheless, that his claws are so sharp that our Tupinamba, who are always naked, do not take much pleasure in playing with him. Now this may sound like a tall tale, but I have heard not only from the savages but also from the interpreters who had lived a long time in that country, that no man has ever seen this animal eat, either in the fields or in a house; so that some think that he lives on air.[10]

The other animal that I also want to speak about, called *coati*[b] by the savages, is of the height of a big hare, with a short coat, sleek and dappled, and small, erect, pointed ears. Its head is not very large; its muzzle from the eyes down is more than a foot long, round as a stick, and suddenly narrowing, being no bigger high up than it is at the mouth (which is so small that you could scarcely put the tip of your little finger in it). This muzzle resembles the drone or the pipe of the bagpipe, and could hardly be more curious or more monstrous in shape. When this beast is caught, it holds all four feet tight together, and thus is always leaning over to one side or the other, or else it lets itself fall flat; you can't make it stand up, and you can't make it eat anything except ants, which are what it ordinarily lives on in the woods. About a week after we had arrived in the island where Villegagnon was staying, the savages brought us one of these *coati*, which, as you can imagine, was greatly admired by all of us. Since all these animals are strangely defective with respect to those of our Europe, I would often ask a certain Jean Gardien, of our company, who was expert in the art of portraiture, to draw this one, as well as many others that are not only rare but even completely unknown over here; to my great regret, however, he was never willing to set himself to it.

---

[a][The sloth.]

[b][Léry has described the *tamandua*, or lesser anteater, not what is now called the *coati*, which is an animal closely related to the raccoon.]

ॐ

# OF THE VARIETY
## OF BIRDS OF AMERICA, ALL
### DIFFERENT FROM OURS; TOGETHER
### WITH THE BIG BATS, BEES, FLIES,
### GNATS, AND OTHER STRANGE VERMIN
### OF THAT LAND[1]

I will also begin this chapter on birds (which in general our Tupinamba call *oura*) with those that are good to eat. First, there are a great many of those big hens that we call "guinea hens," which they call *arignan-oussou*.[2] The Portuguese have introduced among them a breed of ordinary little hens that they did not have before, which they call *arignan-miri*. Although they set great store by the white ones for their feathers, which they dye red and use to adorn their bodies, they seldom eat any of either breed. They even believe that the eggs, which they call *arignan-ropia,* are poisonous. When they saw us eating them instead of having the patience to let them hatch, they were astonished, and would say, "You are too gluttonous; when you eat an egg, you are eating a hen." They keep no more reckoning of their hens than of wild birds, letting them lay wherever they please; the hens most often bring their chicks from the woods and thickets where they have brooded them, so the savage women do not take the trouble that we do over here, raising turkey chicks on egg-yolks. And indeed, the hens multiply at such a rate in that country that there are certain localities and some villages, rarely frequented by foreigners, where for a knife worth about a penny you can have a guinea hen, and for one worth a half-penny—or for five or six fishhooks—you can buy four or five of the small common hens.

Along with these two kinds of poultry our savages raise some domestic ducks, which they call *upec.* But our poor Tupinamba have this foolish idea planted in their brains that if they were to eat of an animal like this that walks so heavily, it would keep them from running when they are being pursued by their enemies; it would take a skilled arguer to make them taste of it. For the same reason, they abstain from all beasts that move slowly, and even from some fish, such as certain rayfish, which do not swim swiftly.

As for wild birds, some that are caught in the woods are as big as capons; they are of three sorts, called by the Brazilians *jacoutin, jacou-pen,* and *jacou-ouassou,*[3] all of which have black and gray plumage. From their taste, I think they are kinds of pheasants, and I can assure you that no better fare can be eaten than these *jacous.*

They have two more excellent kinds, which they call *mouton,*[a] which are as big as peacocks, but with the same plumage as the ones I have just described; however, those are rare, and you come across very few of them.

*Mocacoüa* and *ynambou-ouassou*[4] are two kinds of partridge, as big as our geese, and have the same taste as the birds I have already mentioned.

The same is true of these three: *ynamboumiri,* which is of the same size as our partridges; *pegassou,* of the size of a wood pigeon; and *paicacu,* which is like a turtledove.[5]

For brevity's sake, I will leave off speaking of the game birds, which are in such great abundance, both in the woods and along the seashores, marshes, and freshwater rivers; I come now to the birds which are not so commonly eaten in the land of Brazil. Among others, there are two of almost the same size (that is, bigger than a raven), which, like almost all the birds of America, have hooked feet and beaks like parrots, with which they could be classed. But as for the plumage (as you will judge for yourselves after hearing about it), you could hardly believe that there exist in the whole world birds of more marvelous beauty; in contemplating them, one is moved not to glorify nature, as do the profane, but rather their great and wonderful Creator.

The first one, which the savages call *arat,*[b] has wing and tail feathers about a foot and a half long, one half of each feather as red as fine scarlet, and the other half a sparkling sky-blue (the colors are divided from each other along the quill), with all the rest of the body the color of lapis lazuli; when this bird is in the sunlight, where it is ordinarily to be seen, no eye can weary of gazing upon it.

---

[a][*Mutum* (*Crax*): "a curassow, a forest bird about the size of a small turkey" (Wagley, *Welcome of Tears,* 308).]

[b][The macaw, of the genus *Ara:* the largest South American parrot.]

The other, named *canidé*,[6] has all the plumage under the belly and around the neck as yellow as fine gold; the upper part of the back, the wings and the tail are of a blue as clear as can be. You would think that he was dressed in golden cloth below, and clad in a mantle of violet damask above; one is enraptured by his beauty.

The savages often mention this latter bird in their songs, repeating *canidé-jouve, canidé-jouve heuraouech:* that is, "A yellow bird, a yellow bird," and so forth; for *jouve*, or *joup*, means "yellow" in their language. Although these birds are not domestic, they are more often to be found in the tall trees in the middle of the villages than in the woods, and our Tupinamba pluck them carefully three or four times a year, as I have said, and use their beautiful feathers to make fine robes, headdresses, bracelets, ornaments for their wooden swords, and other adornments for their bodies. I had brought many of these plumes back to France, and especially some of the big tail feathers, which are particolored in red and sky-blue; but upon my return, when I was passing through Paris, a certain person representing the king, to whom I showed them, importuned me until he got them from me.

There are three or four kinds of parrots in the land of Brazil. The biggest and handsomest, which the savages call *ajourous*,[7] have a head streaked with yellow, red, and violet, rosy-tipped wings, a long yellow tail, and a green body. Not many of them arrive over here; and yet, apart from the beauty of the plumage, these are the ones that speak the best when they are trained, and that would give the most pleasure. In fact, an interpreter gave me as a gift one that he had kept for three years; it pronounced both the savage and the French languages so well that if you didn't see it, you would have thought you were hearing the voice of a man.

But I have something still more amazing to tell about a parrot of this kind, trained by a savage woman in a village two leagues from our island; for it was as if this bird had the intelligence to understand and distinguish what was said by the woman who had raised him. When we passed by there, she would say to us in her language, "If you will give me a comb or a mirror, I will make my parrot sing and dance now, in your presence." If thereupon, for our amusement, we gave her what she was asking, as soon as she had spoken to that bird he began not only to dance about on his perch, but also to prattle, whistle, and imitate the savages going to war, in an incredible fashion. When its mistress chose to say "Sing," it would sing, and "Dance," it would dance. If on the contrary she chose not to, because she had been given nothing, as soon as she said brusquely to this bird, "*Auge,*" that is, "Stop," it would fall silent, and not utter a word; whatever we might say to him, it was not in our power to make him move his feet or his tongue. According to Pliny,[a] the ancient Romans, in their wisdom, accorded a sumptuous funeral to a certain raven who greeted them each by name in their palace, and even put to death the person who had killed him; think of the value they would have put on such a well-trained parrot! Likewise, this savage woman, who called him her *cherimbaué,* that is, "thing that I love," held him so dear that when we asked her to sell him to us, and wanted to know the price, she replied mockingly, "*Moca-ouassou,*" that is, a cannon;[8] so we never managed to get him from her.

The second kind of parrots, called *marganas*[9] by the savages, which are the kind most often brought over and seen in France, are not held in great esteem by them. They are in as great abundance over there as pigeons are over here; although the flesh is a little tough, still, since it has the taste of partridge, we would eat them often, and as many as we pleased.

The third kind of parrots, called *toüis*[b] by the savages, and *moissons*[c] by the Norman sailors, are no bigger than starlings; but as for the plumage, except for the tail, which is very long and has some yellow mixed in, the body is as green as beets.

Before I finish this discussion of parrots, being reminded of what someone says in his *Cosmography,* that they build their nests hanging from a tree branch so the snakes don't eat their eggs, I will say in passing, having seen the contrary among those in the land of Brazil, all of which build their nests—round in shape, and quite tough—in the hollows of trees, that I judge this to be one of that author's cock-and-bull stories.[d]

The other birds of the country of our Americans are, to begin with, the one that they call *toucan* (which I have mentioned earlier in another connection), which is of the size of a woodpigeon; all its plumage, except for the breast, is as black as a crow's. This breast patch (as I have said elsewhere) is about four fingers long and three wide, yellower than saffron, and edged with red below. The savages skin it off, and besides using

---

[a][*Natural History*] Book 10, Chapter 43.

[b][The parakeet.]

[c][*Moissons* means "harvests" in French; I have not found an explanation of this Norman usage.]

[d][A reference to Thevet, *Cosmog. univ.,* p. 939.]

it to cover and adorn their cheeks and other parts of the body, they customarily carry it when they dance; for that reason they call it "*toucan-tabourace,*" that is, "dancing feather," and they prize it highly. Still, since they have them in great numbers, they are not reluctant to barter them for the merchandise brought by the French and Portuguese who trade over there.

The beak of this bird the *toucan,* which is longer than the whole body and proportionately thick (I will not compare or contrast it with that of the crane, which is nothing by comparison), must be regarded not only as the beak of beaks, but also as the most prodigious and monstrous that can be found among all the birds in the universe. It is not without reason that when Belon[a] found one, he had its picture placed as a curiosity at the end of his third book on birds; although he does not name it, there is no doubt that what is represented there is meant to be the beak of our *toucan.*

There is another kind of bird in that land of Brazil that is the size of a blackbird, and just as black, except for the breast, which is as red as oxblood, and which the savages skin off like the one I just mentioned; they call this bird *panou.*[10]

Another, which they call *quiampian,*[11] is of the size of a thrush, and its entire plumage is as red as scarlet.

But for a singular wonder, and a masterwork of miniature, there is one that I must not omit, which the savages call *gonambuch,*[b] of whitish and shining plumage; although its body is no bigger than that of a hornet or a horned beetle, it excels in singing. This tiny bird, which hardly ever leaves its perch on that coarse millet that our Americans call *avati,* or on other tall plants, always has its beak and throat open; if you didn't hear it and see it by experience, you would never believe that from such a little body could come a song so free and high, so clear and pure as to equal that of the nightingale.

I could not possibly describe in detail all the birds that can be seen in this land of Brazil. They are not only different in kind from those of our Europe, but are of a wholly different range of colors, such as red, pink, violet, white, ash, and shadings of purple. So to conclude, I will describe one which the savages (for the reason that I will explain) hold in such high regard that they would be very sorry to injure it. Indeed, I think

---

[a][Pierre Belon, *Histoire de la nature des oyseaux* (Paris, 1555), III: 28.]

[b][The hummingbird, or *guanumbi* (*Viagem* 153, n. 318).]

that if they knew that someone had killed one of them, they would make him repent it.

This bird is no bigger than a pigeon, and of an ash-gray plumage. But the mystery that I want to mention is this: his voice is so penetrating—even more pitiful than that of the screech-owl—that our poor Tupinamba, who hear him cry more often in the night than in daytime, have the fantasy imprinted in their brain that their deceased relatives and friends are sending them these birds as a sign of good luck, and especially to encourage them to bear themselves valiantly in war against their enemies. They believe firmly that if they observe what is signified to them by these augurs, not only will they vanquish their enemies in this world, but what is more, when they die their souls will not fail to rejoin their ancestors behind the mountains and dance with them.[12]

I once spent the night in a village which the French call *Upec;* toward evening, hearing these birds sing so piteously, and seeing these poor savages so attentive in listening to them, and also knowing the reason why, I tried to point out to them their foolishness. But while I was speaking to them, I began to laugh at a Frenchman who was with me, and an old man said to me rather brusquely, "Be quiet, and do not prevent us from hearing the good news that our grandfathers are even now announcing to us; for when we hear these birds, we all rejoice, and receive renewed strength." So without replying (for it would have been of no use), and remembering those who believe and teach that the souls of the deceased return from purgatory to warn them of their duty, it occurred to me that what our poor blind Americans do in this respect is more tolerable: for as I shall describe when I speak of their religion, although they confess a belief in the immortality of souls, they do not go so far as to believe that souls return after being separated from their bodies, but say only that these birds are their messengers.

And that is what I had to say concerning the birds of America.

There are, however, some bats in that country almost as big as our jackdaws. They usually enter the houses at night, and if they find someone sleeping with his feet uncovered, they always chiefly attack the big toe, and suck the blood from it; in fact, they will sometimes draw more than a cupful without your feeling anything. So when you wake up in the morning, you are appalled to see the cotton bed and everything near it all bloody. However, when the savages notice it, regardless of whether it has happened to one of their people or to a stranger, they only laugh. And indeed, I myself was thus taken by surprise one morning; besides the ridicule I received for it, the tender extremity of my big toe was hurt, and, although the pain was not great, still, for two or three days I could scarcely put my shoes on.

The people of Cumana, on the coast about ten degrees this side of the Equator, are similarly pestered by these big and nasty bats. On this subject, the author of the *General History of the Indies* has an amusing story. There was, he says, at Saint-Foy of Ciribici a monk's servant who had pleurisy. Since the vein for bleeding him could not be found, he was left for dead. But at night there came a bat, which bit him near the heel, which it found uncovered. It drew so much blood that not only did it slake its thirst, but also left the vein open, so that enough blood spurted out of it to restore the patient to health.[a] To which I will add, with the historian, that it was a comical and gracious surgeon for the poor patient. So that in spite of the annoyance that I have said one endures from these great bats of America, this last example shows that they are far from being as dangerous as those malefic birds, called *striges* by the Greeks, which, as Ovid says in Book Three of his *Fastes*, would suck the blood of children in the cradle (for which reason this name has since been given to witches).

As for the bees of America, they are not like ours over here, but rather resemble those little black flies that we have in the summer, especially in the grape season; they make their honey and their wax in the woods in the hollows of trees, where the savages know how to collect them. When the two are mixed together, they call it *yra-yetic,* for *yra* is honey, and *yetic* is wax. After they have separated them, they eat the honey as we do over here; as for the wax, which is almost as black as pitch, they squeeze it into rolls as big as an arm. However, they don't make torches or candles of it; at night they use no other light but that of certain woods that burn with a very clear flame. They mainly use this wax for caulking the big wooden tubes where they keep their feather-work, to preserve them against a certain kind of moth which otherwise would spoil them.

While I am at it, I will describe a kind of tiny creature which are called by the savages *aravers,*[13] which are no bigger than our crickets. When they come out at night in swarms near the fire, if they find something, they will not fail to nibble it. They would hurl themselves on leather collars or slippers, eating the whole upper side; the next morning their owners would find them all white and chewed over. What is more, if

---

[a][Gómara,] *Histoire,* Book 2, Chapter 80.

in the evenings we left some chickens or other poultry cooked and not properly wrapped up, these *aravers* would gnaw them down to the bone, and we could expect to find skeletons in the morning.

The savages are also persecuted in their persons by another kind of small vermin that they call *ton*,[14] which is found on the ground, and at the beginning is not as big as a little flea. However, it attaches itself under the toenails and fingernails, where suddenly it produces an itch, if you do not take care to remove it. Digging itself still farther in, it soon becomes as big as a pea, so that you cannot pull it out without great pain. And it is not only the savages, naked and unshod, who are bothered and afflicted by it; we Frenchmen, well dressed and well shod as we were, had great trouble fending them off. As for me, however careful I was to be on the lookout for them, they were pulled out of various parts of me in numbers of more than twenty in a day. I have seen people who were lazy about watching out for them, and who were so damaged by these fleas or ringworms that not only were their hands, feet and toes blighted by them, but they were all covered with little bumps like moles, even under their armpits, and on other soft parts of the body. I am sure that it is this little beast that the historian of the West Indies called *nigua,* which is also, as he says, found in Hispaniola. This is what he has written about it: "The *nigua* is like a little jumping flea. It likes the dust, and does not bite except on the feet, where it burrows in between the skin and the flesh. It immediately lays eggs in greater quantity than you would guess, given its smallness; these engender others, and if you leave them there without taking measures, they multiply so fast that you cannot get rid of them or be cured except with fire or iron; but if you remove them early, they do little harm. Some Spaniards have lost their toes to them, others entire feet."[a]

To get rid of them, our Americans rub the ends of their toes or other parts of the body where they try to nest with a thick, reddish oil, made from a fruit that they call *couroq,*[15] which has a husk almost like that of a chestnut; when we were over there we did the same thing. This unguent is such a sovereign remedy for wounds, breaks, and other injuries to the human body, that our savages, knowing its virtue, consider it as precious as some people over here regard what they call holy oil. The surgeon of the ship on which we returned to France, who had experimented with several kinds of it, brought back ten or twelve big jars' full, along with an equal quantity of human fat that he had collected when the savages were

---

[a][Gómara, *Histoire,*] Book I, Chapter 30.

cooking and roasting their prisoners of war, in the manner that I will describe in its place.

The air of this land of Brazil produces a sort of gnat, called *yetin* by the natives, which stings so sharply even through light clothing that you would think it was a needle point. So you can imagine what sport it is to see our naked savages pursued by them: when they go slapping their hands on their buttocks, thighs, shoulders, arms, and on their whole body, you would say that they are carters lashing their horses with the whip.

When you move the soil and lift up stones in our country of Brazil, you find scorpions that, while much smaller than the ones you see in Provence, nevertheless have a venomous and deadly sting, as I learned from experience. This animal seeks out things that are clean; it happened that one day after I had washed my cotton bed and hung it back up in the air in the native fashion, there was a scorpion that had hidden in a fold. As I lay down without seeing him, he stung me in the big finger of the left hand, which swelled up so suddenly that if I had not quickly had recourse to one of our apothecaries, who had some dead scorpions in a phial with some oil and applied one to my finger, without a doubt the venom would have spread throughout my entire body. And indeed, in spite of this remedy, which is regarded as the most sovereign for this ailment, the poison had spread so far that I remained for twenty-four hours in such distress that I could hardly contain myself for the violence of the pain. The savages, too, when they are stung by these scorpions, use the same prescription if they can catch them: that is, to kill them and quickly press them on the affected part of the body.

Furthermore, as I have said elsewhere, they are very vindictive, and even furious, against all things that hurt them; if they even stub a toe against a rock, they will snap their teeth at it like mad dogs. With all their might, they will go to any lengths to track down the beasts that do them harm, and rid their country of them insofar as they can.[16]

Finally, there are terrestrial crabs, called *oussa* by the Tupinamba, which live in swarms like big grasshoppers on the seashore and in other marshy regions. As soon as you approach, you see them flee to one side, and swiftly disappear into the holes that they make in the trunks and the roots of trees, from which it is difficult to pull them without having your fingers pinched with their big hooked feet; however, you can go on dry ground up to the openings, where you can see them clearly from above. They are much leaner than the sea crabs; besides their having little flesh, they smell like juniper root, and are not very good to eat.

# CHAPTER XII

۶۹

# OF SOME FISH
## THAT ARE COMMON
### AMONG THE SAVAGES OF AMERICA,
### AND OF THEIR MANNER OF FISHING[1]

In order to forestall repetitions, which I avoid as much as I can, I will refer the readers to Chapters III, V, and VII of this history, as well as to other places, where I have already mentioned the whales, sea monsters, flying fish, and other fish of various kinds. In this chapter I will treat the ones most commonly seen among our Americans, but which have not yet been mentioned.

First, the savages call all fish *para*. But as to species, they have two sorts of mullet, which they call *kurema* and *parati*, which are excellent for eating, whether boiled or roasted (more the latter than the former). Back over here in the last few years I have seen by experience, both in the Loire and in other rivers of France, where the mullet have come up from the sea, that these fish ordinarily move in schools. The savages, seeing big clouds of them bubbling in the sea, quickly shoot into them, and aim so true that they nearly always skewer several of them with long arrows; when the fish are thus pierced, and cannot go to the bottom, they go gather them by swimming. The flesh of these fish is more friable than any other; when they have caught a certain quantity, dried them on the *boucan,* and crumbled them, they make very good flour from them.

*Camouroupouy-ouassou* (*ouassou* in the Brazilian language means tall or big, depending on the accent) is a very big fish that our Tupinamba often mention when they dance and sing, repeating over and over: "*Pira-ouassou à oueh: Kamouroupouy-ouassou à oueh,*" and so forth; it is very good to eat.

Two others, which they call *oura* and *acara-ouassou,*[2] are almost of the same size as those I just mentioned, but better; I would even venture to say that the *oura* is not less delicate than our trout.

*Acarapep* is a flat fish; when it is cooked it yields a yellow fat that serves as a sauce, and its flesh is wonderfully good.

*Acara-bouten* is a viscous fish of a tan or reddish color; it is of a lesser sort than the others, and is not very palatable.

Another, which they call *pira-ypochi,* is as long as an eel, and isn't good—which is what *ypochi* means in their language.

As for the rayfish that are caught in the bay of Janeiro and the surrounding seas, not only are they broader than those found in Normandy and Brittany and other places over here; they also have two rather long horns, five or six clefts (which have an artificial look) under the belly, and a long and slender tail. What is worse, as I saw once myself from experience when we pulled one into the boat, they are so dangerous and venomous that when it stung the leg of a member of our company the spot immediately became red and swollen.

And there you have a summary of the sea fish of America, which exist in innumerable multitudes.

To go on, the freshwater rivers of that country are full of an infinite number of middling and small fish, which in general the savages call *pira-miri* (for *miri* in their patois means "little"); I will describe only two of them, which are amazingly misshapen.

The first, which the savages call *tamou-ata,*[3] is usually only a half a foot long, with a head that is very big, even monstrous. It has two little barbels under the throat, teeth sharper than a pike's, and prickly bones; the whole body is armed with scales that are so resistant that, as I said elsewhere about the terrestrial beast *tatou,*[a] I don't think that a sword-blow would have any effect. Its flesh is very tender, good, and flavorful.

The other fish, that the savages call *pana-pana,*[b] is of a middling size. As for its form, its body, tail, and skin resemble a shark's, and are as rough; its head is so flat, so irregular and so strangely formed that when it is seen out of the water, it seems to be divided and separated into two parts, as if someone had deliberately split it; a more hideous fish head is nowhere to be seen.

As for the savages' style of fishing, I have already said that they spear the mullet with arrows (which is also true of all other kinds of fish that they go after). It must also be noted that the men and women of

---

[a][The armadillo.]

[b][Possibly a kind of hammerhead shark.]

America all know how to swim, so that they can go get their game and their catch in the middle of the water, like spaniels; even the little children, as soon as they begin to walk, get into the rivers and the water along the seashore, and are already splashing around in it like little ducks.

As an example, I will briefly recount what happened one Sunday morning. While we were strolling around on a bulwark of our fort, we saw a bark boat (made in a fashion that I will describe elsewhere) turn over in the sea; in it were more than thirty savages, adults and children, who were coming to see us. Thinking to rescue them, we made toward them with great speed in a boat. We found them all swimming and laughing on the water; one of them said to us, "And where are you going in such haste, you *Mairs?*" (For so they call the French.) "We are coming," we said, "to save you and to pull you from the water." "Indeed," he said, "we are very grateful to you; but do you think that just because we fell in the sea we are in danger of drowning? Without putting foot to ground, or touching land, we could remain a week on the surface, just as you see us now. So," he said, "we are much more afraid of some big fish pulling us to the bottom than we fear sinking." Thereupon the others, who were, indeed, all swimming as easily as fishes, having been alerted by their companion to the cause of our swift approach, made sport of us, and began to laugh so hard that we could hear them puffing and snorting on the water like a school of porpoises. And indeed, although we were still more than a quarter of a league from our fort, there were only four or five of them who wanted to come into our boat, and that was more to talk with us than from any fear of danger. I noticed that the others who were ahead of us not only swam as smoothly and steadily as they wished, but also would rest on the water whenever they pleased. As for their bark boat, and the cotton beds, supplies, and other things that were in it and that they were bringing to us, which had all sunk, they concerned themselves no more about it than you would about having lost an apple. "After all," they said, "aren't there others in the country?"

While I am talking about the savages' fishing, I don't want to omit an account that I heard from one of them. On one occasion, during a calm, he was with some others in one of their bark boats rather far out in the sea. A big fish came up and seized the edge of the boat with a paw as if he meant either to capsize it or throw himself into it. "When I saw this," he said, "I quickly cut off his hand with a pruning-hook. The hand fell into our boat, and as it lay there we could see that it had five fingers, like that of a man. What is more, when the fish raised its head above the water, we saw that it too had a human form, and uttered a little cry of pain."[a]

After this rather strange narration by this American, I will leave it to the reader to philosophize about the common opinion that the sea contains all the kinds of animals that are to be seen on the land, and especially about what some have written concerning tritons and sirens, and whether it was one of them, or rather some marine monkey or marmot, whose hand the savage claimed to have cut off. However, without prejudging whatever might be true about such things, I will say frankly that during the nine months that I was on the open sea without putting foot to earth more than once, and in all the many navigations that I have made by the shores, I have never observed any such thing, nor, among the innumerable fish of all sorts that we caught, have I seen anything that came so close to a human semblance.

To finish what I had to say concerning the fishing of our Tupinamba: besides the method of skewering the fish on their arrows, which I have described, they also have an old style in which they fashion thorns into fishhooks, and make lines out of a plant they call *toucon,*[b] which is prepared like hemp, and is much stronger; with these they fish on the edges and banks of the waters. They also go out onto the sea and the freshwater rivers on certain rafts, which they call *piperis,* made up of five or six round poles bigger around than an arm, joined and bound together with withes of twisted green wood; seated on these, their thighs and legs stretched out, they go where they please, using a little flat stick for a paddle. However, since these *piperis* are only about five feet long, and only about two feet wide, they could not withstand a storm, and each one of them can hold only one man at a time. So in good weather, when the savages are naked and fishing on the sea separately, one by one, if you saw them from a distance you would say that they were monkeys, or rather (so small do they seem) frogs sunning themselves on wooden logs out in the middle of the water. Since these wooden rafts, arranged like organ pipes, are quickly constructed, and since they float unsinkable on the water like a big trellis, I think that if we made them over here they would be a good and safe means of crossing rivers as well as ponds and lakes of still or gently flowing waters, which can be a hindrance when one is in a hurry to travel. When our savages would see us fishing with the

---

[a][Probably a manatee.]

[b][The *Tucumã* palm, the fiber of which is used for rope.]

nets that we had brought over, which they call *puissa-ouassou,* they took great pleasure in helping us and in seeing us bring in so many fish with a single cast of the net; what is more, if we let them, they quickly managed to fish with them very well by themselves. Just as, ever since the French first started trading there, above all the other commodities that they enjoy in return for their merchandise, they praise them most for this, that, having needed, in times past, to put thorns on the end of their lines rather than fishhooks, they now have, thanks to them, the elegant invention of that little iron barb that one finds so suited to the art of angling.

As I have said elsewhere, the little boys of that country have learned to say to foreigners who go over there: "*De agatorem, amabe pinda*":[4] that is, "You are good, give me some hooks"; for *agatorem* in their language means "good," *amabe* means "give me," and *pinda* is a fish-hook. If you don't give them any, the little rascals will suddenly turn their heads away in vexation, saying "*De-engaipa-ajouca*": that is, "You are a good-for-nothing, you must be killed."

While we are on the subject: if you want to be a "cousin" (as we commonly say) as much with the adults as with the children, you must refuse them nothing. It is true that they are not ungrateful; for the old men especially, even when you aren't thinking about it, will remember the gift that they have received from you, and in recognition of it they will give you something in return. But whatever the case may be, I have observed among them that just as they love those who are gay, joyful, and liberal, on the contrary they so hate those who are taciturn, stingy, and melancholy, that I can assure any who are sly, malicious, gloomy, niggardly, or who munch their bread alone in a corner, that they will never be welcome among our Tupinamba; for by their nature they detest such manner of folk.

# CHAPTER XIII

## ૨ે

# OF THE TREES, HERBS,
## ROOTS, AND EXQUISITE
### FRUITS PRODUCED BY THE LAND
### OF BRAZIL[1]

Having already treated the four-footed animals as well as the birds, fish, reptiles, and things having life, movement, and feeling that are to be seen in America, before I speak of religion, war, civil order, and other customs of our savages that are still to be dealt with, I will continue by describing the trees, herbs, plants, fruits, roots—all the things commonly said to have a vegetative soul—which are to be found in that country.

First, since brazilwood (from which this land has taken the name that we use for it) is among the most famous trees, and now one of the best known to us and (because of the dye made from it) is the most valued, I will describe it here.[2] This tree, which the savages call *araboutan*, ordinarily grows as high and branchy as the oaks in the forests of this country; some are so thick that three men could not embrace a single trunk. While we are speaking of big trees, the author of the *General History of the West Indies* says that two have been seen in those countries, one of which had a trunk more than eight arm lengths around, and the other a trunk of more than sixteen. On top of the first one, he said, which was so high that you couldn't throw a stone to the top of it, a *cacique* had built a little lodge (the Spaniards who saw him nesting up there like a stork burst out laughing); they also described the second tree as a marvelous thing. The same author also recounts that in the country of Nicaragua there is a tree called *cerba*,[a] which grows so big that fifteen men could not embrace it.[b]

To return to our brazilwood: it has a leaf like that of boxwood, but

---

[a][Probably *Ceiba pentandra* (L.) Gaertn., the kapok or silk-cotton tree, which can reach seventy meters in height and have huge buttresses.]

[b][Gómara,] Chapters 61, 85, and 204.

of a brighter green, and it bears no fruit. As for the manner of loading it on the ships, take note that both because of the hardness of this wood and the consequent difficulty of cutting it, and because, there being no horses, donkeys, or other beasts to carry, cart, or draw burdens in that country, it has to be men who do this work: if the foreigners who voyage over there were not helped by the savages, they could not load even a medium-sized ship in a year. In return for some frieze garments, linen shirts, hats, knives, and other merchandise that they are given, the savages not only cut, saw, split, quarter, and round off the brazilwood, with the hatchets, wedges, and other iron tools given to them by the French and by others from over here, but also carry it on their bare shoulders, often from a league or two away, over mountains and difficult places, clear down to the seashore by the vessels that lie at anchor, where the mariners receive it. I say expressly that it is only since the French and Portuguese have been frequenting their country that the savages have been cutting their brazilwood; for before that time, as I have heard from the old men, they had almost no other way of taking down a tree than by setting fire to the base of it. There are people over here who think that the round logs that you see at the merchants' are of the natural thickness of the trees; to show that they are mistaken, besides saying that these trees are often very thick, I have added that the savages round them off and shape them so that they are easier to carry and to handle in the ships.

During the time that we were in that country we made fine fires of this brazilwood; I have observed that since it is not at all damp, like most other wood, but rather is naturally dry, it gives off very little smoke as it burns. One day one of our company decided to bleach our shirts, and, without suspecting anything, put brazilwood ash in with the lye; instead of whitening them, he made them so red that although they were washed and soaped afterward, there was no means of getting rid of that tincture, so that we had to wear them that way.

If the gentlemen over here with their perfectly starched pleats— those who send to Flanders to have their shirts whitened—choose not to believe me, they have my permission to do the experiment for themselves, and, for quicker results, the more to brighten their great ruffs (or rather, those dribble-catchers more than half a foot wide that they are wearing these days), they can dye them green if they please.

Our Tupinamba are astonished to see the French and others from distant countries go to so much trouble to get their *araboutan*, or brazilwood. On one occasion one of their old men questioned me about it: "What does it mean that you *Mairs* and *Peros* (that is, French and Portuguese) come from so far for wood to warm yourselves? Is there none in your own country?" I answered him yes, and in great quantity, but not of the same kinds as theirs; nor any brazilwood, which we did not burn as he thought, but rather carried away to make dye, just as they themselves did to redden their cotton cord, feathers, and other articles. He immediately came back at me: "Very well, but do you need so much of it?" "Yes," I said (trying to make him see the good of it), "for there is a merchant in our country who has more frieze and red cloth, and even" (and here I was choosing things that were familiar to him) "more knives, scissors, mirrors, and other merchandise than you have ever seen over here, one such merchant alone will buy all the wood that several ships bring back from your country." "Ha, ha!" said my savage, "you are telling me of wonders." Then, having thought over what I had said to him, he questioned me further, and said, "But this man of whom you speak, who is so rich, does he never die?" "Certainly he does," I said, "just as others do." At that (since they are great discoursers, and pursue a subject out to the end) he asked me, "And when he is dead, to whom belong all the goods that he leaves behind?" "To his children, if he has any, and if there are none, to his brothers, sisters, or nearest kinsmen." "Truly," said my elder (who, as you will judge, was no dullard), "I see now that you *Mairs* (that is, Frenchmen) are great fools; must you labor so hard to cross the sea, on which (as you told us) you endured so many hardships, just to amass riches for your children or for those who will survive you? Will not the earth that nourishes you suffice to nourish them? We have kinsmen and children, whom, as you see, we love and cherish; but because we are certain that after our death the earth which has nourished us will nourish them, we rest easy and do not trouble ourselves further about it."

And there you have a brief and true summary of the discourse that I have heard from the very mouth of a poor savage American. This nation, which we consider so barbarous, charitably mocks those who cross the sea at the risk of their lives to go seek brazilwood in order to get rich; however blind this people may be in attributing more to nature and to the fertility of the earth than we do to the power and the providence of God, it will rise up in judgment against those despoilers who are as abundant over here, among those bearing the title of Christians, as they are scarce over there, among the native inhabitants. Therefore, to take up what I said elsewhere—that the Tupinamba mortally hate the avaricious—would to God that the latter might be imprisoned among them, so that they might even in this life serve as demons and furies to torment those whose maws are insatiable, who do nothing but suck the blood and marrow of others. To our great shame, and to justify our savages in the little care that they have for the things of this world, I had to make this digression in their favor.

I think it is appropriate to add here what the historian of the West Indies has written of a certain nation of savages living in Peru. When the Spanish were first roaming up and down that country, because they were bearded, and because they were so swaggering and so foppish, the savages did not want to receive them, fearing that that they would corrupt and alter their ancient customs; they called them "seafoam," fatherless people, men without repose, who cannot stay in any one place to cultivate the land to provide themselves with food.[a]

To continue to speak of the trees of this land of America: there are four or five kinds of palm trees; among the most common is one called by the savages *gerau,* and another called *yri;* since I have never seen dates in either of them, I think they produce none. However, the *yri* does bear round fruit resembling sloes, in tight clusters like big grapes, so that in a single bunch there are as many as a man can lift and carry with one hand; but it is only the kernel, no bigger than that of a cherry, that is any good. There is also a white tendril between the leaves at the top of the young palm trees, which we would cut for eating; the Sieur du Pont, who was subject to hemorrhoids, said that it served as a remedy, but that I leave up to the physicians.

There is another tree which the savages call *airy;*[3] it has leaves like those of the palm tree and a trunk with thorns all around it, fine and sharp as needles. It bears a fruit of medium size, in which there is a kernel as white as snow, which, however, is not good to eat. In my opinion it is a kind of ebony; for it is black, and it is so hard that the savages use it for wooden swords and maces, as well as for some of their arrows (which I will describe when I speak of their wars). It can be worked to a very smooth and gleaming finish, and is so dense that it sinks in water.

Furthermore, before I go on, there are many kinds of colored woods in this land of America, but I don't know the names of all of the trees that produce them. Among others, I have seen some as yellow as boxwood; others naturally violet, some sticks of which I brought back to France; some white as paper; and other kinds red as brazilwood, from which the savages also make wooden swords and bows. Then there is one that they

---

[a][Gómara,] *Histoire,* Book 4, Chapter 108.

name *copa-u*,[4] which not only resembles the walnut as a standing tree (although it bears no nuts), but when it is made into wooden furniture, its boards show the same kind of grain. There are some that have leaves thicker than a testoon; others have leaves a foot and a half wide. There are several other kinds, which would be tedious to describe in detail.

But above all, there is a particular tree in that country that is not only beautiful but smells so wonderfully good that if, while the joiners were whittling or planing it, we picked up the chips or shavings, we could smell the true fragrance of a fresh rose. On the other hand, there is another wood, which the savages call *aouai*,[5] which stinks so strongly of garlic that when you cut it or put it in the fire, you can't stay near it; this last tree has leaves like those of an appletree, but its fruit (which somewhat resembles a water-chestnut), and especially the pit, is so venomous that whoever eats it suddenly feels the effects of a true poison. Nevertheless it is from this fruit that our Americans make the rattles that they put around their legs, and for that reason they value it highly. It must be noted here that although the land of Brazil (as we will see in this chapter) produces many good and excellent fruits, there are several trees whose fruit is wonderfully beautiful but that nonetheless is not good to eat. Particularly on the seashore there are many shrubs whose fruits resemble our medlar pear, but which are very dangerous to eat. The savages, seeing the French and other foreigners approach these trees to gather the fruit, say to them in their language "*Ypochi*," that is "It isn't good," thus warning them to be careful.

*Hivouraé*[6] has bark about a half a finger thick, that is rather agreeable to eat, especially when it comes fresh off the tree; I have heard from two apothecaries, who came over with us, that it is a kind of guaicum. The savages use it to treat a disease that they call *pians*,[a] which, as I will recount elsewhere, is as dangerous among them as the pox is among us over here.

The tree that the savages call *choyne*[b] is of medium size. Its leaves are of about the shape of our laurel leaves, and are of the same green; it bears a fruit as big as a child's head, and shaped like an ostrich egg, but which is not good to eat. Because this fruit has a hard rind, our Tupinambas keep some of them whole; piercing them clear through lengthwise, they make from them the instrument called the *maraca* (which I

---

[a][Yaws (see Chap. XIX).]

[b][The calabash (*Crescentia cujete* L.) (Lussagnet 233, n. 3).]

have already mentioned, and of which I will speak again); they also hollow them out and split them through the middle to make drinking cups and other little vessels.

Continuing to speak of the trees of the land of Brazil, there is one that the savages call *sabaucaïë*,[a] bearing a fruit that is bigger than two fists, and made in a cup-like shape, and in which there are little pits like almonds, and of almost the same taste. The shell of this fruit is well suited to making vessels; I think that these are what we call "Indian nuts," which, when they are appropriately turned and shaped, we often have set in silver over here. When we were over there, a certain Pierre Bourdon, an excellent turner who had made several handsome dishes and other vessels both of this *sabaucaïë* and of other wood, presented some of these to Villegagnon, who valued them highly; however, the poor man was so ill rewarded by him (as I will recount in due time) as to be one of those whom he caused to be drowned in the sea because of the Gospel.

There is also in that country a tree which grows very high, like our service trees, and bears a fruit that the savages call *acajou*,[b] which is of the size and shape of a hen's egg. When this fruit has come to maturity, and is yellower than a quince, it is good to eat; also, it has a slightly tart but pleasant-tasting juice, and when you are hot this liquor refreshes you more agreeably than any other. However, since it is difficult to beat them down off these tall trees, we had hardly any unless the monkeys, climbing up to eat them, knocked enough of them down for us to gather.

*Paco-aire*[c] is a shrub that usually grows ten or twelve feet high; although there are some that have a trunk almost as big as a man's thigh, it is so soft that you could cut it down with a single stroke of a well-sharpened sword. Its fruit, which the savages call *paco,* is more than half a foot long; when it is ripe, it is yellow and rather resembles a cucumber. Twenty or twenty-five of them grow close together on a single branch; our Americans gather them in big bunches, as many as they can support with one hand, and carry them off in this way to their houses.

As for the goodness of this fruit, when it has come to its proper ripeness, and the skin lifts off like that of a fresh fig, it is slightly gritty, and as you eat it you would indeed say that it is a fig. For that reason, we

---

[a][The sapucaia nut (*Lecythis zabucajo* Aubl.). The nut has a lid that falls off to leave a cup-like receptacle.]

[b][Acaju, an edible fruit of the *Spondias* genus.]

[c][The banana. Native to southeast Asia; in Léry's time, recently introduced into Brazil.]

Frenchmen called these *pacos* figs; however, they taste even sweeter and more flavorful than the very best figs of Marseilles, and must be considered one of the finest and best fruits of the land of Brazil. The histories recount that when Cato returned from Carthage to Rome, he brought back figs of amazing size;[7] but since the ancients made no mention of the one I am speaking about, it is likely that they were not the same ones.

The leaves of the *paco-aire* are rather similar to those of *Lapathum aquaticum;*[a] but they are so extraordinarily big—each one is commonly six feet long, and more than two feet wide—that I don't believe leaves of such size are to be found in Europe, Asia, or Africa. For although I have heard an apothecary affirm that he had seen lagwort leaves a yard and a quarter wide, that is (since this herb is round) three and three-quarters yards in circumference, still, it doesn't approach that of our *paco-aire*. It is true that the leaves are not thick in proportion to their size, but rather very thin, and rising straight up; when the wind is at all strong (which often happens in that land of America), only the stem in the middle of the leaf holds firm; the rest of the leaf splits so that if you saw these shrubs from a distance you would think that they were decked out in great ostrich plumes.

As for cotton trees, which grow to a medium height, there are many of them in the land of Brazil. The flower comes in little yellow bells like that of our gourds or pumpkins, but when the fruit is formed it has a shape like that of the beechnuts of our forests; when it is ripe, it splits into four, and the cotton (which the Americans call *ameni-jou*) comes out in tufts as big as tennis balls, in the middle of which there are black seeds in a tight bundle in the shape of a kidney, no thicker or longer than a bean. The savage women are skilled at gathering together the cotton and spinning it to make beds of a style that I will describe elsewhere.

Formerly (or so I have heard) there were neither orange nor lemon trees in America; however, the Portuguese have planted and raised some, on or near the seashores that they frequented, which have not only greatly multiplied but also bear sweet oranges (which the savages call *morgou-ia*) as big as two fists, and lemons, which are still bigger and in even greater abundance.

Sugarcane grows very well and in great quantity in that country, but when we were there, we Frenchmen did not yet have either the appropriate people or the necessary things for extracting the sugar from it (as the

---

[a][The herbalists' name for a species of dock, probably *Rumex hydrolapathum*.]

Portuguese have in the places that they possess over there). So, as I said in the ninth chapter concerning the savages' drink, we simply soaked the cane in water to sweeten it, or else if you wanted to you could suck and eat the pith of the stalks. While I'm on the subject, I will mention something which some may marvel at. In spite of the quality of sugar—which, as everyone knows, is sweeter than anything else—we sometimes deliberately left some sugar cane to age and get musty; when it had thus decayed, we left it to soak for a while in water, and it became sour enough to serve us as vinegar.

In certain places in the woods grow many reeds and canes, as big as a man's leg; but, although while they are standing, as I said of the *paco-aire,* they are so soft that you can easily cut one down with a single stroke of the sword, when they are dry they are so hard that the savages split them in quarters, shape them into lancets or serpents' tongues, and arm the tips of their arrows with them so well that when they let fly with them they stop a wild beast at the first hit. Speaking of canes and reeds, Chalcondyle in his history of the Turkish War[a] says that some are found in East India which are of such exceeding height and thickness that you can make skiffs from them for crossing the rivers—in fact, he said, entire boats that can each hold twenty *mines* of wheat, each *mine* being about ten bushels according to the Greek measure.

Mastic also comes in little bushes in our land of America; along with innumerable other odiferous plants and flowers, it gives the earth the sweetest fragrance.

Where we were, under the tropic of Capricorn, while there are great thunderstorms (which the savages call *Toupan*), downpours, and strong winds, nevertheless it never freezes, snows or hails, and therefore the trees are not attacked or damaged by cold and storms as ours are over here; you will never see them bare and stripped of their leaves, and all year long the forests are as green as the laurel in our France.

Since I am on the subject, over here our shortest days are in December, when, benumbed with cold, we blow on our fingers, and have icicles hanging from our noses. But it is then that our Americans have their longest days, and it is so hot in their country that, as my voyage companions and I found by experiment, we could go bathing there at Christmas to cool ourselves off. However, as those who understand the globe can comprehend, the days are neither as long nor as short in the tropics as

---

[a][*Rebus Gestis Turcorum,*] Book III, Chapter 14.

they are in our climate. So those who live there have days of more equal length, and (although the ancients thought otherwise) the seasons are incomparably more temperate.

And that is what I had to say about the trees of the land of Brazil.

As for the plants and herbs, which I also want to mention, I will begin with those which, because of their fruits and their effects, seem to me the most excellent. First, the plant that produces the fruit called by the savages *ananas,*[a] has a form like that of a gladiolus, but with leaves slightly curved and hollowed all around, more like the aloe's. It grows compacted like a great thistle; its fruit, related to our artichoke, is as big as a medium-sized melon, and shaped like a pinecone, but does not hang or bend to one side or the other.

When these *ananas* have come to maturity, and are of an iridescent yellow, they have such a fragrance of raspberry that when you go through the woods and other places where they grow, you can smell them from far off; and as for the taste, it melts in your mouth, and it is naturally so sweet that we have no jams that surpass them; I think it is the finest fruit in America. When I was over there I pressed one of them, and extracted almost a glassful of juice, that seemed to me no less good than malmsey. The savage women brought them to us in great baskets, which they call *panacons,* along with *pacos,* which I have already mentioned, and other fruits, which we got from them in exchange for a comb or a mirror.

As for the herbs produced by that land of Brazil, there is one that our Tupinamba call *petun,*[b] which grows a little higher than our sorrel; its leaves are rather similar, but resemble even more those of *Consolida major.*[c] This herb is greatly prized among the savages because of a singular property, which you will hear about. Here is what they do with it. After they have gathered it and hung it by little handfuls to dry in their houses, they take four or five leaves of it, and wrap them in another big leaf of a tree, like a spice cornet. Then they set the small end of it on fire, and, putting it slightly lit into their mouths, they draw on the smoke, which, though it comes back out through their nostrils and through their pierced lips, nonetheless sustains them so well that if they go off to war, and necessity presses them, they will go three or four days without nourishing themselves on anything else. They use it for another purpose as

---

[a][The pineapple. The other early chroniclers also wrote of it ecstatically.]
[b][Tobacco.]
[c][The herbalists' name for comfrey (*Symphytum officinale* L.).]

well: because it distills the superfluous humors from the brain, not only will you hardly ever see one of them without a cornet of this herb hanging from his neck, but, to enhance their presence while they are speaking with you, they inhale the smoke, which, as I have said, comes back out through the nose and the split lips as from an incense-burner; the smell of it is not unpleasant. I have not, however, seen it used by the women, and I don't know why. I can say, having tried this *petun* smoke myself, that it seemed to satisfy and ward off hunger.

Furthermore, although nicotiana (or the "Queen's herb") is now called *petun* over here, it is by no means the herb I am speaking of; on the contrary, these two plants have nothing in common, either in form or in property. The author of *The Country House*,[8] Book Two, Chapter 79, affirms that nicotiana—which, he says, gets this name from Monsieur Nicot, who first sent it from Portugal to France—was brought from Florida, more than a thousand leagues from our land of Brazil (for the whole Torrid Zone lies between the two). Although I have searched in several gardens where it was claimed that *petun* was growing, I have as yet seen none in our France. And lest he who has lately treated us to his *angoumoise*, which he says is true *petun*, should think that I am ignorant of what he has written about it: if the nature of the herb that he mentions resembles the picture that he had done for his *Cosmography*, I will say about it just what I did about nicotiana. So in this case I do not concede what he claims: that is, that he was the first to bring the *petun* seed to France, where I judge that, because of the cold, this herb could grow only with difficulty.[9]

I have also seen over there a kind of cabbage, which the savages call *cajou-a*,[a] from which they sometimes make soup; it has leaves as large and of the same shape as those of the water lily that grows in the marshes of this country.

As for roots, besides those of *maniot* and *aypi*, from which, as I said in the Chapter IX, the savage women make flour, they have still others that they call *hetich*,[b] which grow in as great abundance in the land of Brazil as turnips in Limousin or Savoie; they are usually as big as two fists, and about a foot and a half long. When you see them pulled out of the ground, you would think at first, from their appearance, that they were all of one kind; however, seeing that during cooking some become

---

[a][Perhaps *taióba* (*Colocasia esculenta* (L.) Schott).]

[b][The sweet potato, *Ipomoea batatas*.]

violet, like certain carrots of this country, others yellow as quinces, and others whitish, I think that there are three kinds of them. But whatever the case may be, I can assure you that when they are cooked in ashes, especially the ones that turn yellow, they are no less good to eat than the best pears that we have. As for their leaves, which trail on the ground like *Hedera terrestris,*[a] they are very similar to those of cucumbers, or the largest spinach leaves that are to be seen over here; but they are not so green, for their color is closer to that of *vitis alba.*[b] Because they bear no seeds, the savage women, taking as much care as possible to make them multiply, do nothing other (and here is a wonderful work of agriculture) than to cut them up into little pieces, as we cut up carrots here to make salads; when they have sown them through the fields, after a certain time they have as many big *hetich* roots as they have sown little pieces. However, seeing that it is the greatest manna of that land of Brazil, and that as you travel through the country you see almost nothing else, I think that for the most part it grows without anyone putting a hand to it.

The savages have likewise a kind of fruit that they call *manobi,*[c] which grows in the earth like truffles, and are connected to each other by little filaments; the kernel is no bigger than that of our hazelnuts, and has the same taste. They are of a grayish color, and the husk is no harder than the shell of a pea; but as to whether they have leaves and seeds, even though I have eaten of this fruit many times, I must confess that I didn't observe it well enough, and I don't remember.

There is also a quantity of a certain long pepper, which the merchants back over here use only for dye; but our savages skillfully pound it and crush it with salt, keeping sea water in ditches for that very purpose. They call this mixture *ionquet,* and they use it as we do table salt. They do not, however, salt their pieces of meat or fish before putting them in their mouths as we do; instead, they first take the piece separately, and then take a pinch of this *ionquet* in their mouths with each bite to give flavor to their meat.

Finally, there grows in that country a kind of bean as thick and wide as a thumb, which the savages call *commanda-ouassou,* as well as little black and gray peas, which they call *commanda-miri,* and certain round pumpkins, called *marongans,*[10] which are very sweet to eat.

---

[a][The herbalists' name for ground ivy.]

[b][Apparently the herbalists' name for white bryony, in the gourd family.]

[c][The peanut (*Arachis hypogaea* L.).]

And there you have not all that could be said of the trees, herbs, and fruits of that land of Brazil, but what I observed during the year I lived there. To conclude, just as I declared before—that there are no four-footed beasts, birds, fish, or any other animals in America that completely resemble in all respects those that we have in Europe—so too, I will say that, as I have carefully observed going and coming through the woods and fields of that country, except for three herbs—purslane, basil, and fern, which grow in several places—I have seen no trees, herbs, or fruits that are not different from ours. Therefore every time that the image of this new world which God has let me see presents itself before my eyes, and I consider the serenity of the air, the diversity of the animals, the variety of the birds, the beauty of the trees and the plants, the excellence of the fruits, and, in short, the riches that adorn this land of Brazil, the exclamation of the Prophet in Psalm 104 comes to my mind: "O Lord, how manifold are thy works! In wisdom hast thou made them all: the earth is full of thy riches."[11]

Thus, happy would be the people who dwell there, if they knew the Author and Creator of all these things; but I am about to treat matters which will show how far removed they are from such knowledge.

ऊ

# OF THE WAR,
## COMBATS, BOLDNESS, AND
### ARMS OF THE SAVAGES OF AMERICA[1]

Our Tupinikin Tupinamba follow the custom of all the other savages who live in that fourth part of the world, which includes more than two thousand leagues of latitude, from the Strait of Magellan, lying fifty degrees toward the Antarctic Pole, to Newfoundland, at about sixty degrees on the Arctic side: that is, they wage deadly warfare against a number of nations of their region. However, their closest and principal enemies are those whom they call *Margaia,* and their allies the Portuguese, whom they call *Pero;*[2] reciprocally, the Margaia are hostile not only to the Tupinamba, but also to the French, their confederates.

But these barbarians do not wage war to win countries and lands from each other, for each has more than he needs; even less do the conquerors aim to get rich from the spoils, ransoms, and arms of the vanquished: that is not what drives them. For, as they themselves confess, they are impelled by no other passion than that of avenging, each for his side, his own kinsmen and friends who in the past have been seized and eaten, in the manner that I will describe in the next chapter; and they pursue each other so relentlessly that whoever falls into the hands of his enemy must expect to be treated, without any compromise, in the same manner: that is, to be slain and eaten.[3] Furthermore, from the time that war has been declared among any of these nations, everyone claims that since an enemy who has received an injury will resent it forever, one would be remiss to let him escape when he is at one's mercy; their hatred is so inveterate that they can never be reconciled. On this point one can say that Machiavelli and his disciples (with whom France, to her great misfortune, is now filled) are true imitators of barbarian cruelties; for since these atheists teach and practice, against Christian doctrine, that new services must never cause old injuries to be forgotten—that is, that men, participating in the devil's nature, must not pardon each other—do they not show their hearts to be more cruel and malign than those of tigers?[4]

Now according to what I have seen, here is how our Tupinenquin assemble to go to war. Although they have neither kings nor princes, and consequently are all almost equally great lords, nevertheless nature has taught them (and this was also strictly observed among the Lacedae-monians) that the old men, whom they call *peore-rou-picheh*, because of their experience of the past must be respected, and thus the elders of each village are generally obeyed. Walking about, or seated in their suspended cotton beds, they exhort the others something like this:

"What!" they will say, speaking each in turn, without interrupting each other by a single word, "have our ancestors, who have not only so valiantly fought, but also subjugated, killed, and eaten so many enemies, left us their example so that we should stay at home, effeminate and cowardly of heart? In the past our nation was so greatly feared and dreaded by all the others that they could not stand their ground before us; must our enemies, to our great shame and confusion, now have the honor of coming to seek us out at our very hearths? Will our cowardice give the Margaia and the *Peros-engaipa,*[5] those two worthless allied nations, the occasion to attack us first?" Then the speaker, slapping his shoulders and his buttocks, will exclaim: *Erima, erima, Toüpinambaoults, conomi ouassou tan tan,* and so forth, that is, "No, no, my countrymen, strong and valiant young men, we must not do thus; we must prepare ourselves to go find them, and either let ourselves all be killed and eaten, or avenge our own."

After these old men's orations (which sometimes last more than six hours), each of the hearers, having listened attentively and not missed a word, would feel heartened and emboldened; sending word to each other from village to village, they would directly assemble in haste, and meet in great numbers in the assigned place. But before we have our Tupinamba march in battle, we must know what their weapons are. First, they have their *tacapes,* that is, swords or clubs, some made of red wood and others of black wood, usually five or six feet long. The end is round or oval-shaped, about two hands wide and more than an inch thick through the middle; the edges are so finely sharpened that the weapon, being made of a wood as dense as boxwood, is almost as keen as an axe, and I think that two of the most skillful swordsmen from over here would find themselves kept very busy if they were dealing with one of our furious Tupinamba with one of these in his hand.

Second, they have their bows, which they call *orapats,* made of those same black and red woods, which are so much longer and stronger than ours that one of our men could not begin to bend it, let alone shoot

113

with it; on the contrary, he would have all he could manage with one used by the boys of nine or ten. The strings of these bows, made of a herb that the savages call *tocon,* are very slender, but so strong that they would resist the pull of a horse. Their arrows are about five feet long, and made of three pieces: that is, the middle is made out of reed, and the two other parts of black wood. These pieces are so precisely fitted together and bound with little peelings of bark that they could not be better joined. Their arrows have only two feathers, each one a foot long, which (since they use no glue) are also very neatly bound with cotton thread. At the tip they put pointed bones on some, on others a half a foot of dried and hardened cane, fashioned like a lancet and just as sharp; and sometimes the end of the tail of a rayfish, which is extremely venomous. Since the arrival of the French and Portuguese, the savages in imitation of them have begun to use an arrowhead of iron, or, failing that, a nail's point.

I have already told how dexterously they handle their swords. As for the bow—and those who have seen them about their business will confirm what I say—with their naked arms they bend their bows and shoot so straight and so rapidly that, with all due respect to the English (who are regarded as such good bowmen), our savages, holding their arrows in the same hand that holds the bow, will have sent off a dozen before the English have loosed six.

Finally, they have their bucklers, made from the thickest dried leather off the back of the animal that they call *tapiroussou* (of which I have spoken earlier); they are large, flat, and round like the bottom of a German drum. When they come to hand-to-hand fighting, they do not cover themselves with them as our own soldiers do; they use them in combat only to ward off the arrows of their enemies.

So those are what our Americans have for weapons. As for the rest, they do not cover their bodies with anything at all; on the contrary (aside from their headdresses, bracelets, and short feather garments), if they were wearing even a shirt, they would strip it off when they go to combat, so as not to be encumbered.

If we gave them keen-edged swords (I presented one of mine as a gift to a good old man), they would immediately throw away the scabbards, just as they do with the sheaths of the knives they are given. At first they took pleasure in seeing them glisten, or in cutting branches with them, rather than considering them fit weapons for battle. And indeed, truth to tell, they handle their own swords so skillfully (as I have said) that the latter are more dangerous in their hands.

We had also brought over there a number of cheap harquebuses for

114

trade with the savages. Such was their skill at this that it took three of them to fire a single cannon: one would hold it, another take aim, and a third ignite it. However, they would load and fill the cannon clear to the end; so that if we had not given them, instead of fine powder, some composed half of crushed coal, they would certainly have been in danger of killing themselves by having the whole thing blow up in their hands.[6]

At first, when they heard the sounds of our artillery, and the shots from the harquebuses that we were firing, they were astonished; when they saw some of us, in their very presence, bring down a bird out of a tree, or a wild animal in the middle of the fields, they were amazed mainly because they didn't see the exit or the passage of the bullet. However, once they had come to understand how it was done, they said that they would have loosed five or six arrows with their bows sooner than you could have loaded and fired one shot with a harquebus—which is true— and they began to be confident about confronting one of these in battle. Now if someone says at this point: "Yes, but the harquebus makes a much bigger hole," I reply that whatever ox-hide collars or even shirts of mail one might have (unless they were made expressly for the purpose), our savages, strong and robust, shoot so straight that they will pierce through the body of a man as easily with an arrow as another will do with a harquebus shot. It would have been more appropriate to treat this point later, when I speak of their combats; therefore, so as not to confuse matters further, I am going to put our Tupinamba in the field to march against their enemies.

So they are assembled, by the means described to you, in the number of sometimes eight or ten thousand men; there are many women along as well, not to fight, but only to carry the cotton beds and the flour and other foodstuffs. The old men who have killed and eaten the greatest number of enemies are ordained as chiefs and leaders by the others, and everyone sets forth under their guidance. Although they keep no rank or order while marching, when they go by land they are in serried troops with the most valiant in the lead; and it is a wonder how that whole multitude, without field-marshall or quarter-master, can so conjoin that, without any confusion, you will always see them ready to march at the first signal.

When they are leaving their territory, or moving on from the places where they stop along the way, some of them issue a trumpet-call in order to get the attention of the troops; these trumpets, which they call *inubia*, are of the thickness and length of a half-pike, and at the bottom end about a half a foot wide, like an oboe. Some of the men even have fifes and flutes made from the armbones and thighbones of those who have been killed and eaten by them, on which—to stir each other up to do the same to those against whom they are advancing—they pipe continually as they march.

If they are going by water (which they often do), they line up in their boats, which they call *ygat,* and hug the shore, hardly venturing into the open sea. Each of these boats is made of the bark of a single tree stripped from top to bottom; nonetheless they are so big that each can hold forty or fifty persons. They customarily move over the water standing up, using a paddle flattened at both ends, which they hold by the middle. These boats, which are quite flat, sit no deeper in the water than a plank, and are very easy to steer and handle. It is true that they could not endure a high and turbulent sea, much less a storm; but when our savages go to war in calm weather, you will sometimes see a fleet of more than sixty, following close on each other, and moving so fast that they are soon lost from view. These then are the land and naval forces of our Tupinenquin.

They ordinarily go twenty-five or thirty leagues to seek out their enemies; when they approach their territory, here are the first ruses and stratagems of war that they use to capture them. The most skillful and valiant, leaving the others with the women one or two days' journey behind them, approach as stealthily as they can to lie in ambush in the woods; they are so determined to surprise their enemies that they will sometimes lie hidden there more than twenty-four hours. If the enemy is taken unawares, all who are seized, be they men, women or children, will be led away; and when the attackers are back in their own territory all the prisoners will be slain, put in pieces on the *boucan,* and finally eaten. Such surprise attacks are all the easier to spring in that the villages—there are no cities—cannot be closed, and they have no doors in their houses (which are mostly eighty to a hundred feet long, with openings in several places) unless they block the entrances with branches of palm, or of that big plant called *pindo.* However, around some villages on the enemy frontier, those most skilled at warfare plant stakes of palm five or six feet high, and on the approaches to the paths they go around and stick sharpened wooden pegs into the earth, with their points just above ground level. If the assailants think to enter by night, as is their custom, the inhabitants, who know the narrow path they can follow without hurting themselves, go out and repel them in such a way that, whether the attackers want to flee or to fight, some of them always wound their feet and fall on the spot, and the others then make carbonadoes of them.

If the enemies are warned of each others' approach, and the two

Portrait du combat entre les sauuages Tououpinambaoults & Margajas Ameriquains.

Ce portraict se doit mettre entre le feuillet 204. & 205. apres Q. iiij.

armies come to confront each other, the combat is cruel and terrible beyond belief—which I can vouch for, having myself been a spectator. For another Frenchman and I, out of curiosity, and taking our chances of being captured and either killed on the spot or eaten by the Margaia, once went to accompany about four thousand of our savages in a battle that took place on the seashore; we saw these barbarians fight with such a fury that madmen could do no worse.

First, when our Tupinamba had caught sight of their enemies from something less than a half mile away, they broke out into such howls (our wolf-hunters over here make nothing like such a noise), and their clamor so rent the air that if the heavens had thundered we would not have heard it. As they approached, redoubling their cries, sounding their trumpets, brandishing the bones of prisoners who had been eaten, and even showing off the victims' teeth strung in rows—some had more than ten feet of them hanging from their necks—their demeanor was terrifying to behold.

But when they came to join battle it was still worse: for as soon as they were within two or three hundred feet of each other, they saluted each other with great volleys of arrows, and you would have seen an infinity of them soar through the air as thick as flies. If some were hit, as several were, they tore the arrows out of their bodies with a marvelous courage, breaking them and like mad dogs biting the pieces; all wounded as they were, they would not be kept from returning to the combat. It must be noted here that these Americans are so relentless in their wars that as long as they can move arms and legs, they fight on unceasingly, neither retreating nor turning their backs. When they finally met in hand-to-hand combat, it was with their wooden swords and clubs, charging each other with great two-handed blows; whoever hit the head of his enemy not only knocked him to the ground but struck him dead, as our butchers fell oxen.

I will not touch on whether they were well or badly mounted, for I assume that the reader will remember what I said earlier: that there are no horses or other mounts in their country; they all went (and still go) on foot. I often wished while I was over there that our savages could see horses; but at that moment I wished more than ever that I myself had a good one between my legs. And indeed, I think that if they were to see one of our men of arms, well mounted and armed with a pistol in his hand, making his horse leap and wheel—if they could see the fire bursting out on one side and the fury of the man and the horse on the other—they would think on first sight that it was Aygnan—that is, in their language, the devil.

118

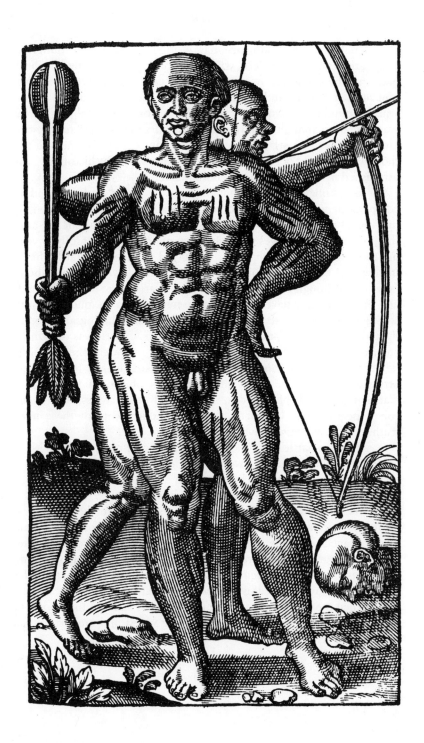

On this subject someone has written a remarkable thing. Atta-balipa, the great king of Peru, who in our time was subjugated by Pizarro, had never before seen horses; the Spanish captain who first went to seek him out, as a trick, and in order to amaze the Indians, made his horse wheel around at a gallop right up to the person of Attabalipa. The latter was so fearless that although drops of the horse's foam spattered onto his face, he showed no sign of discomposure, but gave the command to kill those who had fled before the horse: "a thing," says the historian, "which astonished his people and made ours marvel."[a]

To resume my discussion: if you now ask, "And you and your companion, what were you doing during that skirmish? Weren't you fighting along with the savages?" To make no pretence about it, I answer that, contenting ourselves with having committed that first folly of ventur-ing forth with these barbarians, we stayed in the rear guard where we merely had the pastime of judging the blows. I will say this about it, however: although I have often seen men of arms over here, both on foot and on horseback, nevertheless I have never taken so much pleasure in seeing the infantry, with their gilded helmets and shining arms, as I de-lighted then in seeing those savages do battle.[7] There was not only the entertainment of seeing them leap, whistle, and wield their swords so dexterously in circles and passades; it was also a marvel to see so many arrows fly in the air and sparkle in the sunbeams with their grand featherings of red, blue, green, scarlet, and other colors, and so many robes, headdresses, bracelets, and other adornments of these natural feathers with which the savages were arrayed.

After this battle had gone on for about three hours, and on both sides there were many dead and wounded lying on the field, our Tupinamba finally carried the victory. They captured more than thirty Margaia, men and women, whom they took off into their own territory. Although we two Frenchmen had done nothing (as I have said) except hold our drawn swords in our hands, and sometimes fire a few pistol shots into the air to give courage to our side, still, since there was nothing we could have done to give them greater pleasure than to go with them to war, they continued to hold us in such high esteem that, since that time, the elders of the villages we visited always showed us the greatest affection.[8]

When the prisoners had been placed in the midst of the troops, near those who had captured them, and the strongest and most robust men

---

[a][Gómara,] *Histoire*, Book 4, Chapter 113.

bound and tied with cords for better security, we made our way back toward the bay of Janeiro where our savages lived, a journey of twelve or fifteen leagues. As we passed through the villages of our allies, you can well imagine that they came out to meet us, and applauded and made much of us, dancing, leaping, and clapping their hands. Finally, when we arrived near our island, my companions and I took a boat to our fort, and the savages took off for the mainland, each to his own village.

A few days later, when some of our Tupinamba who had these prisoners in their houses came to see us in our fort, our interpreters entreated them to sell some of them to Villegagnon, and thus a number were rescued by us out of their hands. However, when I bought a woman and a little boy of hers who was less than two years old (who cost me about three francs' worth of goods), I discovered that their captors were of two minds about it: for the man who sold me the prisoners said, "I don't know what will come of all this: for since Paycolas" (meaning Villegagnon) "has come over here, we have scarcely eaten half of our enemies." I had thought to keep the little boy for myself; but Villegagnon made me hand over all my merchandise, and wanted to have everything for himself. What is more, when I told the mother that I would bring him over here with me when I returned across the sea, she replied—so deeply rooted is vengeance in that nation's heart—that she had hoped that when her son grew up he would have been able to escape and go back and join the Margaia so as to avenge them, but that she would have preferred that he be eaten by the Tupinamba than go off so far from her. However (as I have said elsewhere), about four months after we had arrived in that country, out of forty or fifty slaves who were working in our fort (whom we had also bought from the savages who were our allies) we chose ten young boys whom we sent to France in the returning ships, to Henry II, who was reigning at that time.

121

ﾗﾏ

# HOW THE AMERICANS
## TREAT THEIR PRISONERS
### OF WAR AND THE CEREMONIES THEY
### OBSERVE BOTH IN KILLING AND IN
### ~~EATING THEM~~

It now remains to be seen just how prisoners of war are treated in the land of their enemies.[1] As soon as they arrive, not only are they fed with the best food that can be found, but also the men are given wives (the women prisoners, however, are not given husbands); he who has a prisoner will not hesitate to give him even his daughter or his sister in marriage, and the wife that the prisoner gets will treat him well and minister to all his needs. Furthermore, they will keep these captives for greater or lesser periods of time, without any predetermined limit, according to whether they find the men good hunters, or good fishermen, and the women adept at gardening or at gathering oysters;[2] nonetheless, after being fattened like pigs at the trough, the captives are finally slain and eaten, with the following ceremonies.[3]

First, all the villages in the vicinity of the one holding the prisoner are told of the day of execution; men, women, and children arrive from all directions, and begin to dance and to drink *caouin* and revel throughout the morning. Even he who is not unaware that this gathering is on his account, and that in a short time he will be clubbed to death in all his feathered regalia, is by no means downcast; on the contrary, leaping about and drinking, he will be one of the merriest ones there. However, after he has sung and caroused for six or seven hours, two or three of the most respected in the throng will take hold of him, and bind him with ropes made of cotton or of the bark of a tree that they call *yvire*, which is like our linden; without his offering any resistance, even though both his arms are left free, he will be walked for a little while through the village, and displayed as a trophy. But for all that, do you think that he bows his head, as our criminals over here would do? By no means: on the contrary, with an incredible audacity and assurance, he will boast of his past feats of prowess, saying to those who hold him bound: "I myself, who am valiant, first bound and tied your kinsmen." Then, exalting himself more and more, with a demeanor to match, he will turn from side to side and say to one, "I have eaten your father," and to another, "I have struck down and *boucané* your brothers." He will add, "Of you Tupinamba that I have taken in war, I have eaten so many men and women and even children that I could not tell the number; and do not doubt that, to avenge my death, the Margaia, whose nation I belong to, will hereafter eat as many of you as they can catch."[4]

Finally, after he has been thus exposed to everyone's view, the two savages who hold him bound, backing off about five yards from him, one to the right and one to the left, still holding on to equal lengths of rope, each then pull hard enough so that the captive, caught by the middle of the body, is held up short, and cannot move from one side or the other. Next, they bring him stones and shards of broken old pots; then the two who hold the ropes, protecting themselves against injury with shields made of *tapiroussou* skin, say to him, "Avenge yourself before you die." So he throws these missiles, hurling them hard at those who are gathered around him, sometimes in numbers of three or four thousand; you need hardly ask if some carry away the marks of this. In fact, one day when I was in a village called *Sarigoy*, I saw a prisoner hit a woman's leg so hard with a stone that I thought he had broken it.

Now when the captive has hurled everything he could pick up near him on the ground—stones, even clods of earth—he who is to strike the blow, who has not yet shown himself all that day, comes out of a house gripping one of those great wooden swords, richly decorated with beautiful feathers of the finest quality, as are also his headdress and his other adornments. He approaches the prisoner with, for instance, "Are you not of the nation called Margaia, which is our enemy? And have you not yourself killed and eaten of our kinsmen and our friends?" The prisoner, more fearless than ever, replies in his language (for the Margaia and the Tupinenquin understand each other) "*Pa, che tan tan, ajouca atoupave*": that is, "Yes, I am very strong, and have slain and eaten a great many." Then, to spite his enemies still further, putting his hands on his head with vehemence, he says, "O, I have never hesitated: how bold I have been in attacking and seizing your people, of whom I have eaten time and time again," and so he goes on. "And for that reason," says he who is standing there ready to slaughter him, "since you are now here in our power, you will presently be killed by me, and then roasted on the *boucan* and eaten

by all the rest of us." "Very well," replies the prisoner (as resolved to be slain for his nation as Regulus was steadfast in enduring death for his Roman Republic), "my kinsmen will avenge me in turn."

Although these barbarian nations have great fear of natural death, nonetheless such prisoners consider themselves fortunate to die thus publicly, in the midst of their enemies, and are utterly untroubled.[5] In demonstration of this I will cite an example. One day I unexpectedly found myself in a village on the big island called *Piraui-jou*, where there was a woman prisoner all ready to be slain. I approached her, and, trying to adapt my speech to hers, told her to entrust herself to the care of *Toupan* ("Toupan" among them does not mean "God," but rather "thunder"), and to pray to him as I would teach her how to do.[a] Her only response was to shake her head, and say to me in mockery, "What will you give me if I do as you say?" I answered, "Poor wretch, soon you will need nothing more in this world, and therefore, since you believe the soul to be immortal" (which they all confess, as I will recount in the next chapter) "think what will become of it after your death." But she merely laughed again, and was felled with a blow and so died.

But to continue: after these contestations, and most often while they are still speaking to each other, he who is there ready to perform this slaughter lifts his wooden club with both hands and brings down the rounded end of it with such force on the head of the poor prisoner that— just as our butchers slay oxen over here—I have seen some who fell stonedead on the first blow, without ever after moving an arm or a leg. It is true that when they are stretched out on the ground, you see them twitch and tremble, because of the retracting sinews and blood; but whatever the case may be, those who perform the execution usually hit the skull so accurately, and aim so precisely at the spot behind the ear, that, while scarcely shedding any blood, they need no more than one try to end a life. It is the custom in that land to use an expression already habitual with our Frenchmen: in their quarrels, soldiers and others now say to each other instead of "I'll kill you," "I'll break your head."

Now as soon as the prisoner has been thus slain, if he had a wife (for, as I have said, wives are given to some of them), she will perform some slight mourning beside the body—and "slight mourning" is just what I mean. For as one says of the crocodile, that having killed a man, he then weeps just before eating him, so too after the woman has made some

---

[a][Toupan and the use of this concept by Christian missionaries, is treated in Chap. XVI.]

or another lamentation, and shed a few feigned tears over her dead husband, she will, if she can, be the first to eat of him. Then the other women, and chiefly the old ones (who, more covetous of eating human flesh than the young ones, incessantly importune all those who have prisoners to dispatch them quickly),[6] come forward with hot water that they have ready, and scald and rub the dead body to remove its outer skin, and blanch it the way our cooks over here do when they prepare a suckling pig for roasting.

After that, the one who owned the prisoner, with as many neighbors of his own choosing as he pleases, will take this poor body, cleave it and immediately cut it into pieces; no butcher in this country could more quickly dismember a sheep. But even beyond that—O more than prodigious cruelty—just as our huntsmen over here, after taking a stag, give the quarry to their hounds, so, too, these barbarians, in order to incite their children to share their vengefulness, take them one at a time and rub their bodies, arms, thighs, and legs with the blood of their enemies. Since the arrival of Christians in that region, the savages have been using the knives and other iron tools they have received from them to cut up the bodies of their prisoners or of animals, as well as other kinds of food. But before that time, as I have heard from the old men, they had no tools for the task other than sharp-edged stones shaped for the purpose.

Now after all the pieces of the body, including the guts, have been thoroughly cleaned, they are immediately put on the *boucans*. While it all cooks according to their style, the old women (who, as I have said, have an amazing appetite for human flesh) are all assembled beside it to receive the fat that drips off along the posts of the big, high wooden grills, and exhort the men to do what it takes to provide them always with such meat. Licking their fingers, they say, "*Yguatou*": that is, "It is good."

And there you have it, just as I have seen it, the way the American savages cook the flesh of their prisoners of war: that is, on the *boucan*, which is a way of roasting unknown to us.

In Chapter X, on animals, I have explained at length the style of the *boucan* while speaking of the *tapiroussou*; therefore, to avoid repetition I ask the readers, the better to imagine it, to refer to that passage. However, I shall here refute the error of those who, in their maps of the world, have represented and painted the Brazilian savages roasting human flesh on a spit, as we cook mutton legs and other meat; furthermore, they have also falsely shown them cutting it with great iron knives on benches, and hanging up the meat for display, as our beef butchers do over here. Since these things are no truer than the tales of Rabelais about Panurge escaping from the spit larded and half-cooked,[7] it is easy to see that those who make such maps are ignorant, and have never had knowledge of the things they set forth. In confirmation of this, let me add an anecdote to my description of the way the Brazilians cook their prisoners' flesh: while I was in their country, they were so ignorant of our way of roasting meat that one day in a village, when some of my companions and I were cooking a guinea hen with some other poultry on a spit, they laughed at us, and, seeing the meat continually turn, refused to believe that it could cook, until experience showed them so.

To get back to what I was saying. When the flesh of a prisoner, or of several (for they sometimes kill two or three in a day) is thus cooked, all those who have been present to see the slaughter performed gather again joyfully around the *boucans,* on which they gaze with a furious and covetous eye, contemplating the pieces and members of their enemies. However many of them there are, each of them will, if possible, have his morsel. Not, however (as far as one can judge) that they regard this as nourishment; for although all of them confess human flesh to be wonderfully good and delicate, nonetheless it is more out of vengeance than for the taste (except for what I said specifically concerning the old women, who find it such a delicacy); their chief intention is that by pursuing the dead and gnawing them right down to the bone, they will strike fear and terror into the hearts of the living. And in fact, to satisfy their ferocity, everything that can be found in the bodies of such prisoners, from the tips of the toes up to the nose, ears, and scalp, is entirely eaten by them; all except, however, the brain, which they do not touch at all.[8]

Furthermore, our Tupinamba save the skulls, piling them up in heaps in their villages, like the deaths'-heads we see in our cemeteries over here. The first thing they do when the French go to visit them is to recount their valiant deeds, and show them these fleshless skulls as trophies, saying that they will do the same thing to all their enemies. As I said in the previous chapter, they also very carefully save the biggest bones of the thighs and the arms for making fifes and flutes, and they keep the teeth as well, which they pull out and string like rosary beads, and wear wound around their necks. The *History of the Indies,* describing the inhabitants of the island of Zamba, says that they attach to the doors of their houses the heads of those they have slain and sacrificed, and the more to swagger they also wear the teeth hanging from their necks.[a]

---

[a][Gómara,] Book 2, Chapter 71.

As for those who have committed these murders, they think that it is to their great glory and honor; the same day that they have dealt the blow they withdraw and have incisions made, to the point of drawing blood, on their chests, thighs, the thick part of the legs, and other parts of the body.[9] And so that it may be visible all their lives, they rub these slits with certain mixtures and with a black powder that cannot ever be effaced. The more slashes they carry, the more renowned they will be for having killed many prisoners, and they are consequently esteemed the more valiant by the others. (So that you can understand this more clearly, I have repeated the illustration of the savage covered with slashes, next to whom there is another one drawing a bow.)

To conclude this strange tragedy: if it happens that the women given to the prisoners are with child by them, the savages who have killed the fathers, claiming that such children have sprung from the seed of their enemies (a horrible thing to hear, and what follows is still worse to see), will eat them immediately after they are born; or, if they prefer, they will let them get a little bigger before taking that step.[10] And not only do these barbarians delight above all in thus exterminating, so far as is in their power, the race against whom they are at war (for the Margaia offer the same treatment to the Tupinamba when they capture them), they also take a singular pleasure in seeing foreigners who are their allies do likewise. So when they presented us with the human flesh of their prisoners to eat, if we refused it (as I and many others of us have always done, not having, thank God, forgotten ourselves to that point), it seemed to them that we were not showing proper loyalty.

Concerning this, to my great regret I am compelled to recount here that some Norman interpreters, who had lived eight or nine years in that country, accommodating themselves to the natives and leading the lives of atheists, not only polluted themselves by all sorts of lewd and base behavior among the women and girls (by whom one of them had a boy about three years old when I was there), but some of them, surpassing the savages in inhumanity, even boasted in my hearing of having killed and eaten prisoners.[11]

Let me continue describing the cruelty of the Tupinamba toward their enemies. While we were over there, it happened that they remembered there was a village on the Great Island, inhabited by certain of the enemy Margaia, who had surrendered to them as soon as their war began—that is, about twenty years earlier. Since that time they had always let the Margaia live in peace among them; however, one day while

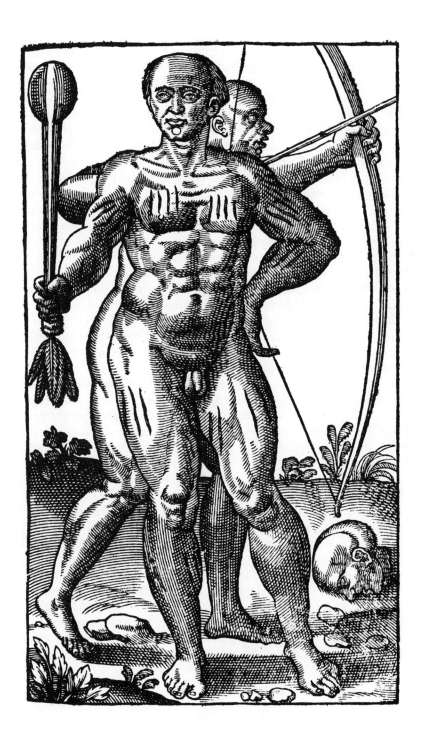

they were carousing and drinking their *caouin*, they began to egg each other on, and to remind each other that these were, as I said, people sprung from their mortal enemies. So they resolved to sack the whole village. And in fact, one night, putting their resolution into practice, they took these poor people by surprise, and wreaked such carnage and such butchery that it was piteous beyond compare to hear the cries.

Several of our Frenchmen were alerted; they left by boat around midnight, well armed, heading in great haste for the village, which was only four or five leagues from our fort. But before they could get there, our savages, enraged and relentlessly pursuing their prey, and having set fire to the houses to force the people out, had already killed so many that it was almost over. I even heard some of our men report, upon returning, that they had seen not only a number of men and women cut in pieces and grilled on the *boucans*, but also little unweaned children roasted whole. There were, however, a few adults who, having thrown themselves into the sea, and having escaped by swimming under the cover of night, came to yield themselves up to us on our island. Our savages, upon discovering this several days later, muttered through their teeth at our keeping them, and were mightily displeased. Nevertheless, after being appeased by some merchandise that they were given, they somewhat grudgingly left them as slaves for Villegagnon.

Another time, when four or five Frenchmen and I were in a village of the same big island, called *Piraui-jou*, there was a prisoner, a handsome and powerful young man, shackled in irons that our savages had obtained from the Christians. He approached us, and said in Portuguese (two of our company spoke good Spanish and could understand him easily) that he had been in Portugal, and had become a Christian: he had been baptized, and was called "Antoni." So although he was of the Margaia nation, by visiting other countries he had shed some of his barbarian ways, and he let us know that he greatly desired to be delivered out of the hands of his enemies. Aside from its being our duty to rescue as many as we could, when we heard these words "Christian" and "Antoni" we were especially moved to compassion for him. So one of our company who understood Spanish, a locksmith by trade, told him that the very next day he would bring him a file to remove his irons. We were to distract the others with conversation while he, as soon as he was free of the irons, was to go hide on the seashore, in a certain thicket that we would show him, where we would, without fail, pick him up in our boat as we left the island. We even told him that if we could get him to our fort, we would come to an agreement with those who held him prisoner.

The poor man, rejoicing at the means of escape that we were offering him, thanked us and promised to do everything just as we had advised him. But the rabble of savages, although they had not heard this conversation, nonetheless suspected that we intended to take him out of their hands. As soon as we had left their village, they quickly called together only their closest neighbors to be spectators of their prisoner's death, and he was immediately slain by them. The next day, pretending to go fetch flour and other supplies, we went back to this village with the file, and asked the savages the whereabouts of the prisoner whom we had seen the previous day. Some of them took us to a house where we saw the pieces of the body of poor Antoni on the *boucan;* they knew they had tricked us, and they showed us his head with great peals of laughter.[12]

Likewise, one day our savages surprised two Portuguese, in a little house made of earth in the woods, near their fort called *Morpion.*[13] The Portuguese defended themselves valiantly from morning to night; after their supply of harquebuses and crossbow arrows was exhausted, they came out with two-handed swords, with which they countered the blows of their assailants so well that many were killed and others wounded. However, the savages, attacking more and more relentlessly, resolved to be cut to pieces rather than withdraw without a victory. Finally they laid hold of the two Portuguese and took them prisoner. Of their spoils, a savage sold me some ox-skin garments, and one of our interpreters obtained a silver plate that they had pillaged, along with some other things from the house that they had broken into; since they were unaware of its value, it only cost him two knives. When they returned to their villages, they tore the beards out of these two Portuguese merely to humiliate them, and then put them cruelly to death. What is more, because these poor tortured men cried out in their pain, the savages mocked them, saying "What is this? Can it be that you have so bravely defended yourselves, and now, when it is the moment to die with honor, you show that you have not even as much courage as women?" And thus they were killed and eaten in the savage style.

I could add similar examples of the cruelty of the savages toward their enemies, but it seems to me that what I have said is enough to horrify you, indeed, to make your hair stand on end. Nevertheless, so that those who read these horrible things, practiced daily among these barbarous nations of the land of Brazil, may also think more carefully about

the things that go on every day over here, among us:[14] In the first place, if
you consider in all candor what our big usurers do, sucking blood and
marrow, and eating everyone alive—widows, orphans, and other poor
people, whose throats it would be better to cut once and for all, than to
make them linger in misery—you will say that they are even more cruel
than the savages I speak of. And that is why the prophet says that such
men flay the skin of God's people, eat their flesh, break their bones and
chop them in pieces as for the pot, and as flesh within the cauldron.[a]

Furthermore, if it comes to the brutal action of really (as one says)[15]
chewing and devouring human flesh, have we not found people in these
regions over here, even among those who bear the name of Christian, both
in Italy and elsewhere, who, not content with having cruelly put to death
their enemies, have been unable to slake their bloodthirst except by eating
their livers and their hearts? I defer to the histories.[16] And, without going
further, what of France? (I am French, and it grieves me to say it.) During
the bloody tragedy that began in Paris on the twenty-fourth of August
1572[b]—for which I do not accuse those who are not responsible—among
other acts horrible to recount, which were perpetrated at that time throughout the kingdom, the fat of human bodies (which, in ways more barbarous
than those of the savages, were butchered at Lyon after being pulled out of
the Saône)—was it not publicly sold to the highest bidder? The livers,
hearts, and other parts of these bodies—were they not eaten by the furious
murderers, of whom Hell itself stands in horror? Likewise, after the
wretched massacre of one Coeur de Roy, who professed the Reformed
Faith in the city of Auxerre—did not those who committed this murder cut
his heart to pieces, display it for sale to those who hated him, and finally,
after grilling it over coals—glutting their rage like mastiffs—eat of it?

There are thousands alive today who beheld these things never
before heard of among people anywhere, and the books about them,
printed long since, will bear witness for posterity.[c] So it is not without
cause that someone (whose name I confess I do not know), after that
execrable butchery of the French people, recognizing that it surpassed all
those that had ever been heard of, wrote the following verses to give it its
due emphasis:

---

[a]Micah 3.3.

[b][The St. Bartholomew Day Massacre.]

[c]*Histoire de notre temps: [contenant un recueil des choses mémorables passées et publiés
pour le faict de la religion et estat de la France, depuis l'Edict de paciffication du 23.jour de
Mars, 1568, iusques au iour présent* (1578)], Book 7, p. 22.

Laugh, Pharaoh,
Ahab and Nero,
Herod too;
Your barbarity
By this deed
Is buried from view.

So let us henceforth no longer abhor so very greatly the cruelty of the anthropophagous—that is, man-eating—savages. For since there are some here in our midst even worse and more detestable than those who, as we have seen, attack only enemy nations, while the ones over here have plunged into the blood of their kinsmen, neighbors, and compatriots, one need not go beyond one's own country, nor as far as America, to see such monstrous and prodigious things.[17]

# C H A P T E R   X V I

 ❧

# WHAT ONE
## MIGHT CALL RELIGION
### AMONG THE SAVAGE AMERICANS: OF THE ERRORS IN WHICH CERTAIN CHARLATANS CALLED *CARAÏBES* HOLD THEM IN THRALL; AND OF THE GREAT IGNORANCE OF GOD IN WHICH THEY ARE PLUNGED[1]

Although the adage of Cicero is held by all as an indubitable maxim—
that there is no people so brutish, nor any nation so barbarous and
savage, as to have no feeling that there is a divinity—nonetheless when I
consider closely our Tupinamba of America, I find myself somewhat at a
loss in applying it to them.[2] Not only are they utterly ignorant of the sole
and true God; what is more, in contrast to the custom of all the ancient
pagans, who had many gods (as do the idolaters of today, even the
Indians of Peru—a land adjacent to theirs and about five hundred leagues
beyond it—who sacrifice to the sun and moon), they neither confess nor
worship any gods, either of heaven or of earth. Consequently, having no
rites nor any designated place of assembly for holding any ordinary service, they do not pray by any religious form to anything whatsoever,
either in public or in private. Likewise, being ignorant of the creation of
the world, they do not distinguish the days by names, nor do they give
one day preference over another, any more than they count weeks,
months or years; they only number and retain time by moons.

They know nothing of writing, either sacred or secular; indeed, they
have no kind of characters that signify anything at all. When I was first in
their country, in order to learn their language I wrote a number of sentences which I then read aloud to them. Thinking that this was some kind
of witchcraft, they said to each other, "Is it not a marvel that this fellow,

who yesterday could not have said a single word in our language, can now be understood by us, by virtue of that paper that he is holding and which makes him speak thus?"

And this is the same idea that the savages of Hispaniola had of the Spaniards who were first there: for he who wrote its history said that the Indians, knowing that the Spaniards understood each other without seeing or speaking to each other but only by sending letters from place to place, believed either that they had the spirit or prophecy, or that the missives spoke. The savages, he said, fearing that they would be caught red-handed, were by this means so firmly held to their duty that they no longer dared to lie to the Spaniards or steal from them.[a]

Here is a fine subject for anyone who would like to enlarge upon it: both to praise and to exalt the art of writing, and to show how the nations that inhabit these three parts of the world—Europe, Asia, and Africa—have reason to praise God more than do the savages of that fourth part, called "America." For while they can communicate nothing except by the spoken word, we, on the other hand, have this advantage, that without budging from our place, by means of writing and the letters that we send, we can declare our secrets to whomever we choose, even to the ends of the earth. So even aside from the learning that we acquire from books, of which the savages seem likewise completely destitute, this invention of writing, which we possess and of which they are just as utterly deprived, must be ranked among the singular gifts which men over here have received from God.[3]

To return to our Tupinamba. In our conversations with them, when it seemed the right moment, we would say to them that we believed in a sole and sovereign God, Creator of the World, who, as He made heaven and earth with all the things contained therein, also now governs and disposes of the whole as it pleases Him to do. Hearing us hold forth on this subject, they would look at each other, saying "Teh!"—their customary interjection of astonishment—and be struck with amazement. As I will recount at more length, when they hear thunder, which they call *Toupan*, they are much afraid. Adapting ourselves to their crudeness, we would seize the occasion to say to them that this was the very God of whom we were speaking, who to show his grandeur and power made heavens and earth tremble; their resolution and response was that since he frightened them in that way, he was good for nothing.[4]

---

[a][Gómara, *Histoire,*] Book I, Chapter 34.

And that, sad to say, is where these poor people are now. "What!" someone will now say, "can it be that, like brute beasts, these Americans live without any religion at all?" Indeed they do, or with almost none; I think that there is no nation on earth that is further from it. Still, let me begin by declaring what light I perceived that they do, nevertheless, possess in the midst of the dense shadows of ignorance where they lie in bondage: in the first place, not only do they believe in the immortality of souls, but they also firmly maintain that after the death of bodies, the souls of those who have lived virtuously (that is, according to them, those who have properly avenged themselves and have eaten many of their enemies) go off behind the high mountains where they dance in beautiful gardens with the souls of their forebears (these are the Elysian Fields of the poets);[5] while on the contrary, the souls of the effeminate and worthless, who have neglected the defense of their fatherland, go with Aygnan (for so they call the devil in their language), by whom, they say, these unworthy ones are incessantly tormented.[6]

And here it must be noted that these poor people are so afflicted throughout their lives with this evil spirit (whom they also call *Kaagerre*)[7] that when the torment comes upon them, they cry out suddenly as if in a fit of madness—as I have seen them do several times even while they were speaking to us, saying, "Alas, defend us from Aygnan, who is beating us." In fact, they would say that they actually saw him, sometimes in the guise of a beast or bird or in some other strange form. They marveled to see that we were not assaulted by him. When we told them that such exemption came from the God of whom we spoke so often and who, being incomparably stronger than Aygnan, kept him from molesting or harming us, it sometimes happened that, feeling hard-pressed, they would promise to believe in Him as we did. But, as the proverb says, "When danger is past we mock the saint," so as soon as they were delivered, they no longer remembered their promises. Nevertheless, to show that what they endure is no child's play: I have often seen them so apprehensive of this hellish fury that when they remembered what they had suffered in the past, they would strike their thighs with their hands, the sweat of anguish beading their brow, and lament to me or to another of our company, saying, "*Mair Atouassap, acequeiey Aygnan Atoupavé,*" that is, "Frenchman, my friend—my perfect ally—, I fear the devil (or the evil spirit) more than any other thing." On the other hand, if the one they addressed said to them, "*Nacequeiey Aygnan,*" that is, "I do not fear him," then, bewailing their state, they would answer, "Alas, how happy we would be if we were saved as you are!" "You would have to believe and trust, as we

do, in Him who is stronger and mightier," we would reply. But although at times, as they saw the evil approaching or already present, they declared they would do so, afterwards it all vanished from their brain.

Before going on, I will add something more to the remark I have made, that our American Brazilians consider the soul immortal. The historian of the West Indies said that the savages of Cuzco, the principal city of Peru, and those of that region, likewise confess the immortality of the soul. What is more (despite the maxim, which has always been commonly held by theologians, that all the philosophers, pagans, and other Gentiles and barbarians had been ignorant of and denied the resurrection of the flesh), they even believe in the resurrection of the body. And here is the example he offers: The Indians, upon seeing that the Spaniards who were opening the sepulchres to get at the gold and riches were scattering the bones of the dead all about, entreated them not to disperse them that way, lest it prevent them from being brought back to life; for they (the savages of that country) believe in the resurrection of the body and the immortality of the soul.[a] There is also another secular author who affirmed that in former times a certain pagan nation had arrived at this belief: "Afterwards Caesar vanquished Ariovistus and the Germans, who were great men beyond measure and fearless; for they attacked boldly and had no fear of death, confident that they would come back to life."[b]

I have wished expressly to recount all of this here, to demonstrate that if those worse-than-devil-ridden atheists, with whom our part of the earth is now covered, share with the Tupinamba the delusion—indeed, even stranger and more bestial in their case—that there is no God, they may at least learn from them, in the first place,[c] that even in this world there are devils to torment those who deny God and His power. They may reply that since there are no devils except the evil impulses of men, the belief in them is but a fantasy harbored by these savages about things that are not. To this I answer that if one considers what I have truly recounted—that the Americans are visibly and actually tormented by evil spirits—it will be easy to judge how wrong it is to attribute these things to human impulses. For however violent those passions might be, how could they afflict men in this way? I will not bother to mention our own

---

[a][Gómara,] *Histoire,* Book 4, Chapter 124.

[b]See Appian, *Of the Celtic War,* Chapter 1. [*De bellis civilibus et de bello celtico,* I: 3.]

[c][The second and third lessons are given in the next two paragraphs: the immortality of the soul and the resurrection of the body.]

experience of these things over here in Europe; and were it not that I would be throwing pearls before swine, I could cite what is said in the Gospel about those possessed by demons who were cured by the Son of God.[8]

In the second place, since these atheists, who, denying all principles, are utterly unworthy of having cited for them what the Scriptures say so magnificently about the immortality of souls, I will rather offer to them the example of our poor Brazilians, who, blind as they are, can yet teach them that there is in man a spirit which not only lives after the body dies, but also, when separated from the body, is susceptible of perpetual felicity or wretchedness.

And in the third place, regarding the resurrection of the flesh: inasmuch as these atheist dogs delude themselves by thinking that when the body is dead it never rises again, I cite the testimony of the Indians of Peru, who, in the midst of their false religion (indeed, having almost no knowledge other than natural feeling) will give the lie to the accursed atheists, and rise up in judgment against them. But since they are worse than the devils themselves—who, as St. James says, believe that there is a God, and tremble[a]—I do them too much honor in offering them these barbarians as theologians. Without speaking further at present of such abominable creatures, I send them straight to Hell, where they will taste the fruits of their monstrous errors.[9]

Let me return to my principal subject, and pursue the consideration of what might be called religion among the savages of America. If one examines closely what I have already touched on—that is, that they would desire to live in repose but are nevertheless forced, when they hear thunder, to tremble under a power they cannot resist—one can gather that Cicero's adage is verified through them after all: indeed, there is no people that does not have the feeling that there is a divinity. Moreover, one can see that this fear they have of Him whom they refuse to acknowledge will render them utterly without excuse. And indeed, it is said by the Apostle that although God in former times let all the Gentiles go their own way, nevertheless, He did not leave himself without witness, in that He did good to everyone, and gave us rain from heaven and the fruitful seasons:[b] this clearly shows us that when men do not recognize their Creator, it is a result of their own wickedness.[10] For further proof, it is

---

[a]James 2.19.
[b]Acts 14.17.

said elsewhere that the invisible things of God are clearly seen in the creation of the world.[a]

So although our Americans do not confess it with their lips, nonetheless inasmuch as they are convinced within themselves that there is some divinity, I concluded that just as they will not be exempt from judgment, so, too, they will not be able to plead ignorance. But beyond what I have said about their belief in the immortality of the soul, about the thunder that terrifies them, about the devils and evil spirits that beat them and torment them (three points to note), I will show in the fourth place how, despite the utter darkness in which they are plunged, the seed of religion (if, after all, what they do deserves that name) germinates in them and cannot be extinguished.[11]

To proceed further into this matter, you must know that there are among them certain false prophets that they call *caraïbes,* who, going and coming from village to village like popish indulgence-bearers, would have it believed that by their communication with spirits they can give to anyone they please the strength to vanquish enemies in war, and, what is more, can make grow the big roots and the fruits (which I have described elsewhere) produced by this land of Brazil.[12]

Now I had heard from the Norman interpreters who had lived a long time in that country that our Tupinamba held a solemn assembly every three or four years; since I once found myself by chance attending one of these, and here is what I can truthfully report. Another Frenchman named Jacques Rousseau and I, with an interpreter, were traveling through the country, and had spent one night in a village named *Cotiva.* The next morning very early, as we were about to move on, we saw the savages from the neighboring regions arriving from all directions, and being met by people of the village, who were coming out of their houses; five or six hundred were soon assembled in a large open place. We stopped and turned back to find out the purpose of this assembly, and saw them suddenly separate into three groups: all the men in one house, the women in another, and the children in a third. Seeing ten or twelve of these *caraïbe* gentlemen who had joined the men, and suspecting that they would do something extraordinary, I urged my companions to stay with me to see this mystery, and they agreed.

The *caraïbes,* before leaving the women and children, had strictly forbidden them to go out of their houses; rather they were to listen

---

[a]Romans 1.20.

attentively to the singing from there. They also ordered us to confine ourselves to the house where the women were. While we were having our breakfast, with no idea as yet of what they intended to do, we began to hear in the men's house (not thirty feet from where we stood) a very low murmur, like the muttering of someone reciting his hours. Upon hearing this, the women (about two hundred of them) all stood up and clustered together, listening intently. The men little by little raised their voices and were distinctly heard singing all together and repeating this syllable of exhortation, *He, he, he, he;* the women, to our amazement, answered them from their side, and with a trembling voice; reiterating that same interjection *He, he, he, he,* they let out such cries, for more than a quarter of an hour, that as we watched them we were utterly disconcerted.[13] Not only did they howl, but also, leaping violently into the air, they made their breasts shake and they foamed at the mouth—in fact, some, like those who have the falling-sickness over here, fell in a dead faint; I can only believe that the devil entered their body and that they fell into a fit of madness.[14] We heard the children similarly shaken and tormented in the house where they were kept, which was quite near us. Although I had been among the savages for more than half a year and was already fairly well used to their ways, nonetheless (to be frank) being somewhat frightened and not knowing how the game might turn out, I wished I were back at our fort. However, after these chaotic noises and howls had ended and the men had taken a short pause (the women and children were now silent), we heard them once again singing and making their voices resound in a harmony so marvelous that you would hardly have needed to ask whether, since I was now somewhat easier in my mind at hearing such sweet and gracious sounds, I wished to watch them from nearby.

When I was about to go out and draw near, the women held me back; also, our interpreter said that in the six or seven years that he had been in that country, he had never dared be present among the savages at such a ceremony: so that, he added, if I went over there I would be behaving imprudently and exposing myself to danger. For a moment I was undecided; however, as I sounded out the case further, it seemed to me that he gave me no good reason for what he said. Besides, I knew I could count on the friendship of certain kindly elders who lived in this village, which I had visited four or five times; so, willy-nilly, I ventured forth.

I drew near the place where I heard the chanting; the houses of the savages are very long and of a roundish shape (like the trellises of gardens over here). Since they are covered with grasses right down to the ground, in order to see as well as I might wish, I made with my hands a little opening in the covering. I beckoned to the two Frenchmen who were watching me; emboldened by my example, they drew near without any hindrance or difficulty, and we all three entered the house. Seeing that our entering did not disturb the savages as the interpreter thought it would, but rather, maintaining admirably their ranks and order, they continued their chants, we quietly withdrew into a corner to drink in the scene.

Now since I promised earlier, when I spoke of the dancing at their drinking bouts and *caouinages,* that I would also tell of their other way of dancing, the more fully to represent them, I will describe the solemn poses and gestures that they used here. They stood close to each other, without holding hands or stirring from their place, but arranged in a circle, bending forward, keeping their bodies slightly stiff, moving only the right leg and foot, with the right hand placed on the buttocks, and the left hand and arm hanging: in that posture they sang and danced.

Because there were so many of them, there were three circles, and in the middle of each circle there were three or four of these *caraïbes,* richly decked in robes, headdresses, and bracelets made of beautiful natural feathers of various colors, holding in each hand a *maraca* or rattle made of a fruit bigger than an ostrich-egg (of which I have spoken elsewhere). So that (as they said) the spirit might thereafter speak through these rattles, to dedicate them to this use they made them sound incessantly. And you could find no better comparison than to the bell-ringers that accompany those impostors who, exploiting the credulity of our simple folk over here, carry from place to place the reliquaries of Saint Anthony or Saint Bernard, and other such instruments of idolatry. In addition to this description, I have tried to illustrate all this for you by the accompanying figure of a dancer and a *maraca*-player.

Moreover, these *caraïbes,* advancing and leaping forward, then drawing back, did not always stay in one place as the others did. I noticed that they would frequently take a wooden cane four or five feet long, at the end of which was burning some of the dried herb *petun* (which I have mentioned elsewhere); turning and blowing the smoke in all directions on the other savages, they would say to them, "So that you may overcome your enemies, receive all of you the spirit of strength." And thus these master *caraïbes* did several times.

These ceremonies went on for nearly two hours, with the five or six hundred men dancing and singing incessantly; such was their melody that—although they do not know what music is—those who have not heard them would never believe that they could make such harmony. At

the beginning of this witches' sabbath, when I was in the women's house, I had been somewhat afraid; now I received in recompense such joy, hearing the measured harmonies of such a multitude, and especially in the cadence and refrain of the song, when at every verse all of them would let their voices trail, saying *Heu, heuaure, heura, heuraure, heura, heura, oueh*—I stood there transported with delight. Whenever I remember it, my heart trembles, and it seems their voices are still in my ears. When they decided to finish, each of them struck his right foot against the earth more vehemently than before, and spat in front of him; then all of them with one voice uttered hoarsely two or three times the words *He, hua, hua, hua,* and then ceased.

Since I did not understand their language perfectly at that time, they had said several things that I had not been able to comprehend, and I asked the interpreter to explain them to me.[15] He told me that at the beginning of the songs they had uttered long laments for their dead ancestors, who were so valiant, but in the end, they had taken comfort in the assurance that after their death they would go join them behind the high mountains, where they would dance and rejoice with them. Likewise, they had pronounced violent threats against the Ouetaca (a nation of enemy savages, who, as I have said elsewhere, are so warlike that they have never been able to subdue them), to capture and eat them, as their *caraïbes* had promised. Moreover, mingled in their songs there was mention of waters that had once swelled so high above their bounds that all the earth was covered, and all the people in the world were drowned, except for their ancestors, who took refuge in the highest trees.[16] This last point, which is the closest they come to the Holy Scriptures, I have heard them reiterate several times since. And, indeed, it is likely that from father to son they have heard something of the universal flood that occurred in the time of Noah. In keeping with the habit of men, which is always to corrupt the truth and turn it into falsehood, together with what we have already seen—that, being altogether deprived of writing, it is hard for them to retain things in their purity—they have added this fable (as did the poets), that their ancestors took refuge in the trees.[17]

To return to our *caraïbes*. They were cordially received that day by all the other savages, who entertained them magnificently with the best food they could find, not forgetting to make them drink and *caouiner*, according to their custom. My two French companions and I, who as I said had found ourselves unexpectedly present at this bacchanalia, were also well feasted by our *moussacats* (that is, by the generous householders who give food to people who are passing through). In addition to all this, after these solemn days have passed (during which, every three or four years, all the mummery you have heard about takes place again among our Tupinamba), and even sometimes before, the *caraïbes* go from one village to another, and have each family adorn three or four of these big rattles that they call *maracas*,[18] using the finest plumes they can find. When the *maracas* are thus decked out, they stick the long end of the rod that runs through them into the earth, and arrange them along the middles of the houses; they then demand that the *maracas* be given food and drink. So these impostors make those poor simpletons believe that these fruits and gourds, hollowed out, adorned, and consecrated, will then eat and drink at night. Since each head of a household credits this, he never fails to put out beside his *maracas* not only flour with meat and fish, but also some of their *caouin*. They usually leave them planted in the earth for two or three weeks, always attended to in the same way; and they have a strange belief concerning these *maracas* (which they almost always have in hand): attributing a certain sanctity to them once this bewitchment has been accomplished, they say that whenever they make them sound, a spirit speaks.

As we passed through their longhouses, if we saw some fine morsels presented to these *maracas* and took and ate them (as we often did), our Americans, duped as they were, and judging that such a deed would bring some misfortune down upon us, were no less offended than those superstitious ones, successors of the priests of Baal, at seeing someone take the offerings brought to their puppets—on which offerings, however, to the dishonor of God, they themselves feed gluttonously and idly with their whores and bastards.[19] If, when we seized the occasion to point out their errors, we told them that the *caraïbes*, who gave it out that the *maracas* ate and drank, were deceiving them; and also, that it was not the *caraïbes* (as they falsely boasted) who caused their fruits and their big roots to grow, but rather the God in whom we believe and whom we were making known to them—well, that had about as much effect as speaking against the Pope over here, or saying in Paris that the reliquary of St. Genevieve doesn't make it rain. Therefore these *caraïbe* charlatans hated us no less than the false prophets of Israel (fearing to lose their fat morsels) hated Elijah, the true servant of God, who similarly revealed their abuses;[a] they began to hide from us, fearing even to approach or to sleep in the villages where they knew we were lodging.

---

[a] I Kings 18.19.

Pursuing what I said at the beginning of this chapter: our Tupinamba (all their ceremonies notwithstanding) do not worship either their
*caraïbes* or their *maracas* or any creatures whatsoever by kneeling or by
any other external gesture; much less do they pray to them or invoke
them. Nonetheless, I will cite another example of what I have perceived in
them concerning religion. I was with some compatriots in a village named
*Ocarentin,* two leagues from Cotiva. As we were having our dinner in an
open area, the savages of that place assembled—not to eat with us but to
view us. For if they want to do honor to a personage they do not take
their meal while he does (not even the old men, who were proud to see us
in their village, and showed us all possible signs of friendship). Each one
had in his hand the nosebone of a certain fish, two or three feet long and
saw-shaped. Rather like our footmen archers, they stood around us to
chase away the children, saying to them in their language: "Get out of
here, you little rascals! The likes of you are not to come near these
people."

After this whole crowd had let us dine in peace without interrupting
a single word of our conversation, an old man who had observed that we
had prayed to God at the beginning and end of our meal asked us, "What
does this mean, this way of doing things, taking off your hat twice, and
remaining silent except for one speaker? To whom was all that addressed,
those things he was saying? Is it to you who are here, or to others who are
absent?" Seizing the occasion that he offered us to speak of the true
religion, and considering that this village of Ocarentin is one of the
biggest and most populated of that country, and that the savages seemed
more attentive than usual and more ready to listen to us, I enlisted our
interpreter to help me make them understand what I was about to say.

I first answered the old man's question by telling him that it was to
God that we had addressed our prayers, and that although He was not
visible, nonetheless He not only heard us but He knew what we were
thinking and what was in our hearts. I then began to speak to them about
the creation of the world. Above all, I insisted on their understanding that
if God had made man excellent above all other creatures, it was so that he
might all the more glorify his Creator. I added that, because we served
Him, He preserved us as we crossed the sea, even as we lived on that sea
continually for four or five months without putting foot to ground, just
so that we might seek them out. We did not fear, as they did, being
tormented by Aygnan, neither in this life nor in the other: so, I said, if
they were willing to turn away from the errors in which their lying and
deceiving *caraïbes* held them captive, and leave their barbarity and no

longer eat the flesh of their enemies, they would receive the same grace whose effects they had seen in us. In short, so that we might prepare them to receive Jesus Christ, having told them of man's perdition, we spent more than two hours on the matter of the Creation, constantly making comparisons with things that were known to them (on which, however, for the sake of brevity, I will speak no further).

All of them, lending ear, listened attentively and with great wonder. Amazed at what they had heard, another old man spoke up: "Certainly you have told us of marvels that we had never heard of. Still, your discourse has recalled to me something we often heard our grandfathers tell of: a long time ago, so many moons ago that we cannot count them, a *Mair*[20] (that is, a Frenchman or a stranger) dressed and bearded like some of you, came into this country, and, thinking to bring them to an obedience to your God, spoke to them in the same manner that you have just done. But, as we have also heard from father to son, they refused to believe. And so there came another who, as a sign of a curse, left them the sword with which we have been killing each other ever since.[21] And we have entered so far into our possession of it that if we were to desist and abandon our custom, all neighboring nations would mock us." We replied vehemently that, far from concerning themselves with the jibes of others, they had only to worship and serve the sole and true God of heaven and earth, whom we were making known to them; then if their enemies came and attacked them, they would overcome and vanquish them all. In short, by the efficacy that God gave to our words, our Tupinamba were so stirred that several of them promised to live as we had taught them, and even to leave off eating the human flesh of their enemies. After this colloquy (which, as I have said, lasted a long time), they got down on their knees with us, and one of our company, giving thanks to God, offered aloud in the midst of this people a prayer, which was then explained by the interpreter. Then they bedded us down in their style, in cotton beds suspended in the air. But before we fell asleep, we heard them singing together, that in order to avenge themselves on their enemies, they must capture and eat more of them than they ever had before.

And there you have the inconstancy of this poor people, a fine example of the corrupt nature of man. Still, I am of the opinion that if Villegagnon had not revolted from the Reformed Religion, and if we had stayed longer in that country, we would have drawn and won some of them to Jesus Christ.

Since that time I have reflected on what they had said they had learned from their forebears: that many centuries earlier a *Mair,* that is, a man from our part of the world (whether French or German hardly matters), had come into their land and had told them of the true God; I have wondered whether he could have been one of the Apostles.[22] Now by no means do I approve of the fanciful books which people have written about the voyages and peregrinations of the Apostles, which go beyond what the Word of God has said on the matter. However, Nicephorus,[a] recounting the story of St. Matthew, says expressly that he preached the Gospel in the country of man-eating cannibals, a people not so different from our Brazilian Americans.[23] But I put much more trust in the passage of St. Paul, taken from the Nineteenth Psalm, which some good expositors apply to the Apostles: "Their sound went into the earth, and their words unto the ends of the world."[b] Considering that they have certainly been in many far-off lands unknown to us, why may we not believe that one of them, or even several, have been in the land of these barbarians? This would serve as an illumination and general exposition of the saying of Jesus Christ, that the Gospel would be preached throughout the world.[c] While I make no claim concerning what happened in the time of the Apostles, I will maintain nonetheless, as I have shown in this history, that in our day I have seen and heard the Gospel proclaimed even to the Antipodes. So that not only will any objection about that passage from the Gospel be answered by this, but also, it will make the savages all the more inexcusable on the Last Day.

As for the other remark of our Americans, that since their ancestors refused to believe him who tried to lead them into the right path, there came another, who, because of this refusal, cursed them and gave them the sword with which they still kill each other every day: we read in the Apocalypse that to him who sat on the red horse—which according to some signifies persecution by fire and by war—was given power "to take peace from the earth, and that they should kill one another; and there was to him given a great sword."[d] There is the text that, to the letter, corresponds to what the Tupinamba say and practice; still, since I am wary of distorting its true sense, and do not want to think that my

---

[a][Nicephorus Callistus Xanthopoulos, *Scriptoris vere catholici ecclesiasticae historiae,*] Book 2, Chapter 41.

[b]Psalms 19.5; Romans 10.18.

[c]Matthew 24.14.

[d][Revelation 6.4.]

interpretations are far-fetched, I will leave the application of this text to others.

I do recall, however, another example that I will put forth here, showing that these nations of savage living in the land of Brazil are teachable enough to be drawn to the knowledge of God, if one were to take the trouble to instruct them. One day, going from our island to the mainland to get provisions, I was accompanied by two of our Tupinikin savages and by another of the nation called *Oueanen* (which is their ally), who had come with his wife to visit his friends and was returning to his own land. As I was passing with them through a great forest, contemplating so many different trees, grasses, and flowers, all green and fragrant, and hearing the songs of the countless birds warbling through the woods in the sunlight, I felt impelled to praise God, and feeling gay of heart, I began to sing aloud Psalm 104, "Bless the Lord, O my soul." My three savages and the woman who walked behind me took such delight in it (that is, in the sound, for they understood nothing of the rest) that when I had finished, the Oueanen, stirred with joy, his face beaming, came forward and said to me, "Truly you have sung wonderfully; your resounding song has recalled to me that of a nation that is our neighbor and ally, and I have been filled with joy at hearing you. But we understand their language, and not yours: therefore I entreat you to tell us what your song was about." So I explained to him as best I could (I was on my way to join two of my countrymen at the place where I was to spend the night, and I was the only Frenchman present) that I had in general praised my God for the beauty and governance of his creatures, and in particular I had attributed to him this: that it was he alone who nourished all men and all animals, and made the trees, fruits, and plants grow throughout the whole world; moreover, that this song I had just sung, dictated by the spirit of this magnificent God whose name I had celebrated, had first been sung more than ten thousand moons ago (for that is their way of counting) by one of our great prophets, who had left it to posterity to be used to that same end. They are wonderfully attentive to what you say to them, and will never interrupt you, so that, as they made their way, it was more than half an hour after hearing this discourse that—using their interjection of amazement, "Teh!"—they said, "O you *Mairs* (that is, Frenchmen) how fortunate you are to know so many secrets that are hidden from us poor wretches!" And to compliment me, saying "Here, because you have sung so well," he made me a present of an *agouti* that he was carrying, which I have described along with other animals in Chapter X.

I have insisted on making this digression to prove that these nations of America, however barbarous and cruel they may be toward their enemies, are not so fierce that they do not consider what is said to them in a reasonable way. And indeed, as far as the natural quality of man is concerned, I maintain that they hold forth better than most of our peasants, and indeed than some others back over here who think they are very clever fellows.

To conclude now, let me touch on a question that one might ask about this whole subject I am treating: that is, from whom are these savages descended? In the first place, they certainly issued from one of the three sons of Noah; but to affirm which one, especially since it could not be proved by Holy Scripture nor yet by secular history, is not easy.[24] It is true that Moses, mentioning the children of Japhet, said that they inhabited the islands; but since, as everyone agrees, what is meant is the countries of Greece, Gaul, Italy, and other regions over here (which, since the sea separates them from Judaea, are called "islands" by Moses), there would be no good reason to take this to mean America or the adjacent lands.

Similarly, to say that they are descended from Shem, from whom issued the blessed seed and the Jews: although the latter too have so corrupted themselves that they have finally been rightly rejected by God, nonetheless for several reasons one could cite, no one, I think, would admit such a thing.

As for blessedness and eternal bliss (which we believe in and hope for through Jesus Christ alone), in spite of the glimpse and the intimation of it that I have said they have, this is a people accursed and abandoned by God, if there be any such under the heavens. (As to this earthly life, I have already shown and will show again that, while most people over here, who are given over to the goods of this world, do nothing but languish, they on the contrary who take things as they come, spend their days and live cheerfully, almost without care.) It seems, therefore, more likely that we should conclude that they are descended from Ham; that, I think, is the most plausible conjecture. For the Holy Scripture testifies that when Joshua began to enter and take possession of the land of Canaan according to the promises that God gave to the patriarchs and the commandment that he himself had received, the people who lived there were struck with such terror that their strength failed them.[a] It

---

[a]Joshua 2.9.

could have happened (I may be wrong in this) that the forebears and ancestors of our Americans, having been chased by the children of Israel from several regions of the land of Canaan, took ship and put themselves at the mercy of the sea, to be cast ashore in this land of America. And indeed, the Spaniard who wrote the *General History of the Indies* (a man well versed in all kinds of knowledge, whatever else he may be) is of the opinion that the Indians of Peru, a land adjacent to that of Brazil, are descended from Ham, and have inherited the curse that God laid on him[a]—a thing that I had also thought and written in the notes that I made for the present history more than sixteen years before I had seen his book. Still, since one could make many objections to all this, and as I do not want to pronounce on it here, I will let everyone believe what he pleases.

However that may be, I take it as resolved that these are poor people issued from the corrupt race of Adam. But having considered them thus void and deprived of any right sense of God, my faith has by no means been in the least shaken on that account. Even less have I concluded from all this, with the atheists and Epicureans,[25] either that there is no God, or that He does not concern Himself in human affairs; on the contrary, having clearly recognized in their persons the difference between those who are illuminated by the Holy Spirit and the Holy Scripture, and those who are abandoned to their own faculties and left in their blindness, I have been greatly confirmed in the assurance of the truth of God.

---

[a][Gómara,] Book 5, Chapter 217.

# CHAPTER XVII

## OF MARRIAGE,
### POLYGAMY, AND DEGREES
### OF CONSANGUINITY OBSERVED BY
### THE SAVAGES; AND OF THE TREAT-
### MENT OF THEIR LITTLE CHILDREN[1]

Now to touch on the marriage customs of our Americans. They observe only these three degrees of consanguinity: no one takes his mother, his sister, or his daughter as a wife, but an uncle may take his niece; aside from this, all the other degrees are of no concern to them.[2] As for ceremonies, they have none, except that he who wants to take a wife, whether widow or maiden, after having ascertained that she is willing, will address himself to the father (or, if that is not possible, the nearest kinsman) and ask that she be given to him in marriage. If the answer is "Yes," then without further contract (for there is no profit in it for notaries) he will take her to wife. If, on the contrary, he is refused, he will desist without further ado. But note that since polygamy, that is, a plurality of wives, is common in their region, men may have as many as they please; in fact, they make a virtue out of a vice, so that those who have the greatest number are deemed the most valiant and bold. I have seen one who had eight, about whom he told tales in his own praise.

And what makes one marvel in this multitude of women is that while there is always one who is the husband's favorite, the others are not at all jealous and do not complain, or at least show no signs of it; all of them, busy with the housework, weaving their cotton beds, tending their gardens, and planting their roots, live together in an incomparable peace. On that point I will let each of you consider whether (even if it were not forbidden by God to take more than one wife) it would be possible for our women over here to live in such harmony. Better to send a man to the galleys than to put him in the midst of such a tumult and uproar as undoubtedly there would be; witness what happened to Jacob for having

152

taken Leah and Rachel, even though they were sisters.ᵃ How could several of our women live together, considering how often she who was especially ordained of God to be man's helpmeet and delight, is instead like a familiar demon in his house?³ In saying this, by no means do I intend to censure in any way those who behave otherwise: that is, who render the honor and obedience that they rightly owe their husbands; on the contrary, when they are dutiful, thus bringing honor upon themselves first of all, I consider them as praiseworthy as I deem the others deserving of all blame.

To return, then, to the marriage customs of our Americans. Adultery on the women's part is held in such horror that, even though they have no other law than that of nature, if a married woman abandons herself to anyone other than her husband, the husband is empowered to kill her, or at least to repudiate her and send her away in shame. It is true that before they marry off their daughters, the fathers and relatives have no great scruples about prostituting them to the first comer; as I have already mentioned elsewhere, although the Norman interpreters had already, before our arrival, taken advantage of them in several villages, nonetheless their reputations were not ruined. But, as I said, once they are married they take care not to stumble, under pain of being beaten to death or sent away in shame.

I will add that, considering the hot region they inhabit, and in spite of what is said of Orientals, the marriageable young people of that land, boys as well as girls, are not so much given over to lust as one might think; and would to God it held no more sway over here. Nevertheless (for I would not make them out to be more virtuous than they are), sometimes when they are greatly vexed with each other they call each other *tyvire*, which is to say "bugger"; one can conjecture from this (for I affirm nothing) that this abominable sin is committed among them.⁴

When a woman is with child, she avoids carrying heavy burdens, but does not abandon her ordinary tasks. Indeed, the women of our Tupinamba work far and away more than the men; for except for a few mornings (and not in the heat of the day) when they cut wood to make gardens, the men do nothing except go to war, hunt, fish, and make their wooden swords, bow, arrows, feather garments, and the other things I have specified elsewhere, with which they adorn their bodies.

---

ᵃGenesis 29 and 30.

Concerning childbearing, here is what I can say as an eyewitness. Another Frenchman and I had bedded ourselves down one night in a village. Around midnight we heard a woman scream; thinking that it was that ravaging beast *Jan-ou-are*[a] (which, as I have said elsewhere, preys on the savages) trying to devour her, we ran to her immediately. We found it was not that, but rather that her labor pains were making her cry out. So I myself saw the father receive the child in his arms, tie off the umbilical cord, and cut it with his teeth. Continuing to serve as midwife, but unlike ours over here, who pull on the noses of newborn infants to make them more beautiful, he, on the contrary, pushed in his son's nose and crushed it with his thumb; this is done over there with all children, who are thought to be prettier when they are snub-nosed.

As soon as the baby has come out of his mother's womb, he is washed clean and immediately painted all over with red and black by the father, who then lays him down, without swaddling him, in a cotton bed hung in the air. If the child is a male, the father makes him a little wooden sword, a little bow, and little arrows feathered with parrot plumes; then, placing it all beside the infant, and kissing him, he will say to him, his face beaming, "My son, when you come of age, be skilled in arms, strong, valiant, and warlike, so that you can take vengeance on your enemies." The father of the child I saw born named him *Orapacen*, that is, the bow and the string: for this word is composed of *orapat*, which is bow, and *cen*, which means its string. And that is how they name all their children, randomly giving them names of familiar things, just as we do to dogs and other animals over here: *Sarigoy*,[b] a four-footed animal; *Arignan*, a hen; *Arabouten*, the brazilwood tree; *Pindo*, a tall grass, and so on.

As for nourishment, it will be some chewed flour, and other soft foods, along with the mother's milk. The mother stays in bed only a day or two, and then takes her baby, suspended from her neck in a cotton scarf made for the purpose, and goes off to the garden or to her other tasks. This is not to disparage the customs of the ladies over here, who, on account of our bad air, stay in bed for two or three weeks, and are for the most part so delicate that, although they have no illness that would prevent them from nurturing their infants as the American women do, as soon as they are delivered of them they are inhuman enough to send them away; so that if the children do not die without their mothers' knowing

---

[a][The jaguar.]

[b][An opossum.]

anything about it, in any case they must be partly grown and old enough to provide some pastime before their mothers will endure their presence.

Now if there are some dainty ladies here who think I do them wrong in comparing them to these savage women, whose rural fashioning (they will say) has nothing to do with their own tender and delicate bodies, I am content, so as to sweeten this bitter pill, to send them to school to the brute beasts, which, even down to the smallest birds, will teach them this lesson: that it is up to each species to take care—indeed, to be at pains—to raise its progeny itself. But to cut short all their retorts, let me ask whether they would be more coddled than a former queen of France, who (as we read in the histories) was impelled by a true maternal passion: when she learned that her child had been suckled by another woman, she was so jealous that nothing would do but that she would make him vomit the milk that he had taken elsewhere than from his mother's breasts.[5]

Now to return to my subject. It is commonly believed over here that if children in their tender and early infancy were not tightly swaddled, they would be deformed and bow-legged. Although that custom is by no means observed for American children (who, as I have said, are from their birth held and laid down without being swaddled), nevertheless you could not find children who walk straighter than they do. I admit that the gentle air and moderate temperature of that land are in part the cause, and I grant that in the winter it is good to keep our children well wrapped, covered, and tucked into their cradles, because otherwise they could not withstand the cold; but in the summer, and even in the temperate seasons, especially when it is not freezing, it seems to me from what I have seen (if I am not mistaken) that it would be better to let the little children caper about freely on some kind of bed one could devise, from which they could not fall, than to keep them so confined. And in fact, it is my opinion that it does great harm to these poor tender little creatures to be sweltering and half-roasted during the hot season in these swaddling clothes where they are bound as if for torture.[6]

In any case, lest you tell me that I meddle in too many things, I will leave the raising of children over here to their fathers, mothers, and nurses, and add the following to what I have already said of American children. Although the women of that country have no clothes to wipe the behinds of their children, and do not even use the leaves of trees and grasses, which they have in such abundance, nevertheless they are so careful that simply by using small sticks of wood that they break off, like little dowels, they clean their children so well that you never see them dirty. This is also what the adults do; of them, however (I digress to treat this foul subject), I will merely say that they ordinarily make water in their houses (since the ground is strewn with sand, and since there are fires burning throughout, there is no bad smell), but go off a long distance to get rid of their excrement.

The savages take care of all their children, which they have in swarms (although you will not find that any single father among our Brazilians will have six hundred sons, as has been written of a king of the Moluccan islands, which must be counted as a prodigy);[a] still, because of their wars, in which it is only the men who fight and who seek vengeance on their enemies, the males are more cherished than the females. You may ask what station of life the children are prepared for, and what they are taught when they are grown. In Chapters VIII, XIV, and XV, and elsewhere in this history, I have spoken of their natural state, their wars, and their eating of their enemies; you can easily imagine, since they have neither schools nor any other means of acquiring the learning of cultivated people—even less the liberal arts—, that their ordinary occupation, both as adults and as children, is to be not only hunters and warriors (true successors of Lamech, Nimrod, and Esau), but also killers and eaters of men.[b]

Taking the discussion of the marriage customs of the Tupinamba as far as one decently can: contrary to what some people have imagined, the men preserve the modesty of nature by never consorting with their wives in public. In that respect, I maintain that they are preferable to that base Cynic philosopher who, caught in the act, instead of being ashamed said that he was planting a man;[7] and surely those stinking billygoats that one sees in our time over here, who have not hidden themselves when committing their lustful acts, are incomparably more disgusting than they are.

To which I will add that during the space of about a year that we lived in that country and spent time in their company, we never saw in the women any signs of their monthly flux. I am of the opinion that they divert that flow, and have another way of purging themselves than that of the women over here. For I have seen young girls, twelve to fourteen years of age, whose mothers or female relatives would stand them up, feet together on a stone, and incise them with an animal's tooth as sharp as a knife, deep enough to draw blood, from the armpit down along the side

---

[a][Gómara,] *Histoire,* Chapter 96.
[b]Genesis 4.23; 10.8–9; 27.23.

156

and thigh, all the way to the knee. The girls, gritting their teeth in great pain, bled for some time. I think, as I have said, that from the beginning they use this remedy to hide the signs of their flow. Physicians or others more learned than I in such matters may reply, "How can you reconcile this with what you said earlier, that when they are married they are very fertile, seeing that when women cease to have their monthly flow they cannot conceive?" If one asserts that these things are contradictory, I reply that my intention is neither to resolve this question, nor to say any more about it.[8]

At the end of Chapter VIII I refuted what some have written and others thought: that the nakedness of the savage women and girls incites men to lust more than if they were clothed. I have also set forth there some other points concerning the food, customs, and ways of life of American children; a reader who requires a fuller development of this subject may turn to that chapter.

# CHAPTER XVIII

### ৯

# WHAT ONE MAY CALL
## LAWS AND CIVIL ORDER
## AMONG THE SAVAGES: HOW HUMANELY
## THEY TREAT AND RECEIVE FRIENDS
## WHO VISIT THEM; AND OF THE
## TEARS AND JOYOUS SPEECHES THAT
## THE WOMEN MAKE TO WELCOME
## THEM[1]

As for the civil order of our savages, it is an incredible thing—a thing that cannot be said without shame to those who have both divine and human laws—how a people guided solely by their nature, even corrupted as it is, can live and deal with each other in such peace and tranquillity. (I mean, however, each nation within itself, or among allied nations: as for enemies, you have seen in another chapter how harshly they are treated.) Nevertheless, if it happens that some of them quarrel (which occurs so rarely that during almost a year I was with them I only saw them fight with each other twice), by no means do the others try to separate them or make peace; on the contrary, even when the adversaries are on the point of putting each others' eyes out, they let them go ahead without saying a word to prevent them. However, if anyone is wounded by his neighbor, and if he who struck the blow is apprehended, he will receive a similar blow in the same part of his body by the kinsmen of the one injured. If the wounds of the latter prove to be mortal, or if he is killed on the spot, the relatives of the dead man will take the life of the killer in the same way. In short, it is a life for a life, an eye for an eye, a tooth for a tooth,[a] and so forth; but as I have said, this is very rarely seen among them.

The real property of this people consists of houses and of many

---

[a] Leviticus 24.19–20.

more excellent pieces of land than they need for their subsistence. In a given village of five or six hundred people, while several families may live in the same house, nevertheless each has its own place, and the husband keeps his wife and children separate; however, there is nothing to keep you from seeing down the full length of these buildings, which are usually more than sixty feet long.

It is a curious fact worth noting that the Brazilians, who usually stay only five or six months in a place, carry with them the big pieces of wood and tall *pindo* plants, with which their houses are made and covered; thus they often move their very villages from place to place. These, however, still retain their former names, so that we have sometimes found villages at a quarter- or half-league's distance from the location where we had visited them before. Their dwellings being so easily transported, you can imagine that they have no great palaces (such as those attributed to the Peruvian Indians, whose wooden houses are so well built that there are rooms one hundred fifty feet long and eighty feet wide);[a] and no one of the Tupinamba nation ever begins a dwelling or any other building that he will not see built and rebuilt twenty times in his life, if he lives to the age of manhood. If you ask them why they move their household so often, they simply answer that the change of air keeps them healthier, and that if they did other than what their grandfathers did, they would die immediately.[2]

With regard to fields and trees, each head of a family will have several acres of his own, in a place that suits him, where he makes his garden and plants his root crops. As for the rest, all the to-do about dividing inheritances, or going to court to place boundaries and separate property—they leave all that to the miserly landowners and wrangling pettifoggers over here.

As for their furnishings, I have already mentioned in several places in this account what they consist of. Still, to omit nothing of what I know about the domestic economy of our savages, I will first speak of the women's method of spinning cotton, which they use to make cord and other things as well, and especially to make the beds, the style of which I will also explain. Here is how they work with it. After they have pulled it from the boll (which I have described in the chapter[b] treating the plant that bears it), they spread it out a little with their fingers, without carding

---

[a][Gómara,] *Histoire,* Book 2, Chapter 60.
[b][Chapter XIII.]

it further, and heap it beside them, either on the ground or on some other object, for they use no distaff as the women do over here. Their spindle is a round stick, no bigger than a finger and about a foot long, which passes through the middle of a little board, round like a wooden trencher and of about that thickness. They attach the cotton to the longer end of this lengthwise stick, spinning it on their knees and releasing it with the hand as spinners do their spindles: with this roller twirling like a top in the midst of their houses or elsewhere, they make the great nets for their beds. I later brought to France some of the finer cord, so well spun and tightly twisted by these same women that when I had a white cloth doublet stitched with it, everyone who saw it thought it was fine purled silk.

As for those cotton beds, which the savages call *inis*,[3] their women make them on wooden looms, which are not laid flat like those of our weavers, nor equipped with so many devices, but are simply raised in front of them at their height. When they have laid the warp in their style, beginning the plaiting from the bottom, they make some of the beds with fishnet, and others more densely like heavy canvas. These beds are for the most part four, five or six feet long and about five feet wide; they have loops at each end also made of cotton, to which the cords are tied for hanging them in the air by attaching them to wooden beams set crosswise in their houses expressly for the purpose.

When they go to war, or sleep in the woods during a hunt, or by the seashore, or by their fishing streams, they hang them between two trees. When these cotton beds are soiled, whether from sweat, or from the smoke of the fires that are burning continually in the houses where they hang, or in some other way, the American women gather from the woods a wild fruit, in form like a flat pumpkin, but much bigger, so that it is all you can do to carry one in your hand. They cut it in pieces, soak it in water in a big earthen vessel, and beating it with wooden sticks, they work up great billows of foam. They use this as soap, and the beds come out as white as snow or as fuller's sheets.

I ask those who have tried them out whether you don't sleep better on these cotton beds than on our ordinary ones, especially in summer; and whether I was not right when I said in the history of Sancerre that in time of war, it is far easier to suspend these sheets in the guardroom for some of the soldiers to sleep on while the others stand guard, than to have them sprawl in the usual way on the straw, where you soil your clothes and get them full of vermin, and find when you get up to be ready for duty that your ribs are bruised from the arms that you must always have at your belt (as we did during the siege of Sancerre, where the enemy did not move from our gates for a whole year).[4]

To sum up the other furnishings of our Americans: the women, who among themselves have all the housework to do, make a great many receptacles and earthen vessels to prepare and store the beverage called *caouin,* as well as cooking pots, both round and oval, and pans of medium and small sizes; although the earthenware is not smooth and even on the outside, it is so polished and sealed on the inside by a certain white liquid that hardens, that our potters over here could do no finer work. These women even dilute certain grayish pigments for their task, and with their brushes they paint a thousand pretty little designs of interlaced curves, tendrils, and other delightful patterns on the inside of these earthen vessels, especially in those that hold flour and other foodstuffs. So you are served quite properly—indeed, more properly than by those over here who serve out of wooden vessels.

It is true that these American painters lack one thing: once they have created with their brushes whatever their fancy has dictated, if you ask them to do the same for you again, they will not be able to imitate the first piece of work, because they have no other plan, model, or sketch than the quintessence of a nimble brain; so you will never see the same design twice.

Our savages also have gourds and other big fruits, split and hollowed out, from which they make their drinking cups, called *coui,* as well as other little containers for other purposes. They also have boxes and baskets, big and small, very neatly woven, some of reeds and some of yellow grasses or straw, called *panacons;* they store flour in them or whatever else they please. I have already described their weapons, feather garments, the device they call a *maraca,* and other utensils, so I will discuss them no further.

With the houses of our savages built and furnished, it is time to go visit them.

Now to take up this subject in a general way: although the Tupinamba receive very humanely the friendly strangers who go to visit them, nevertheless the Frenchmen and others from over here who do not understand their language find themselves at first marvelously disconcerted in their midst. The first time that I myself frequented them was three weeks after we arrived at Villegagnon's island, when an interpreter took me along to four or five villages on the mainland. The first one—called *Yabouraci* in the native language and "Pepin" by the French (because of a ship that loaded there once, whose master had that name)—was only two leagues from our fort. When we arrived there, I immediately found myself surrounded by savages, who were asking me "*Marapé-derere, marapé derere?*" meaning "What is your name? What is your name?"(which at that I understood time no better than High German). One of them took my hat, which he put on his head; another my sword and my belt, which he put around his naked body; yet another my tunic, which he donned. Deafening me with their yells, they ran through the village with my clothing. Not only did I think that I had lost everything, but I didn't know what would become of me. As experience has shown me several times since, that was only from ignorance of their way of doing things; for they do the same thing to everyone who visits them, and especially those they haven't seen before. After they have played around a little with one's belongings, they carry them all back and return them to their owners.

The interpreter had warned me that they wanted above all to know my name; but if I had said to them Pierre, Guillaume, or Jean, they would have been able neither to retain it nor to pronounce it (in fact, instead of saying "Jean," they would say "Nian"). So I had to accommodate by naming something that was known to them. Since by a lucky chance my surname, "Léry," means "oyster" in their language, I told them that my name was "*Léry-oussou,*" that is, a big oyster. This pleased them greatly; with their "*Teh!*" of admiration, they began to laugh, and said, "That is a fine name; we have not yet seen any *Mair* (that is, a Frenchman) of that name." And indeed, I can say with assurance that never did Circe metaphorphose a man into such a fine oyster, nor into one who could converse so well with Ulysses, as since then I have been able to do with our savages.[5]

One must note that their memory is so good that as soon as someone has told them his name, if they were to go a hundred years (so to speak) without seeing him, they will never forget it. Presently I will tell about the other ceremonies they observe when they receive friends who go to see them.

But for the moment I will continue to recount some of the noteworthy things that happened to me during my first journey among the Tupinamba. That same day the interpreter and I were going on to spend the night in another village called *Euramiri* (the French call it "Goset," because of an interpreter of that name who stayed there). Arriving at sunset, we found the savages dancing and finishing up the *caouin* of a prisoner whom they had killed only six hours earlier, the pieces of whom we saw on the *boucan*. Do not ask whether, with this beginning, I was astonished to see such a tragedy; however, as you will hear, that was nothing compared to the fright that I had soon after.

162

We had entered one of the village houses, where each of us sat, according to custom, in a cotton bed hung in the air. After the women had wept (in a manner that I will describe in a moment) and the old man, the master of the house, had made his speech of welcome, the interpreter—who was not new to the customs of the savages, and who, moreover, liked to drink and *caouiner* as much as they did—without saying a single word to me, nor warning me of anything, went over to the big crowd of dancers and left me there with some of the savages. So after eating a little root flour and other food they had offered us, I, weary and asking only for rest, lay down in the cotton bed I had been sitting on.

Not only was I kept awake by the noise that the savages made, dancing and whistling all night while eating their prisoner; but, what is more, one of them approached me with the victim's foot in hand, cooked and *boucané,* asking me (as I learned later, for I didn't understand at the time) if I wanted to eat some of it. His countenance filled me with such terror that you need hardly ask if I lost all desire to sleep. Indeed, I thought that by brandishing the human flesh he was eating, he was threatening me and wanted to make me understand that I was about to be similarly dealt with. As one doubt begets another, I suspected straight away that the interpreter, deliberately betraying me, had abandoned me and delivered me into the hands of these barbarians. If I had seen some exit through which to flee, I would not have hesitated. But seeing myself surrounded on all sides by those whose intentions I failed to understand (for as you will hear, they had not the slightest thought of doing me harm), I firmly expected shortly to be eaten, and all that night I called on God in my heart. I will leave it to those who understand what I am saying, and who put themselves in my place, to consider whether that night seemed long.

At daybreak my interpreter (who had been off carousing with those rascals of savages all night long in other village houses) came to find me. Seeing me, as he said, not only ashen-faced and haggard but also feverish, he asked me whether I was sick, or if I hadn't rested well. Distraught, I answered wrathfully that they had well and truly kept me from sleeping, and that he was a scoundrel to have left me among these people whom I couldn't understand at all; still as anxious as ever, I urged that we get ourselves out of there with all possible speed. Thereupon he told me that I should have no fear, and that it wasn't us they were after. When he recounted the whole business to the savages—who, rejoicing at my coming, and thinking to show me affection, had not budged from my side all night—they said that they had sensed that I had been somewhat frightened of them, for which they were very sorry. My one consolation was the hoot of laughter they sent up—for they are great jokers—at having (without meaning to) given me such a scare.

The interpreter and I went from there to several other villages, but I will content myself with what I have just recounted as a sample of what happened to me during my first journey among the savages, and go on to generalities.

Let me now set forth the ceremonies that the Tupinamba observe when they receive friends who go to visit them. In the first place, as soon as the visitor has arrived in the house of the *moussacat* whom he has chosen for his host (the *moussacat* being the head of a household, who offers food to people passing through the village, and whom one must visit first in each village before going anywhere else if one is not to offend him), he is seated on a cotton bed suspended in the air, and remains there for a short while without saying a word. Then the women come and surround the bed, crouching with their buttocks against the ground and with both hands over their eyes; in this manner, weeping their welcome to the visitor, they will say a thousand things in his praise. For example: "You have gone to so much trouble to come to see us; you are good; you are valiant." And if it is a Frenchman, or some other stranger from over here, they will add: "You have brought us so many fine things that we do not have in this country." Spouting big tears, they will string out this kind of applause and flattery. If the newly arrived guest who is seated in the bed wants in turn to please them, he must assume the appropriate expression, and if he doesn't quite get to the point of tears (I have seen some of our nation, who, upon hearing the bleating of these women next to them, were such babies as to be reduced to tears themselves), at least when he answers them he must heave a few sighs and pretend to weep.[6]

This first salutation having been graciously performed by the American women, the *moussacat,* busy making an arrow or some other object (as you see in the illustration), will meanwhile have spent a quarter of an hour or so pretending not to see you—a blandishment quite contrary to our embraces, hugs, kisses, and handclasps upon the arrival of our friends. Then, approaching you, he will first use this style of speaking: "*Ere-joubé?*" that is, "Have you come?" and then "How are you? What would you like?" and so forth; to which you must respond according to the forms of conversation in their language which you will see hereafter. Then he will ask you if you want to eat; if you reply "Yes," he will immediately have prepared and brought to you, in fine earthen vessels, the flour that they eat instead of bread, as well as meat, poultry, fish, and

other food; but since they have no tables, benches, or stools, the service will be right on the ground in front of your feet. As for drink, if you want a *caouin,* he will give you some if he has any. After the women have wept beside the visitor, they will bring him fruit or some other small gift from their region, to obtain him combs, mirrors, or the little glass beads that they put around their arms.

If, moreover, you want to sleep in that village, the old man will not only stretch out for you a fine white bed, but also, even though it does not get cold in their country, he will place around the bed, against the night's humidity, four or five small fires, which will often be relit in the course of the night, along with some little screens that they call *tatapecoua,* made like the masks that the ladies over here hold in front of them when they are next to the fire, to keep it from spoiling their faces.

Since, in this discussion of the civil order of savages, I have come to the subject of fire (which they call *tata;* and the smoke, *tatatin*), I want to speak of the clever invention, unknown back over here, which permits them to make a fire whenever they please (a thing no less marvelous than the stone of Scotland, which, according to the testimony of the author of the *Singularities* of this country, has the property of lighting a fire in tow or straw without any other device). Since they like fire, they do not linger in a place without having one—especially at night, when they are terrified of being taken unawares by Aygnan, the evil spirit, who, as I have said, often beats and torments them—whether they are hunting in the woods, or fishing by the water's edge, or in the fields. Where we use stone and steel, which is unknown to them for that purpose, they use instead two kinds of wood, one of which is almost as soft as if it were half rotten, and the other as hard as what our cooks use for larding pins. When they want to light a fire, they prepare them in this manner: first, they take a stick of the hard wood, about a foot long, and sharpen one end of it, like the point of a spindle; then they plant this point in the middle of a piece of the soft wood, which they lay on the ground or hold against a trunk or a big log, used for a brace; then they rapidly twirl this stick between the two palms of their hands, as if they wanted to bore clear through the underlying piece. From the rapid and steady motion of these two pieces of wood, the one thrust into the other, there comes not only smoke, but also such heat that if there is any cotton or any dry leaves on hand (just as, over here, one must have a bit of burned cloth or other tinder next to the steel), the fire catches so well that I can assure those who will believe me that I myself started one in this fashion.

However, I do not mean to say, much less do I believe or want you to believe, what a certain person has written: that is, that the savages of America, before this fire-making invention, dried their meat with smoke;[a] for just as I hold that proverbial maxim of physics to be very true—that there is no fire without smoke—also, conversely, I think that he is not a good naturalist who would have us believe that there is smoke without fire. By "smoke" I mean—as did he of whom I am speaking—the kind that cooks meat. If, to get around this, he intended to say that he had heard about vapors and exhalations, he is making fools of us; for while we grant that some of these vapors are hot, they can by no means dry either flesh or fish—they would instead make them moist and humid. Since this author, both in his *Cosmography* and elsewhere, complains so loudly and so often about those who don't speak just as he likes about the matters that he treats (but whose works he admits he hasn't thoroughly read), I entreat my readers to note the ludicrous passage I have cited about his preposterous hot smoke, which I herewith send straight back into his windbag of a brain.

Now to return to the treatment the savages offer visitors. After the guests have drunk and eaten, in the way I have described, and rested or slept in their houses, if they are courteous, they ordinarily present knives to men, or scissors, or tweezers for plucking out beards; to the women, combs and mirrors; and to the little boys, fishhooks. If beyond that there are dealings about food supplies or other things that they have, you ask what they want for it, and upon giving them whatever is agreed upon, you can carry it off and go on your way.

Since, as I have said elsewhere, there are no horses, donkeys, or other beasts of burden in their country, they simply travel on their own two feet. If the foreign visitors are weary, they have only to present a knife or some other object to the savages; the latter, prompt as they are to please their friends, will offer to carry them. In fact, while I was over there, there were those who put us on their shoulders, with their heads between our thighs and our legs hanging against their bellies, and carried us that way more than a league without resting. Sometimes, to give them some relief, we told them to stop; laughing at us, they would say in their language: "What? Do you think we are women, or so slack and weak of heart that we might faint under the burden?" "I would carry you a whole day without stopping for rest," said one of them who had me around his neck. We, for our part, would roar with laughter at these two-footed

---

[a] Thevet, *Singularities,* Chapter 53.

mounts, applauding them and cheering them on, and saying, "Well then! Let's keep going!"

As for their natural fellow-feeling, every day they distribute and present each to each the venison, fish, fruit, and the other good things of their country, and not only would a savage die of shame (so to speak) if he saw his neighbor lacking what he has in his power to give, but also, as I have experienced it, they practice the same liberality toward foreigners who are their allies. As an example of this I will recount the time when, as I mentioned in Chapter X, two Frenchmen and I had lost our way in the woods—when we thought we were going to be eaten by a huge and terrifying lizard—, and moreover, during the space of two days and a night that we were lost, suffered greatly from hunger. When we finally found ourselves in a village called *Pauo*, where we had been on other occasions, we could not have received a better welcome than we had from the savages of that place. To begin with, when they heard us recount the troubles we had endured, and the danger we had been in—not only of being devoured by cruel beasts, but also of being seized and eaten by the Margaia, our enemy and theirs, whose land we had unintentionally approached—and when they saw the state we were in, all scratched up by the thorns that we had gone through in the wilderness, they took such pity on us that I can't help saying that the hypocritical welcomes of those over here who use only slippery speech for consolation of the afflicted is a far cry from the humanity of these people, whom nonetheless we call "barbarians."

They had begun (and here they reminded me of the manner of the ancients) by sending for fine clear water and washing the feet and legs of us three Frenchmen, who were seated each on a separate bed. Upon our arrival the old men had given orders to prepare food for us, and had even ordered the women to prepare quickly some soft flour (which I would as soon eat as good hot white bread); seeing us somewhat refreshed, they immediately had us served, in their style, with many good foods such as venison, poultry, fish, and exquisite fruit, which they are never without.

When evening fell, the elder who was our host had the children taken away from us so that we might rest more comfortably. In the morning when we awoke he said to us, "Well, *Atour-assats* (that is, perfect allies) did you sleep well last night?" We replied that we had, indeed, and he said to us: "Rest some more, my children, because I could tell last night that you were very weary." In short, it is hard for me to express the hospitality that was offered us by those savages, who in truth acted toward us just as, according to Saint Luke in the Acts of the Apostles, the barbarians of the Isle of Malta treated Saint Paul and those who were with him after they had escaped the shipwreck.[a] Now since we never travelled without each having a leather sack full of small merchandise that served us as money in our dealings with this people, at our departure we could give as we pleased: that is (as is the custom) knives, scissors, and tweezers to the elders; combs, mirrors, bracelets, and glass buttons to the women; and fishhooks to the little boys.

So that you may better understand the great store they set by these things, I will recount the following. One day when I was in a village, my *moussacat* (he who had received me into his house) entreated me to show him everything I had in my *caramemo,* that is, in my leather sack. He had brought to me a fine big earthen vessel in which I arranged all my effects. Marveling at the sight, he immediately called the other savages and said to them: "I pray you, my friends, consider what a personage I have in my house for since he has so many riches, must he not be a great lord?" And yet, as I said, laughing with a companion of mine who was there with me, what this savage held in such high esteem was in sum five or six knives with different kinds of handles, and as many combs, mirrors, and other small objects that would not have been worth two testoons in Paris. As I have said elsewhere, they love above all those who show liberality; since I wanted to exalt myself even more than he had done, I gave him freely and publicly, in front of everyone, the biggest and handsomest of my knives, which he set as much store by as might someone in our France who had just received a golden chain worth a hundred crowns.

Now you may want to know whether we felt safe among the savages of America. Just as they hate their enemies so mortally (as you have already heard) that when they have captured them, without any discussion of terms, they slay and eat them, so, on the contrary, they love so dearly their friends and confederates (as we were to the Tupinamba nation) that to keep them safe and spare them any hardship they would have had themselves cut into a hundred thousand pieces. Having had experience of them, I would entrust myself to them, and in fact felt myself safer among this people we call savage, than I would now in some parts of our France, among disloyal and degenerate Frenchmen (I speak only of those who are such: as for worthy people, of whom by the grace of God the kingdom is not yet empty, I would be very sorry to taint their honor.)

However, so that I give both sides, I will recount an event contain-

---

[a]Acts of the Apostles 28, 1–2.

ing the greatest apparent danger I ever found myself in among them. Having met up unexpectedly with six Frenchmen in that fine big village of *Ocarentin,* which I have already mentioned, ten or twelve leagues from our fort, and having decided to spend the night there, we made up a bow-and-arrow shooting match, three against three, to get some wild turkey and other fowl for our supper. As it happened, I was one of the losers. As I was looking through the village for poultry to buy, I came across one of those little French boys whom we had brought along in the ship Rosée to learn the language of the country, and who was now living in this village. "Here is a fine big duck," he said. "Kill it, and you will be quits by paying for it." I had no compunction about doing just that, because we had often killed chickens in other villages, which did not anger the savages since we could content them with a few knives as payment.

The dead duck in my hand, I went into a house where nearly all the savages of the place were assembled to *caouiner.* When I asked who the duck belonged to, so that I might pay him, an old man with a fairly disagreeable mug came forward and said, "It's mine." "What do you want me to give you for it?" I asked him. "A knife," he replied. I offered him one at once; when he saw it, he said, "I want a better one." Which, making no reply, I presented to him; he said he didn't want that one either. "Then what do you want me to give you?" I said. "A pruning hook," he answered. Now aside from the fact that in that country a pruning hook was too much to pay for a duck, I didn't even have one; I told him to content himself with the second knife I was offering him, and that he would have nothing more from me. But thereupon the interpreter, who knew their ways of doing things better than I did (although on this point, as I shall tell you, he was as mistaken as I) said to me, "He is very angry; somehow a pruning hook must be found." I borrowed one from the boy I mentioned, but when I tried to give it to this savage, he refused it more emphatically than he had previously done with the knives. Now I was getting angry, and for the third time I said to him: "What do you want from me?" To which he answered in a rage that he wanted to kill me as I had killed his duck; for, he said, "since it belonged to a brother of mine who is dead, I loved it more than anything else I have in my possession." And indeed, this lout went off to find a sword, or rather a big wooden club five or six feet long; suddenly advancing on me again, he kept repeating that he wanted to kill me. I was dumbfounded; still, I knew that one must not seem to knuckle under or show any fear among these people.

Thereupon the interpreter, seated in a cotton bed suspended between the quarreler and me, and warning me about what I didn't understand, said to me: "Hold your sword in your fist, and show him your bow and arrows, and let him know just who he is dealing with; as for you, you are strong and valiant, and will not let yourself be killed as easily as he thinks." So I bluffed my way through, and after a few more exchanges between this savage and me (without any attempt from the others to reconcile us), he left to sleep off the *caouin* that he had been drinking all day. The interpreter and I went off to dine on the duck with our companions, who were waiting for us in the village and knew nothing of our quarrel.

However, as it turned out, the Tupinamba knew perfectly well that, already having the Portuguese for enemies, if they had killed a Frenchman an irreconcilable war would have been declared between them and that they would be forever deprived of our merchandise; so everything that my man had done was in jest. And in fact, when he woke up about three hours later, he sent a message to me saying that I was his son, and that what he had done to me was only to test me, and to see by my countenance whether I would be valiant in war against the Portuguese and the Margaia, our common enemies. For my part, in order to deprive him of the chance to do the same another time, either to me or to another of our men—for such jokes are not very pleasant—I sent word to him that I would have nothing to do with him, and that I did not want a father who would test me with a sword in his hand. What is more, so as to make him find some better way of dealing with me, and to show him that such a game displeased me, the next day I gave little knives and fishhooks to the others right in front of him, who got nothing.

One can gather, then, as much from this example as from the other I have recounted about my first sojourn among the savages (where, out of ignorance of the standing that our nation had among them, I thought I was in danger), that what I have said about their loyalty toward their friends remains true and firm; that is, they would be very grieved to cause them displeasure.

For a conclusion on this point, I will add that the elders especially, who in the past lacked axes, pruning hooks and knives—which they now find useful for cutting their wood and making their bows and arrows— not only treat visiting Frenchmen very well, but also exhort their young people to do the same in the future.

ॐ

# HOW THE SAVAGES
## TREAT EACH OTHER IN
### THEIR ILLNESSES TOGETHER WITH THEIR BURIALS AND FUNERAL CERE-MONIES AND THE GREAT LAMENTA-TIONS THEY MAKE OVER THEIR DEAD[1]

To conclude my remarks about our savages of America, I must speak of the way they conduct themselves in their illnesses, and at the end of their days: that is, when they are close to natural death. If it happens that one of them falls sick, he points out where he hurts, whether in the arm, legs or other parts of the body, and one of his friends then sucks on this place with his mouth. Sometimes this is done by one of those charlatans among them called *pagés,* that is, surgeons or physicians (these are different from the *caraïbes* whom I spoke of when I discussed their religion);[2] these quacks would have them believe that they are not only extracting their pain, but even prolonging their life.

In addition to their common fevers and illnesses (because of their temperate climate, they are not as subject to them as we are over here), our Americans have an incurable disease that they call *pians.*[a] Ordinarily it is a result of lechery,[3] but I have also seen it in young children, who were covered all over with it just as children over here are afflicted with smallpox. This disease develops into pustules as wide as a thumb, which spread over the entire body, even to the face, so that those who are spotted with it carry the marks of their turpitude and baseness all through their lives, just as our pox-ridden folk do over here. In fact, I have seen an interpreter, a native of Rouen, who had wallowed in all sorts of lechery

---

[a][Yaws, caused by the spirochete *Treponema pertenue.* Unlike *Treponema pallida,* the vector of syphilis, it is mainly carried by flies and is not a venereal disease, as was commonly believed.]

with the savage women and girls, and had so truly received the wages of his sins that his body and face were as disfigured by these *pians* as if he had been a leper; the marks were so deeply imprinted that they could never be effaced. This is the most dangerous disease in the land of Brazil.

But to return to what I was saying. After they have treated someone by suction, the Americans do not give the bedridden invalid anything to eat unless he asks for it, even if he were to go a month without nourishment. And no matter how grave the illness, those who are healthy do not give up their habits of making noise, drinking, singing, and dancing around the poor patient, who, for his part, knowing full well that he has nothing to gain by getting angry, would rather have his ears assaulted with the noise than say a word about it.

However, if it happens that he should die, and especially if he is a respected head of a household, all the singing is suddenly turned to tears, and they lament so loudly that if we were in a village where someone had recently died, either we didn't try to find a bed there, or we didn't expect to sleep that night.

Above all, it is amazing to hear the cries of the women, as loud as the howling of dogs and wolves, wailing these lamentations and responses: "He is dead," say some, trailing their voices, "he who was so valiant, and who gave us so many prisoners to eat!" Then the others will burst out in the same fashion with "O what a good hunter he was, and the best of fishermen!" "Ha!" another one will say, "What a brave slayer of Portuguese and Margaia; he avenged us well!" So that amid these great tears, inciting each other to compete in ever greater mourning and (as you see in the illustration) embracing each other by the arms and shoulders, they will unceasingly recount in detail everything he said and did in his life, and make long chants in his praise, until the body is removed from before them.

They bring to mind the women of Béarn, who, lamenting over their dead husbands, make virtue out of vice, and sing, "*La mi amou, la mi amou: Cara rident, oeil de splendou: Cama leugé, bet dansadou: Lo mé balen, lo m'esburbat; matî depes: fort tard au lheit.*" That is, "My love, my love; laughing face, eye of splendor, light leg, fine dancer, my valiant one, my lively one, early up, late to bed." Some say that the Gascon women add, "*Yere, yere, O le bet renegadou, ô le bet jougadou qu'here.*" That is, "Alas, alas, what a grand swearer, what a fine gambler he was!" And so sing our poor American women, adding at each refrain, "He is dead, he is dead, he whom we now mourn." The men answer with, "Alas, it is true, we will see him no more until we are behind the mountains,

173

where as our *caraïbes* teach us, we will dance with him" and other similar themes.

Now these laments last ordinarily half a day, for they scarcely keep their dead bodies longer. After the grave has been dug (not long, as we dig them, but rather round and deep like a great wine barrel), the body, which immediately after death has been folded with the arms and legs bound around it, will be buried thus almost upright. If it is some worthy elder who has died, he will be entombed in his house, enveloped in his cotton bed; buried with him will be some necklaces, feathers and other objects that he used to wear when he was alive.

One could cite many examples from the ancients, who had similar customs. For instance, Josephus's account of the things placed in David's sepulchre,[a] and the testimony of the secular histories concerning so many great personages: after their death, they are adorned with precious jewels, and it all goes to rot with their bodies.

If we seek other examples, we need not go far from our Americans. The Indians of Peru, a land adjacent to theirs, buried a great quantity of gold and precious stones with their kings and caciques. A number of Spaniards who were among the first in that country searched out the spoils of those dead bodies even into the tombs and grottoes where they knew to find them, and were thereby made immensely wealthy.[4] One can apply to such avaricious creatures the words that, according to Plutarch,[5] Semiramis had engraved in the stone on the outside of her sepulchre:

> If you are a king, of money bereft,
> When this tomb is opened, take all you can heft.
> (Quiconque soit le Roy de pecune indigent,
> Ce tombeau ouvert prenne autant qu'il veut d'argent.)

Then he who opened it, thinking to find rich booty, saw instead this writing inside:

> Were you not a villain, insatiate for gold,
> You would never deposit a corpse dead and cold.
> (Si tu n'étais méchant insatiable d'or,
> Jamais n'eusses fouillé des corps morts le trésor.)

However, to return to our Tupinamba. Since the time that the French have lived among them, they no longer bury things of value with

---

[a] *Jewish Antiquities*, VII: 12.

their dead as often as they were in the habit of doing before. But now—for something much worse—you were about to hear of the greatest superstition imaginable, which holds these poor people are in bondage. They firmly believe that if Aygnan (that is, the devil) were to find no other meat nearby, he would unearth the body and eat it. So from the first night after a body has been buried (in the fashion you have heard described), they put out big earthen plates of flour, poultry, fish, and other well-cooked food, along with some *caouin,* on the grave of the dead person; they continue to perform such truly diabolical services until they think that the body is entirely decayed.

It was all the more difficult for us to lead them away from such an error in that the Norman interpreters who had been in that land before us, like the priests of Baal mentioned in Scripture, had thoroughly maintained and even confirmed them in it; so even though we showed them by experiment that what they put out in the evening was still to be found there the next morning, we could only persuade a few of them, and that just barely.

One can say that this vain imagining of the savages is not very different from that of the Judaic theologians or rabbis,[a] nor from that of Pausanias. For the rabbis hold that the dead body is left in the power of the devil whom they call "Zazel" or "Azazel," who they say is the prince of the wilderness in Leviticus. And to confirm their error, they subvert those passages of the Scripture where it is said to the serpent: "Dust shalt thou eat all the days of thy life." For, they say, since our body is created from the mud and dust of the earth, which is the serpent's meat,[b] it is subject to him until it is transmuted into spirit. Pausanias[6] likewise tells of another devil named "Eurinomus," who, according to the interpreters of Delphi, devoured the flesh of the dead, leaving nothing but the bones; such a belief is the same error as that of our Americans.

In the last chapter we showed how the savages carry their villages from one place to another. Similarly, they put over their graves little coverings of the big plant that they call *pindo;* the passers-by can thus recognize the location of a cemetery, and when the women meet there, or when they are in the woods, if they remember their dead husbands they

---

[a]See Pierre Viret, *La Physique papale* [*faite par maniére de devis et par dialogues* (Genève, 1552),] III: 210.

[b]Leviticus 16.8; Genesis 3.14; Isaiah 65.25.

will break out into their customary lamentations, and howl to be heard half a league away.

So now I will leave them to weep their fill. Since I have followed the savages all the way to the grave, I will here make an end to my discourse on their ways of doing things.

However, the readers will be able to see something more in the following dialogue, which was written while I was in America, with the help of an interpreter who had lived there for seven or eight years and understood the language perfectly. He had studied considerably, and even knew some Greek; therefore, since this nation of Tupinamba has drawn several words from that language (as those who understand it have already been able to observe), he could explain it all the better.[7]

# COLLOQUY UPON THE
## ENTRY OR ARRIVAL IN THE
### LAND OF BRAZIL AMONG THE PEOPLE
### OF THE COUNTRY CALLED TUPI-
### NAMBA AND TUPINIKIN: IN THE
### SAVAGE LANGUAGE AND IN FRENCH[1]

T (TUPINAMBA): *Ere-joubé?* Have you come?

F (FRENCHMAN): *Pa-ajout.* Yes, I have come.

T: *Teh! auge-ny-po.* Well said. *Mara-pé-déréré?* What is your name?

F: *Lery-oussou.* A big oyster.[2]

T: *Ere-jacasso pienc?* Have you left your country to come live here?

F: *Pa.* Yes.

T: *Eori-deretani ouani repiac.* Then come to see the place where you will stay.

F: *Auge-bé.* Very well.

T: *I-endé repiac? aout I-endérépiac aout é éhéraire Teh! Oouéreté Keuoy Lery-oussou yméen!* Look, he has come over here, my son, he has remembered us, alas![a]

T: *Erérou dé caramémo?* Have you brought your chests? (They mean by that any containers for belongings that one might have.)

F: *Pá arout.* Yes, I have brought them.

T: *Mobouy?* How many? (However many one has, one can count the number in words only up to the number five, naming them thus: *Augé-pé,* one; *mocouein,* two; *mossaput,* three; *oioicoudic,* four; *ecoinbo,* five. If you have two of them, there is no need to name four or five. It is enough to say *mocouein* for three or four. Similarly, if

---

[a][The "alas!" probably indicates the weeping greeting described in Chapter XVIII.]

there are four of them you will say *oioicoudic*. And so on for the others. But if there are more than five of them, you must indicate it by your fingers, and by the fingers of those who are next to you, so as to make up the number that you want them to understand; and thus you must do with everything. For they have no other way of counting.

T: *Máé pérérout, de caramémo poupé?* What have you brought in your chests?

F: *A-aub.* Garments.

T: *Mara vaé?* Of what kind or color?

[F:] *Sóbouy-eté.* Blue. *Pirenc.* Red. *Joup.* Yellow. *Son.* Black. *Sobouy, ouassou.*³ Green. *Pirienc.* Multicolored. *Pegassou-aue.* Dove-colored. *Tin.* White. (All these are the colors of shirts.)

T: *Maé pámo?* What else?

F: *Acang aubé-roupé.* Hats.

T: *Seta-pé?* Many?

F: *Icatoupaué.* So many that they can't be counted.

T: *Ai pogno?* Is that all?

F: *Erimen.* No.

T: *Esse non bat.* Name everything.

F: *Coromo.* Wait a little.

T: *Neín.* Go ahead.

F: *Mocap,* or *Mororocap.* A piece of artillery, like a big or small harquebus. (*Mocap* means any kind of artillery, the big ones for ships and others as well. Sometimes they seem to pronounce it *bocap,* with a *b,* and one would do well in writing it to try to use use an *m* and a *b* combined.) *Mocap-coui.* Cannon powder, or gunpowder. *Mocap-couiourou.* Flasks, horns, and so forth, for inserting the gunpowder.

T: *Mara vaé?* What are they made of?

F: *Tapiroussou-alc.* Of oxhorn.

T: *Augé-gatou-tégué.* Very good! *Mâe pè sepouyt rem?* What shall we give you for that?

F: *Arouri.* I merely brought them along with me. (As if to say "I'm in no hurry to get rid of them," so as to increase their value.)

T: *Hé!* (This is an interjection that they are in the habit of making when they are considering what has been said, all the while wishing to reply; however, they remain silent so as not to appear too importunate.)

F: *Arrou-ita ygapen.* I have brought iron swords.

179

T: *Naoepiac-icho péné?* Shall I not see them?

F: *Bégoé irem.* One day, at our leisure.

T: *Néréoùpe guya-pat?* Have you not brought any pruning hooks?

F: *Arrout.* I have brought some.

T: *Igatou-pé?* Are they good?

F: *Guipar-été.* They are excellent pruning hooks.

T: *Aua pomoquem?* Who made them?

F: *Pagé-ouassou remymognèn.* It was he whom you know, of that name, who made them.[a]

T: *Augé-terah.* Very good. *Acepiah mo-mèn.* How I would like to see them!

F: *Karamoussee.* Some other time.

T: *Tâcépiah taugé.* Let me see them now.

F: *Eémbereinguè.* Wait a while.

T: *Ereroupè itaxé amo?* Have you brought any knives?

F: *Arroureta.* I have brought a great many of them.

T: *Secouarantin vaé?* Are they knives with a curved handle?

F: *En-en non ivetin.* With a white handle. *Ivèpèp.* Half-serrated. *Taxe miri.* Little knives. *Pinda.* Fishhooks. *Moutemonton.* Awls. *Arroua.* Mirrors. *Kuap.* Combs. *Moùrobouy été.* Blue necklaces or bracelets. *Cepiah yponyéum.* Such as one rarely sees. These are the finest to be seen since we started coming over here.

T: *Easo ia-voh de caramemo t'acepiah dè maè.* Open your chest so that I may see your goods.

F: *Aimossaénen.* I cannot. *Acépiah-ouca iren desve.* I will show it to you some day when I come to visit you.

T: *Nârour icho p'Irèmmaè desve?* Shall I not bring you some goods on some days?

F: *Mae! pererou potat?* What do you want to bring?

T: *Sceh dè.* I don't know; but you? *Maé peréi potat?* What do you want?

F: *Soo.* Game animals. *Oura.* Birds. *Pira.* Fish. *Ouy.* Flour. *Yetic.* Turnips. *Commenda-ouassou.* Big beans. *Commenda miri.* Little beans. *Morgouia ouassou.* Oranges and lemons. *Maè tirouèn.* Various things.

---

[a][That is, the maker is named *Pagé-ouassou,* or big medicine-man.]

180

T: *Mara-vaé sóo erejusceh?* What kind of animal would you like to eat?

F: *Nacepiah quevon-gouaaire.* I don't want any of those of this country.

T: *Aassenon desve.* Let me name them for you.

T: *Nein.* Go ahead.

T: *Tapiroussou.* An animal so named, half donkey and half cow. *Se-ouassou.* A kind of stag and doe. *Taiasou.* The boar of that country. *Agouti.* A russet-colored beast, the size of a little three-week-old pig. *Pague.* A beast as big as a little month-old pig, with black and white stripes. *Tapiti.* A kind of hare.

[F:] Name me some birds.

T: *Jacou.* (This is a bird as big as a capon, made like a little guinea hen. There are three kinds of them: *Jacoutin, Jacoupem,* and *Jacou-ouassou.* They taste very good, and are as desirable as any birds.) *Mouton.* A wild peacock. (There are two kinds of them, black and gray, with a body the size of one of our peacock's; a rare bird.) *Mócacouà.* A big kind of partridge, with the body bigger than a capon's. *Ynambou-ouassou.* A partridge of the big sort, almost as big as the one just named. *Ynambou.* A partridge almost like those of France. *Pegassou.* The turtledove of that country. *Paicacu.* Another smaller kind of turtledove.

F: *Seta pé-pira sevaé?* Are there many good fish?

T: *Nan.* There are just as many. *Kurema.* Mullet. *Parati.* Another kind of mullet. *Acara ouassou.* Another big fish. *Acara-pep.* A flat fish, even more of a delicacy. *Acara-bouten.* Another fish, tan-colored, of a lesser sort. *Acara-miri.* A very small good-tasting freshwater fish. *Ouara.* A big, good-tasting fish. *Kamouroupouy-ouassou.* A big fish.

[F:] *Mamo-pe-deretam?* Where do you live?

T: (Now he names the place where he lives.) *Kariauh. Ora-ouassou-ouée Jaueu-urassic, Piracan i o-pen, Eiraïa, Itauen, Taracouir-apan, Sarapo-u.* (These are the villages along the shore on your left as you enter the Bay of Janeiro, each given its own name; I do not know that the names can be translated or given any particular meaning.) *Ke-ri-u, Acara-u, Kouroumouré, Ita-aue, Joirâ-rouen,* which are the villages on that bay on the right hand side. The biggest villages farther inland, on either side of the bay, are as follows: *Sacouarr-oussou-tuve, Ocarentin, Sapopem, Nouroucuue, Arasa-tuve, Usu-potuve,* and several others. When we have established communication with the people of this land, and with the heads of households (who are called "kings," which is a misnomer), we will know more about these villages and thus be better able to judge of them.

F: *Móbouy-pé toupicha gatou heuou?* How many chiefs are there here?

T: *Seta-gue.* There are many.

F: *Essenon auge pequoube ychesve.* Name some for me.

T: *Nân.* (This is a word used to get the attention of the person to whom you want to say something.) *Eapirau i joup.* (This is the name of a man who is an interpreter, who is mostly bald.)[a]

F: *Mamo-pè se tam?* Where is his dwelling?

T: *Kariauh-bè.* (In the village that is named after a little river nearby. The name is interpreted "the house of *Karios,*" composed of *Karios* and *auq,* meaning house; removing *os* and adding *auq* gives *Kariauh* and *be,* which is the article of the ablative, used to signify the place one is asking for or where one wants to go.) *Mossen y gerre.* (This is interpreted "keeper of medicines," or the person to whom medicine belongs. They use it when they want to call a woman a witch, or someone possessed of an evil spirit; for *mossen* means "medicine," and *gerre* means "belonging.") *Ourauh-oussou au arentin.* A big feather, chief of this village named "Desestorts." *Tau-couar-oussou-tuve-gouare.* In that village, the place where one gets cane, such as big reeds. *Ouacan.* The chief of that place, that is, their headman. *Soouar-oussou.* The leaf which has fallen from a tree. *Morgouia-ouassou.* A big lemon or orange. *Mae du.* Flame from some fire. *Maraca-ouassou.* A big rattle or bell. *Mae-uocep.* A thing that has partly emerged from the earth or from some other place. *Karaiau-piarre.* The path that leads to *Karios.* Those are the names of the chiefs of the region around the bay of Janeiro. *Che-rorup-gatou, derour-ari.* I am very glad you have come. *Nein téréico, pai Nicolas iron.* Stay with Lord Nicolas.[b] *Nère roupé d'eré miceco?* Haven't you brought your wife?

F: *Arrout iran-chèreco augernie.* I will bring her when my affairs are in order.

T: *Marapè d'erecoran?* What affairs do you have to arrange?

F: *Cher auc-ouam.* A house to live in.

---

[a][In Chapter XVII Léry mentioned that people's proper names are also the names of common animals or objects.]

[b]So they called Villegagnon.

T: *Mara-vae-auc?* What kind of house?

F: *Seth, daè ehèrèco-rem eouap rengnè.* I don't know yet what to do about that.

T: *Nein tèreie ouap dèrècorem.* So think about what you will need to do.

F: *Peretan repiac-iree.* After I have seen your country and dwellings.

T: *Nereico-icho-pe-deauem a irom?* Won't you stay with your own countrymen?

F: *Mara amo pè?* Why do you ask?

T: *Aipo-gué.* I say it for a reason. *Che-poutoupa-gué déri.* I am anxious about it. (As if to say: I would very much like to know.)

F: *Nèn pé amotareum pè orèroubichech?* Do you not hate our chief? (That is, our elder.)

T: *Erymen.* No. *Séré cogatou pouy-èum-été mo?* If it were not a thing that one should guard well, one should say: *Sécouaè apoau-è engatouresme, yporéré cogatou.* It is the custom of a good father to guard well what he loves.

T: Will you not go to war when the time comes?

F: *Asso irénué.* I will go some day. *Mara-pé perouagérre-rèrè?* What are your enemies' names?

T: *Touaiat* or *Margaiat.* (This is a nation which shares their language, who are allies of the Portuguese.) *Ouétaca.* These are true savages who are between the rivers of *Mach-he* and *Paraï. Ouèauem.* (These are savages who are still more savage, who live in the woods and mountains.) *Caraia.* (These are people of a more noble bearing, and richer in goods than those just mentioned, both in food and in other supplies.) *Karios.* (These are another kind of people living beyond the *Touaiaire,* toward the Plata, that have the same language as the Tupinikin Tupinamba.) (There is a difference of tongues, or local languages, among the nations just named. First, the Tupinikin Tupinamba, Touaiaire, Tenreminon, and Kario all speak a same language, or at least there is little difference among them in custom or in any other way. The Karaia have another way of doing and speaking. The Ouetaca differ both in language and in custom from them both. The Oueanen also have a completely different language and way of life.)

T: *Teh? Oioac poeireca à paau ué, iende ve.* A multitude of people seek each other out, and for our good. (This word *iendéve* is a dual number such as the Greeks use when they speak of two. However, here it is used for this way of speaking to us.) *Ty ierobah apòau-ari.* Let us be

183

proud that many people seek us out. *Apóau ae mae gerre, iendesve.* There are people who are here for our good. (That is, who give us of their goods.) *Ty rèco-gatou iendesve.* Let us take care of them well. (That is, let us treat them so that they may be pleased with us.) *Iporenc eté-amreco iendesve.* Here is a fine thing offered to us. *Ty maran-gatou apoau-apé.* Let us be allies of this people. *Ty momour-rou, kmé mae gerre indesve.* Let us do no offense to those who give us their goods. *Ty poih apoaue iendesve.* Let us give them the supplies they need to live. *Ty poeraca apoaué.* Let us work to catch game for them. (This word *yporraca* is used especially for fishing. But they also use it to refer to catching animals and birds.) *Tyrrout maè tyronam ani apé.* Let us bring them everything that we can catch. *Tyre comrémoich-meien dè-maè recoussaue.* Let us not mistreat those who bring us their goods. *Pe-poroinc auu-mecharaire-oueh.* Do not misbehave, my children. *Ta pere coihmae.* So that you may have goods. *Toerecoih peraíre amo.* And so that your children may have, also. *Nyrecoih ienderamouyn maé pouaire.* We received no goods from our grandfathers. *Opap cheramouyn maè pouaire aitih.* I have thrown away everything that my grandfather left me. *Apoau maè-ry oi ierobiah.* Taking pride in the goods brought to us by everybody. *Ienderamouyn-remiè pyac potategue a ou-aire.* Which our grandfathers would like to have seen, yet have not seen. *Teh! oip otarhètè ienderamouyn rècohiara ete iendesve.* This is good, that a trade more excellent than that of our grandfathers has come to us. *Iende pouuar oussou-vocare.* It is what frees us from all sadness. *Iende-co ouassou-gerre.* That lets us have big gardens. *En sassi piram. Ienderè memy non apè.* It no longer hurts our grandchildren when we shave their heads. *Tyre coih apouau, ienderoua gerre-ari.* Let us lead these with us against our enemies. *Toere coih mocap ò mae-ae.* May they have their harquebuses, their own weapons. *Mara mosenten gatou-euin-amo?* Why would they not be strong? *Meme-tae morerobiarem.* It is a nation that fears nothing. *Tysenenc apouau, maram iende iron.* Let us test their strength when they join with us. *Mènre-tae moreroar roupiare.* They are the ones that defeat those who carry off others, that is, the Portuguese. *Agne he oueh.* This is true, all that I have said.

T: *Nein-tyamoueta indere cassariri.* Let us speak together of those who are coming to seek us out. (They mean us, for the most part.)

F: *Nein-che atouu-assaire.* Well, then, my ally! (But on this point one must note that this word *atour-assap* is different from *cotouassap.*

For the first signifies a perfect alliance among them, and between them and us, so that the goods of one are common to the other. And also that they cannot have the daughter or the sister of such an ally. But that is not so of the latter term, which is only a casual manner of naming each other by another name than one's own, as one says "my leg," "my eye," "my ear," and other such expressions.)

T: *Maé resse iende moueta?* What shall we speak of?

F: *Seéh mae tirouen-resse.* Of numerous and various things.

T: *Mara-pieng vah-reré?* How do you say "sky?"

F: Sky.

T: *Cyh-rengne-tassenouh mamaetirouen desve.*[a]

F: *Auge-bè.* It is well said.

T: *Mac.* The sky. *Couarassi.* The sun. *Jasce.* The moon. *Jassi tata ouassou.* The big morning and evening star that is commonly called "Lucifer." *Jassi tata miri.* These are all the other little stars. *Ubouy.* The earth. *Paranan.* The sea. *Uh-etè.* Soft water. *Uh-een.* Salt water. *Uh-een buhc.* Stagnant water, which the sailors usually call "sommaque." *Ita.* Properly, stone. It is also used for all kinds of metal and for the essential parts of buildings, as in *aoh-ita,* the pillar of the house. *Yapurr-yta.* The rooftop. *Iura ita.* The big rafters of the house. *Igourahou y bouirah.* Every kind of wood. *Ourapat.* A bow. The word is made up of *ybouyrah,* meaning wood, and *apat,* meaning curved or split; however, they pronounce it *orapat* by syncope. *Arre.* Air. *Arraip.* Bad air. *Amen.* Rain. *Amen poyton.* The weather when it is on the point of raining. *Toupen.* Thunder. *Toupen verap.* The lightning that precedes it. *Ybuo ytin.* Clouds or fog. *Ybueture.* Mountains. *Guum.* Countryside or flatland where there are no mountains. *Taue.* Villages. *Auc.* House. *Uh-ecouap.* River or flowing water. *Uh-paon.* An island surrounded by water. *Kaa.* All kinds of woods and forests. *Kaa-onan.* Who is nourished by the forest. *Kaa-gerre.* An evil spirit, who does nothing but harm them as they go about their business. *Ygat.* A skiff of bark that can hold thirty or forty men going to war. The word is also used for a ship, which they call *ygueroussou.* *Puissa-ouassou.* A fishing net. *Inguea.* A big fishing boat. *Inquei.* (Diminutive.) A boat used when the waters overflow their banks. *Nomognot mae tasse nom desve.* Let

---

[a][Léry gives no translation. Ayrosa gives: "Let it be said in the first place, among the various things that I will tell you" (my trans.) (*Viagem* 283).]

me stop naming things. *Emourbeou deretaniichesve.* Tell me about your country and the place where you live.

F: *Augébé derenguéepourendoup.* Very well. First ask me questions.

T: *Ia-eh-marape dertani-rere.* Willingly. What is the name of your country and your dwelling?

F: Rouen.[a] That is the name of a city.

T: *Tav-ouscou-pe-ouim?* Is it a big village? (They make no distinction between city and village, because of their own customs: they have no cities.)

F: *Pa.* Yes.

T: *Moboii-pe-reroupichah-gatou?* How many lords do you have?

F: *Auge-pe.* Only one.

T: *Marape-sere?* What is his name?

F: Henry. (It was in the reign of King Henry II that this voyage was made.)

T: *Tere-porrenc.* That is a fine name. *Mara-pe perou pichau-eta enin?* Why do you not have several lords?

F: *Moroér é chih-gué.* . . . We have no more than one . . . *ore ramouin-ave,* since the time of our grandfathers.

T: *Mara-pieuc-pee?* And you others, who are you?

F: *Oroicógue.* We are content this way. *Oree maé-gerre.* We are the ones who have wealth.

T: *Epè-noeré-coih? peroupícgag mae?* And your Prince, does he have any wealth?

F: *Oerecoih.* He has as much and more. *Oree-mae-gerre-a hépé.* Everything that we have is at his command.

T: *Oraiui-pe ogépé?* Does he go to war?

F: *Pa.* Yes.

T: *Mobouy-tave-pe-iouca ny mae?* How many cities or villages do you have?

F: *Seta-gatou.* More than I could tell you.

T: *Niresce-nouih-icho pene?* Won't you name them for me?

F: *Ypoicopouy.* It would be too long and tedious.

---

[a][Rouen is in Normandy, nowhere near Léry's birthplace. This suggests that a Norman interpreter is writing this section.]

T: *Yporrenc-pe-peretani?* Is it beautiful, the place you come from?

F: *Yporren-gatou.* It is very beautiful.

T: *Eugaya-pe-per-auce?* Are your houses like ours?

F: *Oicoe-gatou.* They are very different.

T: *Mara-vaé?* What are they like?

F: *Ita-gepe.* They are all of stone.

T: *Youroussou-pe?* Are they big?

F: *Touroussou-gatou.* They are very big.

T: *Vate-gatou-pé?* Are they very high?

F: *Mahmo.* Very. (This word means more than "very" or "much"; they use it when speaking of a thing to be marveled at.)

T: *Engaya-pe-pet-anc ynim?* Is the inside the same? (That is, as those of the houses here.)

F: *Erymen.* Not at all.

T [F?]: *Esce-non-de-rete renomdau eta-ichesve.* Name me the parts of the body.

F [T?]: *Escendou.* Listen.

T [F?]: *Ieh.* I am ready.

T: *Chè-acan.* My head. *De acan.* Thy head. *Ycan.* His [or her] head. *Oreacan.* Our head. *Pè acan.* Your head. *An atcan.* Their head.

But so that you can better understand these pronouns, I will give the persons, both singular and plural.

### FIRST.

*Ché.* This is the first-person singular, which is used in all kinds of speech, root words, derived words, possessives, or others. That applies to the other persons as well.

| | |
|---|---|
| *Ché-avè.* | My head or my hair. |
| *Chè-voua.* | My face. |
| *Chè-nembi.* | My ears. |
| *Chèsshua.* | My forehead. |
| *Ché-ressa.* | My eyes. |
| *Chè-tin.* | My nose. |
| *Che-jourou.* | My mouth. |

| | |
|---|---|
| *Ché-retoupavè.* | My cheeks. |
| *Chè-redmiva.* | My chin. |
| *Ché-redmiva-avè.* | My beard. |
| *Ché-ape-cou.* | My tongue. |
| *Chè-ram.* | My teeth. |
| *Ché-ajouré.* | My neck, or my throat. |
| *Ché-assoec.* | My gullet. |
| *Ché-poca.* | My chest. |
| *Ché-rocapè.* | The front of me, generally. |
| *Ché-atoucoupè.* | The back of me. |
| *Chè-pouy-asóo.* | My backbone. |
| *Chè-rousbony.* | My loins. |
| *Ché-revirè.* | My buttocks. |
| *Ché-invanpony.* | My shoulders. |
| *Ché-inva.* | My arms. |
| *Chè-papouy.* | My fist. |
| *Che-po.* | My hand. |
| *Chè-poneu.* | My fingers. |
| *Ché-puyac.* | My stomach or liver. |
| *Ché-reguie.* | My belly. |
| *Ché-pourou-assen.* | My navel. |
| *Ché-cam.* | My breasts. |
| *Ché-oup.* | My thighs. |
| *Ché-roduponam.* | My knees. |
| *Chè-porace.* | My elbows. |
| *Che-retemeu.* | My legs. |
| *Ché-pouy.* | My feet. |
| *Ché-pussempé.* | My toenails. |
| *Che-ponampe.* | My fingernails. |
| *Che-guy-eneg.* | My heart and lungs. |
| *Che-eneg.* | My soul, or thought. |
| *Che-enc gouere.* | My soul after it has left my body. |

Names of parts of the body that it is not decent to name:

*Che-rencouem.*
*Che-rementien.*
*Che-rapoupit.*[a]

For the sake of brevity I will give no other definitions. It must be noted that one cannot name most things (those already mentioned as well as others) without adding the pronoun, whether first, second or third person, and whether singular or plural. So that you can better understand each of them separately:

## FIRST.

*Ché,* I. *Dè,* thou. *Ahé,* he.
*Oree,* we. *Peè,* you. *Au-aé,* they.

As for the third person singular, *ahe* is masculine, and for the feminine and neuter they use *aé* without aspiration. In the plural *au-ae* is used for both the masculine and the feminine, and therefore can be common.

Things belonging to the household and the kitchen:

*Emiredu-tata.* Light the fire.
*Emo-goep-tata.* Put out the fire.
*Erout-che-rata-rem.* Bring something to light my fire with.
*Emogip-pira.* Cook the fish.
*Essessit.* Roast it.
*Emous.* Boil it.
*Fa-vecu-òuy-amo.* Make some flour.
*Emogip-caouin-amo.* Make some *caouin* (their drink).
*Coein upé.* Go to the fountain.
*Erout-u ichesve.* Bring me some water.
*Ch-renni-auge-pe.* Give me something to drink.
*Quere me che-remyou-recoap.* Come give me something to eat.
*Taie-poeh.* Let me wash my hands.
*Tae-iourou-eh.* Let me rinse my mouth.

---

[a][Ayrosa (*Viagem* 286, n. 119) identifies these respectively as the male member, the visible female parts, and the internal female parts.]

*Ché-embouassi.* I am hungry.

*Nam-che-iourou-eh.* I have no appetite.

*Ehe-usseh.* I am thirsty.

*Ché-reaic.* I am hot, I am sweating.

*Chè-rou.* I am cold.

*Ché-racoup.* I have a fever.

*Ché-carouc-assi.* I am sad. (However, *carouc* means vespers or evening.)

*Aicouteve.* I am anxious, uneasy. (Whatever the concern may be.)

*Che-poura-oussoup.* I am being inconvenienced, or poorly treated.

*Cheroemp.* I am cheerful.

*Aico memouoh.* I am being ridiculed; people mock me.

*Aico-gatou.* I am doing what pleases me.

*Che-remiac-oussou.* My slave.

*Chere-miboye.* My servant.

*Che-roiac.* Those who are inferior to me, and who are there to serve me.

*Che-porracassare.* My fishermen. (Those who catch fish and other things as well.)

*Ché-mae.* My goods, merchandise, furnishings, and everything that belongs to me.

*Che-rémigmogmem.* It is of my fashioning.

*Che-rere-couarré.* My guard.

*Ché-roubichac.* He who is greater than I: what we call our king, duke, or prince.

*Moussacat.* A worthy head of a household who offers food to travelers, both strangers and others.

*Querre-muhau.* One who is powerful in war, and valiant in his undertakings.

*Tenten.* Strong in appearance, in war and in other things.

Of Lineage:

*Chè-roup.* My father.

*Chè-requeyt.* My elder brother.

*Chè-rebure.* My younger brother.

*Chè-renadire.* My sister.

*Ché-rure.* My sister's son.

*Chè-tipet.* My sister's daughter.

*Chè-aiché.* My aunt.

*Ai.* My mother. (One also says *Ché-si,* my mother, and uses this most often in speaking of her.)

*Ché-siit.* My mother's companion, who is also, like my mother, the wife of my father.

*Chè-raiit.* My daughter.

*Chèrememynou.* The children of my sons and daughters.

It must be noted that the uncle is called the same way the father is; likewise, the father calls his nephews and nieces "my son and my daughter."

What the grammarians call "verb" can be called "speech" in our language;[4] in the Brazilian language *guengave,* which is about like saying speaking or manner of saying. So that one can have some understanding of this, we will put forth some examples.

## FIRST.

Singular indicative or demonstrative: *Aico,* I am. *Ereico,* you are. *Oico,* he is. *Oroico,* we are. *Peico,* you are. *Auraèo ico,* they are.

The third person of the singular and the plural are alike, except that one must add to the plural the pronoun *au-ae,* which means *they,* as is shown.

In the past tense, there is the imperfect for actions not completed. For one can still be what one was at that time.

The singular is modified by the adverb *aquoémè,* that is, "at that time," to form the past: *Aico-aquoémè,* I was then. *Eréico-aquoémé,* you were then. *Oico aquoèmè,* he was then.

Plural imperfect: *Oroico aquoémè,* we were then. *Peico aquoémé,* you were then. *Aurae-oico-aquoémè,* they were then.

To express a time completely past, an action accomplished:

*Singular.*
We will use the verb *oico,* as before, and add the adverb *aquoè-menè,* which amounts to saying that the action took place in a time past and

191

completely over, without there being any hope of things being as they were at that time.

Example:

> *Assauoussou-gatou-aquoémené,* I loved him perfectly at that time; *quouènén-gatou-tègné,* but now not at all. (As if to say: he should have valued my friendship at the time that I bore him friendship. For one cannot return to it.)

For the time to come, called the "future":

*Aico-irén,* I will do it in the future. (And so forth for the other persons as before, both singular and plural.)

For the command called the "imperative":

*Oico,* be. *Toico,* may he be.

*Toroico,* may we be. *Tapeico,* may you be. *Aurae toico,* may they be.

(And for the future, simply add *iren,* as before. For a command in the present, say *taugé,* which means "now.")

To express the desire to do something, which we call the "optative":

*Aico-mo-men,* "Oh, how I would like to" and continuing as before.

For what we call the "conjunctive," to express the idea of joining, they use the adverb *iron,* which means that with which one wants to join.

Example:

*Taico-de-iron,* Let me be with you. (And so on.)

The participle drawn from this verb.

*Chè recoruré,* I being.

(This participle cannot be understood alone; one must add the pronoun *de-ahe-et-aé.* The plural is *Oreé, pèe, an, -ae.*)

The indefinite form of this verb can be taken for an infinitive, but they rarely use it in that way.

The conjugation of the verb *aioüt.*

Example of the indicative or demonstrative in the present tense. The forms are given a double translation into French, of which the second one is a past tense.

192

*Singular.*

> *Aiout,* I come, or I have come.
>
> *Ereiout.* You come, or have come.
>
> *O-out.* He comes, or has come.

*Plural.*

> *Ore-iout.* You come, or have come.
>
> *An-ae-o-out.* They come, or have come.

To form the other tenses, one must simply use the adverbs given below. For no verb can be conjugated without having its meaning completed by an adverb, whether in the preterite, present imperfect, indefinite pluperfect, or the future.

> *Example of the imperfect preterite, to express an action that is not completed:*
>
> *Aiout-aguoème.* I was coming then.

Example of a perfect preterite, for a completed action:

*Aiout-aguoèmènè.* I came, I had come at that time.

*Aiout-dimaè-nè.* I had come a long time ago.

(These tenses can be fairly indefinite, both here and in speaking.)

Example of the future, or the time to come:

*Aiout-Iran-nè.* I will come a certain day. (One can also say *Iran* without adding *né,* as the phrase or manner of speaking requires. Note that when adding the adverbs, one should repeat the persons, as in the present indicative or demonstrative.)

Example of the imperative:

*Singular.*

> *Eori, eyot.* Come. (There is only the second person, for in this language you cannot issue a command to a third person that you do not see.) But one can say:
>
> *Emo-out.* Make him come.
>
> *Pe-ori.* Come.

The sounds written as *eiot* and *pe-iot* have the same sense, but the first, *eiot,* is more appropriate among men, while the last, *Pe-iot,* is ordinarily used when calling domestic animals and birds.

Example of the optative, which seems to issue an order, as a desire for something or as a command:

*Singular.*

*Aiout-mo.* I would like to come or would willingly have come. (And so forth for the other persons, as in the conjugation of the indicative. There is a future tense, formed by adding the adverb, as in the examples given above.)

I do not know any indicative of this verb, but a participle is formed from it.

*Touume.* Coming.

Example:

*Ché-rourmè-Assoua-nitin.*

*Chè-remièreco-pouére.*

While coming, I encountered what I had formerly guarded [someone who was a former guest?].

*Senoyt-pe.* Leech.

*Inuby-a.* Wooden horns that the savages blow on.

# END OF COLLOQUY

So that those with whom I crossed and recrossed the sea, as well as those who have seen me in America (some of whom may still be alive), and even sailors and others who have voyaged and sojourned in the Bay of Janeiro or Guanabara, under the tropic of Capricorn, may judge better and more promptly of the discourses I have made concerning the things I saw in that land, I wished particularly for their sake to add separately, at the end of this colloquy a list of the twenty-two villages that I frequently visited among the American savages.

First, those that are on the left side when one enters the bay:

1. *Kariauc.*
2. *Yaboraci.* (The French call this second village Pepin, because of a ship that loaded there once, whose master was of that name.)
3. *Euramyry.* (The French call it Gosset, because of an interpreter of that name who had stayed there.)

4. *Pira-ouassou.*

5. *Sapopem.*

6. *Ocarentin,* a fine village.

7. *Oura-ouassou-oueé.*

8. *Tentimen.*

9. *Cotiva.*

10. *Pauo.*

11. *Sarigoy.*

12. One named Pierre by the French, because of a little rock, rather like a millstone, which marked the path at the entry to the woods that leads to it.

13. Another called *Upec* by the French, because there were many ducks that the savages call by that name.

14. There is a village that got its name this way: the first time that we were on the path in the woods that leads to it, we shot a great many arrows into the top of a big tall rotted tree, so that we could find it again. Since the arrows remained fixed in that treetop, we named the village "Village of Arrows."

Those that are on the right-hand side:

15. *Keri-u.*

16. *Acara-u.*

17. *Morgouia-ouassou.*

Those of the Great Island:

18. *Pindo-oussou.*

19. *Corouque.*

20. *Pirauijou.*

21. And another whose name has escaped me, between *Pindo-oussou* and *Pirauijou,* which I once helped to buy some prisoners.

22. Then another one between *Corouque* and *Pindo-oussou,* whose name I have also forgotten.

I have already told elsewhere what these villages are like, and the style of the houses.

# CHAPTER XXI

# OF OUR DEPARTURE
## FROM THE LAND OF BRAZIL,
### CALLED AMERICA; TOGETHER WITH THE SHIPWRECKS AND OTHER PERILS THAT WE ESCAPED ON THE SEA DURING OUR RETURN

To understand fully the occasion of our departure from the land of Brazil, one must recall what I said earlier, at the end of Chapter VI: that is, after we had been for eight months on the island where Villegagnon was staying, he became angry with us because of his own revolt from the Reformed Religion, and since he was not able to control us by force, he compelled us to leave. We retreated to the mainland, to a place that we called "The Brickyard," only half a league from Fort Coligny, on the left as you enter the Bay of Guanabara or Janeiro. There we stayed about two months, living in the shacks that the French workmen had built for shelter when they went there for fishing or other business.

During this time Messieurs de la Chapelle and de Boissy, whom we had left with Villegagnon, now abandoning him for the same reason we did—because he had turned his back on the Gospel—came to join us and became part of our company, and were included in our arrangements, which were: six hundred pounds, and food provisions from the region, which we had promised to pay and to furnish—which we did—to the master of the ship that was to take us back across the sea.

But before continuing I must here fulfill my promise to relate how Villegagnon behaved toward us upon our departure from America. Since he acted as if he were viceroy of that country, none of the French seamen who were sailing there would have dared undertake anything against his will. While the ship was at anchor in the Bay of Janeiro, where it was being loaded for the return voyage, Villegagnon not only sent us a permit to leave signed by his hand, he also wrote a letter to the ship's master, saying that he had no objection to our being taken back. "For," he said deceitfully, "just as I rejoiced at their coming, thinking that I had found what I was looking for, so too, since they do not agree with me, I am glad of their departure." Under this fine pretext he had brewed the treachery that you will now hear. He gave the ship's master a little chest wrapped in waxed canvas to protect it from the sea, full of letters addressed to various people over here. In them he lodged an indictment against us without our knowledge, with the express command to the first judge in France who might receive it that we should be seized and burned as the heretics he said we were. So in recompense for the services we had rendered him, he had, as it were, sealed our leave-taking with this betrayal, which, however (as will be seen in due time) God by his wondrous providence made redound to our comfort and to his frustration.

This ship, the *Jacques,* was loaded with brazilwood, long peppers, cotton, apes, marmosets, parrots, and other things, rare over here, which most of us had acquired earlier; we embarked on the fourth of January 1558. But before we put to sea, there is something I want to say, to demonstrate once more that Villegagnon is the sole cause wherefore the French did not establish themselves in that country. A certain Fariban of Rouen, captain of this ship, at the request of several notable personages of the Reformed Religion in France, had undertaken this voyage expressly to explore the land and quickly choose a place to settle. He told us that had it not been for the revolt of Villegagnon, seven or eight hundred people would have been sent in big Flemish ships to begin populating the place where we were staying. I firmly believe that if Villegagnon had remained true to the faith, there would be at present more than ten thousand Frenchman over there who, besides staunchly protecting our island and fort against the Portuguese, who then could never have taken it (as they did, after our return),[1] would now possess under allegiance to our King a great country in the land of Brazil, which one could rightfully have continued to call "Antarctic France."

To get back to my subject. The ship in which we returned was a merchant ship of only middling size; its master, Martin Baudouin of Le Havre, had only about twenty-five sailors, and there were fifteen in our company, making in all forty-five people on board. The same day, the fourth of January, we weighed anchor, and committing ourselves to the protection of God, we set forth on that great and tempestuous Ocean Sea of the West. Not, however, without great fear and apprehension: in view of the hardships we had endured going over, if it had not been for the ill turn done us by Villegagnon, several of us, who had not only found over there the means of serving God as we wished, but had also tasted the goodness and the fertility of the country, might well have stayed on instead of returning to France, where the difficulties were then—and are still—incomparably greater, with respect both to religion and to things concerning this life.

So that saying goodbye here to America, I confess for myself that although I have always loved my country and do even now, still, seeing the little—next to none at all—of fidelity that is left here, and, what is worse, the disloyalties of people toward each other—in short, since our whole situation is Italianized,[2] and consists only in dissimulation and words without effect—I often regret that I am not among the savages, in whom (as I have amply shown in this narrative) I have known more frankness than in many over here, who, for their condemnation, bear the title of "Christian."

At the beginning of our voyage we had to go around the Great Shoals, which is a point of mixed sand and rock projecting around thirty leagues into the sea, which the mariners greatly fear. The wind was keeping us from getting away from land, which, rather than follow the coastline, was what we needed to do; in order to avoid this danger we were almost compelled to put into harbor. We had been afloat seven or eight days, and had been tossed from one side to the other by this unfavorable wind, which had hardly advanced us at all when, at around midnight, we became aware of a much greater danger. The sailors on watch, going as usual to pump out the water, found that they had to stay at it, and although they counted more than four thousand *bâtonnées* (those who have sailed on the Ocean Sea with Normans will understand this term to mean "pump strokes"), it was impossible for them to drain it. When they were very weary of pumping, the master's mate, looking to see where it was coming from, went down through the hatch and found the ship leaking in several places; it was already so full of water, which was still coming in full force, that it could not be steered, and one could feel it sinking little by little.

You need not ask whether, when we were all awakened and made aware of the danger, we were marvelously stunned. In truth, it seemed so likely that we would be submerged any minute that some, suddenly losing all hope of being saved, acted as if they were already dead and at the bottom of the sea.

However, as God willed it, some of us, being resolved to prolong our lives while we could, found courage enough to sustain the ship with two pumps until noon; that is, nearly twelve hours, during which time the water entered in such quantity that we had to keep those two pumps working without a moment's pause. The water rose so high that it covered the brazilwood in the cargo, and ran out through the conduits as red as oxblood. While we were exerting all our strength at this task, as our dire situation required, we had a wind favorable for returning us to the land of the savages, which was not far away, and which we could see from about eleven o'clock on that same day. Determined to take refuge there if we could, we headed straight for it. Meanwhile the mariners and the carpenter were under the hatches looking for the holes and cracks through which the water was coming in and assailing us with such force. They managed to caulk the most dangerous of these with lard, lead, cloth, and so forth, which were provided in abundance; so that when we were at the point of exhaustion we were able to have a little relief from our labor.

The carpenter looked over the ship carefully, and said that it was too old and worm-eaten for the voyage we were undertaking; his advice was that we return to our place of departure and wait there for another ship from France, or else that we build a new one. All of that was debated at length. However, the ship's master objected that if he returned to land, his sailors would leave him, and (so little judgment did he have) that he preferred to hazard his life rather than lose his ship and his merchandise; he concluded that he would continue the voyage, whatever the danger. He said, however, that if Monsieur du Pont and the passengers under his guidance wanted to return to the land of Brazil, he would give them a boat. Du Pont immediately replied that he was resolved to continue on to France, and advised all his people to do the same. Thereupon the master's mate argued that besides the dangers of the navigation, he could foresee that we would be a long time on the sea, and that there was not enough food in the ship to feed all the passengers. At that point six of us, considering the probabilities of shipwreck on the one hand and famine on the other, resolved to return to the land of the savages, which was only nine or ten leagues away.

To put this plan into effect, we quickly put our belongings into the boat that was given us, with a little root flour and some drink. As we were taking leave of our companions, one of them, full of regret at my departure and impelled by a particular feeling of friendship, put out his hand as I was in the boat, and said, "I beg you to stay with us; for even if we cannot get to France, still there is more hope of safety on the coast of Peru, or on some island, than in returning to Villegagnon, who as you very well know will never leave you at peace over here."

Upon these remonstrances, and seeing that there was no time for more discussion, I left some of my belongings behind me in the boat, and, hastily climbing back into the ship, I was thus preserved from the danger that you will soon hear about, and which my friend had clearly foreseen.

As for the five others, whose names (for a reason) I specify here—Pierre Bourdon, Jean du Bordel, Matthieu Verneuil, André La Fon, and Jacques Le Balleur—they took leave of us with tears, and returned to the land of Brazil. As I shall recount at the end of this history, they landed there with great difficulty, and upon their return to Villegagnon, he had the first three put to death for their confession of the Gospel.[3]

Thus having made ready and put our sails to the wind, we again set forth on the sea in this wretched old ship that we thought would be our sepulchre, more expecting to die in it than to live.

Besides the great difficulty we had passing the shoals, the whole month of January we had continual storms; what is more, our ship continued to take in great amounts of water, and if we had not constantly been at the pumps, we would have (so to speak) died a hundred times a day. We sailed a long time amid such hardships.

When, with such labor, we had put the mainland more than two hundred leagues behind us, we sighted an uninhabitable island, as round as a tower, which I took to be about a half a league in circumference. As we were going alongside it—with it on our left—we saw that it was not only full of trees, all green in this month of January, but it was covered with birds. A great flock of them flew out and lit on the spars of our ship, where they let themselves be caught by hand; seeing the island from a distance, you would have said it was a dovecote. Some of the birds were black, others gray, or whitish, or of other colors, and as they were all flying around they seemed very big. However, when those that we caught were plucked, they had no more flesh than a sparrow.

About two leagues away on our right we saw some rocks as sharp as steeples emerging from the water, which made us fear that there might be some just below the surface that could have wrecked our ship—and if that had happened, we would have been quit of water pumps forever.

The whole five months of our return voyage, we saw no land other than these islets, which our masters and pilots did not find marked on their marine maps, and which perhaps had never been discovered.

At the end of the month of February, we arrived at a point three degrees from the Equator. Almost three weeks had passed, and we had not yet completed even a third of our voyage. Our food supply was rapidly diminishing, and we considered making a stop at Cape Saint

Roch,[4] which is inhabited by savages from whom, some of our people said, we could get fresh provisions. However, most were of the opinion that we should, rather, husband the food supplies by killing some of the monkeys and parrots that we were carrying, and sail on; which is what we did.

In Chapter IV I recounted our toil and hardship going over as we were approaching the Equator. I have seen by experience (as have all those who have passed through the Torrid Zone) that it is no less troublesome returning here from the direction of the South Pole, and I will here explain what I think to be the cause of these difficulties.

Let us assume that the Equator, which runs from east to west, is like the backbone of the world to those voyaging from north to south, or vice versa (for I know that a ball considered as such has neither top nor bottom). In the first place, from whichever direction one arrives, there is the difficulty of mounting to this ridge of the world; then there are the sea currents from either direction, indiscernible in the midst of this expanse of water; added to these are the fickle winds that come out of this spot as from their center and blow against each other, pushing back the ships. These three things, in my opinion, make the Equator difficult to reach. And what confirms me in my opinion is that as soon as you are about one degree beyond the Equator as you are going out, or one degree this side as you are coming back, the mariners rejoice at having, so to speak, cleared the hurdle; since they are now hopeful about this voyage, they urge each other to eat the provisions that had been so carefully conserved while getting out of that region had been so uncertain.

So when the ships are on the slope of the globe, they are not hindered gliding down as they are going up. Furthermore, all the seas communicate with each other, and were it not for the wondrous power and providence of God, they could cover the earth. Although they are higher than the land and are supported by it, they only divide it into islands and pieces, which are, I think, likewise all conjoined, and bound together as it were by roots, in the deep hollows of the seas. This big mass of waters is thus suspended with the earth, and turns as if on an axis through two pivots (which I imagine to be at right angles to the poles so that they are found at the full and half circles which surround the whole sphere) in perpetual motion, as the ebb and flow of the tides clearly show. This general movement takes its fulcrum under the line, so when the hemisphere of southern waters (from our perspective) advances, turning almost to its prescribed limits, and the northern waters withdraw by the same amount, those who are in the middle and in the belt of the ball are thus swung and tossed, as if they were on a see-saw or teeter-totter in continual motion, and are thus prevented from going further. And I will add what I have already mentioned elsewhere: the unsettled weather and the calms that one often encounters under the Equator are a great hindrance, and often delay the voyager in the region for a long time.

And there you have, in summary and in passing, my opinion on this high matter, which, moreover, I regard as so disputable that only He who created this great round machine composed of water and earth, and who miraculously sustains it suspended in the air, can understand all there is to know about it. I am certain that in no other spirit can any man, however learned, speak of this without being subject to correction. And indeed one could, with the appearance of reason, contradict most of the arguments of the schools (which, however, should not be scorned, since they awaken the intellect); provided that all this be taken as a second cause, and not as the supreme cause, as it is by the atheists.[5] In conclusion, there is nothing about any of this that I believe absolutely, except what the Holy Scriptures say; for since they proceed from the Spirit of Him upon whom depends all truth, I hold their authority alone to be beyond all doubt.

To resume our journey. Thus, little by little and with difficulty, we approached the Equator, and our pilot, having taken the sun's altitude with the astrolabe, assured us that we were right under that belt of the world on the same equinoctial day that the sun was there, that is, the eleventh of March;[a] this he pointed out to us as a singular event, which happens to very few ships. So, to make matters short, in that place we had the sun at the zenith, directly over our heads, and I will let you imagine the extreme and violent heat that we endured at that time. Furthermore, although in other seasons the sun, drawing alternately from one side or the other toward the tropics, strays and departs from that line, nevertheless it is impossible to be in any part of the world, on sea or land, where it is hotter than under the Equator. Therefore I wonder all the more at something that was said by someone whom I consider reliable. Certain Spaniards, he said, traveling in a region of Peru, were astonished not only to see it snow under the Equator, but also to cross it, with great effort and hardship, while going over snow-covered mountains; in fact, they experienced there a cold so severe that several of them were frozen to death.[b]

---

[a] [On the Julian calendar.]

[b] [Gómara,] *Histoire,* Book 4, Chapter 126.

Now it is the common opinion of natural philosophers that snow is formed in the middle regions of the air. But, given that the sun's rays are always vertical in the Equatorial zone, and thus that the air is always hot—no matter what is adduced about the height of the mountains or the frigidity of the moon—, there could then be no snow there. In respect to this climate (subject always to correction by the learned men), I see no basis for the opinion of the philosophers.

Therefore I conclude, for my part, that we have here an exception in the rule of philosophy, and I think that there is no solution to this question more certain than the one that God himself offered to Job. To show him that men, however subtle they may be, could never comprehend all his magnificent works, much less their perfection, He said to him: "Hast thou entered into the treasures of the snow? Or hast thou seen the treasures of the hail?"[a] As if the Eternal, this great and excellent worker, were saying to his servant Job: "In what garner do you think I store these things? Could you give the reason for them? No, you cannot, you have not the knowledge."

To return to my subject. After the southwest wind had pushed us and drawn us out of this intense heat (in which we were roasted as if in purgatory), advancing in this direction, we began to see the North Pole,[b] which we had lost sight of more than a year earlier. But, to avoid wordiness, I refer the readers to my earlier discussion of the remarkable things that we saw on our way over, and I will not repeat here what I have already touched on concerning the flying fish and other monstrous and strange sea creatures of different kinds that can be seen under this Torrid Zone.

Let me continue, then, recounting the extreme dangers from which God delivered us on the sea during our return. There was a quarrel and a mutual spite between our master's mate and our pilot, which caused them to neglect the duties of their charge. On the twenty-sixth of March the pilot, who was on watch (that is, steering for three hours) had all the sails high and fully spread. Failing to notice the approach of a *grain*, that is, a whirlwind that was coming up, he allowed it to smash into the sails (which he should have lowered earlier) with a violence to heel the ship right over and make the crow's nest and mast heads plunge, so that, indeed, the cables, birdcages, and whatever else was not well lashed down

---

[a]Job 28.32.

[b][That is, Polaris, the North Star, which marks the celestial North Pole.]

were pitched into the sea, and all of it lost; we very nearly capsized. After the rigging and the sheets of the big sail had been cut, the vessel righted itself little by little; but we knew that we had escaped by the skin of our teeth. And yet the two who had been the cause of this danger were by no means ready to be reconciled, as they were vehemently urged to do; on the contrary, as soon as the peril had passed, their way of giving thanks was to seize and pummel each other so hard that we thought they would kill each other.

Moreover, we soon entered into more danger. A few days later, when the sea was calm, the carpenter and some of the other seamen, thinking to relieve us during this time of tranquility and give us some rest from our day-and-night labor at the pumps, went to look around in the bottom of the ship to find the holes through which the water was entering. It happened that as they were working on one that they thought they could mend, right in the bottom of the ship near the keel, a piece of wood came off, about a foot square. The water came in through the hole with such force that it made the seamen flee the spot and abandon the carpenter. When they reached the upper deck, they were incapable of telling us what had happened, except to cry "We are lost! We are lost!"

At this point the captain, the master, and the pilot, seeing the obvious danger, decided to abandon the ship, and escape in the boat. In order to free the boat and get it out as quickly as possible, they threw the panels that covered it into the sea, along with a great quantity of brazilwood and other merchandise, up to the value of more than a thousand francs. The pilot, fearing that the boat would be overloaded by the great number of passengers who would want to throw themselves into it, got in it himself with a great cutlass in his fist, and said that he would cut off the arms of the first person who made a move to board it. So seeing ourselves already, as it seemed, abandoned to the mercy of the sea, and remembering the first shipwreck from which God had delivered us, we were as resolved to death as to life; nevertheless, to sustain the ship and keep it from going to the bottom, exerting all our strength to draw the water out of it, we managed to keep it from covering us. However, not all were so courageous; for most of the seamen, expecting to have to drink more than their fill, were desperate and in such fear of death that nothing else concerned them. I am sure that if the Rabelistes, mockers and scorners of God, who, when they are on land with their feet snugly under the table, idly chatter and jest about the shipwrecks and perils undergone by those who go to sea—if they had been there, their merriment would have been changed to a horrible terror; and I do not doubt that a number of those who will read

204

this (and the other dangers that I have already mentioned and will mention again, that we experienced during this voyage) will say, as the proverb has it: Ha! how good it is to plant cabbage, and much better to hear tales of the sea and of savages than to go see it.[6] O how wise Diogenes was, to esteem those who, having decided to sail, yet sailed not.[7]

However, it is not yet done, for all of this happened to us when we were more than a thousand leagues from the port we were heading for; we still had much ahead of us to endure, and (as you will hear shortly) we even had to go through a grievous famine that carried off a number of us. But meanwhile, this is how we were delivered from the present danger.

Our carpenter, a stout-hearted little fellow, had not abandoned the bottom of the ship like the others; rather, having put his sailor's cloak over that big hole, he planted himself on it with both feet to resist the water (which, as he told us later, knocked him off balance several times by its violence). In that state he cried out to the others, as best he could, to bring him clothing, cotton beds, and other things that would keep the water from entering while he put back the piece that had come loose. This being done, we were saved by his efforts.

After that, the winds were so inconstant that our ship was pushed off course and drifting now to the east, now to the west (neither of which was our path, for we wanted to go south).[a] Our pilot, who was unskilled at his trade, no longer knew how to chart his course, and we sailed thus, in uncertainty, clear to the tropic of Cancer.

Moreover, for about two weeks we were in the midst of some plants floating on the water which grew so thick and in such abundance that if we had not cut them with axes to make way for the ship, which had difficulty breaking through them, I think that we would have come to a dead stop.[8] These plants made the water somewhat murky; perceiving that we were in some muddy marshes, we conjectured that we must be close to some islands. But although soundings were taken with more than fifty fathoms of rope, we found neither bottom nor bank, nor did we sight any land. On this point I will recount here what the historian of the Indies has written about it.[b] He says that Christopher Columbus, during the first voyage of discovery of the Indies in 1492, stopped for fresh provisions at one of the Canary Islands, and after having sailed on for

---

[a][A slip of the pen? They are clearly trying to go north.]
[b][Gómara,] *Histoire*, Book I, Chapter 16.

several days encountered so many plants that it seemed like a meadow: which caused him some fear, even though there was no danger. Now to describe these marine plants I am speaking of: they are connected to each other by long filaments, like *Hedera terrestris*,[a] and float rootless on the sea. Their leaves are rather like those of garden rue, and they have a round seed no bigger than that of the juniper; their color is pale or whitish like that of dried hay. As we discovered, they are not at all dangerous to handle. I have also seen certain filthy red things floating on the sea, shaped like a cock's crest, and so venomous and pestilent that as soon as we touched them our hands became red and swollen.

I spoke just now of the sounding line. I have often heard old wives' tales about it: for instance, that seamen can throw it to the bottom and bring back on the end of it some earth by which to recognize the country where they are. That is false, as far as the Western Sea is concerned; I will tell what I have seen of it, and how it is used. The sounding line, then, is a device of lead, shaped like a medium-sized wooden skittle like the ones we use when we play at ninepins in our town squares and gardens. It is pierced through the more pointed end, and the seamen thread through it as much rope as is needed; they then put suet or some other grease on the flat part of the other end. When they approach the port, or judge that they are in a place where they might anchor, they drop it down and let it go to the bottom. If, upon pulling it back up, they find gravel fixed to the grease, it is a sign of a good bottom. But if it brings nothing back, they conclude that it is mud or rock, in which the anchor cannot catch or get any purchase, and therefore one must go take a sounding elsewhere.

That is what I wanted to say in passing to refute the error I mentioned above. For anyone who has been out in the middle of the Ocean Sea can bear witness that it is utterly impossible to find bottom there, even if one had all the ropes in the world; when there is a wind one must go night and day without stopping, and in time of calm float and remain still (because the ships are not rowed with oars, like galleys). One can see that these abysses and gulfs are altogether unsoundable, and it is nonsense to say that one can bring back up earth by which to recognize what country one is in. If it can be done in other seas, as in the Mediterranean—or by land in passing through the deserts of Africa, where, as it has been written, one is guided by the stars and by the marine compass—I will not dispute the facts

---

[a][Ground ivy.]

in the matter;[a] but as for the Western Sea, I maintain what I have said to be true.

So we left behind us that grassy sea. Because we were afraid of meeting up with pirates, we leveled four or five pieces of such artillery as we had in our ship; also, to defend ourselves if necessary, we prepared our fire arrows and other munitions of war. However, on account of that very thing, here is yet another mishap that befell us. As our cannoneer was drying his powder in an iron pot, he left it so long on the fire that it got red-hot; the powder ignited, and the flame shot from one end of the ship to the other, and even ruined some sails and rigging. Because of the grease and the pitch with which the ship was rubbed and tarred, the whole thing almost caught fire, and we narrowly escaped being burned to death in the midst of the waters. And, in fact, one of the pages and two other seamen were so badly burned that one of them died a few days later. For my part, if I had not immediately put my sailor's cap in front of my face, it would have been damaged or worse; but having thus protected myself, I escaped with only the ends of my ears and my hair singed. That occurred on about the fifteenth of April.

And now to catch a moment's breath at this point, here we are, by the grace of God, not only escaped from shipwreck and from the water (which, as you have heard, we thought several times was about to swallow us up) but also from the fire that just now almost consumed us.

---

[a]Chalcondyle, *De la Guerre des Turcs.*

ॐ

# OF THE EXTREME
## FAMINE, TEMPESTS, AND
### OTHER DANGERS FROM WHICH GOD
### DELIVERED US AS WE WERE
### RETURNING TO FRANCE

Now after all these mishaps, we went, as they say, from the frying pan into the fire. Since we were still more than five hundred leagues away from France, our ordinary allowance both of biscuit and of other food and drink, which was already only too small, was nonetheless suddenly cut in half. This delay was not only because of bad weather and unfavorable winds; for besides that (as I have said elsewhere), the pilot, who had not correctly charted his course, found himself so far off that when he told us that we were approaching Cape Finisterre, on the coast of Spain, we were still at the level of the Azores, which are almost three hundred leagues away.

So because of this navigational error, by the end of the month of April we had completely run out of all provisions. To get the last bits of food, we had to clean and sweep out the hold, that is, the little white-plastered room where the ship's biscuit is kept. There we found more worms and rat droppings than crumbs of bread; nevertheless, separating it with spoons, we made a gruel of it which was as black and bitter as soot; you can imagine what a delightful dish it was. Those who still had monkeys and parrots (for several had already eaten theirs long before), which they had kept so as to teach them to speak a language that they did not yet know, now put them into the cabinet of their memory, and made them serve as food.[1] In short, by the beginning of May, when all ordinary food supplies were exhausted, two seamen had died of hunger and were, as is the custom at sea, cast overboard to be buried in the deep.

Furthermore, during that famine the tempest raged day and night for three weeks, and the sea was so high and so stormy that we were obliged to strike all the sails and tie the rudder; since we could no longer direct the ship, we had to let it drift with the waves and the wind, so that during this whole time, when we were in such distress, we could not catch a single fish.

So there we were once again in famine up to our teeth, assailed by the water from within and tormented by the waves from without. Those who have never been on the sea, and especially in such an ordeal, have only seen half the world; and here must be repeated what the Psalmist rightly says of mariners, who, floating, mounting, and descending thus on this terrible element, abiding in the midst of death, truly see the wonders of the Eternal.ᵃ You need hardly ask if our Papist sailors, seeing themselves reduced to such extremities, promised Saint Nicholas a waxen image as big as a man if he would get them safely to land, and made marvelous vows;[2] but that was about the same as crying out to Baal, who gave them no heed.ᵇ We, however, found far more benefit in calling upon Him whose aid we had already so often experienced, who alone, sustaining us by extraordinary means throughout the famine, could command the sea and appease the storm; it was to Him and to no one else that we addressed ourselves.

We were already so thin and so weakened that we could hardly hold ourselves up to perform the maneuvers for the ship; nevertheless, necessity, in the midst of this harsh famine, prompted each of us earnestly to think and rethink just what he could fill his belly with. Some took it into their heads to cut pieces of the shields made of the hide of the *tapiroussou* and boil them, intending to eat them this way; but this recipe was not found to be good. Others, also seeking all the devices they could invent to remedy their hunger, put these pieces of leather shields on the coals with such success that after the pieces were roasted a little, and the burned part scraped off with a knife, it was as if we were eating carbonadoes of bacon rind. Once this experiment had succeeded, there was a great hoarding of these shields, as hard as dried ox-hide, which were cut up with billhooks or other tools; those who possessed them carried the pieces in their sleeves in little canvas bags, and set no less store by them than our big usurers do by their purses full of crowns.

Even as Josephus said,[3] that the besieged in the city of Jerusalem fed on their thongs, their shoes, and the leather of their shields, so too some among us arrived at the point of eating their morocco collars and their

---

ᵃPsalm 107.23–24.

ᵇI Kings 18.26. ["But there was no voice, nor any that answered."]

shoeleather;[a] even the pages and the cabin boys, pressed by a ravenous hunger, ate all the lantern horns (which are always numerous in a sea-going vessel) and as many tallow candles as they could lay hands on.

Furthermore, our debilitated state notwithstanding, we had to be at the hard labor of the pumps incessantly, night and day, on pain of going to the bottom and having more to drink than we had to eat.

The fifth of May, at sunset, we saw a great flash of fire blazing across the sky, which made such a reflection in the sails of our ship that we thought they had caught fire; however, it passed in an instant without harming us. If you ask where it could come from, it is all the more difficult to explain in that we were at the latitude of Newfoundland (where they fish for cod) and of Canada, regions where it is usually extremely cold, so one cannot say that it came from hot exhalations in the air. And indeed, so that we would have tasted some of everything, in those parts we were battered by a wind from the north-northeast—very nearly a proper boreal storm—, which gave us such a chilling that for more than two weeks we could not get warm.

Our cannoneer had been wasting away from hunger; I once saw him eat the raw guts of a parrot. Around the twelfth of May he finally died of starvation, and like those before him who had died of the same malady, was cast into the sea and buried in the deep. We cared little about the loss of his function as cannoneer; we were so weakened that if we had been attacked, instead of defending ourselves we would have preferred to be taken and carried off by some pirate, provided he would give us something to eat. But, since it pleased God to afflict us the whole length of our voyage, during our return we saw only a single ship; and when we sighted it, we were too weak to raise our sails, and so we could not approach it.

Now the shields that I have spoken of, and all the leather, even the covers of our trunks, along with everything in our ship that could be found for sustenance, had been completely used up; we thought that we were at the end of our voyage. But necessity, inventress of arts,[4] put it into a number of minds to hunt the rats and mice, which (because we had taken the crumbs and everything else they might have nibbled) were running through the ship in great numbers, dying of hunger. They were so intently pursued, and with so many kinds of rat-traps invented by each of us (we would lie in wait for them, vigilant as cats, even at night when they

---

[a][The Jewish Wars,] VII: 7.

came out by moonlight) that however they might try to hide, few of them escaped. And, indeed, when someone had caught a rat, he would value it much more highly than he would a beef if he were on land; I have seen some that were sold at two, three, and even four crowns apiece. Our barber once caught two at once, and one of us offered him, in return for one of the rats, to buy him a complete set of clothes, from head to foot, at the first port; the barber, however, preferring his life to those garments, would not accept the offer. You would also have seen mice boiled in sea water, with the tripes and the guts, and those who could get them set greater store by them than we on land ordinarily do by leg of lamb.

But among other remarkable things, to show that nothing was wasted: one day our master's mate had prepared a big rat for cooking, and had cut off its four white feet, which he threw on the deck; a certain fellow instantly swooped them up, put them to grill over the coals, and, as he ate them, said that he had never tasted partridge wings more savory. In a word, what would we not have eaten, or rather devoured, in such extremity? For in truth, to appease our hunger we craved even the old bones and other offal that the dogs drag off the dung-heaps; without a doubt, if we had had green grasses, even hay, or leaves of trees such as one might have on land, we would have grazed on them like brute beasts. That is not all; for during the three weeks of this harsh famine, we had left not a trace either of wine or of fresh water, and all that remained to drink was a little barrel of cistern water. The masters and the captains husbanded it so thriftily and held on to it so carefully that if, during this distress, a monarch had been on board with us, he would not have had more than anyone else: that is, one small glass a day. Being even more pressed by thirst than by hunger, when it rained we spread out sheets with an iron ball in the middle to funnel the rainwater and catch in it receptacles; we even collected what trickled in little streams on the deck, and though from the tarred caulking and the dirt left by our feet this water was murkier than what runs in the streets, we nonetheless drank it.

In conclusion: although the famine that we endured in 1573, during the siege of Sancerre, must be ranked among the most severe that has ever been heard of (as one can see by the history of it that I have had printed), still, as I have noted in that work, there was no lack either of water or of wine; so, while the famine was longer, I can say that it was not as severe as the one I am treating here. For in Sancerre we at least had roots, wild herbs, vine sprigs, and other things that can be found on land.[5] And indeed, inasmuch as it pleases God to grant his benediction to his creatures, even in those things that are not commonly used for the nourishment of men—as skins, parchment, and other such merchandise that I have listed, and off which we lived in that siege—having, I say, experienced what value they take on in time of need, as long as I have leather collars, chamois garments, and other such things containing juice and moisture, if I were shut up in a place for a good cause, I would not surrender for any fear of famine.

But on the sea, during the voyage of which I speak, we were reduced to such extremity that we had nothing left but brazilwood, which has less moisture than any other; several, however, pressed to the limit, for lack of anything else began to gnaw on it. One day our guide the Sieur du Pont, holding a piece of it in his mouth, said to me with a great sigh, "Alas, Léry, my friend, I am owed the sum of four thousand francs in France; would to God I could acquit my debtor now and have instead some bran bread and a glass of wine." As for Master Pierre Richier, presently minister of the Word of God at La Rochelle, the good man will say that during our misery, stretched out in his little cabin, he was so enfeebled that he could not have raised his head to pray God—whom, however, flat on his back as he was, he ardently invoked.

Before I finish this subject I will speak here in passing of something I have not only observed in others, but felt in myself during these two famines, as harsh as any that man has survived. When the bodies are weakened, and nature is failing, the senses are alienated and the wits dispersed; all this makes one ferocious, and engenders a wrath that can truly be called a kind of madness. The common expression we use for saying that someone lacks food is very accurate: we say that such and such a person is mad with hunger.

Furthermore, as experience makes a fact better understood, one comprehends why it is that God, in the Book of Deuteronomy, threatening to send his people famine if they do not obey him, says expressly that the man who is tender and delicate, that is, of a gentle and benign nature, and who formerly had a horror of cruel things, in the extremity of famine will nevertheless become so denatured that he will look with an evil eye upon his neighbor, even his wife and his children, and desire to eat them.[a,6] In the history of Sancerre I have recounted the examples of the father and mother who ate their own child, and of some soldiers who tasted the flesh of human bodies that had been killed in war, and who have confessed since that if the affliction had continued, they would have

---

[a]Deuteronomy 28.53–54.

hurled themselves upon the living. Besides these prodigious things, I can testify that during our famine on the sea we were so despondent and irritable that although we were restrained by the fear of God, we could scarcely speak to each other without getting angry, and, what was worse (may God pardon us), glancing at each other sideways, harboring evil thoughts regarding that barbarous act.

Now to pursue what is left of our voyage. As we left the Equator even farther behind us, two more of our seamen died of starvation. At this point, given the long time we had been tossing on the sea without sight of land, some of us imagined ourselves to be in the midst of a new Flood; when we saw the bodies of these seamen thrown into the water to feed the fish, we expected nothing else but to join them, all of us, and soon. However, in spite of this inexpressible suffering and famine, during which, as I said, all the monkeys and the parrots that we had brought were eaten, I had nevertheless up to that time kept one, as big as a goose, that uttered words freely like a man, and was of excellent plumage. Out of a great desire to save him to give to my Lord Admiral,[a] I even hid him for five or six days without being able to give him anything to eat; but what with the pressure of necessity, and my fear that someone might steal him from me at night, he had to pass the same way as the others. I discarded nothing but the feathers, so that not only the body but also the tripes, feet, claws, and hooked beak served me and some of my friends to keep ourselves alive for three or four days. However, I regretted it all the more in that five days after I had killed him we saw land; so that since this kind of bird needs very little water, I would only have needed a few nuts to feed him for that time.

"But what!" someone will now say, "when will you stop dwelling on your parrot, which does not concern us? Are you going to keep us in suspense about your state of distress? Won't you soon have endured enough of all of this? Will it never end, by death or by life?" Indeed it will, for God, sustaining our bodies by things other than by bread and common nourishment, was leading us by the hand to the port, and granted by His grace that the twenty-fourth day of that month of May 1558 (when we lay exhausted, stretched out on the deck, almost unable to move arms or legs) we sighted Lower Brittany. However, the pilot had deceived us so many times, showing us passing clouds instead of land, that although the sailor in the crow's nest cried out two or three times,

---

[a][Coligny.]

"Land! land!" we still thought that it was all a hoax. But having a favorable wind, we headed straight for what proved indeed to be the mainland.

To conclude this account of our afflictions, I will here relate something to make you understand still better the harsh extremity into which we had fallen, and how in our need, when we had no more respite, God took pity on us and helped us. After we had thanked Him for our approaching deliverance, the master of the ship said aloud that if we had remained in that state one more day, he had resolved for certain not to cast lots, as some have done in such distress, but, without saying a word, to kill one of us to serve as food for the others; which I feared the less for myself since (although there was not much fat on any of us) unless he had been willing to eat skin and bones, it would not have been me.

Now our seamen had decided to unload and sell their brazilwood at La Rochelle; so when we were two or three leagues from Brittany, the ship's master, with the Sieur du Pont and some others, left us at anchor, and went off in a boat to a nearby place called Audierne to buy provisions. But two of our company, to whom I personally gave money to bring me refreshment, also got into the boat; as soon as they found themselves on land, seeming to think that it was the ship itself that contained the famine, they abandoned the trunks and belongings they had left on board, and swore never to set foot on it again; in fact, they took off at that very moment, and I have not seen them since.

While we were at anchor, there approached some fishermen, whom we asked for food. Thinking that we were jesting, or that under this pretext we meant to do them some injury, they quickly tried to draw back. But we held on to them; pressed by necessity, we were more nimble than they were, and we threw ourselves with such impetuosity into their boat that they all thought they were about to be plundered. However, we took nothing from them except what we paid for, and we found only a few quarter-loaves of black bread. One of them was a base fellow who, notwithstanding our obvious and extreme need, instead of taking pity on us had no compunctions about taking two *réales* from me for a little quarter-loaf that was not worth a *liard* in that country.[a]

Our people came back with bread, wine, and other food, which, as you can imagine, we did not allow to grow mouldy or sour. Intending still to go to La Rochelle, we had sailed two or three leagues when we were

---

[a][A *liard* was a copper coin worth about a quarter of a *réal*.]

214

warned by those on an approaching ship that there were pirates ravaging the length of that coast. Upon hearing that, and considering that, after so many great dangers from which God had granted us escape, it would be tempting Him and looking for trouble to expose ourselves to new hazards, we no longer delayed landing, and that same day, the twenty-sixth of May, we entered the beautiful and spacious harbor of Blavet in Brittany.[a]

There also arrived at that time a great number of vessels of war returning from voyages in various countries; firing their cannons and making the customary show of bravado upon entering a seaport, they were rejoicing in their victories. Among others, there was one from Saint-Malo, whose seamen not long before had seized and carried off a Spanish ship returning from Peru, loaded with good merchandise estimated at more than sixty thousand ducats. This news had been proclaimed all over France, and many merchants—Parisians, Lyonnais, and others—had come to buy things from it. For us, they came at an opportune moment. To our good fortune, some of them happened to be near our ship as we were landing; not only did they help us up by the arm (for we could not even stand up) but also—and very much to the point—hearing of our great hunger, they warned us to take care not to eat too much, and to start by sipping bouillons of old poultry well stewed, and goat's milk, and other things good for enlarging our shrunken intestines. Those who heeded their counsel did, indeed, profit from it; as for our sailors, who insisted on glutting themselves from the very first day, I think that of the twenty who survived the famine more than half ate to the point of bursting, and so died.

But as for us other fifteen passengers, who, as I said at the beginning of the preceding chapter, had embarked in this ship in Brazil to return to France, not one of us died, either on the sea or, now, on land. It is true that we had saved only our skin and bones, and if you had seen us you would have said that we were unburied cadavers. What is more, as soon as we had breathed the air of the land, we were so devoid of appetite, and had such an abhorrence of food, that (speaking for myself in particular) when I came indoors, upon smelling some wine that was offered me in a cup, I fell backward onto a trunk, and it was thought, what with my weakness, that I was about to give up the ghost. I had done myself no great injury, however, and I was put to bed. I had not slept French-style (as one says today) for more than nineteen months; nevertheless, contrary

---

[a][Now the port of Lorient, at the mouths of the rivers Blavet and Scorff.]

to the opinion of those who say that when one is accustomed to sleeping on the ground one cannot sleep on a featherbed for a long time after, I slept so well that very first time that I did not wake up until sunrise the following day.

After spending three or four days in Blavet, we went to Hennebont, a little town two leagues from here, where during the two weeks of our stay we were treated according to the advice of physicians. But however good a diet we followed, most of us became swollen from the soles of the feet to the crown of the head; only I and two or three others were swollen merely from the waist down. Furthermore, all of us suffered from diarrhea and from such weakness of the stomach that it would have been impossible for us to keep any food in our bodies if it had not been for a recipe that was given us: take the juice from *Hedera terrestris*[a] and some well-cooked rice, which, taken off the fire, must be smothered in the pot with old rags; then take egg-yolks, and mix it all together in a chafing-dish over a flame. We ate it with spoons, like a gruel, and felt stronger almost at once; and without this remedy, by which God revived us, I think that ailment would have carried off all of us in a few days.

So that was our voyage, which, in truth, if one considers that we sailed about seventy-three degrees, or about two thousand French leagues north-south, will not be regarded as one of the shortest. But to give honor where it is due, does it compare to the voyage of that excellent pilot, the Spaniard Juan Sebastián del Cano?[b] Having sailed around the globe—that is, having encircled the whole roundness of the universe, which, I think, no man before him had ever done—when he returned to Spain, he justifiably had a globe painted for his coat of arms, around which he put as a device *Primus me circumdedisti:* meaning, you were the first to encircle me.

Now to finish what remains of our deliverance: it would seem that for this time we were quits with all our ills. But if He who had so many times saved us from shipwreck, storms, harsh famine, and the other hardships that assailed us on the sea, had not guided our doings upon our arrival on land, we would not have escaped. For as I mentioned when I was describing our embarkation for the return voyage, Villegagnon, with-

[a] [Ground ivy.]

[b] [When Magellan was killed in the Philippines, del Cano assumed command and completed the first circumnavigation in 1522.]

out our knowing anything about it, had given to the master of our ship (who knew nothing of it either) an indictment that he had formed against us, with the express order to the first judge in France to whom it would be presented, not only to arrest us, but also to put us to death, by having us burned as the heretics that he said we were. But it so happened that our guide the Sieur du Pont knew some of the magistrates in that country who sympathized with the Religion we professed. The chest covered with waxed canvas, containing this indictment along with a number of letters addressed to various personages, was given to them; when they saw what they were ordered to do, by no means did they treat us as Villegagnon desired. On the contrary, they not only offered us the best hospitality they could but, offering their own resources to those of our company who had need, they loaned money to the Sieur du Pont and several others. Thus we see how God, who surprises the devious in their schemes, not only, through these good personages, delivered us out of the danger in which the revolt of Villegagnon had placed us, but what is more, when the treason he had plotted against us had been thus revealed to his confounding, turned it all to our solace.

So after we had received this new benefice from the hand of Him who, as I have said, showed Himself our protector both on sea and on land, our seamen left the town of Hennebont for their Normandy; we departed also, removing ourselves from these Breton-speaking Bretons,[7] whose language we understood less than that of the American savages, and quickly set forth for the city of Nantes, which was only thirty-two leagues away. Not, however, that we went posthaste; for in our weakened state, we lacked the strength to manage the horses with which we had been provided, or even to endure a trot, so each of us had his own man to lead his horse by the bridle.

It was imperative that we restore our bodies; not only did we have fantastic cravings, such as women with child are commonly said to have (were it not for fear of wearying the readers, I could cite strange examples), but some among us also had such a distaste for wine that it was more than a month before they could bear to smell it, let alone taste it. And to cap all our miseries, when we arrived at Nantes it was as if all our senses had been entirely overthrown; for about a week we were so hard of hearing, and our vision was so obscured, that we thought we were becoming deaf and blind. However, some excellent physicians and other notable personages, who visited us often in our lodgings, took such care of us and brought us such aid that in my own case these ailments disappeared without a trace, and a month later I heard as clearly as ever before, and had as good vision. (It is true that as far as my stomach goes, it has been rather weak ever since; the experience having been repeated in the interim, about four years ago during the siege and famine of Sancerre, I can say that I will feel the effects all my life.) Thus after having somewhat regained our strength at Nantes, where, as I have said, we were very well treated, each of us went his own way.

To bring this present history to a close, nothing remains to be told except what became of the five of our company who, as I said, after our first near-shipwreck returned to the land of Brazil; and here is how it came to be known. Certain trustworthy persons whom we had left in that country, from which they returned about four months after we did, met the Sieur du Pont in Paris. They informed him that, to their great regret, they had been spectators when Villegagnon had three of the five drowned at Fort Coligny because of their adherence to the Gospel: that is, Pierre Bourdon, Jean du Bordel, and Matthieu Verneuil. Moreover, these same persons brought back the written confession of faith of those three, as well as the whole indictment that Villegagnon brought against them, and they gave it to the Sieur du Pont, from whom I obtained it soon after. Thus I saw how, while we were sustaining the waves and storms of the sea, these faithful servants of Jesus Christ were enduring the torments, indeed the cruel death that Villegagnon made them suffer; and I remembered that I alone of our company (as has been seen) had left the boat in which I was all ready to return with them. I thus had reason to render thanks to God for my particular deliverance, and also felt myself obliged, more than all the others, to see to it that the confession of faith of these three good persons be inscribed in the roll of those who in our time have steadfastly endured death for the witness of the Gospel. Therefore that same year 1558 I gave it to the printer Jean Crespin, who, along with the narration of their difficulties landing in the country of the savages after they had left us, inserted it in the *Book of Martyrs,* to which I refer the readers; except for the aforementioned reason, I would have made no mention of it here.

Yet I will say one more word: since Villegagnon was the first to shed the blood of the children of God in this newly discovered country, by this cruel act he has justly earned the title that has been given him: "the Cain of America." And to satisfy those who would like to know what has become of him, and what his end has been, we, as has been seen in this history, left him settled in that land in Fort Coligny, and I have heard nothing else of him since, except that when he returned to France, after having done his worst, by word of mouth and by writing, against those of the Evangelical Religion, he finally died, inveterate in his old skin,[8] in a command post of his Order of Malta, near Saint-Jean-de-Nemours. As I learned from a nephew of his whom I had seen with him at Fort Coligny, he ordered his affairs so badly, both during his illness and before, and was so ill disposed toward his kinsmen, that although they gave him no cause for such treatment, they had no profit from his wealth, neither during his life, nor after his death.

To conclude: Since, as I have shown in the present history, I have been delivered, not only with my fellows but also in my single person, from so many kinds of dangers, indeed from so many abysses of death, can I not say, with that holy woman the mother of Samuel, what I have myself experienced: that it is the Eternal who causes us to live and to die, to descend into the grave and to arise from it?[a] Yes, certainly, I have had as good proof of it as any man alive; and if it were pertinent, I could yet add that by his infinite goodness he has rescued me from many straits.

That, finally, is what I have observed, both on the sea, during the voyage to and from the land of Brazil, called America, and among the savages who live in that country, which, for the reasons I have amply set forth, may well be called a new world with respect to us.

I know, however, that having such a fine subject, I have not treated the various matters that I have mentioned in a style or a manner as grave as was required; I admit that even in this second edition I have sometimes overamplified a discussion that should have been cut short, and conversely, falling into the other extreme, have touched too briefly on some matters that should have had a longer treatment. To compensate for these defects of language, I once again entreat the readers to consider how hard and troublesome for me was the experience of this history's content, and to receive my affection as payment. Now to the King of the Ages, immortal and invisible, to God who alone is wise, be all honor and glory, world without end. Amen.

---

[a] I Samuel 2.6. [The Lord killeth, and maketh alive: he bringeth down to the grave, and bringeth up.]

# EDITIONS AND RECEPTION
# OF LÉRY

In the late sixteenth and early seventeenth century, Léry's *Histoire d'un Voyage* became part of an expanding corpus of Protestant texts in a network that covered a large part of Western Europe. After the initial publication in 1578, there were editions in 1580, 1585, 1594, 1599–1600, and 1611.[1] The changes in the succeeding editions were almost always in the direction of augmentation. Some of the additions, particularly those of the 1585 edition, were a continuation of the war with Thevet, who had sniped at Léry in his *Vies et pourtraicts des hommes illustres* of 1584. But chiefly, as time went on, Léry extended the range of his references and comparisons. Less bent on offering a history limited to what he had seen and could personally vouch for, he poured into his text the converging witness and confirmation of other New World chroniclers such as Benzoni and Staden; he sought further comparisons with Turkish, Slavic, and African history. The spectacular section on cannibalism underwent the greatest expansion in the comparisons of barbaric cruelty of various times and places; it eventually reached out to include the horrors of the Spanish conquests in America, as described in the accounts of Las Casas, and the material was so abundant that in the 1599 edition Léry added another chapter to accommodate it. For the modern reader, the inclusion of these compilations of authorities may clutter the text; some critics have regarded this textual development as a regressive tendency, and think of Léry as reverting to an obsolescent style rather like that of Thevet himself. But this development can also be seen as Léry's assumption of a more authoritative voice, as he seeks to demonstrate the world-scale relevance and importance of data from the New World.[2]

Simultaneously, Léry himself was becoming an authority to be used in compilations. He is cited by his friend the formidable polemicist Urbain Chauveton in his lavish annotation to Benzoni's *Historia del*

*Mondo Nuovo.* In Latin translation, his work forms part of the third volume (1583) of the *Grands Voyages* published by the De Bry family, a magnificently illustrated and widely circulated collection of volumes that was part of the great publicity movement to encourage Protestant colonization of the New World. Some of Léry's ethnographic material found its way into an early seventeenth-century version of a hugely successful collection of folkways that, in its original edition, predated Léry: Johann Boemus's *Mores, Leges et Ritus Omnium Gentium* (Geneva, 1604), which appeared in English in 1611. A larger selection from Léry translated into English appears in Samuel Purchas's collection *Hakluytis Posthumus or Purchas His Pilgrimes* (1625). Léry's influence was not confined to Protestant circles: in the early seventeenth century, Claude d'Abbeville, who lived among the Tupinamba of Maranhão, leans heavily on Léry in his report *Histoire de la mission des Pères capucins* (1614). In his work on early French Canada, *Histoire de la Nouvelle France* (1609), Marc Lescarbot borrowed largely from Léry's work in his discussion of the French colony in Brazil.

The work that most effectively bore Léry's vision and spirit down the centuries is one that never names him: Montaigne's essay "On Cannibals," which has been read by every generation from its own time to the present. Montaigne probably read both Thevet and Léry. That he preferred the version of Léry is suggested by a sarcastic reference to the pretensions of cosmographers (for which one can read Thevet), and by the entire moral thrust of the essay.[3]

There seem to have been no full editions of Léry in French in the eighteenth century,[4] but editions did appear in Germany and the Netherlands. Did Rousseau know the *Histoire?* A Swiss Protestant reader of voyage literature (and Rousseau was an enthusiastic one) might well have have come across, in the private libraries of the many houses where he stayed, the work of a frequently reedited Calvinist voyager. In the *Discourse on the Origins of Inequality,* when Rousseau compares his model of primitive man with the descriptions of the newly discovered peoples; when he speaks of preagricultural society as a possible golden age, the point at which cultural development should have remained, it may be that Léry's Brazilians were part of his mental image. The discussions in *Emile* on the care of infants (against swaddling, in favor of breastfeeding) are very close to passages in Chapter XVII of the *Histoire;* but we do not really know whether Rousseau ever read the whole text of Léry, whether he read extracts in compilations of voyage literature, or whether these ideas reached him through various intermediaries.[5] In any case, Rousseau certainly knew Montaigne, and the essay "On Cannibals" was part of his intellectual equipment.

The reeditions of Léry resumed in the late nineteenth century, first through Paul Gaffarel, whose *Histoire du Brésil français au XVIe siècle* (Paris, 1878) brought together many of the key documents concerning the Villegagnon expedition. His 1879 edition of the *Histoire d'un Voyage* was sometimes textually faulty, but it was richly annotated, and subsequent editors have benefited greatly from his work. (The Portuguese translations of Léry are based on Gaffarel rather than on the original editions.) Gaffarel had a specific project: he wanted to give hope and spirit to the French imperial enterprise by demonstrating that the French had talent as colonizers, and to this end he promoted the text of Léry.

More than forty years passed before the next reedition; in 1927, Charly Clerc offered an abridged modernized version, with an introduction dealing in depth with the Villegagnon controversy. In 1957 Olivier Reverdin published some extracts under the title *Quatorze calvinistes chez les Topinambous: Histoire d'une mission genevoise au Brésil (1556–1558);* as the title suggests, he mainly sought to shed some light on the misunderstandings between the Calvinists and Villegagnon. That same year, M.-R. Mayeux published another abridged and modernized version under the title *Journal de bord de Jean de Léry en la terre de Brésil (1557)*. In 1972 there appeared two editions: an orthographically modernized version edited by Michel Contat and J.-C. Wagnières; and selections entitled *Indiens de la Renaissance: histoire d'un voyage fait en la terre du Brésil (1557)*, with an introduction by Anne-Marie Chartier.

In 1975, Jean-Claude Morisot published an annotated critical edition, and offered a facsimile of the 1580 text. For the first time since the early seventeenth century, Léry's book was made widely available in its original form (and without the occasional deformations of Gaffarel's readings).

In 1980 there appeared a complete edition by Sophie Delpech (*Histoire d'un voyage fait en la terre de Bresil* [Paris: Plasma]) in modernized French.

The introductions to these various works are substantial, forming part of a rediscovery of Léry from the early part of this century. In the generation after Gaffarel, Gilbert Chinard published his *L'Exotisme américain dans la littérature française au XVIe siècle* (Paris, 1911), using Léry as a prime example in his exploration of the French mentality confronting the New World. In 1935 there appeared Geoffroy Atkinson's *Les nouveaux horizons de la Renaissance française*, which provided two very important kinds of data: what kind of geographical works were published in the sixteenth century, on what countries, and in how many editions. It also provided a thematic organization (the Golden Age, avarice, civil order, etc.) so that the reader could appreciate to what extent a given passage in a particular work is part of a larger discourse. Atkinson had great admiration for Léry, and provided a context for understanding the degree of his popularity and his relation to other writings about non-European cultures.

Léry's work began to reach a wider public in 1955, with the appearance of *Tristes tropiques,* where Lévi-Strauss referred to it as the *bréviare de l'ethnologue,* and gave his own pithy and incisive version of the Villegagnon episode. The work of Léry now appeared in the setting of Lévi-Strauss's poetic mediation on the anthropologist's enterprise, of which it now seemed an ancestor, or even a companion work.[6] Not only did Lévi-Strauss give Léry his endorsement; his structural anthropology was offering new conceptual tools with which to look at Léry's work (as is evident in the remarkable introduction by Anne-Marie Chartier mentioned above).

Developments in French historiography have favored a continuing and intensifying interest in the *Histoire d'un Voyage.* The attention of the *Annales* school to all kinds of documents from material, everyday life; the studies by Le Roy Ladurie of communities in various kinds of crisis in early modern Europe; the research of Michel Foucault into archaeologies of knowledge, into the "epistemes," into patterns of conception and codes of discourse: all these ways of thinking about the past have enhanced Léry's value as a witness, and are bringing his name into the mainstream of French intellectual life. In 1975 there appeared Michel de Certeau's *L'écriture de l'histoire,* which contains an extremely rich and suggestive chapter on Léry. It speaks of the ideologies of which Léry is the unconscious (and inevitable) emissary, and particularly his role as the historian, the bearer of the written word, confronting an oral culture.

In recent years there has appeared, in the wake of Foucault and Certeau, an impressive body of work by Frank Lestringant, who is frequently cited in the notes to this translation. Lestringant has paid close attention to the Calvinist context of Léry's writing, to the controversies and polemics of the period. He has made important corrections in the publishing history of the *Histoire,* and has shed light on the significance of Léry's long war with Thevet. He has illuminated the contexts in which cannibalism was thought about in the Renaissance and after. His work is indispensable to any student of Léry, Thevet, and the relationship between early French Protestantism and the New World. As this book was going to press, a major new work of Lestringant appeared which shed yet more light on Léry's life and world: *Le Huguenot et le sauvage* (Paris: Aux amateurs de livres, 1990).

The name of Léry is beginning to reach the English-speaking public: through Hugh Honour's iconographic work *The New Golden Land;* through the fine collection of papers edited by Fredi Chiapelli, *First Images of America;* and through Olive Dickason's *The Myth of the Savage.* Colloquia, conferences, and seminars on New World writing, literature, and iconography abound at this moment of writing; and on Léry, there is undoubtedly much more to come.

# NOTES

## INTRODUCTION

1. Trans. John Russell (New York: Atheneum, 1972), 85.

2. The most thorough biography of Léry is that of Géralde Nakam, *Au lendemain de la Saint-Barthélemy* (Paris: Anthropos, 1975). Léry's adversary André Thevet called him a shoemaker; Léry retorted in his Preface to the 1585 edition of the *Histoire* that his rank was far superior to Thevet's, but refused to specify it. Nakam (p. 13) indicates that he was probably of the bourgeoisie or the minor nobility; but Emile Doumergue cites an archival source that suggests that he was in fact a shoemaker (*Jean Calvin, les hommes et les choses de son temps* [Lausanne: G. Bridel, 1899–1905]), III: 221.

3. See Carlos Eire, *War Against the Idols: The Reformation of Worship from Erasmus to Calvin* (Cambridge, U.K.: Cambridge University Press, 1979): 189–193.

4. Nakam (p. 14) states that Léry was studying theology in Geneva at this time; Emile Doumergue claims that Léry joined the group as an artisan (III: 221).

5. For the chronology of Léry's life, I am following Nakam, pp. 19–40.

6. Théodore de Bèze, *Histoire ecclésiastique*, III: 506–507 (edition of 1889, cited in Nakam, p. 21).

7. Nakam's *Au lendemain de la Saint-Barthélemy* contains the complete work on Sancerre in a critical edition. See also Robert Kingdon, *Myths about the Saint-Bartholomew's Day Massacres 1572–1576* (Cambridge, Mass.: Harvard University Press, 1988): 51–62; also my article, "Food and the Limits of Civility: The Testimony of Jean de Léry," *Sixteenth Century Journal* 15 (1984): 387–400.

8. A particularly useful history of early colonial Brazil is John Hemmings's *Red Gold: The Conquest of the Brazilian Indians* (Cambridge, Mass.: Harvard University Press, 1978). See also Charles-André Julien, *Les Voyages de découverte et les premiers établissements* (Paris: PUF, 1948).

9. The polemic was particularly violent in 1560, when Villegagnon and Pierre Richier, the old Calvinist leader of the Brazilian mission, were both back in Europe. For the pamphlet war of that period, see Olivier Reverdin, *Quatorze Calvinistes chez les Topinambous: Histoire d'une mission genevoise au Brésil, 1556–1558* (Geneva: Droz, 1957), 39–49, and Frank Lestringant, "Calvinistes et cannibales: Les écrits protestants sur le Brésil français 1555–

1560," *Bulletin de la société de l'histoire du protestantisme français* 1–2 (1980): 9–26, 167–192.

10. One such influential work was *Histoire nouvelle du nouveau monde* (Geneva, 1579), a translation by another Huguenot pastor, Urbain Chauveton, of an Italian work by Girolamo Benzoni. In the late sixteenth to early seventeenth century, the De Bry family published a lavishly illustrated series of anthologies of New World writing called *Les Grands Voyages,* which was a major component of the Protestant canon. Léry's work received wide dissemination in that form in Latin and German. See Frank Lestringant, "L'excursion brésilienne: Note sur les trois premières éditions de *l'Histoire d'un Voyage* de Jean de Léry (1578–1585)," *Mélanges sur la littérature de la Renaissance à la mémoire de V.-L. Saulnier* (Genève: Droz, 1984), 53–72. See also my article, "*Une révérence réciproque:* Huguenot Writing on the New World," *University of Toronto Quarterly* 57.2 (Winter 1987/88): 270–289.

11. The battle continued through the various editions of Léry's work. Thevet's *Vrais pourtraits et vies des hommes illustres, grecs, latins et païens* (1584) mounted a counterattack, to which Léry responded by an even longer polemic in the preface to the 1585 edition.

12. See Julien, *Les Voyages de découverte,* 373–394 for a balanced assessment of Thevet. Roger Schlesinger and Arthur P. Stabler provide a convenient brief biography in English, in *André Thevet's North America: A Sixteenth-Century View* (Kingston and Montreal: McGill-Queen's University Press, 1986), vii–xli. See also Frank Lestringant's preface to his modernized edition of the *Singularités de la France Antarctique* (Paris: Maspéro, 1983), and, for the Léry-Thevet relationship, "L'excursion brésilienne." Bernard Weinberg looks at precise textual borrowings by Léry from Thevet in "Montaigne's readings for 'Des Cannibales,' " *Renaissance and Other Studies in Honor of William Leon Wiley* (Chapel Hill: University of North Carolina Press, 1968), 264–279.

13. For the French context of these questions, the classic studies are Gilbert Chinard, *L'exotisme américain dans la littérature française au XVIe siècle* (Paris: Hachette, 1911) and Geoffrey Atkinson, *Les nouveaux horizons de la Renaissance française* (Paris: Droz, 1935). A wide-ranging and excellent collection of articles is *First Images of America: The Impact of the New World on the Old,* ed. Fredi Chiapelli (Berkeley, Los Angeles, London: University of California Press, 1976). See Hugh Honour, *The New Golden Land: European Images of America from the Discoveries to the Present Time* (New York: Pantheon, 1975) for a splendid study of the iconography. See also Olive Dickason, *The Myth of the Savage and the Beginnings of French Colonialism in the Americas* (Edmonton: The University of Alberta Press, 1984).

14. One of the best works on early ethnography is Margaret Hodgen's *Early Anthropology in the Sixteenth and Seventeenth Centuries* (Philadelphia: University of Pennsylvania Press, 1964). For the ambiguous heritage of Herodotus and ways of thinking about the "other," see François Hartog, *Le Miroir d'Hérodote: Essai sur la représentation de l'autre* (Paris: Gallimard, 1980), which contains some remarks on Léry.

15. Frank Lestringant traces these relationships with particular care in "Le Nom des 'Cannibales', de Christophe Colombe à Michel de Montaigne," *Bulletin de la Société des Amis de Montaigne* 17–18 (1984): 51–74.

16. See Richard Bernheimer, *The Wild Man in the Middle Ages: A Study in Art, Sentiment, and Demonology* (New York: Octagon, 1970); also *The Wild Man Within: An Image in Western Thought from the Renaissance to Romanticism,* ed. Edward Dudley and Maximillian E. Novak (Pittsburgh 1972), especially the essays of Earl Miner and Hayden White.

17. For a study of the marvelous, the prodigious, and the fabulous in the Renaissance, see Jean Céard, *La Nature et les prodiges: L'insolite au XVIe siècle en France* (Paris: Droz, 1935).

18. See Harry Levin, *The Myth of the Golden Age in the Renaissance* (New York: Oxford University Press, 1972); and Arthur Lovejoy and George Boas, *Primitivism and Related Ideas in Classical Antiquity* (New York: Octagon Books, 1965).

19. See Honour, 53–83.

20. See Lewis Hanke, *Aristotle and the American Indians* (London: Hollis and Carter, 1959) and "The Theological Significance of the Discovery of America" in *First Images of America* 1: 363–390.

21. See David B. Quinn, "New Geographical Horizons: Literature," *First Images of America,* 2: 635–658.

22. For accounts of the "wonder-cabinets" preserving Brazilian artifacts, see Hodgen, 116–124; Honour, 28–51; Steven Mullaney, "Strange Things, Gross Terms, Curious Customs: The Rehearsal of Cultures in the Late Renaissance," *Representing the English Renaissance,* ed. Stephen Greenblatt (Berkeley, Los Angeles, London: University of California Press, 1988), 65–92. For the Brazilian spectacle at Rouen, see Ferdinand Denis, *Une fête brésilienne célébrée à Rouen en 1550* (Paris 1850); Mullaney's article has a fascinating analysis of the same event.

23. For Léry's use of taxonomy, see Marie-Anne Chartier's introduction to selections from Léry in *Indiens de la Renaissance* (Paris: Epi, 1972). Other more general useful works are Paul Delaunay, *La zoologie au seizième siècle* (Paris: Hermann, 1962) and A. G. Morton, *History of Botanical Science* (London: Academic Press, 1981). See also Joseph Ewan, "The Columbian Discoveries and the Growth of Botanical Ideas with Special Reference to the Sixteenth Century," *First Images of America,* 2: 807–812, and Jonathan D. Sauer, "Changing Perception and Exploitation of New World Plants in Europe, 1492–1800," in *First Images of America,* 2: 813–832.

24. See Céard, *La Nature et les prodiges,* 21–24, on St. Augustine and the salutary sense of wonder. See also Calvin, *Institutes:* "in the creation of the universe he brought forth those insignia whereby he shows his glory to us, whenever and wherever we cast our gaze [trans. Battles]" (I: 52). The Chauveton reference is in his translation of Girolamo Benzoni, *Histoire nouvelle du nouveau monde* (Geneva 1579), iii–v.

25. See Frank Lestringant, "Calvinistes et cannibales"; also his "Catholiques et cannibales: Le thème du cannibalisme dans le discours protestant au temps

des guerres de religion," *Pratiques et discours alimentaires à la Renaissance* (Paris: Maisonneuve et Larose, 1982), 233–245. See also "Le cannibalisme des 'Cannibales.' I. Montaigne et la tradition," *Bulletin de la société des amis de Montaigne* 9–10 (1982): 27–40; "Le cannibalisme des 'Cannibales.' II. De Montaigne à Malthus," *Bulletin de la Société des Amis de Montaigne* 11–12 (1982): 19–38.

26. The sixteenth-century sources on the subject of cannibalism—Portuguese, French, English, and German—have been assembled and synthesized by Alfred Métraux in *La Religion des Tupinamba et ses rapports avec celles des autres tribus tupi-guarani* (Paris: Ernest Leroux, 1928) and "L'Anthropophagie rituelle des Tupinamba," *Religions et magies indiennes d'Amérique du Sud* (Paris: Gallimard, 1967), 45–78. See also Florestan Fernandes, "Guerre et Sacrifice humain chez les Tupinamba," *Journal de la société des Américanistes de Paris* (n.s.) 40 (1952): 139–220. For the influence of Thevet and Léry on Montaigne, see Bernard Weinberg, "Montaigne's readings for 'Des Cannibales,' " in *Renaissance and Other Studies in Honor of William Leon Wiley* (Chapel Hill: University of North Carolina Press, 1968), 264–279. For comparisons between Montaigne and Léry regarding their use of the motif of cannibalism, see Gérard Defaux, "Un cannibale en haut de chausses: Montaigne, la différence et la logique de l'identité," *Modern Language Notes* 7.4 (May 1982): 919–957, and Frank Lestringant, "Le cannibalisme des 'Cannibales.' "

27. See Natalie Davis, "The Rites of Violence," *Society and Culture in Early Modern France* (Stanford, Calif.: Stanford University Press, 1975), 152–187.

28. See Robert Kingdon, *Myths about the St. Bartholomew's Day Massacres 1572–1576* (Cambridge, Mass.: Harvard University Press, 1988). Kingdon offers a thorough treatment of Protestant martyrologies and the desire for witness of their travails.

29. See Calvin, *Institutes,* ed. John T. McNeill, trans. Battles (Philadelphia: Westminster Press), I: 44.

30. See Carlos Eire, *War Against the Idols,* especially chap. 6, "Calvin's Attack on Idolatry."

31. Calvin had remarked in the *Institutes* that it was necessary that celestial doctrine be written down, "that it should neither perish through forgetfulness nor vanish through error nor be corrupted by the audacity of men [trans. Battles]" (I: 72). On the significance of the medium of the written word, see Michel de Certeau's important essay, "L'Ethno-graphie. L'oralité, ou l'espace de l'autre: Léry," *L'Ecriture de l'histoire* (Paris: Gallimard, 1975), 215–248 (trans. Tom Conley as *The Writing of History* [New York: Columbia University Press, 1988]). Tzvetan Todorov, in *La Conquête de l'Amérique: La Question de l'Autre* (Paris: Seuil, 1982) discusses the role of presence and absence, the immediate and the mediated, in relation to oral and literate cultures (pp. 162–166). In a famous passage of *Tristes tropiques* Lévi-Strauss shows a Nambikwara chief feigning to understand the written word to impress his own people, and puts forth the hypothesis that "the primary function of writing, as a means of communication, is to facilitate the enslavement of other human beings" (p. 292).

32. See Alfred Métraux, *La Religion des Tupinamba et ses rapports avec celles des autres tribus tupi-guarani* (Paris: Ernest Leroux, 1928); *Religions et magies indiennes d'Amérique du Sud* (Paris: Gallimard, 1967). For a more recent—and revised—treatment of Tupi religion, see Hélène Clastres, *La Terre sans mal: Le prophétisme tupi-guarani* (Paris: Seuil, 1975).

33. In *Sermons on the First Epistle to Timothy,* Calvin writes: "We must pray not only for the faithful who already have some brotherhood with us, but for those who are far removed from it, as poor unbelievers. . . . For we do not know if it will please God to show them mercy and lead them back to the path of salvation. We must even hope for it, since all are created in the image of God [trans. mine]." Cited in E. Doumergue, *Jean Calvin: Les Hommes et les choses de son temps,* Vol. IV: *La Pensée religieuse de Calvin* (Lausanne: Bridel, 1910). Frank Lestringant, in "Calvinistes et cannibales," finds Léry's appreciation of the Tupi to be predicated on their exclusion from God's grace; his enthusiasm and generosity are the "envers paradoxal d'une condamnation sans appel" (p. 21). Questions of Léry's attitude toward the religion of the Tupi, and the degree of open-mindedness, are treated by Michel Jeanneret, in "Léry et Thevet: comment parler d'un monde nouveau?," *Mélanges à la mémoire de Franco Simone. IV: Tradition et originalité dans la création littéraire* (Geneva: Slatkine, 1983), 228–245.

34. This "welcome of tears" has resonances for us that it did not have for Léry; these are spelled out in Charles Wagley's book *Welcome of Tears* (New York: Oxford University Press, 1977), which traces the remnants of Tupi culture in the Brazil of the last generation.

35. See Chap. XX, n. 1.

36. For sixteenth-century views on New World language, and their relation to *The Tempest,* see Stephen Greenblatt, "Learning to Curse: Aspects of Linguistic Colonialism in the Sixteenth Century," *First Images of America,* 561–580.

# PREFACE

1. Written with the very substance of America. The dye of brazilwood was the essential commodity in Brazilian-European relations.

2. For the chronology of Léry's ministry, see the Introduction.

3. The actual title is *Les Singularitez de la France Antarctique* (Paris, 1558). In the Preface, Ambroise de la Porte is said to have "taken entire charge of the present book." For details on Thevet, see the Introduction.

4. Martin Fumée was the translator of the work of the Spanish historian Francisco López de Gómara, which appeared in France in 1569 under the title *Histoire générale des Indes Occidentales et Terres Neuves;* it was reedited several times. Gómara, who had been Cortés's secretary in the New World, is Léry's chief source for Spanish history, and was for Montaigne as well.

5. Pierre Richier was, indeed, a former Carmelite and theologian of the Sorbonne (which is what is meant by "Doctor of Paris"). He was one of the more powerful personalities in the Calvinist mission to Brazil, as will be seen

in subsequent chapters. After the return, he and Villegagnon engaged in a bitter war of pamphlets. He died in La Rochelle in 1580.

6. "Croyez ce porteur": the standard formula for the contents, or conclusion, of a letter of credit, but "used sometimes in a contrary sense for 'believe the liar' " (Cotgrave, *A Dictionarie of the French and English Tongues* [London, 1611].)

7. The Latin original of this letter is in the Bibliothèque de Genève (Reverdin 40).

8. Chronicles II, XXVII: 16–21. In the King James Version, the name is Uzziah; this combining of functions is a transgression against God punished by leprosy.

9. This conspiracy is also described by the Protestant pilot Nicolas Barré, who attributes the instigation of it to one of the Norman interpreters. See his "Deuxième Lettre," in Paul Gaffarel's *Histoire du Brésil français au seizième siècle* (Paris, 1878), 382–383.

10. Renée de France, daughter of Louix XII and of Anne de Bretagne, Duchess of Ferrara (1510–1576); as religious tensions were mounting in France, she was protectress of Calvin, Marot, Rabelais, and others.

11. Jean Crespin, *Histoire des Martyrs persécutez et mis à mort pour la vérité de l'Evangile, depuis le temps des Apostres jusques à présent* (Genève, 1564). This work contains an account by Léry of this execution by drowning. This whole episode, which is important to Léry's view of his mission in writing the *History of a Voyage*, is treated at more length at the end, in Chapters XXI and XXII (this volume).

12. *Cordeliers' Koran: L'Alcoran des cordeliers*, published in Geneva in 1556. Its subtitle is "the sea of blasphemies and lies of that stigmatized idol, known as Saint Francis, collected by Doctor Martin Luther . . . [trans. mine]."

13. Lussagnet (*Le Brésil et les Brésiliens*, 55) notes that *pa* is the affirmative uttered in response to the traditional Tupi question of greeting: *Eraiubé*, or "Have you come?" However, Plinio Ayrosa (*Viagem*, 45 n.51) indicates that *pa* can also have the meaning that Thevet attributed to it.

14. *Singularités*, Chapter 53.

15. François de Belleforest, a fellow cosmographer, had originally admired Thevet and had written a liminary ode of praise for *Les Singularités;* he became an adversary and wrote a satiric epistle on Thevet. He is mentioned by name in the text below.

16. These are *Maire-monan* and *Maire-Pochy* in Thevet's discussion of Tupi's religion, in Chapters IV, V, and VI of Book 21 of the *Cosmographie universelle;* in Chapter XVI of this present work I provide a summary of the role of these figures in the Tupi creation myths as reported by Thevet. Léry is probably excessively severe on this point; modern ethnographers such as Alfred Métraux do not share Léry's contempt for Thevet's treatment of Tupi religion. The elements of his discussion can be found in other sources contemporary with Thevet, although he may have combined them as he pleased. *Maire-monan* seems to mean a creating and civilizing god; *Maire-Pochy* is

230

his familiar and servant. For an assessment of Thevet's chapters on religion, see Lussagnet's notes, pp. 36–48.

17. Allusion to a common sixteenth-century proverb referring to monks. See also Rabelais's *Pantagruel*, XXXIV: "And if you desire to be good Pantagruelists, that is to say, to live in peace, joy, health, making yourselves always merry, never trust those men that always peep out at one hole [trans. Urquhart and Motteux.]." Here, too, the reference is to the opening of a monk's hood.

18. Belleforest was the author of a number of tragedies; "Comingeois" refers to his place of origin, Comminges, in southwestern France.

19. Probably St. Francis of Paola (1416–1507), a member of the Franciscan Order and founder of the order of Minims. He was famous for the miraculous cures attributed to him even during his lifetime. His body was disinterred and burned by the Huguenots in 1562.

20. The name is variously transliterated: Konyanbebe, Cunhambebe, Quoniambec. Quoniambegue was a chief of the Tamoio tribe of Tupinamba, and his exuberant personality left an impression on European travelers. The *Cosmographie universelle* provides an engraving of the episode in question; the text reads, "to give courage to his men in battle, he would take two of the artillery pieces that he had just removed by force from a Portuguese ship, which could fire shot as big as a tennis ball, and set them on his shoulders, turning the mouths of the cannons toward his enemies" [trans. mine]. Hans Staden's *Wahrhaftige Historie* (Marburg, 1557), describing his adventures in Brazil, also contains an anecdote concerning him.

21. Mathieu de Launay, or Launoy, was a Catholic priest and theologian who joined the Reformed Church in 1560. He was banished from it because of a morals charge; he then returned to the Catholic Church, and proceeded to attack his ex-colleagues, the Reformed ministers, and their doctrine. See the Morisot edition of *Histoire d'un Voyage*, 415.

22. Léry gives, "Que l'appétit bouillant en l'homme, / Est son principal Dieu en somme."

23. *Histoire mémorable de la ville de Sancerre* (1574). In Chapter XXII of the present work Léry describes the famine of the return voyage, and compares it with the famine of the siege of Sancerre, which he lived through in 1573.

24. Léry's expression is "mots nouveaux et bien pindarisés." The last word suggests an obscure and inflated lyricism, in the style of Pindar, and is probably a shaft in the direction of Ronsard and the other Pléiade poets, whose program was to enrich the language by borrowings from classical sources. These poets had also written sonnets in praise of the work of Thevet.

25. López de Gómara, whose *General History of the West Indies* is Léry's main source for information about the rest of Latin America.

26. It was not until 1586 that Léry learned of Hans Staden's *Wahrhaftige Historie* (Marburg, 1557). Staden was a prisoner among the Tupinamba, and wrote an account that Léry regarded with favor. He mentions it near the end of the editions of 1600 and 1611.

CHAPTER I

# THE MOTIVE AND OCCASION OF OUR VOYAGE

1. Here and throughout, the French "sauvage" will be translated as its cognate "savage." In the French, however, the primary connotation is not one of cruelty or ferocity: wildflowers are "fleurs sauvages," and an unofficial day nursery is a "crèche sauvage." The word most often means simply "living in a state of nature."

2. Gaspard de Coligny (1519–1572) was one of the greatest of the Huguenot leaders. He became Admiral of France in 1552. At the time of his support of the Brazil colony, doctrinal lines were less clearly drawn in France than they were to be a few years later, which undoubtedly contributed to the misunderstandings surrounding this mission; Coligny did not make his public profession of Protestantism until 1559, after the Villegagnon expedition. He was the first person to be killed in the St. Bartholomew's Day Massacre, of which he was a chief target.

3. These letters have been lost since the sixteenth century. In the violent disputes that took place after the dissolution of the colony, Villegagnon denied having written them, and challenged his adversaries to produce them. There exists a letter from the minister Nicolas Des Gallars to Calvin, written in September 1556, telling him of the departure of the Calvinist group for the New World; it suggests, but is not conclusive evidence, that Villegagnon did ask Calvin for help, and that the latter expected to be kept informed of developments. The issue was important for Léry, in that he saw Villegagnon's subsequent behavior as a real reversal and betrayal rather than the result of a profound misunderstanding, which is at least as likely. See Reverdin, 7, 21–22.

4. When Léry speaks of the "Arctic Pole" and the "Antarctic Pole," he is not speaking of points on the earth, but rather of those points on the celestial sphere about which it appears to revolve. Similarly, he writes of sailing under the equinoctial line and of Brazil lying under the tropic of Capricorn.

5. Bourdon was a turner; Verneuil, David, and Rousseau were joiners; La Fon, a tailor; Bordel, a cutler; Carmeau, a shoemaker. Thevet, in his unpublished *Histoire de deux voyages*, said that Léry was a shoemaker, but Léry made no mention of it himself. All the members of the Calvinist mission were natives of France who were sent by the Church of Geneva.


CHAPTER II

# EMBARKATION, TRAVAILS, AND FIRST DISCOVERIES

1. Psalm 107, 23–30 (King James Version):
   They that go down to the sea in ships, that do business in great
      waters;
   These see the works of the Lord, and his wonders in the deep.
   For he commandeth, and raiseth the stormy wind, which lifteth up
      the waves thereof.


232

> They mount up to the heaven, they go down again to the depths:
> their soul is melted because of trouble.
> They reel to and fro, and stagger like a drunken man, and are at
> their wit's end.
> Then they cry unto the Lord in their trouble, and he bringeth them
> out of their distresses.
> He maketh the storm a calm, so that the waves thereof are still.
> Then are they glad because they be quiet; so he bringeth them unto
> their desired haven.

2. Juvenal, *Satires* XII: 5.
3.

> Quoique la mer par son onde bruyante,
> Fasse hérisser de peur cil qui la hante,
> Ce nonobstant l'homme se fie au bois,
> Qui d'épaisseur n'a que quatre ou cinq doigts,
> De quoi est fait le vaisseau qui le porte:
> Ne voyant pas qu'il vit en telle sorte
> Qu'il a la mort à quatre doigts de lui.
> Réputer fol on peut donc bien celui
> Qui va sur mer, si en Dieu ne se fie,
> Car c'est Dieu seul qui peut sauver sa vie.

4. Job 38, 8–11:

> Or who shut up the sea with doors, when it brake forth, as if it had
> issued out of the womb?
> When I made the cloud the garment thereof, and thick darkness a
> swaddlingband for it,
> And brake up for it my decreed place, and set bars and doors,
> And said, Hitherto shalt thou come, but no further: and here shall
> thy proud waves be stayed?

Psalm 104, 9:

> Thou has set a bound that they [the waters] may not pass over; that
> they turn not again to cover the earth.

## CHAPTER III
# BONITOS, PORPOISES, AND FLYING FISH

1. The common porpoise (*Phocoena phocoena*) has a blunt, rounded face; the common dolphin (*Delphinus delphis*) has a beak-like snout.
2. In both French and English, the word for this animal is based on "pig": *marsouin* comes from the Scandinavian *marsvin*, "sea-swine"; *porpoise* comes from the Low Latin *porcus piscis*, "hog fish."

## CHAPTER IV
# THE EQUATOR, ITS WINDS, AND PESTILENT RAINS

1. These foul, blistering rains are also reported by Gonneville and by Thevet (*Singularités* LXIX). I have been unable to find any meterological explanation of these reports.

2. The cockleshell (or scallop shell) was the emblem of St. James, and was worn by pilgrims to indicate that they had made the journey to his shrine at Compostella in Spain. Mont-Saint-Michel was an important stop along the route. In the present context, the expression "to sell cockleshells to those who have been to Mont-Saint-Michel" means to try to impress another person by feigning a kind of knowledge that the other person really possesses. Cotgrave translates the expression "A qui vendez-vous vos coquilles à ceux qui viennent de Saint-Michel?" by "Why should you think to cozen us, that are as cunning as yourselves?"

3. Léry's expression is "manger de la vache enragée": literally, "to eat of the rabid cow."

4. In the fourth century the Julian Calendar had set the vernal equinox at March 21; however, the Julian year was slightly too long, and by the sixteenth century the accumulation of discrepancy had displaced the vernal equinox to March 11. The Gregorian calendar, introduced in 1582, corrected this error.

5. Psalms 104.24–26:

> O Lord, how manifold are thy works! in wisdom has thou made
> them all: the earth is full of thy riches.
> So is this great and wide sea, wherein are things creeping innumerable, both small and great beasts.
> There go the ships: there is that leviathan, whom thou hast made to
> play therein.

Job 41.5:

> Wilt thou play with him [leviathan] as with a bird? or wilt thou
> bind him for thy maidens?

## CHAPTER V
# OUR FIRST SIGHTING OF THE LAND OF BRAZIL

1. A planisphere is a plane projection of a portion of the celestial hemisphere, as seen from a point on the earth at a particular time.

2. Exactly what Amerigo Vespucci saw and when he saw it has long been open to question. His first New World voyage was in 1497, along the coasts of Honduras and Yucatan and through the Florida Channel; his second, of 1499, seems to have included the discovery and exploration of the mouths of the Amazon. Martin Waldseemüller, in his *Cosmographiae introductio* (1507), first proposed the name "America" for the new continent to honor Vespucci.

234

3. The name is variously transliterated: *Margageat, Markaia,* or *Maracajá.* Thevet uses the term *Margargeat* in *Les Singularitez* (pp. 184, 208) in speaking of the enemies of the Indians that he knew. *Maracajá* is the Tupi word for a large jungle wildcat, now called *Jaaguatirica.* The Maracajá are mentioned in French texts and in that of the German Hans Staden as allies of the Portuguese and enemies of the groups friendly to the French; according to Lussagnet, they are not mentioned by that name in early Portuguese texts (p. 17, n. 1).

4. The proverb appears in Cotgrave as "Plus près est la chair que la chemise."

5. The Ouetaca (or Waitaca) were mentioned by many chroniclers, who attributed to them toughness, elusiveness, and voracious cannibalism. According to Anthony Knivet, "These canibals have no peace with any kinde of Nation, but doe eat all kinds of people, Frenchmen, Portugals, and Blackamoores" (Purchas 16, 252). Léry refers to them again in Chapter VI, in his polemic against Villegagnon.

6. Cotgrave gives as a second meaning for Basque: "A lackey, or footboy: so called, because many that are of that profession in France come from that country." A running footman's job was to run along beside his master's coach.

7. The Roman Catholic sailors observe feast days that are deemphasized or eliminated in Protestant worship. This particular example, Shrove Tuesday, or "Mardi Gras," has a more general observance as a day for parties and carousing than a religious holiday, but Léry is marking here a distance between his group and the sailors in this respect. The day after Shrove Tuesday is Ash Wednesday, the first day of Lent.

8. In this relatively unmarked, unmapped America, it would seem that one can choose the meanings—particularly the religious meanings—to be imposed on it. In this passage Léry is treating the New World as a place as yet uncorrupted by Roman Catholicism.

## CHAPTER VI
# OUR ARRIVAL AND THE BEHAVIOR OF VILLEGAGNON

1. See Chapter I, note 3. In the present chapter, Léry is trying to demonstrate that Villegagnon claimed unambiguously to be of the Reformed persuasion, and that he slid back into Papism shortly after, thereby betraying his promise to the Calvinist mission. In the violent exchange of polemics (particularly with Pierre Richier) after his return, Villegagnon denied any Calvinist theological belief, or any promises to their group.

2. "Epicureans" was a term commonly used in the period (by Calvin, among many others) to denounce free-thinkers. See Lucien Febvre, *The Problem of Unbelief in the Sixteenth Century: The Religion of Rabelais.*

3. Léry has a marginal note to these "apostates": "These were certain Norman interpreters, who, being dispersed among the savages before Villegagnon

went into that country, did not want to submit to his rule upon his arrival."
See the Introduction.

4. Genesis 14.28. Melchizedek was both king of Salem and "priest of the most
high God." He blessed Abraham after a battle, and Abraham gave him tithes
of the spoils. See also Psalm 110.4: "The Lord hath sworn, and will not
repent, Thou art a priest forever after the order of Melchizedek." This saying
is expounded at length by St. Paul (Hebrews 5–7), for whom the priesthood
of Melchizedek prefigures that of Christ.

5. Transubstantiation is a doctrine of the Roman Catholic Church according to
which in the Eucharist the whole substance of the bread is transformed into
the body of Christ and the whole substance of the wine into his blood, with
only the appearance of the bread and wine remaining.

6. Consubstantiation is the doctrine, offered during the Reformation by the
Lutherans, that the substance of the body and blood of Christ coexists in and
with the substance of the bread and wine of the Eucharist.

7. The Ouetaca, treated in Chapter V, represent the extreme of barbarism in
this work; they eat human flesh raw (rather than cooked, as the Tupinamba
do), their language is unknown to their neighbors, and they avoid all contact
with others. In the pamphlet war after Villegagnon's return, the Protestant
polemicists labeled Villegagnon a cannibal: for their rhetorical purposes,
adhering to the Roman Catholic doctrine of transubstantiation amounted to
eating raw the flesh of the Saviour. In comparing Villegagnon to the
Ouetaca, Léry is equating him with the most savage of savages; later, he will
indicate Villegagnon's inferiority to the Tupinamba, who, while also cannibals, are sociable and, within a particular code, trustworthy. See Lestringant,
"Calvinistes et cannibales," 168–177.

8. Chartier never obtained the clarifications he asked for; his communications
with Calvin were impeded by various delays (deliberate and otherwise) and
by the difficulties of communications between Brazil, France, and Geneva
(Reverdin, 65–67).

9. "Old skin" is probably an echo of the references to the "old man" in St. Paul.
Romans 6.6: "Knowing this, that our old man is crucified with him, that the
body of sin might be destroyed, that henceforth we should not serve sin."
Ephesians 4.22–23: "That ye put off concerning the former conversation the
old man, which is corrupt according to the deceitful lusts; and be renewed in
the spirit of your mind; and that ye put on the new man, which after God is
created in righteousness and true holiness."
Colossians 3.9–11: "Lie not to one another, seeing that ye have put off the
old man with his deeds: and have put on the new man, which is renewed in
knowledge after the image of him that created him: where there is neither
Greek nor Jew, circumcision nor uncircumcision, Barbarian, Scythian, bond
nor free; but Christ is all, and in all."
The last passage seems particularly apt, since the issue is the inclusion of the
"savage" or the "barbarian" into the Christian community.

10. The Second Council of Nicaea, in 787. See John T. McNeill's edition of
Calvin's *Institutes of the Christian Religion*, 114 nn. 26, 27.

11. In 1560, after his return to France, Villegagnon wrote to the Church of Geneva, describing his disputes with Richier and Du Pont, and asked to have a formal theological debate with Calvin, to be arbitrated by Lutherans. The Geneva Council did not take the request seriously, and rejected it. The proposed debate was replaced by a war of pamphlets (Reverdin, 68–69).

12. Petrus Richelius is Pierre Richier, who wrote one of the chief denunciations of Villegagnon. The remarks about currying and dusting refer to two anonymous Protestant pamphets of 1561, *L'Estrille de Nicolas Durand, dit le chevalier de Villegagnon,* and *L'Espoussette des armoiries de Villegagnon.* Richier had accused Villegagnon of being marked on the shoulder with the fleur-de-lis, the brand of the convict; the curry-comb and duster of these titles are the instruments that would remove the dust and grime that had obscured the mark, and bring it to the light of day. See Lestringant, "Calvinistes et cannibales," 2d part, 185, n.3.

13. This presentation of Villegagnon is a reference to the iconography of the pamphlet war of 1560/61, in which Villegagnon was represented as a savage anthropophagous Cyclops.

14. Orlando Furioso: a reference to the warrior hero Roland, portrayed as mad in Ariosto's epic poem of the same name (1532).

## CHAPTER VII
# THE BAY OF GUANABARA AND ITS ISLANDS

1. Léry speaks of "la rivière de Ganabara"; the word "rivière" was used at the time to mean various indentations in a coastline, including bays and gulfs. That is clearly what is meant here. "Guanabara" means "A bay that resembles the sea" (Lussagnet, 10 n. 1).

2. The Fort of Coligny fell to Portuguese forces led by the governor Mem de Sá in 1560.

3. *Cosmographie* 910.

4. For the fictions in Thevet's maps glorifying the Valois dynasty, see Frank Lestringant, "Fictions de l'espace brésilien à la Renaissance: l'exemple de Guanabara."

5. One of the numerous gulfs on the Brazilian coast, probably about half way between Guanabara and São Vicente to the southwest (Lussagnet, 8–9 n. 7).

## CHAPTER VIII
# THE BODILY DESCRIPTION OF THE BRAZILIANS

1. Vaz de Caminha, who in 1500 gave one of the earliest written descriptions of Brazilian Indians, spoke repeatedly and glowingly of their handsomeness: "Our Lord gave them fine bodies and good faces, as to good men." (Letter to King Manuel, in *The Voyage of Pedro Alvares Cabral to Brazil and India* [trans. Greenlee], 29).

2. There is a vast literature on the ways in which New World societies were seen as survivals of the Golden Age. Harry Levin's *The Myth of the Golden Age in the Renaissance* is especially useful (pp. 58–83), as in Geoffroy Atkinson's *Les Nouveaux Horizons de la Renaissance française* (pp. 137–168). Atkinson specifically treats the reports of extreme longevity (pp. 118–119) and the frequent criticism of European avarice (p. 133).

3. Many Europeans expected the New World inhabitants to resemble the hairy Wild Man of medieval legend. See Richard Bernheimer, *The Wild Man in the Middle Ages.*

4. See Lévi-Strauss, *Tristes Tropiques:* "It is in fact probable that the penis-sheath, when used, is intended not so much to prevent an erection as to make plain the peaceful condition of him who wears it. Peoples who live entirely naked are not ignorant of what we call modesty: they simply have another frontier line. Among the Brazilian Indians . . . modesty has nothing to do with how much or how little of the body is exposed; tranquility lies on one side of the frontier, agitation on the other" [trans. Russell] (pp. 277–278). See also Wagley, *Welcome of Tears:* "[Tapiripé] men took considerable caution not to be seen without their *chirankonya-chiwawa* (penis band). To be seen without it was analogous to a North American being seen on Main Street without his pants" (p. 127).

5. All these body ornaments are treated in Métraux, *La Civilisation matérielle des tribus Tupi-Guarani* 121–201. Important contemporary sources are Staden II: xv; Magalhães de Gandavo, *Historia* X; Soares de Sousa, *Tratado* CLV; Thevet, *Singularités* XXXIV; and *Cosmographie,* 931.

6. On a number of occasions Léry uses this term either as synonymous with "Tupinamba" or as a qualifier for it. His usage of this term, like that of Thevet, is different from that of the other chroniclers, who identify the Tupinikin as allies of the Portuguese and enemies of the French. (Lussagnet, 299 n.1.)

7. The ostrich, genus *Struthio,* is an Old World bird. The New World genus *Rhea* resembles the ostrich. The former has two toes, the latter three.

8. *Caouin* is a fermented brew, of great importance to the Tupinamba in all their festivities (see Chap. IX). Léry frequently gives this word a French infinitive verb ending (*caouiner*) or a French noun ending (*caouinage*).

9. One of the more sly of Léry's numerous comparisons between Tupinamba and Roman Catholic display and ritual; see Chapter XVI. Such comparisons are common in Huguenot writing of the period.

10. Reconstructed by Plinio Ayrosa as *Mair, nde angaturã, emeén abé morubi* (*Viagem,* 119 n.199). *Mair* was a term used to address Frenchmen; for its implications, see Chapter XVI.

11. Vaz de Caminha has various remarks on female nudity, modesty, and beauty: "one of the girls was all painted from head to foot with that paint, and she was so well built and so rounded and her lack of shame was so charming, that many women of our land, seeing such attractions, would be ashamed that theirs were not like hers" (p. 16).

238

12. The "heretics" are probably such sects as the Adamites. See Thevet, *Cosmographie*, 928. "One should have sent among these savages the Adamites, issued from the school of Wycliff and of John Huss, who imitated their first father by going naked in Bohemia" [trans. mine]. The Adamites were a fringe element of the sect of John Huss in Bohemia and Moravia in the fifteenth century, and a continuation of the secret society known as the Brothers and Sisters of the Free Spirit, which was persecuted in France in the preceding century (Lussagnet, 111 n.1). For Léry, shame is the law of nature: that is, the nature of man after the Fall.

## CHAPTER IX
## ROOTS AND GRAINS THAT THEY EAT, AND THEIR DRINKING

1. For discussions of Tupi agriculture, see Staden II: 20, and 14; Thevet, *Singularités* LVIII, and *Cosmographie*, 948–949; Magalhães de Gandavo, *Historia* V; Soares de Sousa, *Tratado* II: 4.

2. Both *aypi* and *maniot* refer to the same species, *Manihot esculenta* Crantz. Cultivars differ in the amount of cyanide contained in the tubers. The "bitter" types contain large amounts of cyanide and must be detoxified by leaching or cooking before they can be eaten. The "sweet" types have cyanide only in the outermost layers of the tuber and thus may be peeled before being eaten, or else they may contain very low amounts of the poison.

3. The Portuguese called these, respectively, *farinha de guerra* (war flour) and *farinha fresca* (fresh flour); see Magalhães.

4. This is still a common way of making beer, or "chicha," in Latin America. The enzyme ptyalin in saliva converts the starches to sugars for yeast fermentation.

5. However, not only Thevet (*Cosmographie* 916) but also Magalhães de Gandavo (*Tratado* II: 7) and Staden specify that it is the young girls or virgins who chew the roots for the brew.

6. The reputation of the Germans for drunkenness in this period is attested to by Rabelais and Montaigne. The former uses the expression "boire à la tudesque" [drink in the Teutonic fashion]" (*Pantagruel* XXVIII), and the latter refers to the "Germans drowned in wine" (*Essais* II: 2).

7. A very similar remark in Thevet, *Cosmographie*, 930: "During their meal, they observe a marvelous silence, and make fun of us when they hear us chatter at the table."

## CHAPTER X
## THE ANIMALS AND MONSTROUS BEASTS OF AMERICA

1. For comparable descriptions of animals, see Thevet, *Singularités* XLIX and LII, and *Cosmographie*, 936–941; Staden II: xxix–xxx; Magalhães de Gandavo, *Historia* VI: Soares de Sousa, *Tratado* II: xi.

2. As a verb, *sóo* means to feed; as a noun, it means flesh, or, more generally, animals whose flesh is used as food (*Viagem*, 135 n.245).

3. In their attempts to describe the tapir, most of the early chroniclers, including Thevet and Soares de Sousa, resorted to the idea of a combination of a jenny and a bull, or a jack and a cow.

4. The root meaning of *boucan* is "to dry" (*Viagem*, 137 n.248).

5. A reference to Thevet, *Cosmographie* 930.

6. Pierre Belon, *Observations de plusieurs singularitez et choses memorables* (Paris, 1553).

7. *Natural History*, Book V, Chapter 196.

8. Earlier editors and translators have identified this as the *sucuryuba*, or *tapiiara*, a snake that was known to swallow large animals, whole. It was probably, rather, an iguana, some Brazilian species of which do grow to the size that Léry describes; furthermore, the modern ethological descriptions of their threat displays involve a kind of audible, aspirant breathing like that which Léry describes.

9. Clément Marot (1496–1544), French lyric, satiric, and religious poet. The poem is "Fripelipes, valet de Marot, à Sagon."

10. Thevet (*Cosmographie* 940 v.) claims that he kept one for a month, and that it stayed in good health without eating or drinking all that time. Soares de Sousa (*Tratado* II: xii) makes similar remarks.

## CHAPTER XI
# THE VARIETY OF THE BIRDS OF AMERICA

1. Compare Thevet, *Singularités* XLVII, XLVIII, LI; *Cosmographie*, 839, 938–940; Magalhães de Gandavo, *Historia* VII; Soares de Sousa, *Tratado* II: x–xi; Yves d'Evreux, *Voyage* XVIII

2. Thevet uses a similar term, *arignane*, to refer to poultry. It is not clear where he and Léry got this word; the common Tupi word was *çapucai* (Lussagnet, 118 n.2) or *sapukai* (*Viagem*, 147 n.282).

3. The first, the species *Cumana iacutinga*, is blue, black, and white; the second species, *Penelope superciliaris*, has a white line above the eyes; the third species, *Penelope obscura*, is big, as the suffix *-uassu* indicates, and is reddish brown and black (Lussagnet, 158 n.3; *Viagem*, 148 nn. 288, 289, 290).

4. *Mocacoüa* is probably derived from *macuco*, the name of various birds of the Tinamidae family; the *ynambu-guaçú* belongs to the same family (see *Viagem*, 149 nn. 293, 294, 295).

5. *Ynamboumiri* is a little *ynambú*; *pegassou* is of the Columbidae family; *paicacu* is difficulty to identify (see *Viagem*, 149 nn. 295, 296, 297).

6. The species *Ara ararauna*, of the Psittacidae family (*Viagem*, 149 n. 299); it is also described by Thevet, Magalhães de Gandavo, and Soares de Sousa. Most transliterate the name *canindé*.

7. Or *Ajurú*, of the *Amazona* genus. For *a* + *jurú*, "people's mouth," an allusion to the parrot's apparent ability to speak like human beings (*Viagem*, 150 n.304; Lussagnet, 167, n.1).

8. *Mokáb* was the name given to the harquebus; with the suffix *-ouassou*, meaning "big," it indeed designated a piece of artillery (*Viagem*, 151 n.308).

9. The species *Ara maracana* (see *Viagem*, 151 n.310).

10. Perhaps the bird known as *tié-sangue* or *tiépiranga* (*Rhamphocelus bresilius bresilius* L.) (Lussagnet, 168 n.1).

11. Unclear; perhaps *guyrá-pirá* or *Ará* + *pirá*, birds of this Psittacidae family (see *Viagem*, 153 n.317).

12. Compare Thevet, *Cosmographie*, 939, and Yves d'Evreux, *Voyage*, 281, for similar descriptions of birds as communicators with the supernatural. For attempts to identify this bird, see Lussagnet, 105 n.2.

13. This term designates various insects, such as cockroaches, beetles, and scarabs (*Viagem*, 155 n.326).

14. *Tun* or *tung:* the chigoe (*Tunga penetrans*). Staden (II: xxxi), calls it *attun*, and makes similar observations.

15. The species *Myristica officinalis* Mart. (Lussagnet, 153 n.2).

16. Thevet had also remarked on the vindictiveness of the Tupi against anything that hurt them, even thorns or stones (*Singularités* XLI; *Cosmographie*, 947).

CHAPTER XII
# THE COMMON FISH, AND THE MANNER OF FISHING

1. Compare Thevet, *Singularités* XXVI; Magalhães de Gandavo, *Historia* VIII; Soares de Sousa, *Tratado* II: xv, xvi.

2. *Akará* is the generic term for a fish with scales; it is qualified by various adjectives in the names that Léry gives subsequently: *acara-ouassou* is a big fish; *Acarapep* is a flat fish (*peb* means flat); *Acara-bouten* is a red fish (*pytã* means red). See *Viagem*, 162 nn. 342–344.

3. *Tamouhata* or *tamboata* (*Callichthys Callichthys* Linn.). See *Viagem*, 163 n.346; Lussagnet, 306 n.1.

4. *Nde angaturã, emeé abé pinda* (*Viagem*,165 n.353).

CHAPTER XIII
# THE TREES, PLANTS, AND EXQUISITE FRUITS OF BRAZIL

1. Compare Thevet, *Singularités* LIX; *Cosmographie*, 949; Magalhães de Gandavo, *Historia* I, V; Soares de Sousa, *Tratado* II: iv, v.

2. The word *brésil* (*brasile*, etc.) had existed at least since the twelfth century to designate trees that yielded red dyes, the color of glowing coals (*braise*).

Before the New World discoveries, the source of this dye was the heartwood of the tree now known as *Caesalpinia sappan* L. (sappanwood) native to Indomalaya. Upon the discovery in the New World of *Caesalpinia echinata,* the name *brésil* was transferred to the plant and then to the country where it was found. The name Terra do Brasil soon replaced the earlier Portuguese name, Terra da Santa Cruz. Léry's term *araboutan* appears in modern transcription as *ibirapitanga* or *ybra pytã,* meaning "red wood" (Lussagnet, 216–217 n.3; *Viagem,* 167 n.359).

3. It is believed that *genau, airy,* and *iry* are all the same tree: *Astrocaryum ayri* Mart. (Lussagnet, 186 n.2).

4. The copaiba (*Copaifera officinalis* [Jacq.] L. and *Copaifera Langsdorfii* Desf.), described at length by most of the Portuguese chroniclers; its balsam was greatly valued for its medicinal properties (Lussagnet, 319 n.1).

5. *Thevetia ahouai* A. DC, so named because Thevet was the first to describe it (*Singularités* XXXVI; *Cosmographie,* 922). It belongs to the Apocynaceae, or dogbane family, which contains many poisonous plants. Thevet says that husbands and wives sometimes used it to poison each other, and that it also served as an abortifacient.

6. *Pradosia glycyphloea,* a sweet-smelling wood; its common Portuguese name is *buranhém.* The early voyagers frequently confused it with guaicum, a standard antisyphilitic of the sixteenth century brought back from the Caribbean at the time of Columbus's early voyages.

7. Pliny, *Historia naturalis* XV: 20. Bananas were unknown in the Mediterranean in classical times; therefore Pliny's mention of Cato probably refers to the real fig, *Ficus carica* L.

8. Charles Estienne and Jean Liébault, *L'Agriculture et maison rustique* (Paris, 1583).

9. There has been much controversy over which of the two, Thevet or Nicot, should have the credit for introducing tobacco to France. Jean Nicot, ambassador from France to Portugal, received some tobacco that had originally come from Florida. That tobacco plant had probably been introduced in Portugal in the early sixteenth century, but only for ornamental uses. In 1560 Nicot sent seeds to the Queen Mother, Catherine de Medici; the plant was known successively as *herbe à la reine, catherinaire, Médicée,* and *Nicotiane.* If Thevet upon his return from Brazil in 1556 brought back and cultivated tobacco seeds, he was, indeed, four years ahead of Nicot. However, he seems to have remained at the experimental stage of cultivation of the seeds, and the diffusion of tobacco can still be credited to Ambassador Nicot. Léry exaggerates the difference between the plants of Thevet and of Nicot. Nicot's Florida tobacco may be *Nicotiana rustica* L., originating in the West Indies, and Thevet's Brazilian species *Nicotiana tabacum* L. But the species were put to similar use by both Europeans and Indians (Lussagnet, 102–104 n.2). Thevet's initial description of *petun* is in *Singularités* XXXII; it is elaborated with references to the rivalry with Nicot (unnamed), in his *Cosmographie,* 926–927. Angoumois was the birthplace of Thevet, and also the place of origin of the ruling dynasty; hence the name *angoumoisine.*

10. *Moráng:* A species of *Cucurbita.*

11. Psalm 104, v. 24. I have, as usual, given the King James version; Léry uses a
version in rhymed decasyllabic couplets by Clement Marot:

> O Seigneur Dieu que tes oeuvres divers
> Sont merveilleux par le monde univers:
> O que tu as tout fait par grand sagesse!
> Bref, la terre est pleine de ta largesse.

## CHAPTER XIV
## THE WARFARE, BOLDNESS, AND ARMS OF THE SAVAGES

1. See, for comparison, Staden II, Chapter 26; Magalhães de Gandavo, *Historia*
XI; Thevet, *Cosmographie,* 941–944.

2. The origin of this term is uncertain; it may be from the Portuguese name Pero
(cf. Pedro). See Hélène Clastres's edition of Yves d'Evreux's *Voyage au Nord
du Brésil,* 173, note to Chapter XII.

3. See Montaigne "On Cannibals," for a more idealized view: "Their warfare is
wholly noble and generous, and as excusable and beautiful as this human
disease can be; its only basis among them is their rivalry in valor" [trans.
Frame] (p. 156).

4. The work of Innocent Gentillet, *Discours sur les moyens de bien gouver-
ner . . . Contre Nicholas Machiavel* (Geneva, 1576), was highly influential in
creating the image of a villainous Machiavelli; it was especially important in
Protestant circles. Gentillet cites the very passage from Machiavelli that Léry
is paraphrasing here (from Chapter VII of *The Prince*), and ascribes the
atmosphere of vengeance in France to just such a principle. Thus, this sentence of Léry's is probably an allusion to the civil strife in France. (See the C.
E. Rathé edition [Genève: Droz, 1968], 324–335.)

5. *Angaipá* means "bad" (*Viagem,* 184 n.419).

6. This detail is also described in Thevet (*Cosmographie* 942).

7. Compare Thevet, *Cosmographie:* "it is a horror mingled with entertainment
to see these savages when they join battle" (p. 942); "Watching these threats
is the greatest pleasure that one could wish" (p. 943).

8. Ibid.: "by this alone they measure the friendship you bear them" (p. 942).

## CHAPTER XV
## THE CEREMONIES FOR KILLING AND EATING PRISONERS

1. Descriptions of Tupinamba cannibal rites are numerous in the travel reports
of the sixteenth and early seventeenth centuries, particularly those of Nicolas
Barré, André Thevet, Hans Staden, Magalhães de Gandavo, Yves d'Evreux,

Claude d'Abbeville, Fernão Cardim, and Anthony Knivet. From these sources Alfred Métraux has assembled a composite description of the rites, in *La Religion des Tupinamba et ses rapports avec celle des autres tribus Tupi-Guarani* (1928). The chapter "L'Anthropophagie rituelle des Tupinamba" (pp. 124–169) was revised and published in his *Religions et magies indiennes d'Amérique du Sud* (1967), 45–78. See also the study by Florestan Fernandes, "La Guerre et le sacrifice humain chez les Tupinamba," as well as Lussagnet's extensive notes to Thevet's *Cosmographie universelle*.

2. Prisoners were kept for varying lengths of time, even up to fifteen or twenty years for the younger men (Thevet, *Histoire de deux voyages*, in Lussagnet, 273).

3. These ceremonies stretched out over three to five days (there seem to have been regional differences). They involved elaborate adornments of the victim, the executioner, the rope that held the prisoner, and the sword-club with which he was dispatched. See Cardim, *Treatise* (trans. Purchas), 432–439; and Thevet, *Histoire de deux voyages* (Lussagnet, 275–284).

4. Some version of this rhetoric of defiance is to be found in most of the early accounts; it was clearly attractive to the chroniclers, for example, Hans Staden: "Yes, we went forth, as it beseems valiant men, to capture and eat you, our enemies. Now you have gained the upper hand, and have captured us, but we care not for this. Braves die in their enemy's country, and as our land is still large, the others will revenge us well upon you [trans. Tootal]" (p. 103). Compare Montaigne, "Of Cannibals": " 'These muscles,' he says, 'this flesh and these veins are yours, poor fools that you are. You do not recognize that the substance of your ancestors' limbs is still contained in them. Savor them well; you will find in them the taste of your own flesh.' An idea that certainly does not smack of barbarity [trans. Frame]" (p. 158).

5. Compare Thevet, *Cosmographie*, 944: "And do not think that the prisoner is disconcerted by this news [the details of his forthcoming execution]; he believes rather that his death is honorable, and that it is much better for him to die thus, than in his own house, of some contagious disease [trans. mine]." Yves d'Evreux has left a memorable lament of a slave rescued by the Europeans from the ritual cannibal slaughter. When asked if he does not consider himself lucky to be alive, he answers: "I would be sorry to die in my bed, and not die in the manner of the great ones, in the midst of the dances and the drinking, and avenge myself before dying on those who would have eaten me. For whenever I consider that I am the son of a great one of my country, and that my father was feared, and that everyone surrounded him to listen when he went to the *carbet* [assembly], and seeing myself now a slave, without painting, without plumes attached to my head, arms and wrists, as the sons of the great ones of our region are adorned, I wish I were dead [trans. mine]" (p. 55).

6. A particularly sinister role is given to the old women, whose avidity appears as a contrasting element in the generally controlled and ritualized structure of Tupi cannibalism. Thevet (*Histoire de deux voyages,* in Lussagnet, 281–282) and Claude d'Abbeville (p. 294) make similar remarks.

7. *Pantagruel,* Chapter XIV.

8. Métraux (*Religions et magies,* 67–73) and Lussagnet (pp. 192–193 nn. 2, 3) offer interpretations of the significance of Tupinamba cannibalism, both for the early European voyagers and, to the extent that it can be reconstructed, for the Tupinamba themselves. The early chroniclers are unanimous in re-marking that Tupi cannibalism is not a matter of nutrition or sensual greedi-ness (except in the case of the old women); it is a sign of vengeance, and as such is part of a code of honor that the European voyagers were quick to see—rightly or wrongly—as analogous to the feudal *point d'honneur.* There are suggestions in these early sources that the Tupinamba believed that the vital force of the victim could be ingested with his flesh. Métraux (*Religions et magies,* 69–70) endorses the views of the Brazilian sociologist Florestan Fernandes ("A funçao social da guerra na sociedade tupinamba," p. 325), who sees the execution of a prisoner as a religious act, intended to appease the soul of a slain kinsman; what one seeks to appropriate in eating the enemy's flesh is not so much the latter's own energies as the substance of the kinsman that the enemy had eaten.

9. The withdrawal of the executioner to his house was the occasion of another visible phase of ritual, akin to mourning, intended to protect him from the angry spirit of his victim (Métraux, *Religions et magies,* 73–78): he is con-fined to a hammock, and must observe a fast; his pulses are anointed with the filaments from the eye sockets of the victim, and as a bracelet he must wear the victim's mouth, cut in a circle (Cardim [trans. Purchas], 439). He must take a new name: perhaps to escape the wrath of his victim's spirit, perhaps as a sign of rebirth. Cardim treats this whole phrase of ritual as a sort of entrance into nobility: "from thence forward he remains enabled to kill without any painful ceremony being done to him, and he also sheweth himself honoured and contented and with a certain disdaine, as one that hath honour already, and gets it not anew" (p. 440). See also Magalhães de Gandavo: "he [the executioner] eats nothing, but on the other hand orders himself scarified over the whole body, because they consider it certain that he would soon die if he did not spill some of his own blood as soon as he had performed this duty" (*Historia* [trans. Stetson], 106).

10. According to Thevet (*Cosmographie,* 933), the Indians believe that the male alone is the maker of his child; therefore the child of a male captive is by blood entirely an enemy. See also Magalhães de Gandavo, *Historia:* "And if the woman who was the wife of the prisoner is found to be with child, after the child is born and weaned, it is killed and eaten without there being a person to pity so unjust a death. . . . [The grandparents] say that, as it is the son of its father, they are taking vengeance on the father; for they believe that under the circumstances this creature derives nothing from the mother, nor do they think that such unfriendly seed can blend with her blood. . . . But as the mother knows the end which her child must suffer, often when she realizes she is pregnant she kills the child in the womb, so that it will not see the light" [trans. Stetson] (pp. 107–108).

11. See my article, "Food and the Limits of Civility," pp. 391–392.

12. In the *Cosmographie* (p. 947) Thevet also recounts the slaying of a baptized Margaia by the Tupinamba.

13. Morpion was the Portuguese captaincy of São Vicente, south of Rio de Janeiro.

14. The editions from 1585 onward contain additions at this point in the form of many other examples of Old World atrocities. In the 1611 edition a new Chapter XVI was added to accommodate the expansion of this material, including an account of the cruelties of the Spaniards in their conquest of America as reported by the great defender of the Indians, Bartolomeo de las Casas.

15. Probably a sardonic reference to the Catholic doctrine of the Real Presence, that of Christ in the bread and wine of the Eucharist, by transubstantiation.

16. For the background of European cannibalism during the period of the religious wars in France, see Géralde Nakam's introduction to her edition of Léry's *Histoire mémorable de la ville de Sancerre;* the Weber edition of d'Aubigné's *Les Tragiques* (in *Oeuvres,* 913 n.9); Frank Lestringant, "Catholiques et Cannibales: Le thème du cannibalisme dans le discours protestant au temps des guerres de religion"; also his "Le Cannibalism des 'Cannibales' "; my article "Food and the Limits of Civility." For a discussion of this and other forms of violence in this period, see Natalie Davis, "The Rites of Violence," in *Society and Culture in Early Modern France,* and Robert Kingdon, *Myths about the St. Bartholomew's Day Massacres.*

17. Compare Montaigne, "Of Cannibals": "I am not sorry that we notice the barbarous horror of such acts, but I am heartily sorry that, judging their faults rightly, we should be so blind to our own. I think there is more barbarity in eating a man alive than in eating him dead; and in tearing by tortures and the rack a body still full of feeling, in roasting a man bit by bit, in having him bitten and mangled by dogs and swine (as we have not only read but seen within fresh memory, not among ancient enemies, but among neighbors and fellow citizens, and what is worse, on the pretext of piety and religion), than in roasting and eating him after he is dead [trans. Frame]" (p. 155).

CHAPTER XVI

# WHAT MAY BE CALLED RELIGION AMONG THE SAVAGES

1. For an overview of Tupinamba religion, the classic modern study is Alfred Métraux, *La Religion des Tupinamba et ses rapports avec celle des autres tribus Tupi-Guarani;* see also his *Religions et magies indiennes d'Amérique du Sud,* especially Chapter I, "Messies indiens," for a treatment of Indian shamanism. For all Léry's scorn of Thevet, the latter remains one of the most valuable sources of information on Tupi religion; in his *Cosmographie* he provides more detail of Tupi creation and transformation myths than any of his contemporaries. The accounts of Yves d'Evreux and Claude d'Abbeville contain much material on religion; written in 1614, they show us how two

more generations of contact with Christianity had affected Tupinamba religious belief and practice.

2. Cicero, *On the Nature of the Gods,* I. Compare Calvin, *Institution de la Religion chrétienne,* Chapter I: "If ignorance of God is to be looked for anywhere, surely one is most likely to find an example of it among the more backward folk and those more remote from civilization. Yet there is, as the eminent pagan says, no nation so barbarous, no people so savage, that they have not a deep-seated conviction that there is a God. And they who in other aspects of life seem least to differ from brutes still continue to retain some seed of religion [trans. Battle]" (p. 44).

3. From the 1585 edition on, Léry expands his discussion to present the argument of Socrates: that the art of writing degrades the arts of memory: "Writing and letters, far from conserving memory as they are commonly judged to do, on the contrary are injurious to that end . . . Since writing allows one to scorn the observance of memory, the knowledge of things has been less vivified, and consequently each person has known less because of knowing only what is [writing] reminds us of [trans. mine]" (pp. 268–269). Having presented Socrates' argument, Léry then goes on to refute it with allusions to Cicero and to Moses: both history and scripture need writing for their reliable transmission.

4. Toupan (also Tupan, Tupã, Tupä), the Tupi term for thunder, was early seized on by many missionaries as a way of referring to the Christian God. See Métraux, *Religion,* 52–56; also H. Clastres, *La Terre sans mal,* 15–39. Clastres points out the importance of Tupä as a god not of creation but of cataclysms, which have a primary role in the prophetic aspects of Tupi religion. In *Welcome of Tears* (pp. 200–211) Charles Wagley describes a 1940 celebration—perhaps one of the last—of the Thunder ceremonies among the Tapirapé, descendants of the Tupinamba. The creatures of thunder were called *topu,* which is clearly a form of *Tupã.*

5. This is the "Land without Evil," the belief in which, according to Hélène Clastres (*La Terre sans mal*) is at the heart of Tupi religion. The Land without Evil was thought to be accessible in *this* life; a number of long and exhausting migrations, led by Tupi shamans or *caraíbes,* resulted from the search for this land of ease and plenty. See also Métraux, *Religion,* 201–224 and *Religions et magies,* 11–41.

6. Like *Toupan,* the term *Aygnan* was adopted by the missionaries in their conversion efforts; it was identified with the Devil of Christianity. See Métraux, *Religion,* 57–67. The word *anhanga* or *anchunga* is still in use among Brazilian Indians to designate spirits (Wagley, 174ff.)

7. The name indicates "demon of the bush" (Métraux, *Religion,* 63–64); encounters with him (or them) are chiefly to be feared in the forest at night.

8. See Matthew 4.24; 9.32–34; Mark 1.32–34; 5.1–19; Luke 5.33–42; 9.31–42; 11.14–15.

9. For the various meanings of the term "atheism" in the sixteenth century, see Lucien Febvre, *The Problem of Unbelief in the Sixteenth Century: The Religion of Rabelais* (pp. 131–151). See also Stephen Greenblatt's essay "Invisi-

ble Bullets," in *Shakespearean Negotiations*. Greenblatt treats the explorer Thomas Harriott's reputation as an atheist, and points out that atheism "was almost always thinkable only as the thought of another" (p. 22).

10. The idea that no human being can plead ignorance of God is important in the work of Calvin: "But upon his individual works he has engraved unmistakeable marks of his glory, so clear and so prominent that even unlettered and stupid folk cannot plead the excuse of ignorance" (*Institutes* 52). Compare St. Paul, Romans 1.20: "For the invisible things of him from the creation of the world are clearly seen, being understood by the things that are made, even his eternal power and Godhead; so that they are without excuse."

11. Compare Calvin, *Institutes* I: iv: "Experience teaches that the seed of religion has been divinely planted in all men [trans. Battles]" (p. 47).

12. The term *caraïbe* was applied to men who claimed and to whom were attributed prophetic powers. Thevet uses *caraïbe* in speaking of the culture heroes of Tupi mythology. Early Jesuit writers say that *caraïbe* meant "the sacred." The early lexicographer Montoya noted that *carai* was both the title for the great shamans and the name given to the Spaniards, who were in fact sometimes confounded with the civilizing heroes of Tupi myth. See Hélène Clastres, *La Terre sans mal*, Chapter II.

13. From the 1585 edition onward, the musical notation for Tupi chants is included in the text.

14. From the 1585 edition onward, Léry presents an account of a European witches' sabbath from Jean Bodin's *De la démonomanie des sorciers* (1578), with this comment: "I have concluded that they have the same master: that is, the Brazilian women and the witches over here were guided by the same spirit of Satan; neither the distance between the places nor the long passage over the sea keeps the father of lies from working both here and there on those who are handed over to him by the just judgment of God" (pp. 280–281).

15. Hélène Clastres (*Terre*, 61–63) notes the continuity between the topics of these Tupi chants and the preoccupations of some of the modern Guarani tribes, especially the linking of the deluge myth—a cataclysm past or future?—and access to the Land without Evil. Pierre Clastres has recorded some Tupi-Guarani chants of today, and relates them to these early sources, in *Le Grand Parler; Mythes et chants sacrés des Indiens Guarani*.

16. In his *Cosmographie* (pp. 913–915) Thevet gives two versions of the flood in Tupi mythology. In the beginning, the earth was flat and uniform, producing everything for human needs. The first race of people fell into dissolute ways; Monan, the creator, to punish them for their ingratitude, sent fire down from heaven and burned the face of the earth, making it irregular, covered with valleys and mountains. One man, Irin-Mage, was saved; for him Monan sent great rains that filled up the new hollows on the earth and thus created the seas. Two brothers, descendants of Irin-Mage, quarreled bitterly; in his anger, one struck the earth so hard that he opened up a great spring of water, which released a flood over all the earth. The brothers took refuge in separate trees, each with a wife; from these two families descended the warring Tupi tribes.

17. Léry may have been thinking of Ovid's *Metamorphoses,* Book I, which describes the flood of which Deucalion and Pyrrha were the survivors. On the issue of writing as a fixative for truth, see Calvin, *Institutes* (trans. Battles), 72. Michel de Certeau, in *L'Ecriture de l'histoire,* characterizes Léry's attitude to oral and literate cultures: "Thanks to the scriptural standard, Léry knows how to determine what the oral adds to things, and he knows exactly how things had been. He becomes a historian. Speech, to the contrary, has much to do with custom, which 'turns truth into falsehood.' And more fundamentally, the Tupis' account is a fable (from *fari,* parler). So *fable is a drifting away;* adjunction, deviation, diversion, heresy and poetry of the present with respect to the 'purity' of the primitive law [trans. Conley]" (p. 217). Léry's Protestantism undoubtedly plays an important part in the value he places on the idea of a pure, uncorrupted written source; but see also a Catholic contemporary of Léry, Fernão Cardim (trans. Purchas): "It seemeth that this people hath no knowledge of the beginning and creation of the world, but of the deluge it seemeth they have some notice: but as they have no writings nor characters, such notice is obscured and confused" (p. 418).

18. On the cult of the *maraca,* see Métraux, *Religion,* 72–78, and Lussagnet, 118 n. 1. Important primary sources are Thevet, *Cosmographie,* 929; Staden II, Chapter XXIII. The latter's formulation is memorable: "They believe in a thing which grows, like a pumpkin, about the size of a half-quart pot" (p. 145). Probably of Central American origin, the *maraca* is the typical attribute of shamans throughout South America.

19. The successors of the priests of Baal are presumably the Roman Catholic clergy, and the "puppets" religious statues.

20. *Maire* or *Maira* is the generic name of the culture heroes of Tupi mythology; the term was associated with skill in manipulating the material world, and was applied to the newly arrived Europeans as well. Compare Thevet, *Cosmographie:* "Seeing that we know how to do more things then they, . . . they say that we are the successors and true children of Maire-Monan [the first culture hero]" (p. 914).

21. According to Métraux (*Religion,* 20–22), legends concerning New World and Old World weapons sprang up simultaneously after the Conquest in various South American tribes. See Claude d'Abbeville: "These prophets presented to our ancestor two swords: one of wood and the other of iron, and gave him the choice. He found the iron sword too heavy, and chose the wooden one. Upon his refusal, the ancestor from whom you are descended, who was more astute, took the iron one [trans. mine]" (p. 69). Léry seems to be speaking of the indigenous Tupi wooden sword, which, as he recounts in Chapter XIV, was a highly efficient weapon; still, it is presented as an accursed gift that came from a stranger.

22. There was a widespread belief among the early missionaries that the apostle St. Thomas had evangelized the Indies (the East and the West Indies were confounded). This notion was supported by the similarity between the Spanish version of Thomas (Tomé) and a culture hero in Tupi mythology called *Sumé,* or *Zumé,* or, in Thevet, *Sommay* (*Cosmographie,* 914). This belief

allowed the missionaries to see certain elements of Tupi myth as fragments of a largely forgotten Christian revelation; it also made them neglect important aspects of Tupi belief that could not readily be assimilated to a Christian structure. See Métraux, *Religion*, 16–22, and H. Clastres, *La Terre sans mal*, 27–28.

23. Nicephorus Callistus (ca. 1256–ca. 1335) was a Byzantine historian whose principal work, the ecclesiastical history cited by Léry, was translated from Greek into Latin in 1555 and published in Basle; it was important in the religious controversies of the time, not only for the point raised by Léry but also for its arguments concerning images and relics. See *The Oxford Dictionary of the Christian Church* (1985).

24. For Renaissance speculation on the descendants of Noah and the populations of the earth, see Don Cameron Allen, *The Legend of Noah; Renaissance Rationalism in Art, Science and Letters*, especially Chapter 6 (pp. 113–117): "The Migrations of Men and the Plantation of America."

25. "Epicureans" is a common term for free-thinker in the sixteenth century. In his *Excuse aux Nicodémites*, Calvin says: "As for the Lucianics or Epicureans, that is, all scorners of God, who feign adhering to the Word, and in their hearts mock it and regard it as no more than a fable, I refuse to speak about them here. For it would be time wasted, to try to win them by admonition [trans. mine]" (ed. Higman; p. 141).

## CHAPTER XVII
# MARRIAGE, CONSANGUINITY, AND THE CARE OF CHILDREN

1. Compare Staden II: xvii–xix; Thevet, *Singularités* XLII; *Cosmographie*, 916, 932–934; Soares de Sousa, *Tratado* II, 152; Yves d'Evreux XXIII.

2. Thevet and Yves d'Evreux give considerable detail on the laws of marriage and consanguinity. The rules were probably more complex and more strict than the early observers recognized. The Portuguese chroniclers Anchieta and Soares de Sousa noted an absolute prohibition of marriage with a paternal uncle, for whom the niece was regarded as a daughter (Lussagnet, 129 n.2).

3. In "Of Cannibals" Montaigne commented on the absence of jealousy among the women in the polygynous Brazilian household. "Our wives will cry 'Miracle!' but it is no miracle. It is a properly matrimonial virtue, but one of the highest order. In the Bible, Leah, Rachel, Sarah, and Jacob's wives gave their beautiful handmaids to their husbands [trans. Frame]" (p. 158).

4. *Tivîro, tebiró*, etc. (Lussagnet, 136 n. 1; *Viagem*, 224 n. 531.) The same word appears in Thevet as *tevir* (*Cosmographie*, 933). Many early accounts accused the New World peoples of sodomy, which was ferociously punished by the Spaniards.

5. See the famous treatment of breastfeeding in Rousseau's *Emile*, Book I. Affonso Arinos de Mello Franco, in *O Indio Brasileiro e a Revolução*

*Francesa*, traces this theme through major writers of the sixteenth, seventeenth, and eighteenth centuries (pp. 138–148); he believes that Rousseau, who was a great reader of travel literature, knew the work of Léry firsthand (pp. 304–306). Considering that Rousseau shares with Léry a Swiss Calvinist background, the conjecture is not unreasonable. I have been unable to identify the queen of France mentioned here; Léry's reference in the 1611 edition is even vaguer: "as someone has written," rather than "as we read in the histories."

6. Compare Rousseau's similar views on swaddling in *Emile*, Book I.

7. Léry is speaking of Diogenes the Cynic. Thevet makes a similar comparison between the savages and Diogenes: speaking of their burial ceremonies, he finds them "wiser in their brutishness than that stupid philosopher Diogenes the Cynic, who wanted his body to be exposed to the mercy of beasts" (*Cosmographie*, 926). Even more barbarous than the savage, then, is the European who would strip away all ceremony. The main source is Diogenes Laertius's section on the life of Diogenes in his *Lives of Eminent Philosophers*.

8. Thevet gives an even more graphic description of these puberty rites, and of the girls' suffering. He says that he asked an old Portuguese, established in Brazil with his family, to have the women try to persuade the Indians to abandon this custom. After consulting with their *pagés* (shamans), the Indians reported that if they were to change such a ceremony, *Maire-monan* (a divinity/culture hero) would cause them to perish (*Cosmographie*, 947).

## CHAPTER XVIII
# LAW AND CIVIL ORDER AMONG THE SAVAGES

1. Compare Staden II: 4, 5, 12; Thevet, *Singularités* XLIV; *Cosmographie*, 928–929; Yves d'Evreux, L; Magalhães de Gandavo, *Historia* X; Soares de Sousa, *Tratado* II: 315 and 316. For the material aspects of the households, see Métraux, *Civilisation matérielle:* on houses, pp. 47–57; on hammocks, pp. 60–64; on ceramics, pp. 233–247.

2. A principal reason for moving was the loss of fertility of the surrounding land; also disease or death associated with the place itself (Lussagnet, 116–117 n. 1).

3. The word "hammock" (Fr. *hamac*) comes from the Arawak of Haiti; it entered the European languages through Spanish (*hamaca*). The French travelers of the sixteenth century did not use the word *hamac*, but rather the Tupi word *ini* (Lussagnet, 117 n. 2).

4. See Léry's *Histoire mémorable de la ville de Sancerre* (1574), Chapter VII (ed. Nakam [1975], 250).

5. It was a commonplace during the Renaissance to praise voyagers by comparing them to Ulysses; for instance, a liminary poem celebrating Léry, found in the later editions, begins "Si d'Ulysse le grand renom / S'est espandu par tout le monde." What is unusual in this passage is the voyager comparing himself

251

not to Ulysses but to one of the men transformed by Circe into a beast; it is the Tupinamba who have the role of Ulysses.

6. Métraux (*Religion,* 180–188) gives an overview of this ceremony of the tearful greeting, which was widespread among South American tribes east of the Andes, and among some North American tribes (see also Georg Friederici, *Der Tränengruss der Indianer*); it seems to have existed in parts of Australia and New Zealand as well. The Tupi versions were described by virtually all the French and Portuguese chroniclers of the sixteenth and early seventeenth century. As for the content of the welcoming laments (in a "versified prose," according to Fernão Cardim), Thevet and Claude d'Abbeville relate almost the same words as Léry's; Yves d'Evreux says that they repeat the names of their ancestors, and their whole history; various Portuguese sources say that they recount the hardships endured by the guest in his travels, and their own anxiety concerning him. Métraux thinks that this ritual is associated with the cult of the dead, whose names and exploits figure so often in the laments. Wagley, in *Welcome of Tears,* notes the survival of this custom in 1953 in a Tupi-related tribe, the Tapirapé. "To the Tapirapé, such a return mixes emotions of joy at seeing an old friend with the sadness of the memory of those who died during the interim. Both the sadness and the joy are expressed ritually by crying" (p. 238).

## CHAPTER XIX
# ILLNESS, DEATH, AND FUNERALS AMONG THE SAVAGES

1. Compare Thevet, *Singularités* XLIII, XLV, XLVI; *Cosmographie,* 925, 934; Soares de Sousa, *Tratado* II: 165, 175,176; Cardim, *Treatise,* 428–429; Yves d'Evreux, XXIX, XXX, XXXI. See also Métraux's summary of funeral ceremonies, *Religion,* 113–123.

2. For a summary of the activities and functions of the *pagé* of this period, see Métraux, *Religion,* 79–92. Some writers, such as Thevet, use *pagé* and *caraïbe* almost interchangeably; some, like Léry, make a distinction: the *pagé* being a simple shaman, believed to have powers to cure or inflict illness, to influence the health of crops, and so on, and the *caraïbe* being a more powerful figure, believed to have prophetic powers. Of a quasi-messianic prestige, it was the *caraïbes* who led the various migrations to the "Land without Evil" (see Chap. XVI). Among Léry's contemporaries, Fernão Cardim makes the distinction (*Treatise,* 419–420); for a modern anthropologist's treatment, see H. Clastres, *La Terre dans mal,* Chapter 2. Métraux (*Religions et magie* 14) speaks of the prestige that the *pagé* have retained among the Guarani Indians of Paraguay. The word *pagé* survives among today's Tapirapé as *panché;* Charles Wagley describes their function in a community in the 1940s, and the decline of their power over the next two decades (*Welcome of Tears,* Chap. 6).

3. See Francisco Guerra, "The Problem of Syphilis," *First Images of America* 2: 845–851.

4. Gómara, *Histoire,* Chapter 123.

5. Plutarch, *Moralia: Apophthegmata regum et imperatorum.*

6. *Phocis* XXVIII.

7. There were numerous attempts to relate the New World languages to ancient Greek: for instance, Court de Gebelin, *Le Monde primitif* (Paris, 1773–1782), VIII: 515 (Morisot, 439). In "Of Cannibals," Montaigne notes a similarity without suggesting an affiliation: "Their language, moreover, is a soft language, with an agreeable sound, somewhat like Greek in its endings [trans. Frame]" (p. 158).

## CHAPTER XX
# A COLLOQUY IN THE TUPINAMBA AND FRENCH TONGUES

1. In his unpublished *Histoire de deux voyages,* Thevet claimed that this colloquy was actually of Villegagnon's composition, and that Léry had borrowed a copy and passed it off as his own. (See Gaffarel's edition of *Histoire d'un voyage* II, 209). In the *Cosmographie universelle,* Thevet himself had presented translations into Tupi of several prayers (the *Pater,* the *Ave Maria,* the *Sanctus,* and the Apostles' Creed, which he probably got from a Portuguese source (see Lussagnet 94 n. 1). The first Tupi grammar is that of the Jesuit Jose de Anchieta, *Arte de Gramatica da Lingoa mais usada na costa do Brasil,* written in 1555 but published in Coimbra only in 1595 (cited in John Hemmings, *Red Gold: Conquest of the Brazilian Indians* (Cambridge, Mass.: Harvard University Press, 1978, p. 550). In the Brazilian Portuguese translation of Léry's *Histoire* (*Viagem à terra do Brasil*) Plinio Ayrosa offered a restoration and transcription of the colloquy into a more modern spelling of Tupi. However, Ayrosa's work has come under heavy attack by other Tupi scholars. See A. Lemos Barbosa, *Estudos de Tupi: "O Diálogo de Léry" na restauração de Plinio Airosa* (Rio de Janeiro, 1944); Frederico G. Edelweiss, *Estudos Tupis e Tupi-Guarani* (Rio de Janeiro: Livraria Brasiliana Editôra, 1969). For another annotated reconstruction of the dialogue in Portuguese, see Afranio Peixoto, *Primeiras Letras* (Rio de Janeiro: Publicações da academia brasileira, 1923). There are more obscurities in this colloquy than in any other part of the *Histoire,* which suggests that it may indeed be the work of several hands. At several places in the text, the specialists mentioned here disagree among each other regarding both the transcription of the Tupi and Léry's translation into French. The text also appears to contain inconsistencies in the use of accent marks in the transliteration of Tupi words, possibly originating with Léry's printer; I have simply transmitted them. In my attempts to resolve the ambiguity between *i* and *j,* and between *u* and *v,* I have used Ayrosa's transcription. I have added parentheses for what are obviously Léry's own interpretive remarks rather than part of the French translation of the Tupi. I have added in brackets indications of an obvious change of speaker (Tupinamba or Frenchman) that Léry has omitted, or an apparent mistake in the identification of the speaker. Léry's transcription of Tupi sounds is very

253

close to that of modern transcriptions; as a record of the language, this colloquy is considered one of the most valuable documents extant.

2. For this play on Léry's name, see Chapter XVIII. Whether this dialogue is entirely Léry's work or not, this line clearly indicates his hand in it.

3. Léry's text reads *massou*, but is probably a printer's error; see Ayrosa, *Viagem*, 294 n. 10.

4. The terms Léry uses are *verbe* and *parole*.

## CHAPTER XXI
# OUR DEPARTURE FROM BRAZIL AND OUR PERILS

1. Villegagnon's fort fell to the Portuguese governor of Brazil, Mem de Sá, in March 1560. Needless to say, Mem de Sá had his own providential interpretation of the events: "The deed was done by our Lord, who did not want . . . Lutherans and Calvinists to be planted in this land" (letter to Queen Catarina of Portugal, cited in Hemmings, *Red Gold*, 126).

2. A reference to the Queen Regent Catherine de Medici, and her courtiers. She was identified by the Protestants as their arch-enemy, and was largely responsible for the Saint Bartholomew's Day Massacre.

3. The fate of these men is recounted in Chapter XXII. But Léry had also treated this subject earlier in two chapters that he contributed to Jean Crespin's *Histoire des martyrs* (1564), a Protestant martyrology. His contribution was entitled "La persécution des fidèles en terre d'Amérique." In the first chapter he gives a brief history of the Villegagnon colony, and in the second he describes the martyrdom of Bourdon, Du Bordel, and Verneuil. His treatment of this present episode—the abandonment of the ship by a small group and their return to Brazil—is quite different: there it is the leaders Du Pont and Richier who are on the point of leaving the ship to return to the mainland, and who change their minds. Léry himself as an individual does not figure in this text. One cannot be certain how to account for the discrepancy. In the earlier account, Léry may simply have preferred not to speak of himself. In the decade and a half between the pieces for the Crespin collection and the *Histoire d'un voyage*, Léry has come to think of himself as providentially saved to be a witness for the Protestant cause and for a true history of the colony; whether he fabricated this episode or simply made a different narrative choice among real events in the past is probably not knowable. For a treatment of the bibliographical complexities surrounding Léry's contribution to the *Histoire des martyrs*, as well as a discussion of the providential interpretation that Léry gives to his own destiny, see Lestringant, "Calvinistes et Cannibales," 9–26.

4. Cabo São Roque, on the northeast coast of Brazil, at a latitude of 5.29 degrees south. Either Léry is off by two degrees, which is rare for him, or it was a question of backtracking.

5. Léry is stressing that one must understand that these natural phenomena are not self-generating, but are produced by God, the supreme cause. The "athe-

ists" would maintain that Nature herself is the supreme cause. This theme occurs several times in this work. In Chapter XI: "in contemplating them [the beautiful birds], one is moved to glorify not nature, as do the profane, but rather their great and wonderful Creator." And Chapter XIII: "however blind this people may be in attributing more to nature and to the fertility of the earth than we do to the power and the providence of God."

6. On the Calvinist disapproval of Rabelais, see Lucien Febvre, *The Problem of Unbelief in the Sixteenth Century: The Religion of Rabelais*. However, this whole paragraph is full of echoes of Rabelais, especially the Fourth Book of *Pantagruel*, Chapter XVIII: "we shall drink but too much anon, for aught I see. Eat little and drink the more will hereafter be my motto, I fear. Would to our dear Lord, and to our blessed, worthy, and sacred Lady, I were now, I say, this very minute of an hour, well on shore, on terra firma, hale and easy. O twice and thrice happy those that plant cabbages! O destinies, why did you not spin me for a cabbage-planter? O how few are there to whom Jupiter hath been so favourable as to predestinate them to plant cabbages! They have also one foot on the ground, and the other not far from it [trans. Motteux]." See also the end of Chapter XII (this volume). For all Léry's disapproval of the "Rabelistes," he does not hesitate to use Rabelais as part of a fund of proverbial and humorous lore.

7. See Diogenes Laertius' account of Diogenes in his *Lives of Eminent Philosophers*.

8. They have come to the Sargasso Sea, between twenty-five and thirty degrees north, in the stretch of the Atlantic between the West Indies and the Azores. It gets its name from the alga sargasso, or gulf-weed, which grows thickly in it.

## CHAPTER XXII
# THE DIRE FAMINE FROM WHICH GOD DELIVERED US

1. "Cabinet" (the French word is the same) is probably an allusion to the private collections of curiosities (*cabinets de curiosités*) or "*singularités*" assembled in the Renaissance by those interested in natural history, and especially that of the New World; here, the "cabinet de leur mémoire" is the only repository for the monkeys and parrots whose remains should have adorned a more material collection.

2. Compare Erasmus' colloquy "The Shipwreck," which Léry almost certainly knew, and which concerns superstition and the terror of the sea: "I couldn't help laughing as I listened to one chap who in a loud voice . . . promised a wax taper as big as himself to the Christopher in the tallest church in Paris" (*Ten Colloquies* [trans. Craig Thompson], 7).

3. On the importance of Josephus for Léry and the Huguenot public, see Nakam, 136–138; also my article, "Food and the Limits of Civility." In his history of the siege of Sancerre, Léry often links the fate of the besieged town with that of Jerusalem. The beleaguered Huguenots came to think of Jose-

phus's account of Jewish resistance to the Romans as a prototype of their own history.

4. I have preserved the feminine here, which Léry insisted on in a correction (*inventoire* to *inventeresse*). Aside from the fact that *necessité* is a feminine noun, Léry often alludes to necessity as a maternal, generating force. "Necessity is the mother of invention" underlies his description of the response to famine in the Sancerre book: "Necessity mistress of the arts," and so forth.

5. *Histoire mémorable de la ville de Sancerre,* Chapter X.

6. "And thou shalt eat the fruit of thine own body, the flesh of thy sons and of thy daughters, which the Lord thy God hath given thee, in the siege, and in the straitness, wherewith thine enemies shall distress thee: So that the man that is tender among you, and very delicate, his eye shall be evil toward his brother, and toward the wife of his bosom, and toward the remnant of his children which he shall leave."

7. Léry's expression is "ces Bretons bretonnants," which means even today those who keep the traditions and language of Brittany. The Breton language is Celtic; hence its incomprehensibility to Léry and his friends. It is, of course, yet another example of the "strangeness" that can be encountered even on one's own native soil.

8. Léry had used this expression in Chapter VI, in speaking of the recalcitrance of the Tupinamba women regarding conversion to Christianity.

## EDITIONS AND RECEPTION OF LÉRY

1. Paul Gaffarel refers to an edition of 1642, which is mentioned in Jacques-Charles Burnet's *Manuel du libraire et de l'amateur de livres* (Paris: 1860–1865). I find no trace of it in the catalogues of the John Carter Brown Library, the Bibliothèque nationale, the British Museum, or the Library of Congress.

2. See Lestringant, "L'excursion brésilienne."

3. See Bernard Weinberg, "Montaigne's Readings for 'Des Cannibales' ", *Renaissance and Other Studies in Honor of William Leon Wiley* (Chapel Hill: University of North Carolina Press, 1968), 264–179.

4. The catalogue of the British Museum gives a listing of a fragment of Léry's *Histoire* published in the late eighteenth century, apparently called into service for the early romantic vogue of shipwreck: "Situation déplorable du vaisseau français le Jacques à son retour du Brésil, causée par une famine, etc." in *Voyages imaginaires, songes, visions, et romans cabalistiques,* 36 vols. (Paris, 1787–1789).

5. For the image of the Brazilian Indian in relation to Rousseau, see Mello-Franco, *O Indio Brasileiro e a Revolução Francesa* (Rio de Janeiro: José Olympio, 1937).

6. See the unpublished dissertation of Irma Majer, "The Notion of Singularity: The Travel Journals of Michel de Montaigne and Jean de Léry." Ph.D. diss. Johns Hopkins University, 1972.

# BIBLIOGRAPHY

## EDITIONS OF *HISTOIRE D'UN VOYAGE FAIT EN LA TERRE DU BRESIL* PUBLISHED DURING LÉRY'S LIFETIME:[a]

1578: *Histoire d'un voyage faict en la terre du Bresil autrement dite Amerique / le tout recueilli sur les lieux par Jean de Léry.* "[Genève], Pour Antoine Chuppin."[b]

1580: "Seconde Edition." "A Genève. Pour Antoine Chuppin."

1585: "Troisieme Edition." "[Genève,] Pour Antoine Chuppin."

1594: False "Troisieme Edition." "[Genève,] Pour les heritiers d'Eustache Vignon" (A reprint of the 1580 edition).

1599–1600: "Quatrieme Edition. Dediee a Madame la Princesse d'Orange." "[Genève,] Pour les heritiers d'Eustache Vignon" (two printings of the same edition).

1611: "Cinquieme Edition. Dediee a Madame la Princesse d'Orange. A Genève, pour Jean Vignon."

## MODERN EDITIONS[c]

*Histoire d'un voyage faict en la terre du Brésil, avec une introduction et des notes par Paul Gaffarel.* Paris: Lemerre, 1879 (2 vols.).

*Le voyage au Brésil de Jean de Léry, 1556–1558: avec une introduction par Charly Clerc, gravures d'un anonyme du XVIe siècle.* Paris: Payot, 1927.

*Journal de bord de Jean de Léry en la terre de Brésil (1557).* Présenté et commenté par M.-R. Mayeux. Paris: Editions de Paris, 1957. (Text of 1580, abridged and modernized.)

*Indiens de la Renaissance: histoire d'un voyage fait en la terre du Brésil (1557).* Présentation par Anne-Marie Chartier. Paris: Epi, 1972. (Abridged text.)

*Histoire d'un voyage fait en la Terre du Brésil.* Etablissement du texte et glossaire

---

[a]See Lestringant, "L'excursion brésilienne: Note sur les trois premières editions de l'*Histoire d'un Voyage* de Jean de Léry (1578–1585)."

[b]Some copies of this edition give the place as La Rochelle.

[c]Presented chronologically.

de Michel Contat. Postface de Jean-Claude Wagnières. Lausanne: Bibliothéque romande, 1972.

*Histoire d'un voyage fait en la terre du Brésil.* Edition, presentation et notes par Jean-Claude Morisot. Index des notions ethnologiques par Louis Necker. Geneva: Droz, 1975. (Facsimile of 1580 edition.)

*Histoire d'un voyage fait en la terre de Bresil.* Introduction de Sophie Delpech. Paris: Plasma, 1980. (Modernized text.)

# TRANSLATIONS

## Latin

*Historia navigationis in Brasiliam quae et America dicitur. Qua describitur autoris navigatio, quaeque in mari vidit memoriae prodenda: Villagagnonis in America gesta: Brasiliensium victus et mores, a nostri admodum alieni, cum eorum linguae dialogo: animalia etiam, arbores, atque herbae, reliquaque singularia et nobis penitus incognita / a Ioanne Burgundo Gallicè scripta. Nunco vero primum latinitate donata, 7 varii figuris illustrata.* Geneva: Eustathius Vignon, 1586. (Reprinted in 1594 with some slight alterations. It was also issued by the same publisher that same year along with the Latin translation of Benzoni, *Historia Indiae Occidentalis.*)

*Americae tertia pars memorabile[m] provinciae Brasiliae historiam contine[n]s, Germanico primum sermone scriptam a Ioa[n]ne Stadio . . . nunc autem Latinitate donatam a Teucrio Annaeo Privato Colchanthe. Addita est Narratio profectionis Joannis Lerij en eamdem provinciam, quae ille initio Gallicè conscripsit, postea vero Latinam fecit.* Frankfurt: De Bry, 1592. (Reissued in 1597 or later; second edition 1605; third edition 1630.)

*Excerpta quaedam de America sue Brasilia ex Joan. Lerij Historia.* (In Johann Boemus, *Mores, leges et ritus omnium gentium.* Geneva, 1604.)

## German

*Dritte Buch Americae, darinn Brasilia durch Johann Staden . . . aus eigener Erfahrung in teutsch beschrieben. Item Historia der Schiffart Ioannis Lerij in Brasilien, welche er selbst publiciert hat, jetzt von newem verteutscht, durch Teucrium Annaeum Privatim, C. [i.e. J. A. E. Lonicer] . . . Alles von newem mit kunstlichen Figuren in Kupffer gestochen und an Tag geben, durch Dieterich Bry.* Frankfurt: De Bry, 1593.

*Niederlassung der Franzosen in Brasilien. Johanns von Lery Reise.* In *Allgemeine Historie der Reisen zu Wasser und Lande* (1758), 16: 159–182.

*Des Herrn Johann von Lery reise in Brasilien. Nach der von dem herrn verfasser selbst veranstalteten verbesserten und vermehrten lateinischen ausgabe übersetzt. Mit anmerkungen und erläuterungen.* Münster: Im verlag der Platvoetischen buchhandlung, 1794.

*Brasilianisches Tagebuch 1557.* Trans. Ernst Bluth. Tubingen and Basel: Erdmann, 1967.

## Dutch

*Historie van een Reyse ghedaen inden Lande van Bresillien, andersins ghenoemt America* . . . *Alles beschreven door Ian de Léry* . . . *Nu over-geset wt het Franchoiys te Geneve Ghedruckt.* Amsterdam, by C. Claesz, 1597.

*De seer aanmerklijke en vermaarde reys, van Johannes Lerius Brazil in America. Gedaan anno 1556* . . . *Nu aldereest uyt 't frans vertaald, na den laatsten druk.* Leyden: P. van der Aa, 1706.

## English

BOEMUS, JOHANN. *The Manners, Lawes and Customes of All Nations* . . . *The Like Also out of the History of America, or Brasill, written by John Lerius.* Trans. E. Aston. London, 1611. (Excerpts.)

"Extracts out of the Historie of John Lerius a Frenchman, Who Lived in Brasill with Mons. Villagagnon, Ann. 1557, and 58." In Samuel Purchas, *Hakluytus Posthumus or Purchas His Pilgrimes* (1625), reedition of 1906 (Glasgow: MacLehose), XVI: 518–579.

## Portuguese

*Historia de uma viagem feita à terra do Brasil.* Traduiza por Tristão de Alencar Aripe. Rio de Janeiro, 1889.

*Historia de uma viagem feita à terra do Brasil.* Tradução ordenada literariamente por Monteiro Lobato. Rio de Janeiro, São Paulo: Companhia editora nacional, 1926.

*Viagem à terra do Brasil.* Tradução integral et notas de Sérgio Milliet, segundo a edição de Paul Gaffarel com o colóquio na língua brasílica et notas tupinológicas de Plinio Ayrosa. São Paulo: Livraria Martins, 1941, (Second edition 1951; third, 1960; Fourth, 1967. Reissued by Editora da Universidade de São Paulo, 1980.)

## Czech

*Historie o plavení se do Ameriky kteráž i Brasilia slove. Z latiny přel. roku 1590 P. Slovák a M. Cyrus.* K vydáni připravili Q. Hodura, B. Horák. Prague, 1957.

# OTHER WORKS OF LÉRY

*Histoire des choses memorables advenues en la terre du Brésil, partie de l'Amérique Australe, sous le gouvernement de M. de Villegagnon, depuis l'an 1555 jusqu'à l'an 1558.* Genève, 1561.

"La Persécution des fidèles en terre d'Amérique," in Jean Crespin, *Histoire des choses memorables advenues en la terre du Bresil* (Genève, 1564). (Same as above, with minor modifications. An abridged version appeared the following year under the title *Brief Recueil de l'affliction de l'Eglise des fidèles du pays de Brésil.*)[a]

*Histoire memorable de la ville de Sancerre.* 1574.
See Nakam, Géralde. *Au lendemain de la Saint-Barthelemy.* Paris: Editions Anthropos, 1975. (Critical edition of above.)
*Histoire mémorable de la ville de Sancerre: augmentée de deux pièces rares sur le siège de Sancerre.* Marseille: Lafitte, 1980.

# EARLY SOURCES CONSULTED

BARRÉ, NICOLAS. *Copie de quelques lettres sur la navigation du Chevalier de Villegaignon.* Paris, 1557. (Reedited in Gaffarel, *Histoire du Brésil français au XVIe siècle.*)
BENZONI, GIROLAMO. *Histoire nouvelle du Nouveau Monde . . . extraite de l'Italien de M. Hierosme Benzoni, Milanois, qui ha voyagé XIII ans en ces pays-la . . . enrichie de plusieurs discours et choses dignes de memoire, Par M. Urbain Chauveton.* Geneva: Eustache Vignon, 1579. (Italian original, Venice, 1565.)
CALVIN, JEAN. *Institution de la Religion chrestienne.* Ed. Jacques Pannier. Paris: Les Belles Lettres, 1961.
———. *Institutes of the Christian Religion.* Ed. John T. McNeill. Trans. Ford Lewis Battles. Philadelphia: Westminster, 1960, 2 vols.
———. *Three French Treatises.* Ed. Francis Higman. London: Athlone, 1970.
———. *Trois traités.* Textes présentés et annotés par Albert-Marie Schmidt; préface de Jacques Pannier. Paris: Editions "Je sers," 1935.
CAMINHA, PERO VAZ DE. Letter to King Manoel, May 1, 1500. Trans. William Brooks Greenlee, in *The Voyages of Pedro Alvares Cabral to Brazil and India.* Hukluyt Society, 2d ser., 81. London, 1937, pp. 3–33.
CARDIM, FERNÃO. *Do principio e origem dos Indios do Brasil e dos seus costumes, adoração e ceremonias.* Translated as "A Treatise of Brasil, written by a Portugall which had long lived there," in Samuel Purchas, *Hakluytus Posthumus or Purchas His Pilgrimes* (1625), reedition of 1906 (Glasgow: MacLehose), XVI: 418–517.
CLAUDE D'ABBEVILLE. *Histoire de la Mission des Pères Capucins en l'Isle de Maragnan et terres circonvoisines.* Paris: François Huby, 1614. (Facsimile ed., Graz: Akademische Druck-u. Verlagsanstalt, 1963.)
COTGRAVE, RANDLE. *A Dictionarie of the French and English Tongues.* London, 1611. (Facsimile edition, New York: Da Capo Press, 1971.)
ERASMUS, DESIDERIUS. *Ten Colloquies.* Trans. Craig R. Thompson. Indianapolis: The Library of Liberal Arts, 1957.

---

[a] See Lestringant, "Calvinistes et cannibales," 24–25.

GONNEVILLE, BINOT PAULMIER DE. "Voyage du capitaine Paulmier de Gonneville au Brésil (1503–1505)" in Charles-André Julien, *Les Français en Amérique,* 25–49 (Paris: Presses Universitaires de France, 1948).

HATON, CLAUDE. *Mémoires de Claude Haton contenant le récit des événements accomplis de 1553 à 1582, principalement dans la Champagne et de la Brie* (2 vols.). Paris: M. Felix Bourquelot, 1857.

LÓPEZ DE GÓMARA, FRANCISCO. *Histoire generalle des Indes occidentales et Terres Neuves qui jusques à présent ont esté descouvertes.* Trans. M. Fumée. Paris: Michel Sonnius, 1569. (Spanish original Saragossa, 1552).

MAGALHÃES DE GANDAVO, PERO. *The Histories of Brazil.* Trans. John B. Stetson. New York: The Cortes Society, 1922. (Translation of *Historia da Provincia de Santa Cruz* and *Tratado da terra do Brasil,* 1576.)

MARTIRE D'ANGHIERA, PIETRO. *De Orbe Novo* (2 vols.) Trans., ed. Francis Augustus MacNutt. New York: Putnam's, 1912.

MONTAIGNE, MICHEL DE. *The Complete Works of Montaigne.* Trans. Donald M. Frame. Stanford, Calif.: Stanford University Press, 1957.

——. *Essais.* Ed. M. Rat (2 vols.). Paris: Garnier, 1962.

PURCHAS, SAMUEL. *Hakluytus Posthumus or Purchas His Pilgrimes: Contayning a History of the World in Sea Voyages and Lande Travells by Englishmen and Others, by Samuel Purchas.* Glasgow: J. MacLehose and Sons, 1905–07, 20 Vols. Hakluyt Society, extra series.

RABELAIS, FRANÇOIS. *Oeuvres complètes.* Ed. Jacques Boulenger. Paris: Gallimard, 1955.

——. *The Works of Rabelais.* Trans. Urquhart and Motteux. London, n.d.

SOARES DE SOUSA, GABRIEL. *Tratado descriptivo do Brasil em 1587.* Ed. Francisco Adolfo Varnhagen. São Paulo, 1938.

STADEN, HANS. *The Captivity of Hans Stade of Hesse in A.D. 1547–1555 Among the Wild Tribes of Eastern Brazil.* Ed. Richard F. Burton. Trans. Albert Tootal. London: Hakluyt Society, 1st ser., 15, 1874. (Trans. of *Wahrhaftige Historie und Beschreibung eyner Landschafft der Wilden, Nacketen, Grimmigen, Menschfresser Leuten, in der Newen Welt America gelegen . . .* [*Marburg, 1557.*])

THEVET, ANDRÉ. *La Cosmographie universelle.* Paris, 1575. (The Brazilian section of this appears in Lussagnet, *Le Brésil et les brésiliens.*)

——. *Les Singularitéz de la France antarctique.* Paris, 1558. (See also modernized edition: *Les Singularités de la France Antarctique: Le Brésil des Cannibales au XVIe siècle.* Choix de textes, introduction et notes de Frank Lestringant. Paris, 1983.)

——. *Les Vrais Pourtraits et vies des hommes illustres.* Paris, 1584. (Facsimile edition Ed. Rouben C. Cholakian, New York: Scholars' Facsimiles and Reprints, 1974.)

VESPUCCI, AMERIGO. *The Letters of Amerigo Vespucci.* Ed. Sir Clements Robert Markham. London: Hakluyt Society, 1894.

YVES D'EVREUX. *Voyage dans le Nord du Brésil fait durant les années 1612 et 1614.* Ed. Ferdinand-Jean Denis. Leipzig and Paris, 1864. (Original title: *Suitte de l'histoire des choses plus memorables advenues en Maragnan ès annees 1612 et 1614.*) (See also modernized edition: *Voyage au nord du*

*Brésil fait en 1613 et 1614.* Présentation et notes d'Hélène Clastres. Paris: Payot, 1985.)

# MODERN SOURCES ON LÉRY AND HIS TIMES

ALLEN, DON CAMERON. *The Legend of Noah: Renaissance Rationalism in Art, Science and Letters.* Studies in Language and Literature, vol. 33, nos. 3–4. Urbana, Ill., 1949.

ATKINSON, GEOFFROY. *Les nouveaux horizons de la Renaissance française.* Paris: Droz, 1935.

BATAILLON, MARCEL. "L'Amiral et les 'nouveaux horizons' français." *Actes du colloque: L'Amiral de Coligny et son temps.* Paris: Société de l'Histoire du Protestantisme français, 1974, pp. 41–52.

———. "Montaigne et les conquérants de l'or." *Studi francesi* 9 (Dec. 1959): 353–367.

BERNHEIMER, RICHARD. *The Wild Man in the Middle Ages.* New York: Octagon Books, 1970.

BOAS, GEORGE. *Essays on Primitivism and Related Ideas in the Middle Ages.* Baltimore: Johns Hopkins University Press, 1948.

———, Arthur O. Lovejoy, and Gilbert Chinard, Eds. *A Documentary History of Primitivism and Related Ideas.* Baltimore: Johns Hopkins University Press, 1935.

BRANDON, WILLIAM. *New Worlds for Old: Reports from the New World and Their Effect on the Development of Social Thought in Europe, 1500–1800.* Athens, Ohio: Ohio University Press, 1986.

BUCHER, BERNADETTE. *Icon and Conquest: A Structural Analysis of the Illustrations of de Bry's Great Voyages.* Trans. Basia Miller Gulati. Chicago: University of Chicago Press, 1981. Translation of *La sauvage aux seins pendants.* Paris: Hermann, 1977.

CÉARD, JEAN. *La Nature et les prodiges: L'insolite au XVIe siècle en France.* Geneva: Droz, 1977.

CERTEAU, MICHEL DE. *The Writing of History.* Trans. Tom Conley. New York: Columbia University Press, 1988. Translation of *L'ecriture de l'histoire.* Paris: Gallimard, 1975.

CHAUNU, PIERRE. *L'Amérique et les Amériques.* Paris: A. Colin, 1964.

CHIAPELLI, FREDI, ED. *First Images of America: The Impact of the New World on the Old.* Berkeley, Los Angeles, London: University of California Press, 1976 (2 vols.).

CHINARD, GILBERT. *L'exotisme américain dans la littérature française au XVIe siècle.* Paris: Hachette, 1911.

CIORANESCU, ALEXANDRE. "La découverte de l'Amérique et l'art de la description." *Revue des sciences humaines* (n.s.) 106 (1962): 161–168.

DAVIS, NATALIE. "The Rites of Violence." *Society and Culture in Early Modern France.* Stanford: Stanford University Press, 1975. 152–187.

DEFAUX, GÉRARD. "Un cannibale en haut de chausses: Montaigne, la différence et la logique de l'identité." *Modern Language Notes* 7.4 (May 1982): 919–957.

DELAUNAY, PAUL. *La zoologie au seizième siècle.* Paris: Hermann, 1962.

DELUMEAU, JEAN. *La mort des Pays de Cocagne: Comportements collectifs de la Renaissance à l'âge classique.* Paris: Publications de la Sorbonne, 1976.

———. "Les réformateurs et la superstition." *Actes du colloque: L'Amiral de Coligny et son temps.* Paris: Société de l'Histoire du Protestantisme français, 1974, pp. 451–487.

DENIS, FERDINAND. *Une fête brésilienne célébrée à Rouen en 1550.* Paris: J. Techener, 1850.

DICKASON, OLIVE PATRICIA. *The Myth of the Savage and the Beginnings of French Colonialism in the Americas.* Edmonton: University of Alberta Press, 1984.

DOUMERGUE, EMILE. *Jean Calvin, les hommes et les choses de son temps* (3 vols.). Lausanne: G. Bridel, 1899–1905.

DUDLEY, EDWARD, AND MAXIMILIAN E. NOVAK. *The Wild Man Within: An Image in Western Thought from the Renaissance to Romanticism.* Pittsburgh: University of Pittsburgh Press, 1972.

DUPRONT, ALPHONSE. "Espace et humanisme." *Bibliothèque d'Humanisme et Renaissance: Travaux et documents* 8 (1946): 7–104.

EIRE, CARLOS M. M. *War Against the Idols: The Reformation of Worship from Erasmus to Calvin.* Cambridge: Cambridge University Press, 1979.

ELLIOTT, JOHN H. *The Old World and the New, 1492–1650.* Cambridge: Cambridge University Press, 1970.

———. "Renaissance Europe and America: A Blunted Impact?" *First Images of America.* Ed. Fredi Chiapelli. Vol. 1. Berkeley, Los Angeles, London: University of California Press, 1976, pp. 11–23 (2 vols.).

EWAN, JOSEPH. "The Columbian Discoveries and the Growth of Botanical Ideas with Special Reference to the Sixteenth Century." *First Images of America.* Ed. Fredi Chiapelli. Vol. 2. Berkeley, Los Angeles, London: University of California Press, 1976, pp. 807–812 (2 vols.).

FAIRCHILD, HOXIE N. *The Noble Savage: A Study in Romantic Naturalism.* New York: Columbia University Press, 1928.

FEBVRE, LUCIEN. *The Problem of Unbelief in the Sixteenth Century: The Religion of Rabelais.* Cambridge: Harvard University Press, 1982. Translation of *Le problème de l'incroyance au XVIe siècle: La religion de Rabelais.* Paris: Albin Michel, 1942.

GAFFAREL, PAUL. *Histoire du Brésil français au XVIe siècle.* Paris: Maisonneuve, 1878.

GEERTZ, CLIFFORD. *The Interpretation of Cultures.* New York: Basic Books, 1973.

GILMORE, MYRON P. "The New World in French and English Historians of the Sixteenth Century." *First Images of America.* Ed. Fredi Chiapelli. Vol. 2. Berkeley, Los Angeles, London: University of California Press, 1976, pp. 519–528 (2 vols.).

GOMEZ-GERAUD, MARIE CHRISTINE. "Du Verbal au visuel: Sonnets liminaires à l'*Histoire d'un voyage fait en la terre du Brésil* de Jean de Léry." *Renaissance and Reformation/Renaissance et Réforme* 24.3 (1988): 215–222.

GREENBLATT, STEPHEN. "Learning to Curse: Aspects of Linguistic Colonialism in the Sixteenth Century." *First Images of America.* Ed. Fredi Chiapelli.

Vol. 2, Berkeley, Los Angeles, London: University of California Press, 1976, pp. 561–580 (2 vols.).

———. *Shakespearean Negotiations: The Circulation of Social Energy in Renaissance England.* Berkeley, Los Angeles, London: University of California Press, 1988.

GUERRA, FRANCISCO. "The Problem of Syphilis." *First Images of America.* Vol. 2. Berkeley, Los Angeles, London: University of California Press, 1976, pp. 845–851 (2 vols.).

HAMILTON, EARL J. "What the New World Gave the Economy of the Old." *First Images of America.* Ed. Fredi Chiapelli. Vol. 2. Berkeley, Los Angeles, London: University of California Press, 1976, pp. 853–884 (2 vols.).

HANKE, LEWIS. *Aristotle and the American Indians.* London: Hollis and Carter, 1959.

———. "The Theological Significance of the Discovery of America. *First Images of America.* Ed. Fredi Chiapelli. Vol. 1. Berkeley, Los Angeles, London: University of California Press, 1976, pp. 363–390 (2 vols.).

HARTOG, FRANÇOIS. *Le Miroir d'Hérodote: Essai sur la représentation de l'autre.* Paris: Gallimard, 1980.

HEULHARD, ARTHUR. *Villegagnon, roi d'Amérique. Un homme de mer au XVIe siècle.* Paris: PUF, 1948.

HODGEN, MARGARET. *Early Anthropology in the Sixteenth and Seventeenth Centuries.* Philadelphia: University of Pennsylvania Press, 1964.

HONOUR, HUGH. *The New Golden Land: European Images of America From the Discoveries to the Present Time.* New York: Pantheon, 1975.

JEANNERET, MICHEL. "Léry et Thevet: comment parler d'un monde nouveau?" *Mélanges à la mémoire de Franco Simone, IV: Tradition et originalité dans la création littéraire.* Geneva: Slatkine, 1983, pp. 228–245.

JOHNSON, HILDEGARD BINDER. "New Geographical Horizons: Concepts." *First Images of America.* Ed. Fredi Chiapelli. Vol. 2. Berkeley, Los Angeles, London: University of California Press, 1976, pp. 615–634 (2 vols.).

JULIEN, CHARLES-ANDRÉ. *Les Voyages de découverte et les premiers établissements.* Paris: PUF (Presses Universitaires de France), 1948.

———. *Les Français en Amérique pendant la première moitié du XVIe siècle.* Paris: PUF, 1946.

KEEN, BENJAMIN. "The Vision of America in the Writings of Urbain Chauveton." *First Images of America.* Ed. Fredi Chiapelli. Vol. 1. Berkeley, Los Angeles, London: University of California Press, 1976, pp. 107–120 (2 vols.).

KINGDON, ROBERT. *Church and Society in Reformation Europe.* London: Variorum, 1985.

———. *Geneva and the Coming of the Wars of Religion in France, 1555–1563.* Geneva: Droz, 1956.

———. *Myths about the St. Bartholomew's Day Massacres 1572–1576.* Cambridge, Mass.: Harvard University Press, 1988.

LESTRINGANT, FRANK. "Calvinistes et cannibales: Les écrits protestants sur le Brésil français (1555–1560)." *Bulletin de la société de l'histoire du protestantisme français* 1–2 (1980): 9–26, 167–192.

———. "Le cannibalisme des 'Cannibales'." I. Montaigne et la tradition. *Bulletin de la société des Amis de Montaigne* 9–10 (1982): 27–40.

———. "Le cannibalisme des 'Cannibales'." II. De Montaigne à Malthus. *Bulletin de la société des Amis de Montaigne* 11–12 (1982): 19–38.

———. "Catholiques et cannibales: Le thème du cannibalisme dans le discours protestant au temps des guerres de religion." *Pratiques et discours alimentaires à la Renaissance*. Paris: Maisonneuve et Larose, 1982, pp. 233–245.

———. "L'excursion brésilienne: Note sur les trois premières éditions de l'*Histoire d'un Voyage* de Jean de Léry (1578–1585)." *Mélanges sur la littérature de la Renaissance à la mémoire de V.-L. Saulnier*. Geneva: Droz, 1984, pp. 53–72.

———. "Fictions de l'espace brésilien à la Renaissance: l'exemple de Guanabara." *Arts et légendes d'espace: figures du voyage et rhétoriques du monde*. Ed. Frank Lestringant and Christian Jacob. Paris: Presses de l'Ecole normale supérieure, 1981, pp. 206–256.

———. "Le nom des 'cannibales' de Christophe Colomb à Michel de Montaigne." *Bulletin de la Société des Amis de Montaigne* 17–18 (1984): 51–74.

———. "Récit de quête/Récit d'exil: Le retour de la terre promise (XVIe siècle)." *Revue des sciences humaines* 214 (1989): 25–41.

LEVIN, HARRY. *The Myth of the Golden Age in the Renaissance*. New York: Oxford University Press, 1972.

LOVEJOY, ARTHUR AND GEORGE BOAS. *Primitivism and Related Ideas in Classical Antiquity*. New York: Octagon Books, 1965.

MAJER, IRMA STAZA. "The Notion of Singularity: The Travel Journals of Michel de Montaigne and Jean de Léry." Ph.D. diss. Johns Hopkins University 1982.

———. "La fin des voyages: écriture et souvenir chez Jean de Léry." *Revue des sciences humaines* 214 (1989): 71–83.

MANDROU, ROBERT. *Introduction à la France moderne (1500–1650): Essai de psychologie historique*. Paris: Albin Michel, 1962.

MORISON, SAMUEL ELIOT. *The European Discovery of America. The Southern Voyages, 1492–1616*. New York: Oxford University Press, 1974.

MORTON, A. G. *History of Botanical Science: An Account of the Development of Botany from Ancient Times to the Present Day*. London, New York: Academic Press, 1981.

MULLANEY, STEVEN. "Strange Things, Gross Terms, Curious Customs: The Rehearsal of Cultures in the Late Renaissance." *Representing the English Renaissance*. Ed. Stephen Greenblatt. Berkeley, Los Angeles, London: University of California Press, 1988, pp. 65–92.

NAKAM, GÉRALDE. *Au lendemain de la Saint Barthélemy: Guerre civile et famine: Histoire mémorable du siège de Sancerre (1573) de Jean de Léry*. Paris: Anthropos, 1975.

OLSCHKI, LEONARDO. "What Columbus Saw on Landing in the West Indies." *Proceedings of the American Philosophical Society* 84 (1941): 633–659.

QUINN, DAVID B. "New Geographical Horizons: Literature." *First Images of America*. Ed. Fredi Chiapelli. Berkeley, Los Angeles, London: University of California Press, 1976, pp. 635–658 (2 vols.).

REVERDIN, OLIVIER. *Quatorze Calvinistes chez les Topinambous: Histoire d'une mission genevoise au Brésil, 1556–1558.* Geneva: Droz, 1957.

SAUER, JONATHAN D. "Changing Perception and Exploitation of New World Plants in Europe, 1492–1800." *First Images of America.* Ed. Fredi Chiapelli. Vol. 2. Berkeley, Los Angeles, London: University of California Press, 1976, pp. 813–832 (2 vols.).

SCAGLIONE, ALDO. "A Note on Montaigne's *Des Cannibales* and the Humanist Tradition." *First Images of America.* Ed. Fredi Chiapelli. Vol. 1. Berkeley, Los Angeles, London: University of California Press, 1976, pp. 63–70 (2 vols.).

STURTEVANT, WILLIAM C. "First Visual Images of Native America." *First Images of America.* Ed. Fredi Chiapelli. Vol. 1. Berkeley, Los Angeles, London: University of California Press, 1976, pp. 417–454 (2 vols.).

TODOROV, TZVETAN. *The Conquest of America: The Question of the Other.* Trans. Richard Howard, New York: Harper and Row, 1984. Translation of *La Conquête de l'Amérique: La Question de l'Autre.* Paris: Seuil, 1982.

WASHBURN, WILCOMB E. "The Clash of Morality in the American Forest." *First Images of America.* Ed. Fredi Chiapelli. Vol. 1. Berkeley, Los Angeles, London: University of California Press, 1976, pp. 335–350 (2 vols.).

WEINBERG, BERNARD. "Montaigne's readings for 'Des Cannibales.' *Renaissance and Other Studies in Honor of William Leon Wiley.* Chapel Hill: University of North Carolina Press, 1968: pp. 264–279.

WHATLEY, JANET. "Food and the Limits of Civility: The Testimony of Jean de Léry." *Sixteenth Century Journal* 15 (1984), 387–400.

———. "Impression and Initiation: Jean de Léry's Brazil Voyage." *Modern Language Studies* 19.3 (Summer 1989): 15–25.

———. "Savage Hierarchies: French Catholic Observers of the New World." *Sixteenth Century Journal* 17 (1986): 319–330.

———. "*Une révérence réciproque:* Huguenot Writing on the New World." *University of Toronto Quarterly* 57.2 (Winter 1987/88: 270–289.

WHITE, HAYDEN. "The Noble Savage Theme as Fetish." *First Images of America.* Ed. Fredi Chiapelli. Vol. 1. Berkeley, Los Angeles, London, University of California Press, 1976, pp. 121–135 (2 vols.).

# MODERN WORKS ON BRAZIL AND THE TUPINAMBA

BARBOSA, A. LEMOS. *Estudos de Tupi: "O Diálogo de Léry" na restauração de Plinio Airosa* (Rio de Janeiro, 1944).

CLASTRES, HÉLÈNE. *La Terre sans mal: Le prophétisme tupi-guarani.* Paris: Seuil, 1975.

CLASTRES, PIERRE. *Le Grand Parler: Mythes et chants sacrés des Indiens Guarani.* Paris: Seuil, 1974.

EDELWEISS, FREDERICO G. *Estudos Tupis e Tupi-Guaranis: Confrontos e revisõs.* Rio de Janeiro: Livraria Brasiliana Editôra, 1969.

FERNANDES, FLORESTAN. "La Guerre et le sacrifice humain chez les Tupinamba." *Journal de la Société des Américanistes de Paris* (n.s.) 40 (1952): 139–220.

FREYRE, GILBERTO. *The Masters and the Slaves: A Study in the Development of Brazilian Civilization.* Trans. Samuel Putnam. New York: Knopf, 1946. Translation of *Casa-Grande e senzala: Formacão da familia brasileira sob o regime de economia patriarchal.* Rio de Janeiro: José Olympio, 1943.

FRIEDERICI, GEORG. *Der Tränengruss der Indianer.* Leipzig: Von Simmel, 1907.

HEMMINGS, JOHN. *Red Gold: The Conquest of the Brazilian Indians.* Cambridge, Mass.: Harvard University Press, 1978.

HOEHNE, F. C. *Botánica e agricultura no Brasil (século XVI).* Bibliotheca pedagógica brasileira, Brasiliana, no. 71. São Paulo: Cia Editora Nacional, 1937.

IHERING, RODOLPHO VON. *Dicionário dos animais do Brasil.* São Paulo: Editora Universidade de Brasilia, 1968.

LAPOUGE, GILLES. *Equinoxiales.* Paris: Flammarion, 1977.

LEVI-STRAUSS, CLAUDE. *Tristes tropiques.* Paris: Plon, 1955. Trans. John Russell. New York: Atheneum, 1972.

LUSSAGNET, SUZANNE. *Le Brésil et les Brésiliens.* Paris: PUF, 1953. Vol. 1 of *Les Français en Amérique pendant la deuxième moitié du XVIe siècle* (2 vols.), 1953–1958.

MELLO FRANCO, AFONSO ARINOS DE. *O indio Brasileiro e a Revolução Francesa.* Rio de Janeiro: José Olympio, 1937.

MÉTRAUX, ALFRED. *La Civilisation matérielle des tribus Tupi-Guarani.* Paris: Geuthner, 1927.

———. *La Religion des Tupinamba et ses rapports avec celles des autres tribus tupi-guarani.* Paris: Ernest Leroux, 1928.

———. *Religions et magies indiennes d'Amérique du Sud.* Paris: Gallimard, 1967.

PEIXOTO, AFRANIO. *Primeiras Letras.* Rio de Janeiro: Publicações da academia brasileira, 1923.

WAGLEY, CHARLES. *Welcome of Tears: The Tapirapé Indians of Central Brazil.* New York: Oxford University Press, 1977.

# INDEX

Designer: Linda M. Robertson
Compositor: Huron Valley Graphics, Inc.
Text: 10 / 12 Sabon
Display Caslon
Printer: Maple-Vail Book Mfg. Group
Binder: Maple-Vail Book Mfg. Group